VOID

Library of
Davidson College

THE PHILOSOPHY OF WILLIAM JAMES

The Philosophy of William James

Walter Robert Corti, Editor

Felix Meiner Verlag
Hamburg

Bibliographie von Charlene Haddock Seigfried

CIP-Kurztitelaufnahme der Deutschen Bibliothek

The philosophy of William James / Walter Robert Corti, ed.
1. Aufl. — Hamburg: Meiner, 1976
   ISBN 3-7873-0352-9

NE: Corti, Walter Robert [Hrsg.]

© Felix Meiner, Hamburg 1976
Alle Rechte, auch die des auszugsweisen Nachdrucks, der photomechanischen Wiedergabe und der Übersetzung, vorbehalten
Herstellung: CVB Buch+Druck, Zürich
Printed in Switzerland

CONTENTS

Preface by S. Morris Eames 7

Notes on Contributors 9

1 Van Meter Ames, William James and the Open Universe 17

2 V. Donald Oliver, James' Cerebral Dichotomy . . 33

3 David L. Miller, William James and the Specious Present 51

4 John J. McDermott, A Metaphysics of Relations: James' Anticipation of Contemporary Experience . . 81

5 Edward H. Madden and Peter H. Hare, A Critical Appraisal of James's View of Causality 101

6 Elisabeth R. Eames, A Pragmatic Concept of Causation 119

7 Keith R. David, Percept and Concept in William James 133

8 Gustav Emil Mueller, On William James' "Radical Empiricism" 147

9 S. Morris Eames, The Meaning of Truth in William James 157

10 Elisabeth F. Flower, The Unity of Knowledge and Purpose in James' View of Action 179

11 Felicia Czerwionka, The Self in William James'
    Psychology 201

12 George Francis Cronk, James and the Problem of
    Intersubjectivity: An Interpretative Critique . . . 221

13 Abraham Edel, Notes on the Search for a Moral
    Philosophy in William James 245

14 John Albin Broyer, William James' Theory of
    Education 261

15 John K. Roth, William James and Contemporary
    Religious Thought: The Problem of Evil 283

16 Hans F. Geyer, Eight Spotlights on "The Will
    to Believe" by William James 307

17 Gérard Deledalle, William James and his Father:
    A Study in Characterology 317

18 Victor Lowe, The Relation between James and
    Whitehead 331

19 Mohammed Fahdel Jamali, An Appreciation of
    William James: Philosopher, Psychologist and
    Educator 347

20 Herbert W. Schneider, Healthy Minds with Sick
    Souls 357

Walter Robert Corti, Nachwort 379

Bibliography of Writings by and about William James
    by Charlene Haddock Seigfried 385

Index 395

PREFACE

The Fourth Seminar in American Philosophy was held in Winterthur, Switzerland, September 3–7, 1973. Dr. Walter Robert Corti, Director of the Archiv für genetische Philosophie, was the sponsor of this seminar, as he was also sponsor of the previous ones.

I was designated as the one to assemble, edit, and prepare the papers of the seminar for publication. I was ably assisted in this task by John A. Broyer whose scholarship and editing skill made my task much easier. The typing of the final manuscripts was done by Elaine Stonemark, and all of us are appreciative of her careful work. I want to thank Dr. David S. Clarke, Chairman of the Department of Philosophy, Southern Illinois University, Carbondale, for aid in many ways.

All of the participants are indebted to Dr. Corti for his vision and enthusiasm for these international seminars in American Philosophy. He is an inspiration to all of us. The generous hospitality of Dr. Corti, Mrs. Corti, and Hans Iklé is greatly appreciated by all of the participants.

The discussions of the seminar were taped, and the tapes are deposited in the Philosophical Archives of Southern Illinois University, Carbondale.

S. Morris Eames

NOTES ON CONTRIBUTORS

WALTER ROBERT CORTI is Director of the Archiv für genetische Philosophie, Winterthur, Switzerland. He is internationally known as the founder of the Pestalozzi Children's Village of Trogen. His interest in philosophy has resulted in one of the largest collections of philosophical works for the establishment of an international Akademie für Philosophie. He holds the degree of Doktor Honoris Causa, University of Tübingen. Author of Die Mythopoese des werdenden Gottes (1953), Der Weg zum Kinderdorf Pestalozzi (1955), Plan der Akademie (1955), Heimkehr ins Eigentliche (1969).

VAN METER AMES is Emeritus Professor of Philosophy and former head of the department at the University of Cincinnati. He is a former student of George Herbert Mead's and has published numerous articles on Mead's philosophy. A past president of the American Philosophical Association (Western Division), whose presidential address was on "Zen and Mead"; a past president of the American Society for Aesthetics and a delegate to the American Council of Learned Societies. Author of *Aesthetics and the Novel* (1928), *Introduction to Beauty* (1931), *Proust and Santayana* (1937), *André Gide* (1947), *Zen and American Thought* (1962), *Japan and Zen* (with Betty B. Ames (1962), Editor of *Beyond Theology: The Autobiography of Edward Scribner Ames* (1959). Visiting Professor at the University of Aix-Marseilles; Fulbright Research Professor, Komazawa University, Japan; Visiting Professor, University of Hawaii. Ph. B., Ph. D., University of Chicago.

W. DONALD OLIVER is Emeritus Professor of Philosophy, University of Missouri, Columbia. Author of *Theory of Order* (1951) and of numerous articles in philosophic journals; contributor to several cooperative volumes. He has taught at the University of Minnesota and held a Visiting Lectureship at

Princeton University. Guggenheim Fellow, A. C. L. S. Study Fellowship, Fellowship to Advance Original Work in Philosophy; former president of the Missouri Philosophical Association. Ph. B., M. A., Ph. D., University of Wisconsin.

DAVID L. MILLER is Professor of Philosophy, University of Texas. He is a former student of George Herbert Mead's and has published numerous articles on Mead's philosophy. He is the author of *Individualism: Personal Achievement and the Open Society* (1957), *Modern Science and Human Freedom* (1959), *George Herbert Mead: Self, Language, and the World* (1973). He was a collaborator with the editor of Mead's *The Philosophy of the Act,* a contributor to a symposium on Philosophy of Creativity in George Herbert Mead. He holds an award from the Texas Institute of Letter, and he received the Alexander von Humboldt Award from the Government of West Germany, 1969. Ph. D., University of Chicago.

JOHN J. McDERMOTT is Professor of Philosophy at Queens College, New York City, and a member of the Doctoral Faculty at the City University of New York. He is the editor of *The Writings of William James* (1967), *The Basic Writings of Josiah Royce,* 2 vols. (1969), *The Philosophy of John Dewey,* 2 vols. (1973). In 1964, he received a postdoctoral fellowship to do research in American religion and culture and in 1969 was a recipient of the "E. Hollis Harbison Award for Gifted Teaching". He has lectured at many American universities and has published a monograph on *The American Angle of Vision* (1965), as well as other articles and reviews on American philosophy, contemporary culture and urban aesthetics. M. A., Ph. D., Fordham University; LL. D., University of Hartford.

EDWARD H. MADDEN, Professor of Philosophy, State University of New York at Buffalo, was Visiting Professor at the American University of Beirut in 1969–70. He has written articles and books in metaphysics, philosophy of science, and the history of American philosophy. He is past president of the C. S. Peirce Society and General Editor, Harvard University Press, Source Books in the History of Science. B. A., M. A., Oberlin College; Ph. D., University of Iowa.

PETER H. HARE is Professor and Chairman of Philosophy, State University of New York at Buffalo. He specializes in recent American philosophy, and is presently doing research on James' ethics of belief. He is Secretary-Treasurer of the Charles S. Peirce Society and co-author with E. H. Madden of *Evil and the Concept of God* (1968). B. A., Yale University; M. A., Ph. D., Columbia University.

ELIZABETH RAMSDEN EAMES is Professor of Philosophy at Southern Illinois University, Carbondale. She is the author of numerous articles on pragmatism, and of *Bertrand Russell's Theory of Knowledge* (1969); co-author of *Logical Methods* (1971). She has held a Carnegie Fellowship for study of education in Great Britain, and a research grant from the American Philosophical Society. A. B., M. A., University of Toronto; Ph. D., Bryn Mawr College.

KEITH R. DAVID is Associate Professor of Philosophy at William Jewell College, Liberty, Missouri. His doctoral dissertation was written on William James' theory of knowledge. He prepared for archival use at Southern Illinois University the correspondence and manuscripts of Paul Carus, editor of Open Court Publishing Company. He is the co-author of three aero-engineering research reports. He has served as lecturer in American Philosophy at Wichita State University, and has taught philosophy in state and federal prisons in Illinois. B. A., Oklahoma Baptist University; M. A., Wichita State University; Ph. D., Southern Illinois University, Carbondale.

GUSTAV EMIL MUELLER, native of Bern, Switzerland, Research Professor of Philosophy at the University of Oklahoma. Chairman of the Department of Philosophy and the

School of Letters at O. U. President Southwestern Philosophical Society. Publications: *Dialectic, The Interplay of Opposites, Discourses on Religion. Plato – The Founder of Philosophy as Dialectic. Hegel – The Man, his Vision and Work, Origins and Dimensions of Philosophy*. In German: *Amerikanische Philosophie, Dialektische Philosophie. Querschnitt, Gedichte und Doppelreime*, Universitätsverlag Wagner, Innsbruck. Numerous articles in America and Europe. Stories, Plays, Poems. Data in *Who's Who in America, Who's Who in Europe, Who's Who in Switzerland, International Biography*. In more detail: *Instead of a Biography*, Philosophical Library.

S. MORRIS EAMES is Professor of Philosophy at Southern Illinois University, Carbondale. Author of numerous articles, poems, reviews, and of *The Philosophy of Alexander Campbell* (1966); co-editor of *The Early Works of John Dewey, 1882 –1898;* co-editor and contributor to *Guide to the Works of John Dewey* (1970). An Oreon E. Scott lecturer at Bethany College and a former president of the Missouri State Philosophical Association. A. B., Culver-Stockton College; M. A. in philosophy and M. A. in sociology, University of Missouri; Ph. D., University of Chicago; Litt. D., Bethany College.

ELIZABETH F. FLOWER is Professor of Philosophy at the University of Pennsylvania. Her major academic work is in Ethics, Legal Philosophy, and the History of Philosophy especially in Anglo- and Latin America. She wrote, with Murray Murphey, *Principales Tendencias de la Filosofia Norteamericana* for the Pan-American Union (1963); it will appear shortly in English in a much expanded form. B. A., Wilson College; M. A., Ph. D., Bryn Mawr and University of Pennsylvania.

FELICIA CZERWIONKA, OSM, is Assistant Professor of Philosophy, Siena Heights College, Adrian, Michigan. She wrote her doctoral dissertation on the Self in William James's Psychology (1973). This dissertation explicates the relation between continuity and self, particularly continuity's role in James's characterization of the 'ME' and 'I', in self-knowledge, and in self-identity. B. S., Loyola University, Chicago; M. A., Ph. D., Notre Dame University.

GEORGE FRANCIS CRONK is Assistant Professor of Philosophy and Comparative Religions at Bergen Community College, Paramus, New Jersey. He wrote his doctoral dissertation on George Herbert Mead's philosophy of time and action and is currently at work on a book intitled, *The Philosophical Anthropology of George Herbert Mead.* He has published several articles on social philosophy, philosophical anthropology, and American philosophy. B. A., William Paterson College; M. A., Rutgers University; Ph. D., Southern Illinois University, Carbondale.

ABRAHAM EDEL is Emeritus Distinguished Professor of Philosophy, The City University of New York, and former Executive Officer of the CUNY Doctoral Program in Philosophy. His writings in ethical theory include: *Ethical Judgment: The Use of Science in Ethics* (1955), *Anthropology and Ethics* (co-author, 1959), *Science and the Structure of Ethics* (1961), *Method in Ethical Theory* (1963). He is currently serving as President of the American Section of the International Association for Legal and Social Philosophy. B. A., M. A., McGill; B. A., Oxford; Ph. D., Columbia.

JOHN ALBIN BROYER is Associate Professor of Philosophy at Southern Illinois University, Edwardsville. He is the author of numerous articles on American Philosophy, on Pragmatism, and on Philosophy of Education. He is the compiler of a comprehensive bibliography of writings of George Herbert Mead published in *The Philosophy of George Herbert Mead.* B. S., M. S., Pacific University; Ph. D., Southern Illinois University, Carbondale.

JOHN K. ROTH is Associate Professor of Philosophy, Claremont Men's College. He is the author of *Freedom and the*

Moral Life: The Ethics of William James (1969), *Problems of the Philosophy of Religion* (1971), and (with Frederick Sontag) *The American Religious Experience* (1972). He has edited two collections of the writings of William James: *The Moral Philosophy of William James* (1969) and *The Moral Equivalent of War and Other Essays* (1971). He is also editor of *The Philosophy of Josiah Royce* (1971). A Graves Award in the Humanities enabled him to study at Harvard University in 1970–71. He was Visiting Professor of Philosophy at Franklin College (Lugano, Switzerland) in the spring of 1973, and served as Fulbright Lecturer in American Studies at the University of Innsbruck (Austria) during the 1973–74 academic year. B. A., Pomona College; M. A., Ph. D., Yale University.

HANS F. GEYER of Uster, Switzerland, is an author who has devoted over twenty years to writing books on philosophy. His thesis at the University of Zurich was on Fichte, Schelling, and Hegel. He is the author of *Gedanken eines Lastträgers* (1962), *Philosophic Journal* Tome I *(Von der Natur des Geistes,* 1969), *Philosophic Journal* Tome II *(Arbeit und Schöpfung,* 1970), *Philosophic Journal* Tome III *(Das Kontinuum* der Offenbarung, 1971) *Philosophic Journal* Tome IV (Biologie der Logik, 1972), *Philosophic Journal Tome V* (Dialektik der Nacktheit, 1973), *Philosophic Journal* Tome VI (Gedanken des Leibes über den Leib, 1974).

PROFESSOR GERARD DELEDALLE, who is Docteur ès Lettres of the Sorbonne with a thesis on *L'Idée d'expérience dans la Philosophie de John Dewey* (Presses Universitaires de France, 1967), is currently Director of the French Institute in Tokyo. He has written several other books and a number of articles on Dewey and American philosophy, especially a *Histoire de la philosophie américaine* (P. U. F., 1954) and *Pragmatisme* (Bordas, 1970). He is presently working on Peirce's writings. His latest book is on *Peirce et les signes* (Gallimard, 1974).

VICTOR LOWE is Emeritus Professor of Philosophy, Johns Hopkins University. He took his Ph. D. in 1935 at Harvard, where he was a student of Whitehead, Lewis, Perry Hocking, and Sheffer. He contributed to *Classic American Philosophers* (1951), and to the volumes on Whitehead and Lewis in the *Library of Living Philosophers*. Lowe has published articles on James, Peirce, and general issues in metaphysics and epistemology. He is the author of *Understanding Whitehead* (1962, 1968). He is writing a biographical study of Whitehead, for research on which he was awarded an NEH Senior Fellowship in 1968–69.

MOHAMMED FADHEL JAMALI is Professor of Education, University of Tunis. He was educated at the Teacher Training College of Baghdad, the Khalisi School of Divinity, Kadhimain, the American University of Beirut, Lebanon, the School of Education at the University of Chicago, and Teachers College of Columbia University. He was eight times Foreign Minister and twice Prime Minister of Iraq. He signed the Charter of the United Nations on behalf of Iraq, and was many times head of the Iraqi delegation to the United Nations. He is the author of numerous articles and books in English and Arabic, among which are the following: *The New Iraq: Its Problems of Bedouin Education*, Teachers College, Columbia University; *Letters on Islam* published in English by Oxford University Press. Two most recent books are *The Education of the New Man* (1967) and *Horizons of Modern Education for Developing Nations* (1968).

HERBERT W. SCHNEIDER is Emeritus Professor of Philosophy, Columbia University. Author of *A History of American Philosophy* (1946) and of numerous articles and reviews. Woodbridge Lecturer at Columbia University, *Ways of Being* (1961); author of Introduction to Vol. II, *The Early Works of John Dewey, 1882–1898*. He served in the UNESCO Secretariat in Paris in 1953–56, and since his retirement from Columbia University in 1957, has continued to teach at

Colorado College, Claremont Graduate School, and Oregon State University. B. A., Ph. D., Columbia University; L. H. D., Union College, Baldwin-Wallace, Colorado College; LL. D., Claremont Graduate School.

1

WILLIAM JAMES AND THE OPEN UNIVERSE

Van Meter Ames

William James blazed the way to the future. He was against systems. He was dead against determinism. He wanted an open, draughty universe, with nothing settled, everything in question. He exulted in change and novelty, which he always found at hand in the "pure experience" of the "immediate flux of life". He affirmed Emerson's joy in the "eternal now," and anticipated Mead's "philosophy of the present," the present where everything happens and comes to a focus. He wanted freshness, playfulness, and appreciated the way art played with things, to turn up the unexpected.

The humanity of the man was infectious. A student thought of him, approaching Harvard Yard, as "an irresistible gust of life coming down the street."[1] To be a man, James thought, was first to be an animal. He said what would he have given to have been educated in healthy animality. His receptiveness to all impressions made him quick to respond. He said: "In the healthy-minded... the sensations that pour in from the organism only help to swell the general vital sense of security and readiness for anything that may turn up."[2] James was so open that he was not afraid to risk his scientific standing by investigating psychical phenomena, though he never found anything to addle his sanity.

James felt that man's place in nature is one of congeniality rather than one of dominance, a view more Oriental than Western. The James outlook had been anticipated in the Orient, with its living in the moment, its Thoreau-approaching love of nature, and the Thoreau-realization that "No method or discipline can supersede the necessity of being ever on the alert." Nothing can be alien to an interested and responsive person. William James would agree completely with Thoreau's saying in *Walden:*[3] "What is a course of history or philosophy, or poetry, no matter how well selected, or the best society, or the most admirable routine of life, compared with the discipline of looking always at what there is to be seen?" James knew that one must keep one's eyes open and watch everything with no priorities, getting away from the neurosis of needing to make a profit or having to learn something.

As a "natural born" artist, he noticed everything around him, and loved to sketch his family and friends. Scarcely capable of writing a dull sentence, not only were his popular lectures a sure success, but his scholarly *Psychology* is full of refreshing observations. He did not like warmed-up experience, or expression which had cooled off. His writing was like talking and his talk gave a lift even to a boarding house dinner. His wit and thought sparkled with the unanticipated. He loved "the quip, the prank, the merry jibes, the flash of poetry . . ."[4] His humor and gaiety made him a delightful conversationalist and companion. Henry's envious impression was that he had never seen anything "like William's unawareness of exertion after having helped the lame dog of converse over stile after stile."[5] William knew his own secret when he wrote: ". . . conversation does flourish and society is refreshing, and neither dull on the one hand nor exhausting from its effort on the other, wherever people forget their scruples and take the brakes off their hearts, and let their tongues wag automatically and irresponsibly as they will."[6]

The most unexpected thing he did as a psychologist was to question the existence of a psyche. He asked, "Does Consciousness Exist?" and said it did not, as an entity or stuff. In his famous introspection, when he tried to turn on himself and get a look at himself, he had found nothing of what he sought, and thought a full fledged self or person to be. We must recall that Hume too had failed to find a self in himself, after careful introspection. He found nothing but impressions and ideas, which might be assumed to cohere in an identity but were never known to. When William James tried to come upon himself he found nothing more than movements in his throat and chest, which formed a poor substitute for the self he had thought he had as a member of the James family where he had loved to argue and discuss and make fun.

For James the self could not be a mysterious something behind the scenes. For him the word "I" does not stand for a ghost, but is a term of position indicating where the writer's or speaker's body is when he refers to himself. While individuals have bodies, they are not confined to bodies, but join hands with other people, so that the "I" is literally another, many others. The absence of distinct characters in the *new novel* in France since 1956 is a consequence of something like James's denial of consciousness as a separate entity, and his idea of individuality as a function of conversation and community, not a phantom. Some French authors write off people as interchangeable, assuming that Man with his vaunted individuality and rationality is on the way out. To some it may seem worse if the ego of Man is dead with his eternal verities, values and standards than for God to be dead. If the *new novel* goes too far in doing away with characters and their names, this is only an overdue swing of the pendulum away from over-emphasis on the individual since the Renaissance. The self James recognized in others was a way of looking, talking, walking, and various kinds of acting. In his own case, the self must be made up of its interests and pursuits, as he made clear in his chapter on the "Self". For James, "In its widest sense . . . a man's Self is the sum total of all that he can call his . . . his wife and children, his ancestors and friends." In addition to his body, family, and home, "is the recognition he gets from his mates . . . a man has as many social selves as there are individuals who recognize him."[7] French writers of the new novel and critics of the Structuralist school come to James's support in socializing, not liquidating the self. James was a forerunner of Charles Horton Cooley who pointed out the importance of sociability to personality, saying, ". . . the mind lives in perpetual conversation."[8] Developing his view of the social nature of man, Cooley came to his 1909 book on *Social Organization*[9] where he moved the individual "slightly in the background" of society. In *Social Process* he shows that the procedure of the intelligent mind "is a participation in the social process ... the work not only of my own private mind but of a social group. My information comes to me through other people, and they share in forming my ideas."[10] But Cooley thought of each self as complete prior to the social process, instead of seeing clearly that the self results from social process.

Mead makes the same criticism of James (as David Miller has noted)[11] though it may be said that James was working toward a social self by acknowledging the relations going into it, as Betty Flower has suggested (in the Seminar on William James). It was left to George Herbert Mead, James's student and friend, to develop the idea that no self is separate from the first, since self and mind are inherently social. William James had reduced the romantically inflated ego to a modest size except as the individual may gain the strength of ten or ten thousand in the outreach of his interests and associations. James saw how the proportions of social process, as relationships with other selves, become bound up with one's own being and becoming. Like the men of Zen, James had the sense that the individual in his depths draws support from a great mother sea.

This was akin to his father's Swedenborgian teaching of a sea of divine-natural humanity, which would be mystical though understood in social terms. When Henry James Senior denounced self and personality as a stage to be left behind, he was interpreted by his philosopher son to mean not simply that the individual is nothing, but that he is nothing without society. What he gives up in a false sense of self-sufficiency is more than compensated by the sense of being buoyed up by the divine immensity of humanity. The self is indeed open. Here is the saving realization of the Buddhist that he is one with the universal and eternal Buddha (though, with Mead in mind, it would be better to say *becomes* one.) Buddhism in denying the importance or reality of an egoentity, seems close to the teaching of James and his father, Cooley and Mead, that there is no separate self. Neither in Zen nor in American counterparts does promoting the social above the individual mean downgrading qualities of the spontaneous and humorous which appeal to us as human. These qualities flourish more fully and freely when people are not divided by property and status, when the self is truly open.

James had such zest for life that he did not think it needed a meaning or purpose to justify it. He was as free from the doctrine of teleology as from theology, though he did have ends and respected the ends of others. He wanted an American Tolstoy who would show how to take life neat and drink it all down. He loved a good fight and scorned the Roycean idea of a foregone conclusion in the Absolute, with safety nets and guarantees. This sounds like Zen, as does his deploring "American over-tension and jerkiness and breathlessness and intensity and agony of expression," which he laid to "bad habits."[12] Because he was too high-strung and restless for his own good, he was really admonishing himself.

The essence of religion for him was release from uneasiness. While he could sympathize with putting this in theological terms, what he valued was the experience itself, the mystical experience of being saved, not in theories built upon it, but in the immediate sense that everything is all right, which he shared with all manner of ordinary persons, when they are not upset. It was the Zen sense of the present moment, forgetting all but the fundamental ongoing of life, with no goal but the going. The mystical experience of the open self gave the individual the Zen sense of being great enough to be God or Buddha, and interior enough to be himself.[13]

What is this but a belated Orientalizing of the West, coming around to the Buddhist denial of a separate self? The going home of the lonely individual to the mother-sea of humanity is a kind of natural mysticism like that of Zen Buddhism. It is no more a turn to the One than a return to the Many. James welcomed the "Anaesthetic Revelation" of Benjamin Paul Blood as a "mystical verification" of his own pluralism, saying: "Monism can no longer claim to be the only beneficiary of whatever right mysticism may possess to lend *prestige*."[14] In

Zen even the Buddha is nothing but what each of us is. The lift of realizing this gives the release that for William James is the essence of religion. James argued in *Varieties of Religious Experience* that the saving experience called mystical is common to everyone who wakes up to the wonder of ordinary living.

The trouble with the West is that it has been too earnest and serious, too intent upon getting ahead to appreciate taking time out to look around, relax, meditate, and play. William James says in his chapter on "Instinct" that the impulse to play "is certainly instinctive," and continues: "As a boy can no more help running after another boy who runs provokingly near him, than a kitten can help running after a rolling ball." After speaking of the zest of competition in games, he says: "There is another sort of human play, into which higher aesthetic feelings enter. I refer to that love of festivities, ceremonies... which seems universal in our species... The immense extent of the play-activities in human life is too obvious to be more than mentioned."[15] Yet in the West the tendency has been to depreciate play as unworthy, as in the contempt of playboys. For the Puritan ethic, games were frivolous, but they must be taken seriously when seen to involve all of life.

Anyone absorbed in what he is doing is unmindful of what may be happening around him, and forgetful of himself. The same thing occurs in play as in work that is as absorbing as play. This has been notably the case in producing or appreciating a work of art. The idea that art is a form of play goes back to Kant's *Critique of Judgment,* where play as an agreeable occupation was contrasted with onerous labor, attractive only in being rewarded.

Friedrich Schiller developed the identification of art with play, stressing the freedom involved and the harmonious fusion of man's rational nature with the imaginative and the sensuous.[16] Schiller contended that man is whole only when engaged in such activity. Man is completely man only when he plays. Schiller also held that the artist is concerned with appearance rather than "reality." Konrad Lange regarded art as a mature form of child's play in still being a kind of make-believe or "conscious self-deception," affording escape from ordinary existence into an ideal world.[17] What he says about boys running at random and impersonating animals approaches James's account of the play of boys chasing one another, like a kitten after a ball. Samuel Alexander adds that semblance can be enjoyed with full realization that it is mere appearance.[18] James's understanding of play thus backs up traditional writers on aesthetics.

Johan Huizinga remarks that formerly the importance of the play-element was not acknowledged. He says: "The fact that play and culture are actually interwoven with one another was neither observed nor expressed, whereas for us the whole point is to show that genuine, pure play is one of the main bases of civilization."[20] Roger Caillois, following Huizinga, derives most social institutions from play, regarding civilization itself as passing from a disordered to a more balanced and regulated state of privileges and responsibilities, as life approaches the playing field where rules hold sway. For Caillois, although play is not directly useful, it sharpens the physical and intellectual abilities, teaches the acceptance of setbacks with good humor and victory without vanity. To get rid of envy and hate is surely a contribution of play to decent living. But one must deplore the sad effect of professionalism and commercialization upon sportsmanship. Caillois notes that not all games are regulated by rules. There are none for playing dolls or soldiers. Rules are replaced by the fiction of playing a role. But either way, whether rules or the free-wheeling of fiction dominates, play is not only a pastime, not only for fun, but life-giving.[21] But if Man, in the Renaissance conception of him, is disappearing, *people* are still here, playing the games that people play. As Robbe-Grillet, one of the writers of the New novel, says: "Love is a game, poetry is a game, life should be a game."[22] Mead, of course, found play basic in the development of the self. Recent French writers support William James in his love of playfulness. Avant garde writing today, not only in France, provides the experience of what does not exist. In the New Novel there is no subject matter and no goal save the free deployment of words, the interplay of word against word. There is nothing to look for beneath what is written. A text refers only to itself and other texts. "In so far as the New Novel ist genuinely 'ludic,' it seems to be doodling, rather self-indulgently, off the point," John Weightman says in "Refrigerated Dreams."[23]

William James did not easily put the moral will over feeling. He could not accept spontaneity unless "pledged to righteousness." Yet he admitted in a letter: "To you gifted ones who can float and soar and circle through the sky of expression, so freely, our slow hobbling on terra firma must sometimes be a matter of impatience. I think the power of *playing* with thought and language such as you possess is the divinest of gifts."[24]

Michel Butor asks in *La Modification*, "What is the way to Rome?" The traditional novel reader is looking for the way to Rome. Marguerite Duras, like Alvin Toffler in *Future Shock*, is against knowledge as an accumulation to be held on to. People ask, "What is the purpose?" But, as for Cage, music is just sound,[25] so writing is just writing for writers, an endless referring and supplementing, with erasing and subtracting. It is the idea of calligraphy and graphic space.

Calligraphy is not only beautiful brush writing and ink painting (the Japanese word for writer and painter is the same), but is done with curves and flourishes and variations of brush strokes to delight the eye rather than to convey a message. Graphic space is also pure articulation done for the joy of doing and not for spreading information. This means not less but more, primarily more fun. There need be nothing to comprehend in a work of art, which need not express a view of the world. When we enjoy calligraphy, we care about connections, splicings and articulation in space. If more is wanted, what more could there be than the vastness of the void which is always there? It is not an empty emptiness but pregnant with all there is, in the endless articulation of James's open universe. We do not have any text that we can trust to take ahead with us. The way to Buddha is each person's own creation.

As James's father did not like to exalt the self, so William James wanted to honor the common, the shared, in opposition to privilege and supposed superiority. He, like the French Structuralists, wanted to do away with the evils of inequality, economic and social. Their attack upon traditional conceptions of literature is allied with Marxist hostility to the bourgeois economy, and bound up with the rejection of individualism. The idea that literature is created by an isolated individual as his property is outmoded. The author or writer vanishes. Instead of a work's being signed by an author, the text is self-sufficient, which has already happened in the case of a *nom de plume* or pseudonym. The notion that a work is caused by an individual author is associated with the old theological notion that the universe must have an author.

If, as things are, in our system of private property, a work must have a name attached, it should be that of an editor. After all, Schopenhauer had recognized that the title page should carry the names of those whom the supposed author had read, while his own name should appear in a footnote if at all. A writing or text should not be thought of as expressing a field of reality outside itself, but as an active part of the whole encompassing text which never stops being written.[26]

It is maintained that, to produce a text, a piece of fiction must be confined within a formal space, a frame, a grille arbitrarily cut out of the usual space where we get our bearings and keep our balance. The formal space is freed from beginning or end. Detached from unlimited space, within a grille of limited space, grammatical structures function as a text which after all is not fenced off but is a fragment of a potentially infinite text. Each fragment of the grille has the same relation to the whole grille as the finite whole has to the infinite textual ensemble. So a linear reading is impossible. There are no one-way streets in space.

James's long chapter on "The Perception of Space" holds that even in the voluminousness of space at large there is "no order of parts."[27] There would seem to be here the same absence of beginning or end as within the enclosure of "formal space". In fact, there seem to be no real differences between formal and actual space, and James doubts that we have the experience of "the infinite unitary space of the world." All we can do is to "add one image of sensible extension to another until we are tired."[28] As the same inter-textuality which binds any text to other texts would seem to make for one all-encompassing text, so for the new writers, writing is more than writing, taking in all articulation; as the individual is merged with others in the social conception of the self.

James approaches the writers who seem to follow Kant, Schiller *et al.,* in exalting play, i. e., writing for its own sake as needing no justification, simply being the fulfilment of life. Mead carried on the James idea of creative expression as the power of playing. Mead liked to say that the achievement of the artist is so to construct the object "that the enjoyed meanings of life may become a part of living," and called this the attitude of appreciation. The thirst for such enjoyment, frustrated in an industrial society, leads to day-dreaming as a leap to fulfilments which cannot be fused with the boring detail of most work. Mead agrees with James that it is "silly and inept" to hope that the spread of so-called culture will replace men's reveries with the work of great artists, or that machine production can take the place of medieval artisanship.

The Industrial Revolution and mass production pushed art aside, driving the artist to resist by becoming Bohemian and neurasthenic. William Morris's attempt to revive handicraft was futile except for a few. Lewis Mumford in *Technics and Civilization,*[29] wich came out in the same year as Dewey's *Art As Experience* (1934),[30] noted that early machinery was built for action, leaving out the human factor of form and grace; also that it did not help when manufacturers tried to touch up bridges and radiators with imitation hand work, and put floral designs on sewing machines. Men like Frank Lloyd Wright saw that the machine itself could be an instrument of art, with more imagination than slapping on fake designs. But this called for a new set of aesthetic values, eliminating the non-essential and erasing the personal touch of hand-work. The economy of the impersonal would prevail, in slickness and smoothness.

A. N. Whitehead[31] did not agree with the new aesthetics of Mumford any more than with Morris's effort to turn the clock back to the hand-art of the Middle Ages. Whitehead's view is that science and industry have emphasized things and abstractions at the expense of human values. To him values, to be genuine, must be fresh and vivid like the talk of William James. Whitehead asks which is prettier, a cottage in the English countryside or a factory, and answers that the factory might be. It might, with all its machinery, be an organism of vivid values, as cathedrals were in the years when they were a-building, when whole communities joined in the work on them. Like cathedrals, when they were going up, factories are great centers of cooperative activity in the service of society, supplying human needs. Too much of our professional and practical training stresses the abstractions of methodology instead of what is fresh and vital. James denounces the "Ph. D. octopus," thriving now in art history.

James quickly tired of Europe and was eager to get back to his own pursuits, "... but he had friends in every European country: especially in Switzerland, where he spent his happiest years as a student..."[32] Although he stoutly opposed his brother in preferring his native land to Europe, Perry could say: "The lack of art in the environment made it impossible that James should ever be completely reconciled to the ‚American scene.' ... If James felt the futility of theoretical aesthetics, it was not, then, for lack of artistic sensibility or owing to any disparagement of the value of art." Yet he found it impossible to write on aesthetics. While he felt that the aesthetic: experience "was insuperably personal and subjective," he did not think it should be undiscriminating. Perry quotes his feeling that an old couple entranced for an hour by Titian's "Assumption" in Venice, "had missed the point," having no perception of the right relations involved.[33] Perry is referring to the chapter on "The Emotions" in the *Psychology* where James recalls hearing the woman murmur: "How *unworthy* she feels of the honor she is receiving!"[34] Since James felt that aesthetic experience consisted of feeling, and trusted the richness of his own experience over any possible formula, he did not try to write about art. Perry observes that, whereas James could not write about aesthetic experience because he had it, he could write about religious experience because he lacked it. What turned him against "the cult of art lovers" was their association with traditionalism. He was all for "the boundless future or the opportune present... This worship, this dependence on other men is abnormal. The ancients did things by doing the business of their own day, not by gazing at their grandfathers' tombs, – and the normal man today will do likewise."[35]

The points in Mead's paper "The Nature of Aesthetic Experience" were developed in Dewey's book *Art As Experience,* which in turn brought forward James's conviction that gaping at the treasures of the past is no substitute for the aesthetic satisfaction to be had in one's own efforts when they can be at all free and self-fulfilling, that is, when men can work at putting things together with a sustaining sense of the outcome. William James would recognize his own feeling here. Mead could have been thinking of this when he wrote that under favorable conditions "a man's work would in itself be interesting" and his sense of producing something whole would "give him aesthetic delight."[36] In responding to an artwork, especially a work in progress rather than a "treasure" of the past, we can feel that this is what our senses and capacities are for: not only to appreciate this drawing, this music, this poem, but, it may be, this table, this set of knives and forks, or anything pleasing in itself. Indeed, the fascination of the *nouveau roman* is its open secret of making literature out of the little things that happen, that are being done and said every day, in the intertextual text that all our living is ever writing, with no beginning and no end.

What is called James's *primitivism* by Perry, "relish for the *unformed* – the raw and crude"[37] is not consistent with a passage in the *Psychology:* "it is notorious how seldom natural experiences come up to our aesthetic demands."[38] Perhaps some avant garde art would satisfy James, in seeming to be unformed and yet rising above merely natural experiences. Presumably, he would not object to the search for the new in art, since he easily became bored with repetition and always welcomed novelty. Merleau-Ponty says that museums and libraries transform works born in the warmth of life into things no longer breathing under glass.[39]

James would surely like Dewey's contention that aesthetic experience need not be something strange and remote but any normal experience when complete and clarified. James did exclaim with Zen insight: "As if the common-sense world and its duties were not eternally real!"[40] He might have said, "the really aesthetic." This has been the case with primitive people and in the traditional civilizations of India, China, and Japan, where there has been a close relation between art and life. This has been true of Western antiquity, the Middle Ages, and the Renaissance. The things people used, and were used to, had the benefit of the loving touch of art, in work or war or leisure. Men took pride in what they did and had. What they worked with and lived with, they played with.

Today in painting and plastic art, as in writing, the idea of copying or representing reality is rejected. James, always attracted by the new, would have been interested in the rush of non-art or anti-art that has followed Dada and Surrealism. No doubt, Duchamp, Cage, and others have enjoyed astonishing the bourgeois. James would have been delighted by the fooling as well as by the serious part. If it is play, much of it is of a high order, in a structure of signs pointing to signs, in a process that would appeal to Peirce. The avant garde has all but finished off the history of art and its accompanying aesthetics, symbolized by Irwin Edman as "the stained glass attitude" toward cathedrals and museums of Europe which charmed Henry James as wonderfully superior to the "cruelty and barbarism" of his native country. But William James, after he "had especially looked forward to seeing the art treasures of Florence which had so thrilled Henry... could not thoroughly enjoy even these without wondering whether great art were not a thing of the past ... Like Emerson he felt that it was important not that poets had written poems or sculptors had carved statues but that poems and statues could be and were being created still. William respected artistic creation as activity but not as artefact."[41] In line with his love of an open universe he felt that finished works of art were sterile in contrast to the unpredictable truly creative process.

It is not to be forgotten that William James was an artist himself, not only in love with sketching but in his stirring prose. While his moral earnestness kept him from being an aesthete, his aesthetic nature kept coming to the fore, as in his susceptibility to the seductions of Italy and in his reluctant admiration of Santayana. Incidentally, he agreed with Santayana that volumes of aesthetics rest upon moments of aesthetic experience. James said: "... the experience of a single strain of melody or verse of poetry, of a single square foot of genuine color, is more important to the soul than the reading of all the books on beauty ever composed."[42]

William James recognized that life is a Zen flux with no stopping place. So Eastern sages say, "Just go on with your life." As James meant to show in his *Varieties of Religious Experience,* the saving experience, commonly called mystical, is common, available whenever anyone wakes up to the wonder of ordinary experience. His ultimate wisdom, in perhaps the last thing he wrote, was to let his last word be the (Zen) word of his friend Blood: "There is no conclusion. What has concluded that we might conclude in regard to it? There are no fortunes to be told, and there is no advice to be given. – Farewell!"[43]

NOTES

1. Gay Wilson Allen, *William James: A Biography* (New York: The Viking Press, 1967), p. vii.
2. William James, *Talks to Teachers* (New York: Henry Holt and Company, 1908), p. 204.
3. Thoreau, *Walden*, Chapter on "Sounds."
4. Allen, *William James*, p. 126.
5. *Ibid.*, p. 90.
6. James, *Talks to Teachers*, p. 222.
7. William James, *The Principles of Psychology* (New York: Henry Holt and Company, 1890), I, Chapter on "The Consciousness of Self."
8. Charles Horton Cooley, *Human Nature and the Social Order* (New York: Scribners, 1902), p. 54.
9. Charles Horton Cooley, *Social Organization* (New York: Scribners, 1909), Preface.
10. Charles Horton Cooley, *Social Process* (New York: Scribners, 1918), p. 354.
11. David L. Miller, *George Herbert Mead: Self, Language, and the World* (Austin: University of Texas Press, 1973), p. 48. See Miller's reference to p. 173 of Mead's *Mind, Self and Society*.
12. James, *Talks to Teachers*, p. 212.
13. William James, *The Varieties of Religious Experience* (New York: Longmans, Green and Co., 1902), p. 509.
14. Ralph Barton Perry, *The Thought and Character of William James* (Boston: Little, Brown & Co., 1935), II, p. 659.
15. James, *The Principles of Psychology*, II, pp. 427—429.
16. Friedrich Schiller, *Letters on the Aesthetic Education of Mankind* (1795).
17. Konrad Lange, *Das Wesen der Kunst* (1901).
18. Samuel Alexander, *Space, Time and Deity* (London: Macmillan and Co., Ltd., 1920).
19. Melvin Rader, *A Modern Book of Esthetics*, 3rd ed. (New York: Holt, Rinehart & Winston, 1962), pp. 4—19.
20. Johan Huizinga, *Homo Ludens* (Boston: Beacon Press, 1955), p. 5.
21. See Roger Caillois, *Les Jeux et les Hommes* (Paris: Gallimard, 1958).
22. Alain Robbe-Grillet, in *Le Nouvel Observateur*, 23 June, 1970.
23. John Weightman, *The New York Review of Books*, 1 June, 1972, p. 10.
24. R. B. Perry, *The Thought and Character of William James*, II, pp. 257; 258; 259.
25. See John Cage, *M: Writings, '67—'72* (Middleton, Conn.: Wesleyan University Press, 1973), Foreword, p. v.

26 See Jean-Louis Baudry, "Ecriture, Fiction, Idéologie," in *Théorie d'Ensemble* (Paris: Ed. du Seuil, 1968), pp. 136—137.
27 James, *The Principles of Psychology*, II, p. 145.
28 *Ibid.*, p. 275.
29 Lewis Mumford, *Technics and Civilization* (New York: Harcourt, Brace and Company, 1934).
30 John Dewey, *Art as Experience* (New York: Minton, Balch and Co., 1934).
31 A. N. Whitehead, *Science and the Modern World* (New York: The Macmillan Company, 1925).
32 Allen, *William James*, p. x.
33 Perry, *The Thought and Charakter of William James*, II, pp. 254—255.
34 James, *The Principles of Psychology*, II, p. 472.
35 Perry, *The Thought and Character of William James*, II, p. 258.
36 George Herbert Mead, *International Journal of Ethics*, XXXVI, No. 4, (1926), 382—393.
36 Perry, *The Thought and Character of William James*, II, p. 257.
38 James, *The Principles of Psychology*, II, p. 672.
39 Maurice Merleau-Ponty, *Signes* (Paris: Gallimard, 1960), pp. 96; 78; 79.
40 *Letters of William James,* Edited by his son, Henry James (Boston: The Atlantic Monthly Press, 1920), II, p. 199.
41 Allen, *William James*, pp. 186—187.
42 Perry, *The Thought and Character of William James*, II, p. 127; from the *Nation*, LIX, 1894), 49—50.
43 William James, *Memories and Studies* (New York: Longmans, Green and Company, 1911), p. 411.

2

JAMES' CEREBRAL DICHOTOMY

W. Donald Oliver

My title refers not to the division between the two halves of the physical brain, but to a dichotomy peculiar to James. The opposite lobes of the physiological brain normally work in harmony with one another. This is not the caise with the division I detect in James. He is a philosopher with a divided mind. Two distinct themes run through his philosophical writings, which at certain points are in fundamental opposition. In a broad way, the tension between these themes shows itself in the young James' range of interests and the deep psychological cleft he had to leap before he could enter upon the successful career which eventually he did consummate. He was not one of those facile students who absorb the verbal form of what is presented as indispensable to mastery of their chosen profession. What he read he had to *believe*. Philosophy, or any knowledge, was for him something to live by, to be lived, to be evidenced in his course of life. It had either to become integral to the corpus of his personality, or to be rejected, externalized as academic chaff. In some men a similar strain of deep seriousness yields humorlessness and unimaginative combativeness. What cannot be assimilated must be destroyed. Not so with James. He did have his combativeness – he could never let slip an opportunity to deliver a blow to what he called absolutism and idealistic logic – but instead of destroying all that he could not assimilate to himself, he sacrificed the unity of his world, or, at the least, of *the* world, to make room for a plurality of centers of assimilation, so that what had been excluded from one might be left available for inclusion in others. Indeed, his combativeness is aroused against just those philosophical systems that reduce to nothingness what they cannot assimilate.

Still, James has his own difficulties with assimilation. Sometimes what he is anxious not to destroy exerts destructive pressure on what, by his native propensities, he has thoroughly assimilated. In a sense, we could say that James is a victim of his own tolerance. He would have been better organized as a person had he been less tolerant of diverse opinions. Thus when, in a moment of personal crisis, he found it imperative that he reject the postulate of determinism, because its assimilation would have destroyed all that was fecund of meaning in life, he did not pose to himself the question what would become of the scientific venture on which he was already launched, if this postulate were withdrawn – a question which Peirce did raise and face in all seriousness, and one which Dewey raised and faced too. That is to say, James neither fully rejected nor fully assimilated either horn of the determinism-indeterminism dilemma. In a sense which I shall make explicit as I proceed, he tried to see it as no dilemma at all, but the interpretation he adopted so to see it backfired and bid fair to destroy one half – to my mind the most important half – of his philosophy. Let us take a look at that "most important half" – his pragmatism and its requirements.

A central notion of pragmatism is that "thought makes a difference," a difference in the behavior of men who take thought about what they are doing, and hence a difference in the course of events in parts of the world inhabited by men. All of James' pragmatic essays emphasize this: the individual is faced with options, options in belief and action, and the former are not without effect on the latter. The choice between options is free, not wholly, but sufficiently to give the individual some control over the physical and social world, as well as over his "inner life" of thought, expectation, and, ultimately, his happiness. James' "meliorism," his preference for a world in which all has not been perfected in advance, but challenging work is left for man, entails the concept of man as an active being with a choice of the acts he shall initiate and those he shall eschew.[1] Man as actor is indissociable from James' pragmatism, and we might well conclude that the doctrine of determinism, which James had once found so oppressive as to engender thoughts of suicide, was rejected for no other reason than that of clearing the way for this pragmatic conception of man, one which James evidently felt he had to have of himself, were he to continue in life.

And yet, James is remarkably chary of speaking of action in direct language. In the years before his famous attack on mind-body dualism, the sort of free action he most often mentions is mental, rather than physical, and is patterned after Renouvier's definition of the free act: "The sustaining of a thought *because I choose to* when I might have other thoughts." He obviously thinks of this act of sustained attention as sometimes having physical effects, and these, apparently, would issue through muscular acts mediated by nerve currents. James deals always with the determinism-indeterminism issue on a global scale, and a subjective one at that. The question, in his hands, becomes one of, first, what kind of universe man could live in with the fullest development of his powers and aspirations, and, second, what effects *belief* in one or another kind of universe would have upon his mode of life. He never faces the question of how the relatively mechanical account of man's physiological equipment, given in *The Principles of Psychology* is to be squared with his doctrine of free will.[2] James is no epistemologist, despite his interest in meaning and truth; certainly not an epistemologist of the sort we have come to expect within the tradition of empiricism. He is curiously dead to the issues which his friend C. S. Peirce was working his way through with so much hard intellectual labor, and he seems to be wholly unaware of what Peirce had already accomplished by the time that he, James, expressed himself, loosely and impressionistically, on these same issues. I suggest two considerations that excuse James for his very sloppy treatment of determinism and freedom within the intimate context of body and mind: First, his direct appeal to experience, which, as he describes it, reveals the looseness of

.tion between episode and episode, makes it seem .essary to *argue* indeterminism; and second, his propensity, which comes to full bloom in his radical empiricism, to replace "oldfashioned" notions of causality by the Humean one of constant correlation, destroys any possible motive to spell out in detail a *mechanism* of interaction between body and mind. Correlation is a relation that can hold between any pair of elements whatever; it therefore undercuts the need for mechanical explanation, or, we could say, it places all modes of explanation on the same level, and therefore fits beautifully James' later accounts of the concatenated universe, wherein no single type of relation, explanatory or merely observed, extends throughout.[3]

Once James had become clear about the "artificiality" of the mind-body problem, and formulated his own, for him final, disposition of it in "Does Consciousness Exist?"[4] there was no need for a doctrine of causal interaction. The distinction between the mental and the physical is now to be expressed in terms of two distinct sets of relations into which the same "neutral stuff" can fall; entering into one type, it is physical reality, entering into the other, it is mental. The two types of relation are equally possible, and equally real, as offered in experience, hence there is no reduction of mind to matter or matter to mind. Nonetheless, I do detect a reduction of what we, in a common-sense way, identify as mental and physical, not, as I have said, of one to the other, but of *both* simultaneously. There does not appear to be anything causal (in a non-Humean sense of causality) about the coming in one set of relations or the other. The same item can, indeed, appear in both, or can pass over from the one to the other. In which it occurs is a matter of experience: "where" it occurs in the "matrix of experience." The distinction, in other words, is one that is found, not one that is caused by anything either within or without this world of pure experience. No explanation need be sought for the occurrence of an item of experience in the one or the other set of relations. Indeed, the very notion of explanation is deprived of meaning, hence to seek one is to fail to understand the import of James' radical empiricism. Things happen, yes. There are changes, of many kinds. The kaleidoscope of experience is open to an indefinite variety of content, including feelings of effort, of imposed force, of intent, of desire. Still, the latter are feelings, and there is no reason why they should attach to one distinguishable item of experience rather than another, and their attachment means nothing more than that is where they have appeared. There can be a Humean causality in this world, to be sure, i. e. a regularity of sequence. I can "make an effort," "will an act," but this means no more than that a certain feeling is followed by a certain change, or sequence of changes, in the content of experience.[5]

To be sure, we don't understand how we move our limbs, or why a feeling of effort, or will, is followed by a certain sequence of experiences, but still, we don't doubt that *we* have done something, have worked a change in a world we inhabit. A mystery is tolerable in a world in which further investigation might dispel it. In the world of pure experience there are no mysteries. There are regularities of sequence still to be discovered, to be sure, but there is no mystery that they would dispel. But then, is there really any sense in talk about discovering such sequences? With nothing behind experience, there is nothing to look for. Far more importantly, there can be no sense in making discoveries, in seeking, looking. There is, in fact, no one who could seek. There may occur feelings of puzzlement, feelings of awaiting expectantly, etc. But they are only feelings, and they cannot provide evidence of the presence of an active being who is doing something or preparing to do something. What follows on these feelings, however regularly, cannot provide evidence of such a being either. A feeling of puzzlement is not equivalent to a puzzled man, a feeling of searching is not equivalent to a man engaged in searching, and no nest of relations can make it so. Relations that terminate merely in items of experience can yield the feeling of leading, of revealing, of doing, etc. Or do they? Isn't it the case that feelings associated with them merely come attached to the relations, together with their termini? It appears that there has been a reduction, not of mind to matter, or matter to mind, but of what we in our daily experience and our ordinary talk believe to be real, substantial objects and men. These are reduced to a special, philosophical, variety of experience, which is not at all what we naïvely think ourselves to be experiencing.

Just what is James attempting to do? I have implied that he was concerned to solve the mind-body problem, with its apparently insoluble puzzle of interaction between mind and body. Perhaps he was attempting something more than this. He tells us that his radical empiricism is more akin to "natural realism" than to the idealism of Locke and Berkeley. By "idealism" he here obviously means the reduction of the content of experience to ideas, not that cosmic idealism he so violently rejected in such thinkers as Hegel and Royce. What he means by "natural realism" one must gather from what else he has written. It should be obvious, from what I have already said, that he does not mean naïve or common-sense realism. He wants to restore the immediacy of experience, he says, and by immediacy he seems to mean first-hand acquaintance with whatever is experienced. I think this an admirable goal, yet the question remains, just what do we experience with this desired immediacy? Or, since it is implied that, as philosophers, we don't, then what is it that we should? And why don't we? We will never discover what James is about if we insist on comparing James' philosophical description of experience with that experience you and I enjoy every day of our lives. The fact is that James' radical empiricism is set within the tradition of Anglo-American empiricism, and makes no sense outside of it. From Locke on, the selfstyled empiricists have shown no interest in truly examining experience to discover what it is like. For all their diatribes against the a priori, their account of the elements of which experience is composed is as dogmatically unempirical as any doctrine found in the history of philosophy. It derives from that arch-rationalist, Descartes, from whom we have inherited both the mind-body problem, and the still more troublesome doctrine of the privacy of ideas.

Few empiricists have thought of going behind Descartes, to

ask whether he could have been wrong. James did, and he appears to have done this by a direct scrutiny of experience. What he found when he looked was that the elements of experience are not as discrete as classical empiricism had taken them to be. He had observed, in *The Principles of Psychology*, that ideas tend to be sharp at their "centers" and to shade off into vague, diffused "margins", wherein they often overlap one another.[6] Hence experience can possess a continuity that is not derived solely from the intellectual process of the unfoldment of ideas, called deduction, that characterizes Descartes' philosophy. Subsequently, James observed, and emphatically insisted that relations as well as their terms are given experience.[7] This strengthened his protest against the rationalistic delegation to mind, or reason, of all connective functions, on which the continuity of our world had been asserted to depend. It also weakened the grip of rationalism by making it a question of observation whether our world constitutes a seamless whole of elements bound together by transitive relations over which reason can travel unimpeded. Since it is obvious enough to him who looks, that the relations offered in experience are of many kinds, this opened the way to James' pluralism and his notion of the concatenated universe, and at the same time strengthened his conviction of indeterminism in nature. These are the major changes he induced in the doctrines of classical empiricism. They are all moves in the direction of a genuine empiricism,[8] opposed to the pseudo-empiricism of Locke, Berkeley and Hume.

Nonetheless, James did not succeed in wholly divorcing his thought from the empirical tradition in which he worked these significant changes. His continued reliance on the tradition is evidenced by what I cannot but regard a blindness to certain aspects of experience, which, to my mind, are as readily observed as those which James had pointed out. He challenged the Cartesian postulate of the privacy of ideas in "How Two Minds Can Know one Thing,"[9] but he seemed to think that this dogma could be successfully rejected only by disposing of mind altogether. In the *Psychology* he indulges in an essentially

Humean search for the self, with consequences similar to those Hume arrived at.[10] That is to say, he was working within the restrictive tradition of classical empiricism. The changes he made in that tradition, which I have noted above, did not suffice to lift him completely out of it, and his continued allegiance to it is clearly evidenced in the conception of experience that emerges in his radical empiricism.

Since James says that he wants to restore the immediacy of experience, let us take a brief look at one of the original triumvirate of empiricists, George Berkeley, who professed to be doing the same thing. I think that we can find in Berkeley a truly empirical observation that would go a long way toward restoring what I feel to be missing in James', as well as Locke's and Hume's account of experience.

Berkeley does feed on Locke's initial analysis of experience, and it is easy to see why James could not see Locke as defending experience's immediacy. In Locke, ideas are figures cast upon a screen of mind. They rest there as representatives of something not themselves: substances lying behind and beyond experience. By eliminating one category of unknowable substance, matter, Berkeley did get rid of one "de-realizing" (James' term) factor. To be sure, he did retain the other, mind, but there is a question whether he placed the latter wholly beyond the limits of experience. Certainly it is beyond the comprehension of ideas, for they are passive, innert and discrete, while mind is active and creative. But ideas do not, for Berkeley, make up the whole of experience. He employs his own term, "notion," to fill the gap left by ideas. We do have experience of active beings, he says, of ourselves directly, and, by analogy, of God and other men.[11] It is probably because this move of Berkeley's seems so much like a verbal trick, that it has attracted so little attention. And then, there was Berkeley's strong religious bias. The "notion" was just the sort of thing that would permit him to bridge the gap between human experience and God, and so it was reasonable to suppose it had been invented for this purpose alone. Nonetheless, it could also have been the record of a genuine empirical observation, and if Locke has not already convinced us a to the nature of experience, we ought not to reject it out of hand as nothing more than a clever device.

Berkeley's tentative and undeveloped suggestion that relations also be regarded as notions surely does not make this term look like an *ad hoc* invention. That there is insight in it should suggest itself to anyone who has looked long and hard at Locke's philosophy of ideas. Locke is admittedly full of contradictions, but nowhere in his pages are they more glaring than in his treatment of relations. Once it is admitted that ideas are passive and discrete, and that relations, as they enter into experience, are ideas, all of the paradoxes which F. H. Bradley was so fond of playing on follow automatically.

Ideas are directly experienced in Locke and Berkeley and make up all there is of our experience of nature. Still they are not all there is of our experience of mind in Berkeley, and though they are passive and discrete, they are not deprived of a cause that is active and, by the self-direction of its action, able to think them in ordered relationships. Properly speaking, the order of ideas – the order which science searches for, for example – is imposed on them. They cannot order themselves because they are passive and discrete, and hence are indifferent to whatever order they are found in.[12] Mind, for Berkeley, is an active ordering, as well as a creating, principle, and if we are to hazard a guess as to why he said that relations should be regarded as notions, it ought to be because they bear meaning and purpose. They are not accidental in the way that ideas are. The latter could come in any order, but the order in which they do come is expressive of the intent of the Divine Mind. Perhaps we could even say it *is* that intent, as embodied purpose, hence is active purpose itself.

We cannot impose this somewhat speculative analysis of Berkeley on James, of course, but I think it does reveal what is lacking in James' empiricism, and is utterly essential to his pragmatism. I have always regarded Berkeley as the originator of the pragmatic theory of meaning. Meaning, for him, is constituted by a relation between what is present and what is yet do come; the present idea is a sign of ideas to follow, and no other consideration enters into the notion of meaning, except, as I have just suggested, the activity of a mind that has generated meaning by thinking ideas in a particular order. Up to a point, radical empiricism resembles this Berkeleyan scheme. The order of elements of experience determines the import of the latter. Certain orders characterize these elements as belonging to the mental, others as belonging to the physical.[13] Thus far, the theory of meaning is practically identical in both philosophies, but when we consider James' fullbodied pragmatism, important differences appear. Here there is no universal ordering principle. That experience does come in certain orders is not denied, but individual men are granted a privilege that is reserved for God by Berkeley. Our beliefs, our thought, make a difference in the general order of experience. Where for Berkeley the relations in which God thinks His ideas fixes the order of nature, for James the way individual men conceive nature, themselves, and the possibilities inherent in both, have something to do with the course of future events. Belief is the leaven which brings the ferment of human conceptualization into association with the ongoing processes inherent in the human environment, rendering the former actively productive in redirection of the latter. Here there is no God imposing on experience the order in which it comes to us. Where in Berkeley it is the Divinely imposed order that injects meaningfulness into the world, in pragmatism whatever meanings there are in the world are humanly generated, by our expectations, hopes and fears, conceptualizations, plans and purposes; and belief is associated with all of these.

There are difficulties associated with this philosophical process of humanization which James' radical empiricism, taken strictly as he has expressed it, cannot deal with. It is absurd to suppose that we can make the world into what we would like it to be just by thinking it that way and then by believing that it is so. Of course, no such assertion is found in the radical empiricism, though, speaking loosely and carelessly, James has given some of his critics the impression that this is what he intended in some of his pragmatic writings, especially *The Will to Believe*. The trouble is that the radical empiricism does not lend support to even a moderate and reasonable claim that human thought, action and belief can have some effect on the natural course of events. The doctrine of this phase of James' thought is one of purely descriptive phenomenalism. We *find* certain orders obtaining in our experience, and attach certain labels to them. Even this labeling is not, in all strictness, possible, because *we* are merely segments of the order of experience. Experience just comes. It may display certain orders, but in cannot *be* ordered in the absence of an ordering being who is something more than a mere fragment of its order. I doubt even that order could be discerned if there were no such being, capable of contemplating, thinking over, abstracting, conceptualizing and re-arranging in part the experiences it has had. James has indulged a propensity which philosophers who write in this vein almost always display: he has exempted himself, as describer, from the description he offers.

On the other hand, the same difficulty appears in his description of our experience of nature. On this I have already commented. Radical empiricism not only makes it impossible to consistently conceive an active self, but also active natural objects. Though James can speak of feelings of resistance, of force, of constraint, etc., he cannot convert these into real things affecting us, resisting our efforts, aiding our plans, etc. The absence of such real objects from experience makes nonsense of such talk as Dewey indulges in about the potentialities inherent in natural objects, which could be utilized by man. Phenomenological description misses all that is *practical* in our experience of objects, while pragmatism plays up the role of the practical. James has concentrated his attention too narrowly upon the conventional ontological distinction between mind and matter in "Does Consciousness Exist?" to the exclusion of roles played by the mental, on the one hand, and the physical, on the other, in our dealings with the world. Consciousness, if it can claim a place in our ontologies, must make its case in terms of the essentiality of a "consciousness of": consciousness of entities external to the consciousness, which, though not reducible to the conciousness, can be accepted into our plans, are to be acted on, and can reciprocally act on us.[14] We can utilize these objects only if we know where they are, what they are like, what action we can take on them, and what consequences will follow from this or that act performed on them. James believes that in reducing consciousness to a function, he is not eliminating any of these essential roles, but I cannot convince myself that this is so. Relations integral to experience are supposed to turn the trick, but the relations that James "restores" to experience are those which classical empiricism had excluded from it, and which German idealism had thought it necessary to replace at the expense of making them products of mental activity. James simply observes that they are there, in experience as it comes. This is an effective answer to the atomists and idealists, I think, but then, why should he have stopped with relations? Why shouldn't he have gone all the way with his appeal to experience, and said that objects, too, are given with experience, and men, and the self? Only then could he have made the unabashed claim that he was examining experience and reporting what he had found. The relations that are essential to the claims he makes in his essays on pragmatism hold between objects, thinkers and perceivers of objects, and between the thoughts of thinkers about objects and other men, as well as about themselves.

To summarize: My criticism of radical empiricism is that, though I do not doubt that James can name all those factors in experience that go to make up an act, he is still giving a description, and the latter is not the act. We can read James understandingly because we see him as describing a world that all of us take for granted. All goes well, so long as our belief in this world is unchallenged. James may not have intended to challenge it, yet I cannot but feel that he does. Perhaps the question should be, "Can any theory about experience be equivalent to experience itself?" It would be silly to suppose that James, of all people, thought it could. And yet, he certainly does think that his theory will modify experience. If it didn't, it would not satisfy the pragmatic criterion of meaning. In the end, I strongly suspect that what James did hope to modify was not the experience of "common sense," but that of certain philosophers – i. e., the interpretations of experience given in certain philosophies. Philosophical behavior, even though it is almost entirely verbal. It no doubt does have its effects on action, and if James was seeking a philosophy that man could live by, I remain unconvinced that radical empiricism is that philosophy, though his pragmatism can justly make that claim.

We should not forget that James was a pluralist as well as a pragmatist and radical empiricist. He even offers his radical empiricism as a form of pluralism.[15] It is, but in a limited sense. Observe that, despite his diatribes against idealistic monism, he is a monist himself of a sort, else there would be no sense in his attempt to eliminate mind-body dualism, which is itself a limited kind of pluralism. The theory of a neutral stuff is distinctly monistic when considered in relation to mind-body dualism. To be sure, there is no reason to suppose that any kind of pluralism is a good thing, and Cartesian dualism is surely not radically pluralistic. Most significantly, it excludes the possibility of a concatenated universe, and that may be James' most worthy contribution to contemporary thought. If we read James' pluralism and radical empiricism as intimately related to one another, we will perhaps see better what James was trying to do. Rejection of non-neutral ontological stuffs levels many barriers of ontological prejudice. Those who think they know what the world is made of, deduce from that "knowledge" what can and cannot exist in the world. They cannot accept the evidence of experience, if the latter seems to entail the existence of entities and events that their ontology tells them could not be. Thus James' monism has the effect of unfreezing conventional dualism, and sanctioning a less prejudiced scrutiny of experience to determine what is to be found there. The result is radical pluralism, if scrutiny does yield great variety. Though I have complained that James rejects much of what I find when I look to my experience – objects, animate and inanimate, other men, myself, action and active beings, specifically – and I am not convinced that James can reconstruct these contents of experience out of what his notion of pure experience provides, I must admit that the move he has made does yield great freedom from ontological prejudice, and is, in this respect, an improvement in philosophical method. Nor would I recommend a return to some conventional ontology to correct James' "excesses." I believe that a few rather simple modifications in the philosophical concept of substance, which would result in a radical pluralism of substances, rather than of phenomena, would obviate the difficulties I find in James. But that is another story, and not part of the task I set out to accomplish in this paper.

I cannot resist, though, one last critical comment. Had I conceived the theme of this paper somewhat more broadly, I might have observed a trichotomy of warring themes in James, rather than a dichotomy. James began his career as a physiologist and soon undertook the task of setting psychology up as a science. What is the effect of his radical empiricism and pluralism upon the very considerable contribution he made in this direction? *The Principles of Psychology* is frankly dualistic, and one gathers, from the role assigned in it to man's physiological and neurological equipment, that it has strong leanings to materialism. It exhibits tendencies toward reduction of the mental to the physical; also tendencies toward a Humean phenomenalism in the search for the nature of the self, both of which I believe to be incompatible with James' pragmatic humanism. Thus James' psychology incorporated incompatible themes, and might have destroyed itself. However that may be, his radical empiricism would surely have destroyed it if, as I have argued, the latter provides no ground for an active, materialistic ground for man's thought and action. Surely, his early work would have had to be re-thought and re-written after the appearance of his radical empiricism, and it would have assumed a very different form in the re-writing.

That James' thought developed and suffered change is nothing against him, yet we could feel happier about his undeniable contributions, had he voiced a few rejections himself. What did he think of his early work?[16] Where would he have begun a reconstruction of it? All this is but to repeat the frequently made assertion that James is not a systematic philosopher. It would be unjust to demand that he be what he is not. The value of his contributions may lie in the wealth of rich and bold suggestions he advances for others to develop. Still, one can scarcely down the urge to put the pieces of this complex puzzle that is William James together to see what kind of picture they compose.

NOTES

1 See William James, *Pragmatism* (New York: Longmans, Green and Co., 1907), pp. 290—291.
2 To be sure, James carefully dissociates psychology, as he is dealing with it in the "Principles," from metaphysics. See William James, *The Principles of Psychology* (New York: Henry Holt and Company, 1890), Vol. I, Preface. He does not decry metaphysics, but on the contrary asserts its necessity, yet thinks it should be excluded from scientific psychology. This is one of the things that makes it so difficult to interpret James. His addresses are tailored to specific audiences. He says not only what he thinks they will understand, but what he thinks they "need." In the case of the *Psychology*, he caters to what he takes to be the needs of science and the positivistic prejudices of the scientist, but reserves to himself the right to entertain whatever metaphysical beliefs he may subsequently choose to about "mind," the "soul," etc. This has the admirable effect of reducing any air of dogmatism that might be attached to what James has to say, but it also prevents us from knowing what James truly believed. For himself, it has the advantage of permitting him to leave open the more important metaphysical issues, some of which he had not fully settled in his mind even by the date of his death.
3 Hume asserted himself to be a determinist, yet I can discover no reason why he should have been. I conclude that determinism was, in him, nothing more than one of those "natural" — and irrational — beliefs which he sees as responsible for all forms of "imagined" continuity in our experience.
4 William James, *Essays in Radical Empiricism* (New York: Longmans, Green and Co., 1912), Essay I, pp. 1—38.

5 *Ibid.*, Essay VI, "The Experience of Activity." This is a reprint of his presidential address to the American Psychological Association. Note 2 to page 184 of this address contains the following passage, which is a re-assertion of what he had to say on this subject in *The Principles of Psychology,* though with the limitation I have stated above in my note 2. "I have found myself more than once accused in print of being the assertion of a metaphysical principle of activity ... I should like to say that such an interpretation of the pages I have published on Effort and on Will is absolutely foreign to what I meant to express. [*The Principles of Psychology,* II, Ch. 26.] I owe all my doctrines on this subject to Renouvier; and Renouvier, as I understand him, is (or at any rate then was) an out and out phenomenist, a denier of 'forces' in the most strenuous sense."

6 James, *The Principles of Psychology,* I, pp. 258—260.

7 The "statement of fact," from the preface to *The Meaning of Truth,* quoted by R. B. Perry in his preface to *Essays in Radical Empiricism,* p. x, reads: "The statement of fact is that *the relations between things, conjunctive as well as disjunctive, are just as much matters of direct particular experience, neither more so nor less so, than the things themselves.*"

8 I take it that a genuine empiricism is one in which experience would be left to decide of what it is composed.

9 James, *Essays in Radical Empiricism,* Essay IV, pp. 123—136.

10 James, *The Principles of Psychology,* I, Chapter X, pp. 291—401. But see note 2 above.

11 "We comprehend our own existence by inward feeling or reflection, and that of other spirits by reason. We may be said to have some knowledge or notion of our own minds, of spirits, and of active beings, whereof in a strict sense we have not ideas. In a like manner, we know and have a notion of relations between things or ideas, which relations are distinct from the ideas of things related, inasmuch as the latter may be perceived by us without our perceiving the former. To me it seems that ideas, spirits and relations are all in their respective kinds, the object of human knowledge and subject of discourse: and that the term *idea* would be improperly extended to signify everything we know or have any notion of." *Principles of Human Knowledge,* 2d ed., Part I, Sect. 89.

12 See my *Theory of Order* (Yellow Springs, Ohio: Antioch Press, 1951), pp. 37—38.

13 James, *Essays in Radical Empiricism,* "Does Consciousness Exist?", pp. 27—33.

14 James often speaks of "things" in just this way, but the question

is, whether they are granted a home in the world of pure experience in a more than Pickwickian sense.

15 "In my own mind such a philosophy [of pure experience] harmonizes best with a radical pluralism period...." *Essays in Radical Empiricism,* "A World of Pure Experience," p. 90.

16 He did call *The Principles of Psychology* "dry." But this is not the sort of rejection I have in mind.

3

WILLIAM JAMES AND THE SPECIOUS PRESENT

David L. Miller

James took the expression "the specious present," from Edmund R. Clay, a British psychologist who explained what he meant by it in a book entitled *The Alternative: A Study in Psychology* (1882).[1] Clay contrasted the time period required for experiencing change with what he considered to be real time. He believed we experience change, such as the flying of a bird, not in a real or ontological present but in a specious or phenomenological (psychological) present.

Obviously it takes time for a bird to fly and it takes time to experience the flight. But, Clay contends, the flight has past in it and we cannot experience the past part of the flight in a real present. Nevertheless, since we do experience the flight and since we cannot, so Clay argues, experience it in a real present, we experience it in what he called a "specious present." Clay does not say we do not experience anything in a real present, but he argues that we cannot experience change in a real present. He believed a real present consists of an instant analogous to a spatial point, and what one experiences in a real present is a bird at rest or a bird confined to a static space.

It is clear that Clay believed space is made up of discrete points or discrete atomic places and that time is made up of discrete instants. He believed, accordingly, that we experience, in what he called a real present, a thing that exists in a discontiuous space. He held that motion consists in the occupation by a body of discrete successive points in discrete successive moments of time. Clay, along with many others of his time, was still influenced by Zeno who assumed that a spatial line and a temporal duration are divisible into an infinite number of points and instants which constitute a dense series. But Clay did not understand the meaning of duration as a continuum, and it is obvious that neither a continuum nor a duration can be constructed out of discrete points, instants or moments.

Clay's notion of "the specious present" was based on the assumption that real, "objective," ontological time is identical with abstractions or concepts used by mathematicians and physicists in their treatment of time. He was confusing experienced change and time with concepts by which we understand it. Clay's conclusion seems to be that if experience does not conform to these abstractions, then so much the worse for experience, whereas, as we will see, James assumes that if certain abstractions or concepts are not adequate for interpreting experience, then so much the worse for these particular abstractions, and we must search for others.

James' Concept of the "Specious Present"

Although James and many after him used the expression "the specious present," they did not mean by it what Clay meant. Clay meant a present that is only apparent; a present infected with subjectivity and the sensuous. To Clay the specious present is phenomenal or psychological, relative, but not real, objective, or ontological. James, on the other hand, resorted to what he called a "radical empiricism" and, as a consequence, he claimed that we experience real, objective change and that what is experienced in the so-called specious present is what it is experienced to be. Which is to say, the real has a durational component which cannot be analyzed into or equated to discrete, isolated atomic instants or points. This leads easily to the conclusion that the points and instants as used by mathematicians and physicists are abstractions, methodologically useful, and their use is methodologically justifiable. In brief, Clay mistook abstractions for concrete reality, he mistook an instant of time, which is an abstraction, for a concrete present, which is real, ontological time, having of necessity a durational dimension. Hence "the specious present" as used by James, cannot be assimilated to discrete instants which succeed one another. Rather events or happenings constitute a continuum or, as James says, a flux,[2] but the flux in and by itself is not divided nor does it consists of an aggregate of discrete components. James says: "It is just intellectualism's attempt to substitute static cuts for units of experienced duration that makes real motion so unintelligible."[3]

James holds that the "flux" is experienced directly. He says, "'Pure experience' is the name which I gave to the immediate flux of life which furnishes the material to our later reflection with its conceptual categories."[4] James emphasizes that the flux, though it is experienced in "drops" or "pulses" (each drop being confined to a specious present), is to be contrasted with conceptualizing about it. "The concrete pulses of experience appear pent in by no such definite limits as our conceptual substitute for them are confined by."[5] He believed the world as experience is real, and it is a continuum, no two contiguous phases of the flux are in fact separated. "You cannot separate the same from its other, except by abandoning the real altogether and taking to the conceptual system."[6] "Their *names*, to be sure, cut them into separate conceptual entities, but no cuts existed in the continuum in which they originally came."[7] From this it is clear that conceptualizing and categorizing alone are responsible for cuts within the flux.

The Nature of a Real Present

James, in his use of the idea of the specious present indicates a basic tenet of all process philosophies. Briefly, every process philosopher accepts the fundamental claim that the real has a durational spread, that mathematical points and instants are abstractions, and as a corollary, anyone who believes that the real can be simply located in a space and a time is mistaking mathematical abstractions for concrete reality or, as Whitehead says, they commit the fallacy of misplaced concreteness. James would agree, since he believes the real is an undivided continuum, a flux, and it is experienced or experienceable.

It is unfortunate that what James and others mean by a real present continues to be called by some a specious present. However, most process philosophers use a different more appropriate term. For example H. N. Lee[8] calls it "a concrete present," G. H. Mead calls it "the undifferentiated now," F. S. C. Northrop speaks of "the undifferentiated aesthetic continuum," and Kant, who of course was not a process philosopher, makes reference to the "sensuous manifold." All process philosophers emphasize the reality of becoming and all maintain that whatever exists has temporal extension. For example, Mead[9] holds that the act, not the moment, is the unit of existence, and Whitehead speaks of events and actual occasions as units of existence. James, Bergson, Whitehead, Dewey, Mead, Lee, and others hold that the real (ontological), like the phenomenal, has a durational spread, and there is nothing specious or subjective about what is experienced in a present, inasmuch as both a present and experience are phases of nature. "What really *exists* is not things made but things in the making. Once made, they are dead, and an infinite number of alternative conceptual decompositions can be used in defining them."[10]

James' Main Contention

James' main contention, as advocated in *Principles of Psychology, Radical Empiricism,* and *A Pluralistic Universe,* is that ontology or metaphysics must be founded in experience, in what has been called the phenomenal. "When we conceptualize, we cut out and fix, and exclude everything but what we have fixed."[11] Implications of his view for process philosophy, which is a revolt against atomism and Cartesian dualism, are momentous. Here I hope to take some of these implications into account.

First, one must found ontology on what is experienced, and such terms as "events," "actual occasions," "the social act," and "duration," serve to indicate units of experience or concrete reality, and many terms such as "instant," "point," "stimulus," "response," will be found to refer either to abstractions, which are not a part of the flux, or else they will refer to phases of the flux or phases of more inclusive units or wholes. Anything and everything that is real belongs to the natural continuum, or it is a phase of the continuum, not a disconnected entity having existence apart from the flux. The flux is a continuum not made up of discrete atomic units. There is nothing in the continuum which cuts itself off from other phases of the continuum. And although such philosophers as Berkeley and Hume, Cartesian rationalists and mechanists, commit the fallacy of misplaced concreteness, they also, if James is correct, commit another fallacy, namely "the fallacy of misplaced discreteness."[12]

The Fallacy of Misplaced Discreteness

Change and the flux have meaning only over against the permanent or the relatively permanent. James recognized this when he wrote:

> Conceptions form the one class of entities that cannot under any circumstances change. They can cease to be, altogether; or they can stay, as what they severally are; but there is for them no middle way. They form an essentially discontinuous system, and translate the process of our perceptual experience, which is naturally a flux, into a set of stagnant and petrified terms. The very conception of flux itself is an absolutely changeless meaning in the mind: it signifies just that one thing, flux, immovably. *(Principles of Psychology,* I, 467–8).

It is clear that James contrasted conceptions with the flux and that the changeless or permanent is located in conceptions, not in pure experience of the flux. Concepts, abstractions when applied amount to an interpretation of the flux, the given, the undifferentiated aesthetic continuum or, if you will, they amount to a cutting of the flux. Only by names do we cut them into separate *conceptual* entities.

Here I want to emphasize that every concept and every abstract term is designed to effect a cut within the continuum, the flux, and that without transactions[13] between an organism and its environment no such cuts would be effected. Concepts, conceptions, and abstractions are discrete, but according to James, the discrete is not in the flux, which is a continuum. It would be a mistake to conclude that because James holds that experience comes in "pulses," therefore, first-hand pure experience of the flux gives us distinct separate parts. Discreteness is effected only by transactions between an organism and its environment, including the transaction of conceptualizing. Several erroneous philosophic systems have arisen because the conceptual, the discursive, has been substituted for the flux.[14] It follows that those who claim that the aesthetic continuum, the flux, is made up of discrete or atomic parts have committed the fallacy of misplaced discreteness.

The real, the actual, is not in itself atomic, as Whitehead would have it. To cut it requires transactions between an organism and its environment, and when these transaction become lawful, we have habits, and when they become habits of which we are aware, then we have concepts, abstractions, and concepts are a means, a method of cutting the flux. But there is no discretion, no discernment, no cutting apart from transactions, and the locus of the discrete is the habit, the concept, generality, universality, or what Peirce called Thirdness, which applies to rules and laws as well.

Process philosophers should think of concepts and abstractions as devices by which we cut the flux. They are means, instruments. And the actual cutting must be understood in terms of habits and other transactions connected with habit, such as universals, Thirdness, etc., mentioned above. A habit is itself a concrete, specifiable way of acting on the flux. A kind of habit expresses a way of making a cut. Insofar as nature is a continuum, the actual application of an idea or a habit, or a concept or an abstraction, is a phase of the process of adjustment. Their application in each instance is a transaction within the continuum, the flux, and the transaction is a part of the natural process. To be aware of a method of cutting is to have an idea, a concept, which is a species of generality or Thirdness.

Discreteness and Methods of Cutting the Continuum

Zeno's paradoxes and the whole of mechanistic philosophy along with the atomic philosophy of such men as Berkeley and Hume, as well as the metaphysics of the early Wittgenstein and the early Russell (which was founded on logical atomism), all result from a failure to make a distinction between the nature of concepts and ideas, on the one hand, and that to which they apply on the other. These philosophers assumed that inasmuch as concepts are fixed and stable that, therefore, what is known by means of them must itself also be fixed and discrete. They assumed that there is an isomorphic relation between the known and the means by which it is known. Nature, they assumed also, is real only insofar as it conforms to static concepts or to immutable forms. Thus Zeno held that the concepts "point" and "instant" refer to actual entities in the spatio-temporal world, entities that are discrete, whereas James argues that "there is no such objects as the present moment except as an unreal postulate of abstract thought."[15] Zeno rightfully argued that if points and instants refer to real parts of space and time, then no object can move or get from one point to the next. His argument is based on the fallacy of misplaced concreteness.

If nature is a continuum, both spatially and temporally, then it cannot be built up out of discrete entities and space and time cannot be made up out of what is referred to by "points" and "instants." "When you have broken the reality into concepts you never can reconstruct it in its wholeness."[16] These concepts are abstractions and as used by mathematicians and scientists they are means of conceptually making cuts within a continuum.

Before discussing conceptualization in its general form, let us indicate the mathematical meaning of cutting a continuum. Richard Dedekind says:

> If all points of a straight line fall into classes such that every point in the first class lies to the left of every point of the second class, then there exists one and only one point which produces this division of all points into two classes, this severing of a straight line into two portions.[17]

Dedekind formulated this statement in the 1870's and it is known as a *"Schnitt"* or "Dedekind cut." I conceive of the Dedekind cut as a conceptual means or method of cutting into parts or of making conceptually discrete what is in fact a continuum. This was done by Dedekind by use of numbers, both rational and irrational. Thus neither a line nor a duration is to be thought of as consisting of discrete points or instants; that is, of atomic parts. Rather "points" and "instants" are conceptual devices enabling us to conceive of the flux or to divide it conceptually and, finally, practically, into different kind of things, such as before, after, contemporary, etc., even as ordinary classifications such as, say, "dog" or "cat" enable us to conceive of particular phases of nature in discrete terms. To conceive of phases of nature in discrete terms means to act or respond implicitly to these phases in habitual, general ways of which we are aware. The application of a concept amounts to an overt response to a particular (object or situation) according to a rule.

Had such men as Georg Cantor and Richard Dedekind not shown how it is possible to cut conceptually, at any selected place, what is in fact a continuum which does not by itself furnish the cuts, then we would still be unable to offer a scientific defense of the claim that a bird actually flies and that we experience its flight. It is only by interpreting the Dedekind cut as a method of conceiving of the flight as being divisible conceptually (though not actually) into parts that we can justify both our experience of the flight and our knowledge of it. Conception is related to what is experienced as is a cut to a continuum. The Jamesian flux is a continuum, and no cuts are furnished by it as such, and no cuts are applied to the continuum unless there is experience, and experience is a transaction between phases of the flux. Every such cut occurs not to the flux but within the flux, since neither experience, habit nor conceptualizing can stop the flux.

How Cuts Within the Flux are Made

James' philosophy rests on "The postulate that *the only things that shall be debatable among philosophers shall be things definable in terms drawn from experience.*"[18] James says: "To be radical, an empiricism must neither admit into its constructions any element that is not directly experienced, nor exclude from them any element that is directly experienced."[19] Now no cut is made within the flux apart from transactions. Experience is a species of transaction. Pure experience happens in pulses, each pulse being confined to a specious present, a concrete present. Cognition emerges from pure experience and all cognition refers to something beyond what is immediately experienced or it refers to something beyond a concrete present, that present, that now, in which the flux is directly experienced. Knowledge had in a concrete present is not confined to what is experienced in that concrete present. For this reason I do not agree with James' belief that there is knowledge by acquaintance,[20] which means immediate or discrete knowledge during a given concrete present of what is experienced in that present. It means knowledge had in pure experience. The sense datum theory is based on the false assumptions, first, that there are discrete elements *given* in immediate experience; i.e., that discreteness is given with an immediate experience of the flux and, second, that we have immediate and, therefore, certain knowledge of what is given, which means that we can know and know with certainty within a concrete ("specious") present what is sensed in that present.

However experience of what is in a concrete present cannot include a knowledge of what is experienced in that present. The word "knowledge" should be reserved for experience that requires concepts.

But let us get back to what it means to cut the flux. First of all, we cannot stop the flux by thinking about it or by conceptualizing, anymore than Dedekind could break the continuity of a line or a duration by applying such mathematical concepts as "points" and "instants" to them. It may be that C. I. Lewis is correct in saying we never experience the given, the flux, uninterpreted, but it seems to me we can know after the fact what phase of the experiencing transaction should be called the given and what phase should be called the interpretation. Also, there are times when one's experience should be called (Peirces') Firstness; i. e., an experiencing of the presence of something without knowing what it is, without classifying it. We can, in that case, feel or, if you will, intuit that it is without knowing what it is, without classifying it. In fact this is what James calls "pure experience." Again, we often experience something (or at least feel or intuit its presence in a noncognitive way) that suggests conflicting meanings, or evokes incompatible meaning (responses). Be that as it may, my contention is that in general, experience, habits, and cognition are breaks (cuts) within the flux, the continuum, but not breaks of the continuum.

Here I shall consider experience which is confined to living organisms, and I will not, as apparently Whitehead does, enlarge the meaning of experience so as to include transaction between and among inorganic elements or entities. However, it may be said parenthetically that all transactions between and among inorganic particles, if intelligible, are understood in terms of laws or Peirce's Thirdness. And, in general, a knowledge of any and every particular must be stated in terms of the lawful (or habitual) manner in which it reacts (transacts) with other particulars, each particular being thought of, therefore, as a phase of a more inclusive process.

In speaking of experience had by a living organism we are, *ipso facto,* speaking of a relationship between an organism and its environment neither of which actually exists apart from the other and both of which belong to a process, namely a process of adjustment. At the lowest level of such experience the organism, by virtue of a present sensed object or state, takes into account, by its action, something that is outside or beyond that present. It is reacting by way of the given to something not then given; an interpretation is made of the given. Whenever such an interpretation becomes habitual it is a kind of generalization (Thirdness) and might well be called a proto-generalization.[21] Every interpretation, whether at the noncognitive or cognitive level, is a cutting of the flux, it is a reaction within the flux, a kind of reaction, and the locus of discreteness is the lawful or habitual way in which a reaction is effected. Every cut is discrete in the sense that it is an instance of a kind of transaction.

We consider such things as habits, rules, and laws to be relatively permanent. At least this much can be said: every habit is applicable in principle to an indefinite number of cases or situations, and the same is true of rules and laws. Also, no two cases or situations are existentially identical since they belong to different phases of the flux. Discreteness or absolute identity is found in habit, etc., and habits are ways by which cuts are made or ways in which an organism and its environment interact or transact. But the application of a habit does not stop the flux; it is in fact a part of the flux. Habits arise out of the flux and are additional phases of the flux. Concepts, which amount to an awareness of habits or how cuts are made, are sharable and in them we find universality, discretion, and discreteness. It is in them that we find what is communicable from one person to another. In them we have a common world.

Awareness, Cognition, and the Flux

Both Bergson and James make a clear distinction between duration or the flux as directly experienced and our statements about what is so experienced. Both agree that conceptualization and symbolization cannot portray that firsthand feeling we have of the flux. James calls this firsthand experience "knowledge by acquaintance"[22] and he holds that such knowledge cannot be assimilated to knowledge by description. Bergson contends that knowledge by direct intuition cannot be understood by symbols and that symbols distort the real.[23] Whitehead points out that most philosophers, including the British empiricists, were traditional rationalists at heart, since they mistook abstractions, the static, for concrete reality which consists of events or actual occasions having a durational spread. No doubt, James was influenced by Bergson in his claim that concepts or knowledge by description is not faithful to pure experience; that is, concepts do not arouse in us that firsthand experience with concrete reality. On this point both men are correct. And although James says in effect that it is not the function of concepts to portray feelings we have in direct experience of the flux, he could well have shown more fully that concepts are for the sake of action. Concepts give us the form of acts, and thus we can, by symbols for concepts, communicate or convey concepts from one person to another. Our common world is not and need not be a world in which we share feelings, but it is a world in which we share meanings, concepts, which give us the general, the universal, the form of acts.

I have already stated that I do not believe there is knowledge by direct acquaintance or by what Bergson calls intuition. I do not deny that organisms experience directly such things as pains, tastes, odors, sounds, and feelings. But in themselves these are merely felt or experienced, not known.

It is only because an organism uses something in immediate experience as a stimulus or as a sign that habits are possible. For an organism to use something immediately experienced as a sign (or stimulus) means that the organism, by way of the sign, responds toward some mediate object, situation, or thing; e. g., the directly experienced sound (of, say a buzzer) evokes a response by the dog toward the meat, which is in a future relative to the sound. In brief, in the exercise of any habit, an organism takes into account, by its present action (which has been evoked by a sign or stimulus) some distant, oncoming object or situation. That present in which the organism experienced the sign is a concrete present, and the consummatory phase of the act evoked by the sign lies in a later concrete present. For this reason, every habit, which is a kind of generalization, involves more than the experience had in that concrete present, more, namely, than that sensed sign or stimulus which incites the habit.

Although we conceive of a habit as permanent or relatively fixed, we cannot conceive of a particular application of it as fixed; it is a transaction, a phase of the flux. A particular application of a habit, or the application of a habit to a particular phase of the flux, by no means stops or conceptually distorts that to which it is applied, namely a phase of the flux itself. Symbols cannot distort that to which they do not refer. Conceptualization and cuts of any kind are not aimed at depicting the concrete, which is process, lest we commit the fallacy of misplaced concreteness.

Many habits are formed and applied without cognition, without an awareness of how they are formed, without an awareness by the organism of their nature, or without concepts and symbols for these habits. This applies to the habits of all lower animals and it applies to the early life of the child and, in fact, to much of the life of persons even after they are able to be aware of what they are doing. But I shall defend the claim that awareness arises only when the organism can indicate to itself (and an other) (1) the kind of stimulus that will evoke a response, (2) the kind of response so evoked and, (3) the character of the object to which the response answers. This can be done only at the cognitive level by use of symbols, and, more, specifically, by language symbols. Under these conditions only does one have knowledge of the flux or any phase of it.

This means that one can, in the absence of the stimulus, the response it evokes, and the object to which the response answers, nevertheless have a conception of them. To have a conception of a stimulus etc., is different from a direct experience of it. And no concept is equal to or identifiable with those various and numerous phases of the flux (particulars) to which it applies. Each phase of the flux passes away, but nevertheless a concept, which is applicable to the many, does not pass, even as a habit remains after each particular application of it. We speak of a person as being discrete, as using discretion, when he acts according to a rule or a principle, and in fact we find discreteness in concepts, rules, universals, the general, thirdness. But concepts or thirdness cannot distort the flux. Men's minds can be distorted by believing that since a concept is fixed, therefore that to which it is applied, the flux, is thereby also fixed. Every concept, insofar as it is applicable to the flux, serves as a control over transactions between the organism and its environment. A concept both indicates a habitual way of acting and it controls that action.

There is discreteness only insofar as there are kinds of reactions. A concept does not vanish when it is applied any more than does a hammer when used to drive a particular nail. The driving of the nail passes away and no particular driving is repeatable. But we cannot argue that because the hammer is relatively permanent or static, so the driving is static.

Ontology and Epistemology

Everything that was, is, or will be, everything that exists, must be in some concrete present and it must be a part of the flux. The ontological commitment of every thoroughgoing process philosopher after James is that there is a flux and it is a continuum. Still there are qualitative phases within the flux, lest time be monotonous and not a continuum. A continuum cannot be built out of numerically identical events, pulses, or phases.

Consider a string of a musical instrument such as a violin. When the string is vibrating with its fundamental, every part of the string moves. When it vibrates with its fundamental and its first overtone, still every part of it is in motion and to conceive of the string in that condition as having nodes or parts which do not move is to make an ideational or conceptual cut. This cut is made at a so-called point, which is at the middle of the string. But there is no part of the string that can be said to be located at that point. Nor is this conceptual point mirrored by a part of the string. The point does not give an iconic representation of a part of the string, since every part of the string moves.

So it is with the ontological and epistemology, the thing known, the flux, and the means by which it is known, concepts. Epistemology is an enterprise by which we invent concepts, categories, which enable us to conceptually cut the flux. These cuts, when applied, control the way in which the organism transacts with the environment. Conceptual cuts enable us, for example, to classify, and to put two or more existentially different things, such as particular dogs, in the same class. This is not because there exists in each dog something that is substantially (essentially) identical with something that exists in each other dog. Rather it is because the different dogs are functionally (neither substantially nor existentially) identical. That is, the same habit or set of habits, or the same concept or set of concepts, applies to each dog indifferently. Classifying is a way of cutting the flux conceptually, but to say that x is a dog does not cut the dog off from its environment nor does it mean that the dog exists apart from transactions. If habits and concepts are expedient and justifiable, then conceptual cuts are justifiable. This means that epistemology is similarly justifiable, though we should not believe that cuts, made through the epistemological enterprise, have an isomorphic relation to the flux.

[k]nowledge is conceptual and concepts are discrete. But this affords no warrant for assuming that that which knowledge is about is composed of discrete elements. The fallacy of misplaced discreteness consists of hypostatizing the discrete elements of knowledge and reading them back into that which knowledge is about – ultimately into the matrix-reality which is the source and ground of all knowledge – and supposing that there is a Reality composed of discrete units.[24]

I have emphasized that the locus of discreteness is in the relatively permanent, in Thirdness, of which concepts are a species. Also, that only by discretions can the flux be cut conceptually, but not actually. Which is to say once more that breaks or cuts are not of the continuum but arise within the continuum. Our task now is to explain why and how breaks occur, or why and how concepts arise from the flux and how they are related to the flux. Unless conceptualization or thinking is explained as arising out of the flux and, in turn, as being related to the flux, we cannot escape a dualism in which there would be, on the one hand, a flux and, on the other, minds that simply cut the flux. That would be a case in which action presupposes a conscious actor. If we are to evade Bergson's conclusions that symbols distort reality, with its entailed dualism, it must be shown that concepts emerge from experience and are phases of acts of adjustment, related to transactions involved in the adjustment of the organism to its environment and the environment to it. Just as exercising a particular habit is a transaction in a continuum, so it must be argued that thinking and conceptualizing which result in the discrete, are to be explained in terms of process and they must be considered phases of a more inclusive process. Unless this is done, once more, dualism will again raise its head because of an unwarranted bifurcation of nature. The ontological and the epistemological must be integrally related.

My thesis is that there is a flux before there is experience and that the latter emerges from the former, and is an addition to and a part of the flux. Similarly, there is experience before there are habits and there are habits, kinds of transaction, before there is cognition, and the latter emerge from the former. Knowing emerges from the flux and cognition is a transaction, it is a reaction of the individual self to the flux. There is a continuity about the self and something about it that is relatively permanent. But these must be explained in terms of Thirdness, not in terms of substances. Thinking and knowing emerge only when a previously established habit or concept, or a previously established cut, does not apply adequately to a novel phase of the flux. This novel phase is experienced or felt in a concrete present but an interpretation of it and knowledge always refer to some later phase of the flux, a phase that must exist in a later concrete present. Since cognition presupposes prior experience, every interpretation involves a concrete present, a past, and a future. All knowing involves present past and future and all knowing emanates from a concrete present not known at the time it is directly experienced.

When the individual can indicate to himself the kind of a cut that has been made, namely concept, then he has a mind. He has a mind because he is aware of a kind, a universal, and by language symbols he can indicate that kind to himself and to others. In short, one's mind in its beginning is made up primarily out of concepts that are sharable with others, and, therefore, a mind is not only integrally related to the flux but it is a phase of a process, a social process of adjustment.

Although Peirce and James had shown earlier that the function of thinking is to establish habits and that, therefore, thinking is not separable from action, it was left to George Herbert Mead[25] to explain that thinking begins when established habits are not adequate when applied to a new situation. When a transaction is temporarily checked, thinking intervenes and serves as a mediator between the old and the newly established transaction, a new kind of cut. Successful thinking, therefore, results in a concept that applies to the flux and, *ipso facto,* the flux answers to it.

The Self and the Continuum

I have merely indicated above that the flux, which is a continuum, cannot be homogeneous, lest we have monotony and nothing would pass away; there would be no change. If we consider the visible spectrum as seen in the rainbow we realize that there is no point which sharply and clearly divides, say, yellow from orange or orange from red. Still there are qualitative differences in the spectrum. There can be no temporal continuum, no events, actual occasions, or acts of adjustment unless there are phases composing them, and these phases mark qualitative differences, which fact entails that every unit of existence is heterogeneous. Also, experience shows that a given rainbow is similar (functionally identical) to other rainbows, though no two are existentially identical, since they are different phases of the spatio-temporal continuum. In this sense there are repetitions of events, or the same kinds of events recur, despite and because of the existential differences between any two or more of the events.

Also, in accordance with process philosophy, which accepts the theory of evolution, emergence, and an open universe, there are new kinds of events, objects, and transactions which, from time to time, emerge from the flux and remain within what is, therefore, a more inclusive flux and a richer flux. Notable among these emergents are selves, minds, and reflective intelligence. Again, unless it can be shown that these are phases of nature, arising out of the flux and in turn concerned with the flux, we cannot escape some sort of dualism.

Acquiring habits often takes place at the noncognitive level, but the application of any habit requires that the organism use something in its present experience (in a given concrete present) as a stimulus to respond toward something in a later present. But a lower animal has no self and, consequently, it cannot indicate to itself in the absence of the stimulus the kind of stimulus that will release an impulse or an prepotent response. That is, it cannot, within a given concrete present, present to itself, or represent to itself, ideationally or imaginatively, the various phases of an act, including both the stimulus phase and the response phase. Of course a lower animal can make a response by virtue of the presence of the stimulus, but it cannot respond to its own responses, i. e., it cannot, in the absence of the stimulus nevertheless present to itself the kind of stimulus (and the kind of response that answers to it) that will evoke a response necessary for completing transactions.

But this is precisely what a self can do: it can respond to its own gestures, to its own responses. A symbolic presentation of a kind of response is a concept, it is an implicit response presenting the form of an overt response. By means of concepts one can, so to speak, cut the flux, and commit oneself, in the absence of a particular stimulus, to the kind of stimulus that will answer to that response, to a kind of stimulus necessary for completing an act. Habit is a readiness to act in an orderly way when an overt stimulus is present; by symbols one can be aware, prior to the overt response, of the kind of response to be made and the kind of stimulus that will evoke it.

This means, of course, that one can, by use of symbols, have in his own experience in a given concrete present (through cognition) those phases of the act that lie in a future. He can, by symbols, present to himself at once the entire act with all of its phases. This is what is meant by awareness and cognition. It is a breaking out of a given specious or concrete present so that the act represented by symbols has past, present and future in it. Thus, conceptually the flux is divided and space is conceptually separated from time. Space and time are separated simply because a present stable or static space is necessary for the completion of an act whose consummatory phase can be effected only in a future, that is, *future* with reference to the conception of the act.

Mead has shown that a self arises when the organism is able to incorporate within a single experience (cognitive act) both the stimulus phase and the response phase of an act. This one can do because he can take the role of the other, that role which is the response phase of the act which transpires after the stimulus phase, and it is always future with reference to the concept and corresponding symbol that evokes it. When one's own gesture (word) evokes a response made by another, and when one can anticipate that response (or its kind), then one (by the anticipation) is responding to his own behavior (gesture) as does an other later. Thus the kind of act conceptually presented to oneself with its various phases is a social act.

Conceptualizing is a kind of transaction, the kind that results in discreteness. It results in a way of cutting the flux, and it applies to various phases of the flux because there are phases in the flux that are similar to each other. Since also there are phases of the flux that are different in kind from previous phases, thanks to evolution and emergence, new kinds of cuts are called for and, therefore, the formation of new concepts are relevant.[26] By virtue of similarities of phases in the continuum, proto-generalizations or, as James says, recepts, habits are possible, i.e., a kind of transaction is conceivable. Because of the possibility of new habits, creative thinking is possible, since thinking is for the purpose of establishing new habits. Both habits and concepts are kinds of transactions whose counterpart are other phases of the flux, i.e., when that phase of a transaction effected by an organism has answering to it another phase in its environment, then adjustment is the result.

Can One be Directly Aware of His Self?

How can a subject be an object to itself? How can a subject experience itself? Can one, within a concrete present be aware of both an object not the self and also the self that is being aware? Can one be directly and immediately aware of his self? In Meadean terms, these last two questions amount to asking whether the "I" component of the self can, in a given concrete present, be aware of itself. We must answer in the negative. There is no knowledge of the self by direct acquaintance; the action of the "I" is not experienced in its immediacy, but only mediately and indirectly. Specifically, the self can get at itself and know itself only by way of the role of the other.

Since the time of Descartes most philosophers erroneously accepted the belief that absolutely certain knowledge must begin with a direct knowledge of the self, of that which cogitates or thinks. The task of many, then, has been to show how we reach a knowledge of self, a knowledge believed to be prerequisite for knowledge of anything not the self. Husserl and his followers claim to offer us a method, *phenomenology*, by which this task can be accomplished.

Franz Brentano[27] held that three factors are involved in every mental act, namely, the act of intending, the actor (self), and the object intended. If I interpret him correctly he also believed that when one is aware of an object one is also and immediately, or within that concrete present, aware of the self whose awareness it is, or one is aware, in a concrete present, of both are awareness and the object of awareness. Brentano believed, with Aristotle, that direct awareness of the act of awareness is essential if we are to avoid an infinite regress. But if Brentano is correct, then one is a direct object to himself. I reject this hypothesis since it requires that there be knowledge by acquaintance. It requires that one, within a given concrete present, have knowledge of something confined to that present.

Brentano is very close to Descartes on this point. Descartes says: "It is impossible for us to have within us any thought, without having actual knowledge of it at the very moment it is in us." Husserl, in contrast with Aristotle, Descartes and Brentano, held that one is not necessarily aware of himself, or of the act of intending when thinking about natural objects; he believed correctly that there is no necessity in being aware of the self whenever there are mental acts. One can rather, be completely unaware of himself when, say, he loses himself in reading a book, or in repairing a chronometer. Husserl believed we must get at the self by reflection, and if I understand him he thought that through transcendental reductions we can bracket both natural objects and even ideal objects, universals, and finally have a face to face meeting of the self, that one can have immediate knowledge of intentional acts.

I believe that the entire phenomenological approach to a knowledge of the self as carried on by Brentano, Alexius Meinong and Edmund Husserl is based on the false assumptions that, first, if we are to have knowledge at all about matters of fact, we must begin with knowledge that is certain in the same sense that a priori knowledge of logical statements is certain. Second, the factual knowledge with which we must start is a knowledge of the self. Third, only of immediate knowledge and what is derived from it can we have certainty. Fourth, we can have immediate or direct experience of the self or the self can be directly acquainted with itself, and such direct acquaintance is knowledge. Husserl says: *"Every intellectual process and indeed every mental process whatever,* while being enacted, *can be made the object of a pure ‚seeing' and understanding, and is something absolutely given in the ‚seeing.'"*[28]

Apparently, Husserl believed that one could "bracket" that part of the world which lies outside of that of which we have direct experience and concentrate on the awarer and the awareness itself. Which is to say, he believed that in cognition it is possible to experience one phase or analytic part of it, the awareness, apart from anything beyond the awareness, as if, so to speak, awareness and the object of awareness could be experienced as a single phase and, therefore, within a given concrete present. In that case the self could reflect directly on itself or the reflector and the act of reflection would be one and the same.

Brentano, Husserl, and Mead each tried to show that Hume's approach to a knowledge of the existence and nature of the self was wrong. One cannot look into the mind and expect to find an impression or an idea of the mind. First, because mind is a process, not static as are Humean impressions, and second, mind consists of intending or thinking about objects and is clearly distinct from natural objects intended. However, if that is the case, it seems that the Husserlian approach to a knowledge of the existence of the intending process, or an immediate knowledge of the self, cannot succeed. He wants the evidence for the existence of the self to be self-given. Only the self-given is ultimate. Such an ultimate, according to him, is essential to a knowledge of natural objects and other selves. In contrast to both James' and Mead's approach, Husserl wants to begin with a knowledge of intentionality, the self, and forthwith show that each self, complete in itself, devoid of a social component, furnishes meanings, universals, which are prerequisite for experiencing natural objects. Accordingly, he holds, universals and meanings do not emerge from or grow out of pre-cognitive experiences, but are furnished by the mind and are logically prior to experiences of natural objects. Mead, on the other hand, begins at the "other end" so to speak. He shows that selves, minds, concepts, universals, emerge out of non-cognitive, social experience and, consequently, that every self of necessity has a social component. He agrees with Husserl that one must get at or know his self by reflection, but contrary to Husserl, reflection is not a conversation of the "I" with the "I" but a conversation of the "I" with the other, the generalized other. It is the other that reflects the self and vice versa. One can become aware of his self only if he "sees" himself, his action, as a phase of a more inclusive social process. To "see" oneself as a phase of a wider social act requires that he respond to his own behavior as does another; i. e., one anticipates in a concrete present the response his gesture will evoke in another in a later concrete present. Still, during the time of the anticipation the act of anticipating cannot be the object of cognition.

As stated above, every act of cognition or awareness is a case in which something experienced in a given concrete present is used as a sign (stimulus, symbol); which means it evokes a response toward an oncoming object (situation or event) not in that present. All experience, whether at the perceptual or cognitive level, is a phase of a transaction within the flux. At the level of awareness, the self, by use of a present symbol, takes into account something not then present. To indicate, by a symbol, the kind of thing taken into account is identical with being aware of a kind of object not present. Every awareness has that characteristic and, consequently, the self cannot encounter itself directly and without involving another item. In brief, at least two phases of the flux or two phases of a process are essential to awareness, and this precludes a direct knowledge of the self, say nothing of a knowledge of the self exclusive of all other things. Husserl's phenomenological approach was, to begin with, similar to James' radical empiricism, but his aim, which was identical with Descartes' aim, leads to solipsism. It is impossible, in arriving at a knowledge of the existence of one's self or its nature, to bracket all other items and all other selves. Also, James' belief that there is knowledge by acquaintance could easily mislead one to conclude that the self is directly experienced and known. This would amount to the phenomenological fallacy.

It is to the noteworthy credit of G. H. Mead that he explained the genesis of the self or selves.[29] In doing so he also accounted for its nature. The different phases of a social act cannot be carried out in the same concrete present. When the behavior of one individual serves as a stimulus for another individual to carry out its phase of the social act, then we have what Mead calls the stimulus phase and the response

James and the Specious Present

phase, or the sign (gesture, stimulus) phase and the meaning of the sign (the response). Such behavior takes place among lower animals, but if an individual can anticipate the kind of response his behavior or gesture will evoke in another, i. e., if he knows the meaning of his behavior or gesture (the stimulus phase of the social act) then he is responding (cognitively, implicitly) to his gesture, his own phase of the social process, as does or as will another.

One can respond to his own gesture (sign, symbol, words) only by way of another phase of the process, only by taking the attitude (taking the role) of another. This response to one's own gesture by way of another is equivalent to being aware of one's own behavior or one's own cognition by way of the same kind of response to it as another makes to it. This means that one can be aware of himself only insofar as he can, through awareness, or ideationally, get outside a given concrete present. Awareness of anything, including the self, therefore, involves more than one concrete present, since every interpretation of what is present refers to something beyond. A knowledge of one's self involves a knowledge of another participant in the social process, a participant who carries out another phase of that process. Awareness is a transaction between phases of a social process, and the self can be defined in terms of the social process. It is that phase of the process which is both able to conceive, within a single conspectus of thought, the various phase of the social process and it mediates between a past phase which has been frustrated and a future phase which, through reconstruction (mediation), continues satisfactory. The self is not only a reflection of social roles, as is a Leibnizian monad, but it is able, through the creation of new meanings, to help control the social process, including that phase of the process, that role which it carries out.

This is not the place to make the nature of the self more explicit. But it should be noted that James' radical empiricism, by which he claimed to experience connections as well as disconnections between and among things, including before and after, did not show how awareness emerges out of experience had at the precognitive level. Awareness is a qualitatively different kind of reaction within the flux. It is an emergent not, however, unrelated to nor disconnected from phases of the flux experienced at the precognitive level. Awareness requires a self. Awareness is a transcendence of a concrete present in which it takes place, since it involves reference to something beyond that present. The bird does fly and we experience its flight. But to be aware of either a bird or a flight is an interpretation involving something beyond what is here – now in experience. Interpretations are mental, but the mental is a phase of nature and the social process of adjustment.

NOTES

[1] Edmund R. Clay, *An Alternative: A Study in Psychology* (London: Macmillan and Company, 1882).
Regarding motion Clay says: "A motion is coincidence for an instant with each place of a continuous series of mutually equal, absolute, places, without the intervention of a divisible part of time between any two of the instants." *Ibid.*, p. 150.
"Experience of time-series, e. g., motions, music, days, nights, seasons, customs, comprehends a species of which the *differentia* is, that the whole of the object seems (inconsistently) to exist at the present instant; e. g., motion that seems to be occurring at the present instant, increase of light, heat, pleasure, or pain, that seems to be occurring at the present instant. When we watch the flight of a bird, a part of the flight seems to be occurring at the present instant, and a part to have occurred prior to the present instant. Experience of this pre-present part exemplifies the species of experience opposed to that which I am putting in relief. All experience of time-series save what refers to those that are extremely brief, e. g., a flash of forked lightning, consists of experiences of both kinds, one referent to a series given as occurring at the present instant, and the other as referent to a series given as having occurred prior to the present instant. The whole object, if the time of the experience does not exceed a few seconds, seems to be contained in a larger present of which the present instant seems to be the term. Let us distinguish these two species of experience, the one as *paradoxic*, because it apprehends

as occurring at an instant what coincides with a divisible time, the other as *anti-paradoxic.*" *Ibid.,* p. 151.

"It follows that the whole of the motion is not immediately visible at any instant whatever, and that the immediate object of the perception must be unreal, must be a mental modification serving as vicar or symbol of a remote object, viz. the motion, and that the beginning of the immediate object must be either coincident with or posterior to the end of the remote one. Several successive perceptions, each having for object a part of a motion, however rapidly one may follow another, are not a perception of the motion, and, if a perception of the motion obtain, it must be by means of a modification of consciousness symbolic of the motion, — an immediate unreal object symbolic of a remote one." *Ibid.,* p. 152.

There is a review of Clay's book in *The Academy,* Vol. 23, April 21, 1883. The reviewer, James Sully, does not seem to understand Clay and he says: A book with the characteristics just described is as difficult for the reviewer as for the reader. If there were some one idea developed throughout its pages, it might be possible to estimate its value." P. 278.

In *The Encyclopedia of Philosophy,* there is a discussion of why both Clay and James used the expression "the specious present." Vol. 8, pp. 135 ff.

2 James uses the word "flux" in *The Principles of Psychology* (New York: Henry Holt and Company, 1890), I, p. 468, and in *A Pluralistic Universe* (New York: Longmans, Green and Co., 1909), p. 272, to indicate raw, uninterpreted experience. Also, in *Essays in Radical Empiricism* (New York: Longmans, Green and Co., 1912), he devotes all of Chapter II to a discussion of pure experience or to an experience of the flux. I am intrigued by F. S. C. Northrop's expression, "the undifferentiated aesthetic continuum" in referring to this same thing. See his *The Meeting of East and West* (New York: The Macmillan Company, 1946), pp. 335 ff.

3 James, *A Pluralistic Universe,* p. 254.

4 James, *Essays in Radical Empiricism,* p. 93.

5 James, *A Pluralistic Universe,* p. 282.

6 *Ibid.,* p. 284.

7 *Ibid.,* p. 285.

8 See Harold N. Lee, *Percepts, Concepts and Theoretic Knowledge* (Memphis: Memphis State University Press, 1973), p. 216. See also George Herbert Mead, *Mind, Self and Society* (Chicago: The University of Chicago Press, 1934), p. 351. See also reference to F. S. C. Northrop in note 2 above.

78   David L. Miller

9 See George Herbert Mead, *The Philosophy of the Act* (Chicago: The University of Chicago Press, 1938), p. 65.
10 James, *A Pluralistic Universe*, p. 263.
11 *Ibid.*, p. 253.
12 I am indebted to Harold N. Lee, *Percepts, Concepts and Theoretic Knowledge*, pp. 195; 237; 240f., for the expression, "misplaced discreteness." Although I had used the idea earlier in my writings, Professor Lee's expression helps illuminate that idea; it immediately calls to mind a contrast between concreteness and discreteness, and it suggests at once that Peirce's Thirdness (habit, universality, law, rule, concept) is the locus discreteness.
13 The word "transaction" is used here, instead of "interaction," in the same sense in which and for the same reason Dewey used it. See his use of it in the collection of his essays, *On Experience, Nature, and Freedom*, ed. Richard J. Bernstein (Indianapolis: The Bobbs-Merrill Company, Inc., 1960), pp. 97; 113; 244; 261. In the introduction, Bernstein says that, for Dewey, "Transaction is a generic trait of existence." P. xl. This means, in compliance with process philosophy, and in contrast with mechanistic philosophy, that the phases (not atomic parts) of a unit of existence mutually affect each other and are what they are because of transactions. To think of objects or things as *interacting* suggests that these things have independent existence and remain what they were even after interaction takes place. Dewey uses the term in order to eliminate connotations of mechanism. James also uses the term. See James, *Essays in Radical Empiricism*, p. 56.
14 James, *A Pluralistic Universe*, p. 272.
15 *Ibid.*, pp. 282—283.
16 *Ibid.*, p. 261.
17 Richard Dedekind, *Theory of Numbers* (Chicago and London: Open Court Publishing Company, 1924), p. 11.
18 James, *Essays in Radical Empiricism*, p. ix.
19 *Ibid.*, p. 42.
20 James, *The Principles of Psychology*, I, p. 221.
21 Lee, *Percepts, Concepts and Theoretic Knowledge*, pp. 12ff; 52f; 61; 83; 89; 148; 160; 170.
In *The Principles of Psychology*, II, p. 327, James also recognizes this kind of generalization that takes place at the precognitive level. He calls these generalizations "Recepts." He says: "In these first and simplest inferences the conclusions may follow so continuously upon the 'sign' that the latter is not discriminated or attended to as a separate object by the mind.... The objects, too, when thus inferred are *general* objects. The dog crossing a scent thinks of a deer in general, or of another dog in general,

not of a particular deer or dog. To these most primitive objects, Dr. G. J. Romanes gives the name of *recepts* or *generic* ideas, to distinguish them from concepts and general ideas properly so called. They are not analyzed or defined, but only imagined."

22 See James, *Principles of Psychology*, I, p. 222; *Essays in Radical Empiricism*, pp. 54 ff.

23 Henri Bergson, *An Introduction to Metaphysics* (New York, London: G. P. Putnam's Sons, 1912), pp. 1—9.

24 Lee, *Percepts, Concepts and Theoretic Knowledge*, pp. 240—241.

25 See Mead, *Mind, Self and Society*, pp. 308—309; *The Philosophy of the Act*, pp. 462 ff.

26 Also, old kinds of phases that are repetitive might be responded to more adequately, and this requires new concepts, a new cutting.

27 Franz Brentano, *Psychologie vom empirischen Standpunkt* (Leipzig: Duncker and Humblot, 1874).

28 See William Alston and George Nakhnikian, *Readings in Twentieth Century Philosophy* (Glencoe: The Free Press, 1964), "The Idea of Phenomenology," p. 649.

29 See George Herbert Mead, *The Philosophy of the Present*, ed. by Arthur E. Murphy (Chicago: Open Court Publishing Co., 1932), 176—195.

4

A METAPHYSICS OF RELATIONS: JAMES'S ANTICIPATION OF CONTEMPORARY EXPERIENCE

John J. McDermott

> You see also that it stands or falls with the notion I have taken such pains to defend, of the through-and-through union of adjacent minima of experience, of the confluence of every passing moment of concretely felt experience with its immediately next neighbors.[1]   William James

I

Switzerland is an eminently fitting place for a seminar on the thought of William James, for as his commentators know, this country occupied much of his attention and was the subject of life-long affection. It was in Switzerland that he prepared intellectually and personally for his Gifford Lectures on *The Varieties of Religious Experience,* and one of his very last letters was written to his dear friend, the Swiss philosopher, Theodore Flournoy, as James left Geneva on his trip home to die. Perhaps then, in this environment, we can recapture through access to "the halo of relations," some of James's enthusiasm and his highly imaginative approach to the complexities of the human condition.

The decided increase in publications, both editions and commentaries, have pointed to a definite renascence of interest in American classical philosophy as represented by Peirce, James, Royce, Santayana, Dewey, and Mead. Two major tasks await such a revival of interest; first, to present and clarify the textual tradition; second, to utilize the insights of that tradition in an effort to confront the significant problems of our time. In this essay, I shall try my hand at the second task, relating James's fundamental metaphysics to some of the new concerns in social psychology, communication theory and environmental aesthetics. The intention here is clearly suggestive and exploratory rather than definitive or exhaustive.

Before proceeding to the substance of these issues, two methodological concerns are in order. First, care must be exercised that in formulating relationships between contemporary concerns and the thought of William James, we do not wrench his language and ideas out of their setting so as to create anachronistic and misleading patterns of influence. It cannot be contended, for example, that James anticipated the specifics of new developments in depth psychology, theories of interpersonal relations or proxemics, the new subtleties of cultural anthropology, and the vast import of developments in transportation and electronic media. James was a man of the industrial revolution, of steamships, the telegraph and the train. His experienced sense of time while "speeded up" was fundamentally antique, that is, measurable by the traversing of space.

Despite these cautions, James's thought nonetheless functions in an extraordinarily anticipatory way. For one thing, if not the first, James was the most outspoken proponent of a distinctively contemporary view of cosmology, unabashedly post-Copernican and highly sensitized to the role of novelty and the constitutive role of human life. He was also committed to an overthrow of the centuries old "substance" oriented description of reality, attempting to replace it with a relational and process oriented metaphysics, far more flexible and in keeping with the subsequent developments in the disciplines of our own time. James's critique of previous positions paved the way for a more free-wheeling approach to the problems of inquiry and description and while not worked out in detail, his own theories and approaches, however inadvertently, foreshadowed major shifts in priorities and concerns in psychology, the arts and social psychology.

The significance of James's thought for social psychology leads to the second methodological question. How, it may be asked, can such significance be ascribed to a thinker so notoriously concerned with the individual and so singularly free of apparent insight to matters social or to the sociological context for inquiry, later explicated so brilliantly by John Dewey? A first response to this question has to do with James's language. Granted that he does not invoke a sociological vocabulary, he nonetheless assumes a fundamental social matrix in his epistemology, for the pragmatic method has to do with consequences, testing and experimentation as subject to verifying in a world of experience other than one we simply think about. Put another way, James was adamantly opposed to evaluating ideas relative only to other ideas, professing that ideas carry their weight as applied to actual situations, many of them inevitably social.

Secondly, unless a sociology is explicitly reductionistic, it must honor some assumptions about the nature of human activity from a philosophical and psychological perspective. James's thought on human behavior, while nurtured on his abiding sensibility to individual experience is yet characterized by perceptions significantly germane to social psychology. And as both G. H. Mead and John Dewey have attested, their own developments in social theory would be inconceivable without James's breakthroughs in psychology and his metaphysics of relations.

With these methodological cautions behind us, let us set up the approach to our present concerns. After a brief reminding exposition of James's doctrine of relations, we shall examine in some detail a series of contemporary problems in what is hopefully the Jamesian manner. An attempt will be made to recast the diagnosis of our present situation, characterized as it is by the language of alienation and anomie, in the direction of less emphasis on the quest for human certitude and more emphasis on affectivity and the texture of our actual experiences. For James, after all, "experience itself, taken at large, can grow by its edges."[2] The manifestations of living occur in time, with both events and meanings internal to that process, never yielding to a transcendent point of view.[3]

II

As is well known, James stated the basic contentions of his philosophy, that is, radical empiricism, on a number of occasions. Despite some surface ambiguity, a careful reading of James will show it to be clear, both textually and thematically, that for him pragmatism is a methodological application of his radical empiricism. In that sense, to call James simply a pragmatist is misleading and, indeed, without radical empiricism as a metaphysical base, pragmatism is subject to the savage philosophical critique it has received.

In 1897, as part of the "Preface" to *The Will to Believe,* James wrote:

> Were I obliged to give a short name to the attitude in question, I should call it that of *radical empiricism* ... I say 'empiricism' because it is contented to regard its most absurd conclusions concerning matters of fact as hypotheses liable to modification in the course of future experience; and I say 'radical,' because it treats the doctrine of monism itself as an hypothesis ...
> He who takes for his hypothesis the notion that it [pluralism] is the permanent form of the world is what I call a radical empiricist. For him the crudity of experience remains an eternal element thereof. There is no possible point of view from which the world can appear an absolutely single fact.[4]

In 1904, James wrote to François Pillon that "my philosophy is what I call a radical empiricism, a pluralism, a 'tychism,' which represents order as being gradually won and always in the making."[5] And finally in 1909, James offered his clearest version of radical empiricism when he wrote a "Preface" to *The Meaning of Truth*, significantly, a book intended to answer the critics of his *Pragmatism:*

> Radical empiricism consists first of a postulate, next of a statement of fact, and finally of a generalized conclusion.
>
> The postulate is that the only things that shall be debatable among philosophers shall be things definable in terms drawn from experience. [Things of an unexperiencable nature may exist ad libitum, but they form no part of the material for philosophic debate.]
>
> The statement of fact is that the relations between things, conjunctive as well as disjunctive, are just as much matters of direct particular experience, neither more so nor less so, than the things themselves.
>
> The generalized conclusion is that therefore the parts of experience hold together from next to next by relations that are themselves parts of experience. The directly apprehended universe needs, in short, no extraneous trans-empirical connective support, but possesses in its own right a concatenated or continous structure.[6]

Now for our present purpose, two major themes emerge; first, the contention that in our experience at large we are given continuity but not Unity and second, this continuity is due to our affective or feeling grasp of the relationships which set up in all of our activities, conceptual as well as perceptual. This second claim is what James calls a "statement of fact" and what Arthur Bentley[7] calls the "Jamesian datum," capable of experimental verification. If it is not so that relations are equally and affectively experienced as are the poles of the relationship then James's thought is but a string of brilliant asides, declining considerably in positive and philosophical merit. Further, given that his negative statement about no possibility of seeing the world whole or as a single fact is obviously true, as twentieth century thought attests over and over, his doctrine of relations provides the only meaningful source of intelligibility. The accuracy of James's "statement of fact" is, therefore, no idle matter, for with the rejection of over-arching, transcendent principles of explanation, man is forced back into an unreflective "taking things as they come" or the intellectual encapsulations of a solipsism. Accepting James's radical empiricism and consistent with its claims, let us sketch an approach to the discussion of three contemporary concerns: alienation, repression, and technological artifact.

III

One of the cardinal concerns of our century has been the increased presence of the experience of alienation. The language of articulation for this situation has been either Marxist, following the renewed awareness of the *Economic and Philosophic Manuscripts (1844)*, or Existentialist, following the writings of Camus, Sartre, Marcel, Jaspers and Heidegger. In both Marxist and Existential traditions, however profound their differences, there exists the common theme of deep distrust of the classical European institutions, the Church, class structure, and philosophy, especially the claims fostered by centuries of confidence in the ultimate intelligibility of nature as open to reason. The collapse of these claims in a series of intellectual revolutions, from Copernicanism, through Luther, Hume, Kant, the Romantic poets, Marx and Nietzsche, abetted by the irrational terrors of the holocaust have generated a rootlessness and despair in much of Western contemporary thought. The writings of Cioran and Ellul are a witness to the loss of hope, and the vigorous interest in Eastern thought as well as the writings of Joyce and N. O. Brown, yield a return to the doctrine of the cycle and the rejection of historical novelty.

By contrast, an analysis of alienation from the perspective of James's experience and thought will prove illuminating. Although James[8] has said that a man is not educated unless he has "dallied" with suicide, as he did, and although most interpreters focus on James's multiple neurosis, such as his psychosomatic neurasthenia, insomnia, and transcontinental restlessness, leading Gay Wilson Allen[9] to imply that James was on the edge of a nervous breakdown all his life, nonetheless his anthropology was not characterized by alienation. The reasons for this are extremely instructive, not only relative to an interpretation of James's life but as a harbinger to a creative response to our own problems. Taking fundamental issue with the interpretation of James as a neurotic and insecure person, I offer that the key to his anthropology can be phrased as first, his rejection of a derivative ethics and of a derivative sense of self, and second, his affirmation of local intelligibility as present in the experience-continua of human activity.

For James, alienation is the inability to make relations. To accept a derivative ethics or an a priori meaning of the self, as in the classical doctrine of the soul, is to abort the making of relations. On the other hand, to be without such an inheritance is not to be cut completely adrift, for while "my belief, to be sure, *can't* be optimistic... I will posit life (the real, the good) in the self-governing *resistance* of the ego to the world. Life shall [be built in] doing and suffering and creating."[10] In effect, James sees the human task as constituting meaning, not *ab ovo* from the power of the mind as in philosophical idealism but in selective and rejective response to the press of events upon us.

Alienation can be described as the experience of disconnections in those areas of life in which we are vulnerable. No event, situation or circumstance is by nature alienating. Human beings have withstood, nay flourished under the most objectively dehumanizing and terrifying of experiences. Just as the "liver" is the relational manifold of our bodies so too do we have a psychological relational manifold, which has as its task to anticipate needs, set balances, and warn us against misleading directions. James writes in the *Pragmatism:* "Woe to him whose beliefs play fast and loose with the order which realities follow in his experience; they will lead him nowhere or else make false connexions."[11] He is not pointing to ultimate alienation, that is, the inability to make sense of the world, for that is a result of an illegitimate expectation in the first place. Rather, he is pointing to the instances of alienation which occur when we do not guard against the twin dangers of prometheanism and the laissez-faire acceptance of the world as conceived by others.

When James states that "the inmost nature of the reality is congenial to powers which you possess,"[12] he affirms a metaphysical possibility but he offers no guarantee. Although James is fond of talking about powers, energies and leads, he also assumes a highly developed sense of self-awareness. After all, the abandonment of an inherited self, while liberating is nonetheless challenging and even dangerous. If the world is not given as meaningful and the self is but our capacity to be meaningfully present, then we must guard against both relation-starvation and relation-seduction.

A telescoped statement of James's fundamental anthropology would read as follows: reality is a network of concatenatedly related objects or things, rendered as such by human conceptual decision, in keeping with the possibilities and limitations structured by nature on its terms and historically rendered by previous human activity. Human experience is an aware flow within the activities of reality at large, which in turn is also in process, unfinished and broken into by novelties relative to the patterns already set up. For the most part we live our lives focally, that is, within a familiar range of experiences rendered clear to us by our conceptual systems or simply accepted by habituation. Ideally this focus opens outward, reaching towards a fringe of experiences, often vague and inarticulate but subtly continuous and profoundly meaningful. Religious experience, unusual psychic experiences, aesthetic experiences, drug experiences, psychophysical breakthroughs as in Yoga and the range of allegedly neurotic and psychotic experiences are potentially rich possibilities at the fringe.

Speaking diagnostically, then, about human well-being, James's philosophy offers the following cautions and suggestions. First, if the focus is concave, we tend to duplicate our experiences or at a minimum, no matter their actual differences, they are slotted in an already articulated and accepted conceptual scheme. James refers to this as "vicious intellectualism," which is "the treating of a name as excluding from the fact named what the names' definition fails to include..."[13] This attitude becomes increasingly defensive, overestimating the importance and reach of our focus and in time develops a hostility to experiences not already included within our range. In effect, we tend to identify and evaluate experiences only in terms already familiar to us and sanctioned by us.

Self-encapsulating, this approach results in relation-starvation and in an increasing narrowness of person. What is to be lamented is not the decrease in the quantity of relations formulated, although that is often, if not necessarily, a factor, but in the absence of novelty, differentia and, in short, the developing in ability to be open to experience.

By contrast, if our focus is convex, we have the advantage of reaching out and thereby reconstituting our frame of reference, flooding us with enormous possibilities for, as James tells us, anything that makes a difference anywhere, makes a difference elsewhere.[14] But James cautions us here as well, for he warns against radical discontinuities as, for example, is found in the "leap" experience of the existentialists. To leap over the relationships at work in our experiencing is to be seduced by the drama of radical novelty, as in some drug experiences, and thereby become "cut off" or "strung out." Even more revealing is the experience of suicide, which must be continuous with the needs and patterns of our life, otherwise it is the supreme insulating cut, marked by the presence of no return.

James's view of the fringe is not that of a world separate or totally unknown. It resides within the possibilities of the perceptual field, linked by relationships open to human awareness, even if not to clear and define statement. We make our way to and throughout the fringe hand over hand as it were, with all senses on the *qui vive*, alert to pitfalls and dead-ends, ever within hailing distance of our point of origin. Just as we have no inherited self, so too do we not have a permanent foothold. We do, however, "selve" ourselves in the vast, teeming flow of experience and in so doing, we constitute a foothold, ever-changing but ever-present. Alienation, in an ultimate sense of that term, is an abstract and even artificial problem. It has to do with the language of being and non-being, of meaning and nihilism. For James, the basic language is one of nutrition and starvation, of liberation and entrapment, that is, the language of affairs and processes rather than of traditional metaphysics. He is a philosopher of descriptions and diagnoses, a philosopher of the kind that phenomenologists claim to be but rarely are. And, in the long run, the import of James's philosophy is that an analysis of human activity turns out to be an "ultimate" metaphysics for there is no reality to be discussed apart from our participation and formulation. In *The Varieties of Religious Experience,* he writes, "so long as we deal with the cosmic and the general, we deal only with the symbols of reality, but *as soon as we deal with private and personal phenomena as such, we deal with realities in the completest sense of the term.*"[15]

IV

Turning now to a second contemporary concern, the problem of repression, we find James's thought to be helpful. Beginning for the most part with Freud, the notion of repression has been associated with sexual activity. Without gainsaying the significance of Freud's insight to repression, we cannot accept the patterns of human sexuality as the exclusive root cause. In the area of pedagogy, for example, both Maria Montessori and John Dewey have elucidated the repressive implications of traditional educational institutions and practices.[16] And from Rousseau through Marx to more recent critics, such as Sartre, the repressive penalties of political institutions are well detailed. With regard to Freud, James would reject any explanation that hinges on a single factor, however plausible. For James, repression is a reality but it functions differently for different persons and differently for the same person in different situations.

It is to be noted that James, despite his affection for the mysteries of the fringe of consciousness, did not hold to the presence of a secret self, whether it be traceable to the classical claim of a "soul" or the Freudian claim of an unconscious "id". James would regard the layers of consciousness, *id, ego,* and *superego* as abstractions, devoid of subtlety. So too, would he regard as reductionistic the flock of post-Freudian nostrums, each of them giving a different single principle of accountability. Perhaps we can say that for James, there is no salvation, rather only saving experiences.

In the stream of consciousness, clarity is attained by negation, that is, by cutting off the myriad of relations that proceed from any given experience and by suturing these cuts so that one can name the remainder. Such clarity is often necessary to prevent us from being overwhelmed by the implicitness and inferentiality of our experiences. What we call knowledge is a pragmatically inspired compromise to enable us to hold our own somewhere between our need for identity and our need to grow, that is, to be open to leads and ramifications. *In the Jamesian context, repression means the shelving of an event such that it is banished from the realm of its own implications.* Such an approach need not be dangerous to the person, for within the functional exigencies of human activity some leads should not be followed, dependent upon the overall assessment of the weakness and capacity of the person involved.

It has to be granted that Freud's contention that repression leads to a festering and sublimated articulation, often violent, has considerable empirical support. The major reason for this situation, however, is that within the fabric of Western culture, human beings are burdened by the pressure to come clean, to have our experiences hang together in a causal and rational sequence. Psychoanalysis and its more recent offshoots, such as encounter groups, transactional analysis and varieties of psychodrama, have as their predecessor the resolute possibilities of the long-standing tradition of Christian confession. Despite the claim of an aggressive unconscious at work in human life, ironically, contemporary therapy from Freud forward is addressed to a rational resolution of these hidden difficulties. James would reject both ends of this description. He uses terms such as fringe and sub-liminal to accentuate the reaches of conscious life, holding that we have access to all aspects of our experience while at the same time denying that we can account for any experience undergone in any final or complete sense.

If we take the pragmatic method in a wider sense than that dealing with the question of truth and apply it to human inquiry more generally understood, we could then state the significance of repression as functional. In the welter of experiences to which we have access, repression becomes justifiable and even necessary in the following situations: First, we point to those experiences to which we look forward with considerable anticipation but prove abortive. Unless we are very strong, we run the risk in such situations of tying failure to intensity of effort, a crippling relationship. In short, we should then shelve or "repress" our failure until we set up subsequent of resolution following upon intention. In educational language patterns we call this the need for success experience. Second, we cite those experiences whose implications are so extensive that a vast rearranging of our priorities and sensibilities would be required if we were to absorb them into our immediate frame of reference. In these instances, time is necessary to set up reparations for absorption, requiring us to manage rather than be managed by the events in question. Third, we should consider also those experiences which now stand outside the possibilities of remediation or resolution because of the passing of time, as for example, guilt attendant upon the death of others or frustration due to forever missed opportunities. James would see these situations as involving relations of discontinuity, rooted at one end in our experience but at the other, floating loose, unrealizable warnings to the fact that "whatever separateness is actually experienced is not overcome, it stays and counts as separateness to the end."[17]

As with our earlier discussion of alienation, so too with a

consideration of repression it is necessary to realize the importance of James's functional approach and his steadfast suspicion about apodictic judgments. No experience is unrelated as undergone, for at the minimum the "haver" of the experience proceeds from a perceptual point of view and thereby constitutes a context for and to some extent the quality of the experience. How the experience is had is inseparable from our knowledge of the experience. In his essay on "The Thing and Its Relations," James writes:

> In a concatenated world a partial conflux often is experienced. Our concepts and our sensations are confluent; successive states of the same ego, and feelings of the same body are confluent. Where the experience is not of conflux, it may be of conterminousness (things with but one thing between); or of contiguousness (nothing between); or of likeness; or of nearness; or of simultaneousness; or of in-ness; or of on-ness; or of for-ness; or of simple with-ness; or even of mere and-ness; which last relation would make of however disjointed a world otherwise, at any rate for that occasion a universe 'of discourse'.[18]

The upshot of this is that for James, repression need not have its point of origin in an unintelligible motivation or irrational source. Similar to all of our experiences, repression occupies a role in the sliding stream of events, which for reasons of deep personal self-awareness, functions on behalf of quiescence, hiddenness and a time-biding until the organism can relate the repressed event to a more ongoing, obvious dimension in the flow of our experience. Furthermore, in a world riven with tychastic events, experiences rendered out of sorts, repressed or held at arm's length can be recovered and rejuvenated due to favorable and surprising interventions in our lives. In James's philosophy, no experience can be spoken for once and for all. Opposing the absolutistic arrogance found in the conceptual systems of the philosophers, James writes in a "Notebook" in 1903 that:

All neat schematism with permanent and absolute distinctions, classifications with absolute pretensions, systems with pigeonholes, etc., have this character. All 'classic,' clean, cut and dried, 'noble,' fixed, 'eternal,' *Weltanschauungen* seem to me to violate the character with which life concretely comes and the expression which it bears of being, or at least of involving a muddle and a struggle, with an 'ever not quite' to all our fomulas, and novelty and possibility forever leaking in.[19]

V

Martin Buber once wrote that "in the beginning is the relation."[20] His emphasis on the importance of *zwischenmenschen* as the primary source of meaning contrasts with the traditional emphasis on the knowing subject, knowing about the world. John Dewey, in one of his last written statements, a letter to Arthur Bentley in 1951, states presciently the task of a contemporary epistemology. "If I ever get the needed strength, I want to write on *knowing* as the way of behaving in which linguistic artifacts transact business with physical artifacts, tools, implements, apparatus, both kinds being planned for the purpose and rendering *inquiry* of necessity an *experimental transaction.*"[21] Such a relation-oriented or transactional epistemology, depends on a very different metaphysical underpinning than that dominated by the notion of substance in the history of Western philosophy. Thinkers as diverse as James, Bergson, Whitehead and Dewey each have emphasized the move from substance to process as the basic metaphor in a metaphysics. Of these, James's thought was the most decisive for he offered both the first and the most explicit statement that the most fundamental characteristic of reality is not substance, essence or thing but a relational manifold. James held that things were nothing "but special groupe of sensible qualities, which happen practically or aesthetically to interest us, to which we therefore give substantive names, and which we exalt to this exclusive status of independance and dignity."[22] And later on he tells us that *"there is no property* ABSOLUTELY *essential to any one thing."*[23]

Implicitly with James and explicitly with Dewey, inquiry becomes a transaction between the knowing self and the transactions carried on within the affairs of nature and culture. "Knowledge" then is knowing of processes rather than of objects, the latter being definitional loci, pragmatically contructed to effect optimum management of the transactional relationship between awareness and decision. Put differently, James contends that "perception and thinking are only there for behavior's sake."[24] Rather than set over against the world, we find ourselves within its concatenated fabric, having to hook onto its flow so as not to be bypassed, while yet structuring a self-presence for purpose of evaluation and identity. In a series of previous essays, I have attempted to show the relevance of James's relational metaphysics to the areas of aesthetics, urban experience and the patterns of diagnosis in some forms of interpersonal relations.[25] Continuous with those efforts, I turn here to a brief analysis of James's potential contribution to the problem hinted at in the earlier text from Dewey, namely, the significance of technological artifact in the activity of human inquiry.

While proceeding to this issue, in addition to James's novel doctrine of relations as "radically empirical," we have to remind ourselves of his other controversial assertion that matter and mind are only functionally different. Without commenting on the difficulties involved in his underlying notion of "pure experience," James, in denying an ontological division between matter and mind, points to the extraordinary quality of the human being who has experience in both ways, simultaneously. Just as there is no ontological dualism within the self, classically known as body and soul, so too there is no ontological dualism between the self and the world. Now the startling consequence of this view is that if man and the world are made of the same reality and only function differently, then ontologically similar also are the things of reality as made by man. Artifacts, then, are human versions of the world acting as transactional mediations, representing human endeavor in relational accordance with the resistance and possibility endemic to both nature and culture.

So long as artifacts remained as obvious "utiles," enhancing human activity by virtue of increased leverage, strength, durability or accessibility, the man-world polarity held firm as an exhaustive description. We can refer to this centuries long tradition in terms of the human use of tools. Regarded for the most part as necessities, unless occasionally bestowed by the aesthetic criteria of specific cultures, as, for example, culinary utensils, the presence of such artifacts rarely gave rise to philosophical discussions. Perhaps, this is due in part to the fact that Western philosophy has been concerned far more with the eyes than with the hands, speaking of vision rather than of touch. It is noteworthy that the two most remarkable inventions of the early modern period, the telescope (1590) and the microscope (1608), both have to do with vision. And despite the enthusiastic response to the marvels revealed by these super-eyes, the epistemology remained the same, that is, man the viewer "unhiding" layers and outer reaches of the external world. Until the twentieth century, it did not occur to us to realize that not only did we see "more" but that the viewer beacme profoundly transformed at the level of consciousness. If, as I believe, Kant is correct in his assertion that consciousness informs the world "sensuously," prior to its being known specifically, then transformations of consciousness, are, in effect, transformations of the world. Taking artifacts as "relatings" in the Jamesian sense, gives us the history of artifact as a major strand in the history of the formulation of the meaning of the world.

The significance of James's relational metaphysics for an understanding of artifact becomes much clearer when we cite the move from industrial, machine oriented technology to that of electronic technology which has occurred within the past century. Electronic technological artifacts, such as the telephone, radio, television and computer terminals are "things" in the Jamesian sense, that is, perches or gathering places for ongoing relational processes. As perches they exist in time and space, classically understood relative to motion and dimension, but as activities they defy those limitations and create for us entirely novel sense relations to the world. What James regarded as the fringe of consciousness or the wider range of consciousness, becomes concretized by the presence of electronic media, with Telstar acting as a global cerebral cortex. He waged a life-long assault on the notion of consciousness as a container and on the description of the self as a box from which would spring ideas, conforming to an already explicit external world. The idealists tempted him because of their contention about the vast range of human consciousness, but he distrusted their lack of empirical data and was deeply suspicious of the *deus ex machina* character of the "absolute mind." Aware of the ignorance of the human brain and convinced as few other philosophers of its limitless potential in explicating the mysteries of knowing, James would have been delighted to see the artifactual rendering of the human brain, the computer, turn out to be a miniature version of the concatenated world.

Born at the dawning of electronic technology, he was unaware of how dramatically his most speculative fancies could be realized and how his version of man as a processive field, shifting with relations made and unmade would become commonplace. He would not, however, become a victim of future shock for in this area as well as in other contemporary breakthroughs, James was anticipatory and he welcomed surprises, holding them to be more likely than our certainties. As late as 1909, near the end of his life, undefensively he writes:

> In principle, then, as I said, intellectualism's edge is broken; it can only approximate to reality, and its logic is inapplicable to our inner life, which spurns its vetoes and mocks at its impossibilities. Every bit of us at every moment is part and parcel of a wider self, it quivers along various

radii like the wind-rose on a compass, and the actual in it is continuously one with possibles not yet in our present sight.[26]

NOTES

Unless otherwise cited, references to William James will be to John J. McDermott, ed., *The Writings of William James — A Comprehensive Edition* (New York: Random House, 1967; The Modern Library, 1968), pp. li, 858. This volume contains complete editions of *Pragmatism, Essays in Radical Empiricism, A Pluralistic Universe,* as well as extensive and individually complete selections from all of Jame's major works. It also has a virtually complete "Annotated Bibliography." (Subsequent references will list the title of the essay or book, the abbreviation *W. W. J.* for *The Writings of William James* and the page number)

[1] "*A Pluralistic Universe,*" *W. W. J.*, p. 808.
[2] "A World of Pure Experience," *W. W. J.*, p. 212.
[3] Cf. James, *ibid.*, p. 201. "Knowledge of sensible realities thus comes to life inside the tissue of experience. It is *made;* and made by relations that unroll themselves in time."
[4] *W. W. J.*, pp. 134—135.
[5] "The Letters of William James," *W. W. J.*, pp. xxxvi—xxxvii.
[6] *W. W. J.*, p. 136.
[7] Cf. Arthur Bentley, "The Jamesian Datum," *Inquiry into Inquiries,* ed. Sidney Ratner (Boston: The Beacon Press, 1954), pp. 230—267.
[8] "The Letters of William James," *W. W. J.*, p. xiv.
[9] Cf. Gay Wilson Allen, *William James — A Biography* (New York: The Viking Press, 1967), pp. vii, xii.
[10] "Diary," *W. W. J.*, p. 8.
[11] "Pragmatism," *W. W. J.*, p. 432.
[12] "The Sentiment of Rationality," *W. W. J.*, p. 331.
[13] "A Pluralistic Universe," *W. W. J.*, p. 503.
[14] "Pragmatism," *W. W. J.*, p. 379.
[15] "Varieties of Religious Experience," *W. W. J.*, p. 768.
[16] From a Freudian point of view, it is, of course, not without interest that neither James nor Dewey have even an incipient sexual ethic while Montessori's occasional references to sex are bizarre.
[17] "A World of Pure Experience," *W. W. J.*, p. 212.
[18] *W. W. J.*, p. 221.
[19] Cited in Ralph Barton Perry, *The Thought and Character of*

William James (Boston: Little, Brown and Co., 1935), Vol. II, p. 700.

20 Martin Buber, *I and Thou*, translated by Walter Kaufmann (New York: Charles Scribner's Sons, 1970), p. 69.

21 *John Dewey and Arthur F. Bentley, A Philosophical Correspondence, 1932—1951*, edd., Sidney Ratner and Jules Altman (New Brunswick: Rutgers University Press, 1964), p. 646.

22 "The Stream of Thought," *W. W. J.*, p. 71.

23 William James, *The Principles of Psychology* (New York: Henry Holt and Co., 1890), Vol. II, p. 333.

24 William James, "Reflex Action and Theism," in *The Will to Believe and Other Essays in Popular Philosophy* (New York: Longmans, Green and Co., 1897), p. 114.

25 Cf. John J. McDermott, "To Be Human is to Humanize: A Radically Empirical Aesthetic," *American Philosophy and the Future* (New York: Charles Scribner's Sons, 1968), pp. 21—59; "Celebration and Deprivation: Suggestions for an Aesthetic Ecology," *New Essays in Phenomenology* (Chicago: Quadrangle Books, 1969), pp. 116—130; "Nature Nostalgia and the City: An American Dilemma," *The Family, Communes and Utopian Societies* (New York: Harper and Row, 1972), pp. 1—20; "Feeling as Insight — The Affective Dimension in Social Diagnosis," *Hippocrates Revisited* (Washington: Medcom, 1973), pp. 166—180.

26 "The Continuity of Experience," *W. W. J.*, pp. 296—297.

5

A CRITICAL APPRAISAL OF JAMES'S VIEW OF CAUSALITY

Edward H. Madden and Peter H. Hare

We are convinced that James saw the issues of causality in the proper light and correctly estimated the direction in which their solutions lie. He was right in arguing that potentiality and counterfactuality are irreducible ontological concepts and that the Humean is unable to make sense of them. Moreover, both his earlier and later efforts to supply the needed alternative analysis, though inadequate by themselves, provide genuine insights into a more adequate view. In his discussions of causality and objective reference James, as elsewhere in his writings, makes useful reading for the contemporary philosopher.

1.

As early as the 1870's James held that properties and events are not always logically and physically independent of each other and that the British empiricists were wrong in thinking they always are. If connections are always de facto as Hume claimed, then the concepts of potentiality and possibility become metaphysical phantoms. Yet commonsense statements about physical objects and scientific laws both entail something about what could, would, or might happen. James is on the side of commonsense and science.

James' commitment to the non-independence view and to the categories of potentiality and possibility is everywhere evident in his early piece called "Against Nihilism": "The British School say that laws are nil-*nomines umbra*," whereas in fact they "are as real as the phenomena which they unite"[1]; the thing operates, or is in some way effective or recognized, where it does not actually and plenarily exist"[2]; the positivist "thinks that there is no *nature* in things," while "we say that things behave so and so because of their nature or properties"[3]; "nihilism [positivism] denies continuity" but commonsense is right in holding a thing "to exist potentially or in substance where its antecedent is..."[4]; and "dynamic connection with other existences becomes the test of substantial reality; or, in other words, a thing only has being at all as it enters in some way into the being of other things, or constitutes part of a universe or organism."[5] James hastens to clarify his concept of a substance. Insofar as being continuous "is what people mean when they affirm a substance, substance must be held to exist."[6] But frequently philosophers mean by substance "a primordial *thing* on a plane behind that of the phenomena, and numerically additional to them."[7] James rejects this concept.

James never developed this embryonic analysis of causality in terms of 'the nature of a particular' and 'substance,' where these concepts are empirically conceived, and it is useful to see what kept him from developing them. James seemed to think that the concept of the "nature" of a particular meant "essential nature," and he became increasingly unwilling to believe that particulars have any essential nature. He eventually formulated his teleological analysis of "essential" characteristic, the classical formulation of which appears in the chapter on reasoning in *The Principles of Psychology,* according to which any property taken as essential simply reflects the interests or intent of a person on that occasion and hence that there are as many essential properties as there are human interests and occasions for acting toward a thing with any given property as a "handle."[8] It seems unfortunate to us that James' teleological analysis of "essence" led him away from an empirically conceived and aposteriori grounded concept of the nature of a particular that was genuinely promising.[9]

At an equally early date James, encouraged by the work of such philosophers as Renouvier and Hodgson,[10] held that spatial and temporal relations are an irreducible part of "the given" and saw this view as reinforcing the non-independence claim. "If each representation is totally independent," James asks, "how does it ever come into collision with any other, how can it be synthetized with another?" James answers, "Space and time, at least... they have in common."[11] James realized that spatial and temporal relations are not enough to yield the required counterfactuality, but thought they helped: "And although these are not dynamic or substantial bonds of union, yet they in some sense unite the heterogenous into a universe period...."[12]

To achieve the full goal James eventually added causal connections as an irreducible element to "the given."[13] Like the experience of spatial and temporal relations, the experience of the causal relations cannot be conceptually decomposed. According to James, the volitional context is the place to look for the causal experience. For example, I directly experience my seeking to remember a forgotten name and my remembering it as causally related. The perception of such causal relations "is clear to anyone who has lived through the experience, but to no one else; just as 'loud,' 'red,' 'sweet' mean something only to beings with ears, eyes, and tongue."[14] Just as spatial and temporal relations are basic and unanalysable so are the experiences of causal relatedness irreducible to anything else.

If the meaning of direct experience of causality is as clear to those who have lived through it as the meaning of 'red,' why, one might ask, don't we have names to denote such experiences? James replied that to ask for separate names is to presuppose separate facts, which is precisely the assumption that *radical* empiricism challenges. "[T]he conceptualist rule," James says, "is to suppose that where there is a separate name there ought to be a fact as separate; and Hume, following this rule, and finding no such fact coresponding to the word 'power' concludes that the word is meaningless."[15] But, James objects, "By this rule, every conjunction and preposition in human speech is meaningless – *in, on, of, with, but, and, if* are as meaningless as *for* and *because*. The truth is that neither the elements of fact nor the meanings of our words are separable as the words are."[16]

James frequently warns against the tendency to reify causal connections, to set them apart from what they are experienced to be. James writes, "If there is anything hiding in the background, it ought not to be called causal agency, but should get itself another name."[17] In his usual colorful way he advises us that "the healthy thing for philosophy is to leave off grubbing underground for what effects effectuation, or what makes action act, and try to solve the concrete questions of where effectuation in this world is located, of which things are the true causal agents there, and of what the more remote effects consist."[18]

However, the direct-experience-of-causality view still does not yield the required sense of counterfactuality. As long as the experience of causal connection is restricted to volitional contexts, we do not have the non-independence of properties and events in the physical world that we need to turn the laws of science into something more than summaries of actual events. The causal connection experienced between my striving to remember a name and my remembering it does not help in the least to get causal connections between such things as x's being unsupported and x's falling, or between the atmospheric pressure and water going up a pump. Since James discusses the experience of causality only in volitional contexts, he is apparently committed to the notion that one must *infer* its existence between physical events.[19] An example supposedly would be this: we experience an exertion of power when we bend a young tree, and when we feel the wind blow and see the trees bend, we infer the exertion of such power on the part of the wind. We have got to the physical world at last and hopefully the causal relation there secures ontologically the concepts of potentiality, possibility, and counterfactuality!

2.

In order to understand and appreciate James' view of causality, we need to see how it fits with other major themes of his mature philosophy.

i) James is everywhere a staunch empiricist where this means that all nonlogical truths are known aposteriori. He unequivocally rejects the rationalist notion that there can be apriori knowledge of matters of fact. It is clear that his view of causality qualifies on this score. Since knowledge of causal relations is a matter of immediate acquaintance, it is wholly aposteriori. James, however – and this point is important – equally rejects the Humean contention that there is a material equivalence between 'p is aposteriori' and 'p is contingent' on the one hand, and between 'p is apriori' and 'p is necessary,' on the other. James crosses the lines in his analysis of the causal relation: causal relations are dynamic nonlogical connections but they are known in no other than aposteriori ways.

ii) James is committed to the concept of a plural, open, ambiguous future, and his view of causality, not being a version of the determinist thesis, fits this commitment admirably. Causal connections exist wherever they are experienced – there is that much non-independence of properties and events in the world. In many contexts of deliberation, however, there is no such experience and hence no ground for ascribing a causal connection. There is, then, an admirable escape from the concept of a "block universe." Let us examine this point more closely.

Say that p at t_1 is choosing between a and b and that if he chooses a consequence x will follow at t_n, while if he chooses b consequence y will follow at t_n. Now if at t_0 God or anyone else knows that x will occur at t_n – or even if the proposition at t_0 'x occurs at t_n' is in fact true whether anyone knows it or not –, then it would follow that at t_1 p must "choose" a – it is the only possibility open to him since x in fact is what will be. But then p could not have been said to have chosen anything at all. However, since deliberation does make a difference in the future, the future in certain respects must be conceived as open, plural, and ambiguous.

On the ontological level, then, James can best be understood as steering a middle course between the completely loose universe of the positivist and the block universe of the determinist. There must be enough connection in the world to account for the potentiality and counterfactuality but not so much connection in the world that it is impossible to say of anything that it could have been otherwise. Either too little or too much connection loses some precious aspect of that metaphysically profound concept of possibility. James' middle way may best be stated in the following way: he believed both in the partial dependence of various properties and events (not all conjunctions are coincidental) and in the partial plurality of the future (not all propositional truth values are antecedently determined).

iii) James' middle way, in turn, is supported by his theory of truth. At least part of the meaning of 'p is true' is that p leads us prosperously from one part of our experience to another and that it coheres with the great body of propositions that have already qualified on this count. This p, then, can be said to "become true" as it grows in this way. A proposition, then, is not antecedently true or false; truth or falsity is something that happens to propositions. Hence James is able to say in the case of propositions about future events like x and y dependent upon deliberation that they are not at t_o either true or false because what is needed to make them either one or the other has not yet been determined and will not be until the person decides at t_1. An ambiguous or open future requires the present indeterminacy of the truth values of certain propositions, and James' view of truth provides the ground – though not the only ground – for such indeterminacy.

3.

In spite of the way James' view of causality fits other aspects of his mature philosophy, and so receives support via the coherence route, it remained unsatisfactory in its own right – – and we are not referring here simply to its lack of development. The lack of development follows rather from intrinsic difficulties with view itself, one of which James himself keenly realized. Not knowing how to meet this difficulty, he never developed his view, though he never doubted he was on the right track and was at work on causality when he died. The major difficulties with James' analysis of 'causality' are these:

a) It is not clear that the causal concept is even applicable in volitional contexts. The supposition that a motive is always the cause of a person doing whatever he intentionally does has come under vigorous attack in recent years. The model offered instead of "x caused y to do z" is "y decided to do z," where 'y' refers to a self that initiates causal sequences but is not causally activated itself. This notion of a self with effective powers might still provide the original of 'making x occur' that is the model followed by the pan-psychists. But the important point is that however one construes intentional acts, whether along the motive model or the self model, the notion of cause involved in these contexts is invariably characterized as a subspecies of 'cause' significantly different from the sub-species that includes physical objects and events.

b) The inference claim is highly doubtful. It is contrary to appearances to claim that we only infer causal connections in the physical world. No one is aware of inferences like "me-bending tree, wind-bending tree." The reply to such a criticism is that one is unaware of the inference because it is automatic, telescoped, and non-discursive. To an eye unprejudiced by previous commitments, this reply seems equivalent to saying they aren't inferences at all.

c) The inference claim is highly doubtful in yet another way. On James' view all causal powers of a physical sort supposedly have to be inferred. One is no more directly aware of the force of the hurricane bending the trees than one is directly aware of the pressure of the atmosphere pushing the water up the pump. Such a view seems *prima facie* absurd, however, since we do ordinarily usefully distinguish between inferred and experienced physical powers. If one adopts James' way of talking, he has the difficult problem in his new way of speaking of making this useful distinction.

d) The extrapolation from volitional contexts to the physical world entails the disastrous consequence of pan-psychism. We will not argue that pan-psychism is a disaster but shall simply assume it to be so. It is this difficulty of which James was aware and about which he worried.[20] James in fact was not wholly unsympathetic to pan-psychism and was occasionally on the brink of accepting it, but he was never willing to make the required jump into this sort of metaphysics.[21] Not seeing how to reject the premise that we experience causality only in volitional contexts, worried about supposing a full analogy with physical power, and unable to develop a limited analogy, James was unable to advance any further in anchoring the concepts of possibility and counterfactuality in the physical world.

e) James' premise that we are directly aware of causality only in volitional contexts seems in fact false. Not only are we not confined to volitional contexts for our experiences of causal power, we discover them less easily and quickly there than in physical contexts. According to Sterling Lamprecht, "... instead of going from the psychical facts of volition to the physical thrusts of things (so that belief in causality would be a kind of lingering animistic interpretation of the material world), we begin with the experience of causality in bodily thrusts and only later extend the notion to our own mental life (and the degree to which such extension is legitimate is still to some philosophers an open question)."[22] Indeed, the idea of causality first arises not even from an awareness of things bumping, banging, and pushing on the child, but from his awareness of things banging, bumping, and clashing among themselves. Only gradually does he learn to isolate his own body for special attention, learn its prowess and various kinds of skill, and eventually arrive at an understanding of his own mental powers and the efficacy of his will.

Such a theory of the external origin of the notion of causal power receives strong support from the experimental findings of the Belgian psychologist A. Michotte.[23] We need not describe his experimental apparatus and procedures here, but simply note that they are highly ingenious and well worth close study.

What is significant for our purposes is his finding that the experience of purely mechanical causality (i. e., causation in which one moving object causes another object to move) external to the perceiver is primary. Moreover, he shows, contrary to Hume, that habit and expectation are not necessary conditions for the perception of mechanical causation.

The upshot of our criticism is this: James was wrong in limiting causality in the physical world to what is known inferentially. He was right in being worried about pan-psychistic notions of causality but he cannot avoid them if he keeps his premise that we are aware of causal connections only in volitional contexts. James in principle is correct in claiming that causal connections are an irreducible part of the immediately given.[24] He simply identified or located the irreducible causal relation incorrectly or too parochially. We join Lamprecht and Michotte in claiming that the experience of objective causal connection is an irreducible aspect of the immediately given. In this way, then, we would emend and extend James' view of causality.

4.

The immediate response of the Humean is not hard to guess. He may well agree that the emendation of James' view is all to the good but would argue that ultimately any claim about the ontological irreducibility of causal connections is doomed to failure. The Humean tradition claims to show that the direct perception of causal power is *in principle* impossible. The argument for this conclusion is very simple: one cannot perceive what is not there; 'causal power' entails 'necessary connection'; there are no necessary connections between matters of fact; therefore one cannot perceive causal power. The heart of this argument, and the backbone of the Humean tradition, is that there are no necessary connections between matters of fact. This contention is supported by the familiar Humean dialectic: If there were a necessary connection of any kind between C and E, then the conjunction of C . ~ E would be self-contradictory; but such a conjunction is not self-inconsistent since it is always logically possible that nature may change its course. Moreover, the Humeans do not deny that we have a phenomenologically irreducible experience of causal power; what they deny is that this sort of experience corresponds to any irreducible physical reality. The second part of the Humean argument, then, is to show why one mistakenly thinks his irreducible experience points to physical reality, and it is to this end that Hume introduces his associationistic explanation in terms of custom and its projection onto objects and events. Contemporary Humeans add other projective explanations.

The immediate response is that the second part of the Humean argument is without doubt wholly inadequate. This second claim is not a philosophical one but a factual one, psychological in nature, which common-sense observation and the experiments of Michotte tend to show to be false. Michotte's findings effectively show not only that the Humean associationistic explanations are likely factually false but also that the pan-psychist's genetic explanations of inferential causal knowledge are also. We have argued elsewhere that contemporary Humean projective explanations are no more successful than Hume's or the pan-psychists, and we will not repeat ourselves here.[25] The upshot, then, is that the Humean's system is not without difficulty. However, unless the in-principle argument is countered neither is James' nor any non-Humean analysis adequate. The crucial point, then, is wether the Humean in-principle argument is valid or not.

What sort of reply to this argument is possible, by James or anyone else? The following reply is our own but is certainly in the spirit of James and the main outline is no doubt implicit in much of his writing. As we shall see, even some of the details are there.

The crucial point of our reply is that Hume's in-principle argumentes is really superfluous in the context of his own ontology. The argument supposedly stablishes the independence of events by showing that there are no necessary connections between matters of fact. In fact, however, the very concept of an event in the Humean ontology is identical with the concept of the independence of events, properties, and predicates. It is generally supposed that the in-principle argument of the Humean is not ontology bound, that is, is relevant to all ontologies. In fact the independence of properties, etc., and hence the in-principle argument, is simply a consequence of a particular ontology which there seems little reason to hold. Hume's argument, in short, is ontologically bound in a damaging way. To document these claims, of course, we need to examine the concept of an "event."

In the ordinary and scientific view 'event' is construed in terms of an ontology of enduring things, while on the Humean view enduring things are conceived to be constructions out of "events." An event in the Humean sense must be seen as a temporal cross-section of what we would ordinarily call a physical object. 'x is red at t_1,' 'x is round at t_1,' 'x is sweet at t_1,' etc. would each be an event in this sense. The only connection this sense of 'event' has with the ordinary one is that all Humean events are momentary "happenings" in consciousness, the immediate awareness of the moment. A physical object, then, is construed as a construction out of such events; it is a collection of such events bound together only by temporal continuity and identity, or continuous change of place. For the Humean, in short, all events are logically and physically independent of each other.

There seems little reason nowadays to hold such an ontology. Humeans begin with an epistemic atomism and think it entails an ontological atomism; but Dretske and Joske have shown that the former does not entail the latter at all.[26] And we have seen how James effectively attacks the epistemic atomism of the Humean. Moreover, the efforts to contruct physical object sentences from sentences about events in the Humean sense are notorious failures. The trouble with such "constructions" is that they ignore the fact that what we sense depends upon the state of the observer and the conditions of observations as well as other factors, some reference to which is required *before* one can contruct physical object sentences. Hence such constructed physical object sentences presuppose the very thing they are trying to eliminate. Finally, the antimetaphysical bias of the Humean is already violated in his effort to interpret physical objects as collections of events in his sense bound together by temporal continuity or continuous change of place. This effort requires the assumption of both the density and continuity of time, neither of which are empirical concepts. James, then, was on sounder ground than even he supposed when he claimed that communality in space and time alone, even without causal considerations, goes a long way toward making the concept of a physical object unconstructable out of atomic impressions, and thus essentially presenting the ontology of enduring things as the required framework for securing the required concepts of potentiality, possibility, and counterfactuality.

5.

There is good evidence that James *intended* to meet the Humean thrust by avoiding a phenomenalistic ontology in which the independence of events is simply a corollary and defending instead an ontology of enduring physical objects in which some properties are bound together and in which changes, or events, consequently are sometimes connected. We must be careful on this issue, however, since James is sometimes interpreted as a phenomenalist, A. J. Ayer being a recent example.[27] That this interpretation is false is suggested by taking seriously James' own explicit declarations.

First, James unambiguously announces his aversion to phenomenalism as a satisfactory way of understanding the nature of physical objects. In his Notes for a "Seminary" on "Philosophical Problems of Psychology" given at Harvard in 1897–98, he writes: "The great difference between the phenomenalist and the common-sense view is that the latter gives *stable* elements whilst the former is affected by a restlessness which is painful to the mind. In it one never gets out of the conception of flux, or process; although it might well seem that all the *actual* found its place in the flux . . . ."[28] Thus James both early and late tied together phenomenalism, Humeanism, and actualism, on the one hand, and common-sense enduring objects and potentiality, on the other, and always maintained allegiance to the latter. Second, James on numerous occasions referred to himself straightforwardly as a natural realist and a defender of common-sense ontology. These statements of allegiance come to the fore forcefully in the discussions in those parts of his *Essays on Radical Empiricism* devoted to the concept of pure experience. "Radical empiricism has, in fact, more affinities with natural realism than with the views of Berkeley or of Mill, and this can be easily shown."[29]

We need to examine this issue in detail, however, since it is not enough to know only what James said but what he meant and what he was committed to. We want to get to the center of James' vision and not simply string together quotations from him that fit our thesis. Moreover, in order to make headway in analysis we need to say precisely what *we* mean by key terms, so that whatever others may mean by them the *issues* involved are clear and all of us avoid misunderstandings and disguised arguments about what some terms *really* mean.

The naive or presentational realist believes that we are directly aware of physical objects and their properties, a view which seemingly founders on the issues of false appearances and the mediation of stimuli. The traditional epistemic alternative has been that the only things we are directly aware of are our own sensations, either actual or possible, or sense-data, or whatever else we choose to call the particulars of direct acquaintance. Three issues immediately arise on this alternative: 1) are the particulars of direct awareness public or private?; 2) what level of complexity are the particulars – red patches, etc., or apples?; and 3) is there any objective reference from such particulars to physical objects? There are numerous historical permutations of answers to these questions, but for our purposes only one permutation is important: 1) the particulars of direct awareness are private (held by some phenomenalists and sense-data theorists but by no means by all); 2) such particulars are "atomistic" and physical objects must be construed as "constructions" out of them (held in one version or another by all phenomenalists); and 3) such particulars have no "objective reference" to physical objects in addition to whatever "construction" is involved (again common to all forms of phenomenalism). James can be understood best as accepting 1) and firmly rejecting 2) and 3). That he accepted 1) is clear from the fact that he believed no two observers can have numerically the same percept. The particular you are directly aware of when you look at Memorial Hall from angle x is numerically distinct from the particular I am directly aware of from angle y. That he rejected 2) is apparent from his constant rejection of epistemic atomism in all forms and the absence of any "constructions" out of sense-data in his radical empiricism essays. That he rejected 3) is clear from his repeated claims that the different percepts different people have of the same object are in identically the same place in public space. James' natural realism, then, is his effort – whether successful or not – to introduce objective reference into a private data scheme and hence make room for the enduring objects of science and ordinary life for the sake of accounting for potentiality and counterfactuality – something that phenomenalism, positivism, actualism, and Humeanism are unable to do.

While James' objective, in our view, is a worthy one, he was not, it seems wholly succesful in his efforts; the task of reconciling private data with public, enduring objects is a difficult one indeed. James is committed to the view that the different particulars different people are aware of are in identically the same place in public space. The jarring consequence of this view, however, is that numerically distinct contents can occupy the same place – a consequence that most philosophers would like to avoid. E. g., G. E. Moore shared James' commitment to private data but not being able to accept the jarring consequence concluded that space as well as data must be in some way private.[30] That way out was of no help to James, however, since public space was the only way he could see to achieve objective reference and hence an adequate analysis of potentiality. On our view, the best way out for James would be to reject 1) – deny the private premise – and substitute in its place the more adequate presentational view already present in Reid and developed fully in the recent writings of C. J. Ducasse and Roderick M. Chisholm – namely, the adverbial view of sensing and the dispositional analysis of properties.[31] There are, of course, other alternative epistemic possibilities, including perspectival realism, but whatever alternative one might choose to help James avoid the jarring consequence it should be abundantly clear that James was serious about natural realism and objective reference and was serious about these views because he was deeply concerned throughout his philosophical career to make sense of potentiality and counterfactuality and saw these commitments as necessary to that end.

NOTES

1 "Against Nihilism," in Ralph Barton Perry, *The Thought and Character of William James* (2 vols.; Boston: Little, Brown and Co., 1935), I, p. 525.
2 *Ibid.*
3 *Ibid.*, pp. 525—26.
4 *Ibid.*, p. 526.
5 *Ibid.*, p. 525.
6 *Ibid.*
7 *Ibid.*
8 Cf. James' Chapter on "Reasoning" in Vol. II of *The Principles of Psychology* (2 vols., New York: Henry Holt and Co., 1896).
9 We have developed this concept ourselves in "The Powers That Be," *Dialogue*, X (1971), 12—31. Cf. also E. H. Madden, "A Third View of Causality," *Review of Metaphysics*, XXIII (1969), 67—84, and "Hume and the Fiery Furnace," *Philosophy of Science*, 38 (1971), 64—78.
10 For a thorough treatment of the relation between Renouvier and James see Wilbur H. Long, "The Philosophy of Charles Renouvier and Its Influence on William James" (Unpublished doctoral dissertation, Harvard University, 1925). Unfortunately what appears to be the only copy extant of this useful piece of

11 "Against Nihilism," in Perry, *op. cit.*, p. 526.
12 *Ibid.*
13 Cf. William James, "The Feeling of Effort" in *Collected Essays and Reviews* (New York: Longmans, Green and Co., 1920), pp. 151 ff; "The Experience of Activity" in *Essays in Radical Empiricism* and *A Pluralistic Universe* (New York: Longmans, Green and Co., 1947), pp. 155 ff; and "Novelty and Causation — the Conceptual View" and "Novelty and Causation — the Perceptual View" in *Some Problems of Philosophy* (London: Longmans, Green, and Co., 1916), pp. 189—207 and 208—219, respectively.
14 James, *Essays in Radical Empiricism* and *A Pluralistic Universe*, p. 168.
15 James, *Some Problems of Philosophy*, p. 199.
16 *Ibid.*
17 *Ibid.*, p. 213.
18 James, *Essays in Radical Empiricism* and *A Pluralistic Universe*, pp. 185—186.
19 Cf. James, *Some Problems of Philosophy*, pp. 208—219.
20 *Ibid.*, pp. 218—19. He refers to pan-psychism as a "complication" and the discussion rather abruptly ends.
21 Later Whitehead, accepting the same premises as James, drew the pan-psychic consequence.
22 Sterling Lamprecht, *The Metaphysics of Naturalism* (New York: Appleton-Century-Crofts, 1967), pp. 136—37.
23 A. Michotte, *The Perception of Causality* (New York: Basic Books, 1963), esp. "Commentary" by T. R. Miles, pp. 373—415.
24 Association of James' theory of causality with Bergson's metaphysical intuitionism and romantic evolutionism has regrettably discredited it with some readers who might otherwise have recognized its basic soundness. For James' generous but seriously misleading acknowledgement of Bergson see *Some Problems of Philosophy*, p. 219, footnote.
25 Madden and Hare, "The Powers That Be," pp. 28—31.
26 Fred I. Dretske, *Seeing and Knowing* (London: Routledge and Kegan Paul, 1969); W. D. Joske, *Material Objects* (London: Macmillan, 1967).
27 A. J. Ayer, *The Origins of Pragmatism* (San Francisco: Freeman, Cooper, 1968), pp. 215—324, *passim*.
28 In R. B. Perry, *The Thought and Character of William James*, II, p. 370.
29 *Essays in Radical Empiricism* and *A Pluralistic Universe*, p. 76.

James's View of Causality

30 Cf. Robert G. Meyers, "Natural Realism and Illusion in James's Radical Empiricism," *Transactions of the Charles S. Peirce Society*, V (1969), pp. 211—223.

31 Cf. C. J. Ducasse, *Nature, Mind, and Death* (La Salle, Ill.: Open Court, 1951), pp. 246—290; *Truth, Knowledge and Causation* (London: Routledge and Kegan Paul, 1968), pp. 42—60, 60—72, 90—131; and Roderick M. Chisholm, *Perceiving: A Philosophical Study* (Ithaca, N. Y.: Cornell University Press, 1957); "Theory of Knowledge" in *Philosophy, The Princeton Studies* (Englewood Cliffs, N. J.: Prentice-Hall, 1964), esp. pp. 261—286, 312—344.

6

A PRAGMATIC CONCEPT OF CAUSATION

Elizabeth R. Eames

There is much in what William James says on the subject of cause that is provocative, and much that is elusive. He did not attempt any integration of scattered references, or any comprehensive theoretical analysis on the topic, although it was involved in many subjects which he treated at length such as the concept of "pure experience," the problem of determinism, and continuity of experience. His work is thus open to a variety of interpretations, according to the context selected for discussion, or to the perspective from which a synthesis of his different statements is attempted. It would not be in the spirit of William James to search for one final, correct, and authoritative version of his view of causation from which all different interpretations are revisionist. James' openness of attitude, his willingness to find new truth in every philosophy, and his spontaneity of expression encourage a variety of interpretations of his meaning; in addition we can assume some change in his views from one time to another in his work. In his spirit I propose to review the different contexts in James' work in which causal notions are discussed, to bring these fragmentary discussions under the synthesizing rubrics of pluralism, radical empiricism, and pragmatism, to show to what degree conflicts, unresolved problems, or incompleteness leave room for further work in the pragmatic analysis of causation, and finally, to suggest the direction in which this work might proceed. Perhaps it would not be unwelcome to William James to have an emerging concept of causality attributed to his influence, even if it is, in fact, in conflict with some of his own expressed positions.

There seem to be three areas in which James makes significant use of causal concepts. The first is in the context of what might be called scientific common sense. As a working scientist he assumes that there are causes for events and that these must be investigated, that inferences must be made concerning them, and that, when this is done, patterns or general principles will be seen to emerge which could be called scientific causal principles. Examples of assumption of this kind concerning causes can be found throughout James' writings on physiology and psychology: he assumes the importance of correlation in data in reports of the experiences of normal persons and paraplegics when they resolve to move their bodies,[1] or the occurrence of dizziness in deaf persons[2]; he assumes the significance of temporal sequences as indicating cause and effect relations, as in the relation of sensory stimulation to overt bodily response[3]; he assumes that in causal contexts the search for a mechanism of control will yield the final step in the causal explanation, as the function of a brain structure will solve a causal problem of sensory response[4]; he assumes that in cases of a series of events linked in a causal sequence, the observed parts of the sequence give grounds for making inferences concerning the unobserved part of the sequence,[5] as a neutral process in the brain cells may be inferred from the observations of repeated stimuli and repeated "habitual" reactions to those stimuli under different normal and abnormal conditions. Although in the passages in which such causal assumptions are present he usually does not raise a philosophical issue of the analysis of the causal concept, yet the philosophical implications of his assumptions are important, and have a bearing on the other causal contexts in his writing.

A second context in which James discusses causal concepts is that of the description of experience, especially the experience of doing, acting, or "the feeling of effort." This is an experiential analysis designed to describe in careful language what a causal situation feels like to one who believes himself to be functioning in that situation as a cause, "making something happen." From "The Feeling of Effort" of 1880 to "The Experience of Activity" of 1904, James strives to find clues in this distinctive human experience which would tell us something of how human beings come to believe they cause things to happen. Early and late, James recognizes the philosophical debates that raged around this concept, and he attempts to deal in empirical and noncontroversial terms with the phenomena of experience as a preliminary to giving, first, a psychology of acting, and second, a philosophical clarification of causal issues, arguing against hard-headed Humean positivists, against absolutistic idealists, and against determinists of one kind or another.

The issue of the description of feelings of causal efforts, is of vital importance because of the third major context in which James considers the concept of cause, that is, the context of the living, forced, and momentous options of free will versus determinism. This concern is obvious in the early essays on Renouvier and on the feeling of effort, and it takes classic form in "The Dilemma of Determinism" of 1884.[6] James takes it that there are two possibilities: either every event, including the precursor of the idea which determines the action in a given situation of deliberation, is causally determined by a preceding event, in which case each event forms part of an "adamantine and eternal uniformity" and it is not the case that something else could have happened than did in fact occur; or, in certain cases, there are, prior to the representation which produces this action rather than that, "an original commencement of phenomena" in which case there is a real freedom of the will to determine the outcome in this way rather than in that.[7] According to the famous argument of the "Dilemma" these mutually exclusive and exhaustive alternatives cannot be settled by argument or inquiry, and it is left for the will by its own commitment to make the reality of its own freedom in the assertion of that freedom. Thus a causal determinism, whether hard or soft, is rejected, and a universe of some degree of openess, or, at least, with chinks in the causal network, left in possession of the field.[8] As we shall see, the later discussion of the experience of activity may make a significant difference but, in this early discussion, a dualism of causal concepts seems to be the outcome: a concept of universal and determining causal laws holds throughout nature, and is evidenced in the physiological and some of the psychological mechanisms of habit and of the determination of action, and a different concept of self-determination by causation *ab initio,* a creative and original operation of a cause is essentially linked to intellectuation, choice, and deliberation. It thus appears that the causal concept assumed by James as a working scientist, and the similar causal concept of determinism may be contrasted with the experience of oneself as acting which appears to bear its own authentication and which is closely related to the creative causality of free will identified by James in this essay with indeterminism. In order to see what kind of consistency and philosophical integration James achieves with these conflicting concepts we turn to a discussion of the three themes of his philosophy, pluralism, radical empiricism, and pragmatism as these relate to this conceptual conflict.

James' pluralism is essentially an argument against other kinds of monistic philosophy, especially that of absolutistic idealism, which held the stage during the time that James wrote. His objections to monistic idealism are carefully worked out and deeply felt, as they are the record of his own conversion, and as he himself had felt the appeal of the unifying intent of philosophy in his own thought.

James' criticism of monistic idealism may be summarized: he sees that it neglects the discrepant data, the things that don't fit in with the hypothesis, "sweeping the litter of the world under the rug." He finds that idealism generalizes from situations of intimate and causal relations to the world as consisting of a network of internal relations such that every part of the universe affects every other part.[9] This defies scientific knowledge and common sense. Idealists employ what James called "intellectualist logic" to prove the internalism of the object of knowledge to the knowing relation. James tells us that he first tried to argue down this logic in its own terms, but came to reject both its method and its conclusions in favor of the logic of pragmatism.[10] He concludes that the world has a loose, strung-along character, exhibiting connections and disjunctions, with causes operating where they are found to operate and how they are found to operate, but not everywhere and not always the same.

The criticism of the causal conception in the history of philosophy is pursued in James' last book, although one would wish the alternative had been developed more clearly. The tradition which began with the Aristotelian emphasis on causes came to mean that every event has a cause, there is no more in the effect than in the cause, and this equivalence of cause and effect came to mean denial of any novelty in the world. Whether rationalist, idealist, or materialist the universality and necessity of causation was not disputed. The Humean criticism of the universality and necessity of the causal nexus had as its outcome the denial of "real causes" in nature on the one hand, and the assertion of uniform sequence on the other, with still no room for the reality of novelty. James suggests that the history of philosophy is in conflict with human experience and that it is to experience that we must turn for a proper view of cause.[11] This brings us to radical empiricism.

What makes James' radical empiricism "radical" is that it eschews the atomistic sensationism of the tradition of Locke, Berkeley, and Hume which finds experience to be made up of units given only in temporal succession and spatial contiguity but otherwise with no continuities, in favor of looking at experience as given, starting with the buzzing, blooming confusion of the infant and gradually accumulating relations-structures and a variety of qualities and meanings. James writes:

> Every examiner of the sensible life *in concreto* must see that relations of every sort, of time, space, difference, likeness, change, rate, cause, or what not, are just as integral members of the sensational flux as terms are, and that conjunctive relations are just as true members of the flux as disjunctive relations are. This is what in some recent writings of mine I have called the 'radically empiricist' doctrine (in distinction from the doctrine of mental atoms which the name empiricism

so often suggests). Intellectualistic critics of sensation insist that sensations are *dis*jointed only. Radical empiricism insists that conjunctions between them are just as immediately given as disjunctions are, and that relations, whether disjunctive or conjunctive, are in their original sensible givenness just as fleeting and momentary (in Green's words), and just as 'particular,' as terms are. Later, both terms and relations get universalized by being conceptualized and named.[12]

James' position explicitly undermines the Humean analysis of cause on the basis of experience in its natural state having causal relations embedded in it. This is not to say, as James points out, that experience is never wrong, that sometimes causes are experienced where no causes are, but it does mean that causality can have no meaning anywhere if it does not have it somewhere in experience. If we then look to experience to see what causes are experienced as, we find ourselves again inspecting the vital homeground of the concept of cause, our own experience of ourselves as acting. Here the description that James gives of the ingredients of the experience are parallel to his early "Feeling of Effort," but the essay on "The Experience of Activity" some twenty years later, has also some important differences from the argument of the 1880's. In both cases we are aware of the intent, the end previewed as desired, the effort, the resistance, the end felt as achieved or the effort felt as frustrated. In both cases it is argued that if there is any empirical basic for the concept of cause it is here. James says:

> Whosoever describes an experience in such terms as these describes an experience *of* activity. If the word have any meaning, it must denote what there is found. *There* is complete activity in its original and first intention. What it is 'known-as' is what there appears. The experiencer of such a situation possesses all that the idea contains. He feels the tendency, the obstacle, the will, the strain, the triumph, or the passive giving up, just as he feels the time, the space, the swiftness or intensity, the movement, the weight and color,

the pain and pleasure, the complexity, or whatever remaining characters the situation may involve. He goes through all that ever can be imagined where activity is supposed. If we suppose activities to go on outside of our experience, it is in forms like these that we must suppose them, or else give them some other name; for the word 'activity' has no imaginable content whatever save these experiences of process, obstruction, striving, strain, or release, ultimate *qualia* as they are of the life given us to be known.[13]

It would seem that the rebuttal of traditional causal concepts is now complete: the pluralistic rejection of monism with its universality and necessity of cause-effect relationship, the double rejection of Hume both because of the assumed uniformity of sequence inferred from sensations and because of his failure to recognize that, as radical empiricism shows, causes are real as they are found and where they are found in experience. What will these perspectives on the ancient concept of cause do to the traditional problem of free will and determinism?

James wrote "The Dilemma of Determinism" soon after the essay on "The Feeling of Effort" and the review of Renouvier in 1884. In this essay he relies on a dualism similar to that of the physiological-psychological dualism noted above in reference to Renouvier. He argues that the crucial question is whether there can be an origination of actions without a preceding necessary and sufficient cause. Experience indicates that we have experiences of the expenditure of effort and the achievement of ends, but both the soft and hard determinist theorize that these experiences are themselves the causal product of preceding causes. If this is true, James argues, then there are no free acts and the nerve of moral responsibility is cut. There is no conclusive evidence or argument to settle the issue between the determinist and the person who asserts that a new causal sequence may come into being with the act of the person who makes the decision.[14] His arguments against monism and against Hume are seen really as counter arguments to determinism, but the radical empiricist view of causal experiences is not invoked to decide in favor of novelty and free will.

James argues that such an undecided case leaves room for a pragmatic perspective to assert, act upon, and make true the free will or indeterminist hypothesis.

There are many things that can be said against this argument, such as denying that there is any necessary incompatibility between determinism and free will.[15] But in the context of this discussion the natural question seems to be: When James rejects the traditional conception of cause, is he not rejecting the basis of the determinist argument with it? The quotation from "The Experience of Activity" seems to suggest this, especially in saying that "real effectual causation ... is *just what we feel it to be.*"[16] Can the apparent discrepancy between the argument of "The Dilemma of Determinism" and the later article be explained by the interval of twenty years? Perhaps James came to see just how "radical" empiricism is and the quotation just referred to reflects this. From this later point of view perhaps he could give an affirmative support to "freedom of the will," or at least to causal action as initiated by the person having the experience, as indefeasible by any argument since it is given in direct experience. From this standpoint any form of determinism would be rejected if it conflicted with the direct authority of experience itself. If one could explain a certain discrepancy in the views of cause, between the concept of more traditional determinism as in "The Dilemma of Determinism" and the more radical claim that it is the experience which is itself the very basis of any causal concept, as belonging to different stages in the development of James' philosophy, there would be no problem. James' own footnote to the later essay seems to imply a continuity between his earlier and later views on free will:

Single clauses in my writing, or sentences read out of their connection, may possibly have been compatible with a transphenomenal principle of energy; but I defy anyone to show a single sentence which, taken with its context, should

A Pragmatic Concept of Causation

be naturally held to advocate that view. The mis-interpretation probably arose at first from my defending (after Renouvier) the indeteriminism of our efforts. 'Free will' was supposed by my critics to involve a supernatural agent. As a matter of plain history the only 'free will' I have ever thought of defending is the character of novelty in fresh activity-situations. If an activity-process is the form of a whole 'field of consciousness,' and if each field of consciousness is not only in its totality unique (as is now commonly admitted) but has its elements unique (since in that situation they are all dyed in the total) then novelty is perpetually entering the world and what happens there is not pure *repetition*, as the dogma of the literal uniformity of nature requires. Activity-situations come, in short, each with an original touch.[17]

It seems, then, that James has a discussion of cause in the context of pluralism, according to which he finds a universe with gaps and discontinuities in it, and a similar discussion of cause in the context of radical empiricism according to which these discontinuities are directly experienced as disjunctions, and according to which the experience of activity itself is the experience of cause on the most fundamental level. But, in other contexts, James reverts to a traditional view of causal determinism, as he does when he is concerned with the moral and personal issues of free will and optimism about the world; here he makes less use of his pluralistic and radical empiricist view of cause than he might have. Perhaps in following the determinist argument as far as he did, he was falling back on an uncriticized scientific common sense concept of causality, such as we saw him assuming in his psychology. But before his view is adjudged flawed by a real contradiction, we ought to evaluate his position in the light of his pragmatism.

It would be easy to overlook the pragmatic aspect of the discussion of cause in James. For one thing, James seems to be groping for a better concept by way of a rejection of certain traditional philosophical alternatives. Hence, he and we may become enmeshed in the traditional terminology from which he is attempting to free himself. We may tend to force James into choosing between assigning cause to the experiential, volitional, and subjective realm or to the real, objective, and physical realm; we may argue that he must either defend free will in the context of a physical and causally determined world within which it too is a cause, or adopt an irresponsible indeterminism in which anything is as likely to happen as anything else. But, in fact, James regarded pragmatism as a way of escape from these confining dichotomies.[18] In the process of inquiry, the real and objective is that which gets itself validated in the course of experience while the subjective is that which does not stand the test of leading experience on to the consummation sought; James believes this pragmatic insight allows him to escape the alternatives of objective and subjective. In a similar way, determinism and indeterminism may be thought of as mutually exclusive, the one presupposing a world of ordered cause and effect relations, the other a world of accident and pure and unpredictable spontaneity. But, in fact, the part of our experience which we have succeeded in ordering has the former aspect, and the still unfinished and in process part of our experience the latter. Neither excludes the other but each represents a phase of experience. If experience has aspects which show us that given such and such earlier events, only such and such later events can follow, then this belongs to the continuities of experience and gives us the foresight and control which science has always sought. But, for the rest of experience, the chancy, the self-chosen, the creative, novelty is its characteristic and this is grounded on the discontinuities, disjunctions, and now and then parts of experience which are as really there as are the regularities and continuities. In all cases we must keep our attention on the direction in which activity is moving, and that is always toward the attempted achievement of certain goals. In this attempt some of the regularities of causal "laws" support us, some defeat us, and at other times we have to hazard, leap, and choose, making our own regularity as we go, and as we go making and showing the freedom of the will. It is to this pragmatism of philosophical method that James referred when he said he had to end by rejecting intellectualistic logic; pragmatic logic is always temporal rather than timeless, tested by outcomes rather than by simultaneous correspondence, by fruitfulness rather than by static identities.[19]

Is what we have said sufficient to absolve James of any confusions or inconsistencies in his view of cause? We will have to say that that concept as he left it has confusions within it. There seem still to be residual problems with the concept of "determinism" itself. One is still inclined to say on the basis of both pragmatism and radical empiricism that a view of the compulsiveness of causality ought not to survive James' own analysis. Causes should be imputed, it seems, only where experience shows them to be present and fruitful in leading to desired outcomes or in forewarning us of undesired ones. If so, then the bugaboo of determinism could be defeated more directly in terms of its empirical warrant than in terms of the application of faith in the forced, vital, and momentous option of the early essay. Perhaps had James finished *Some Problems of Philosophy* the full outline of a pragmatic concept of cause would have emerged, but, at least, his ideas are suggestive of new directions in the analysis of the concept. To the directions suggested to me, I devote the last part of this study.

One aspect of James' discussion of the experience of cause which seems undeveloped, and could easily suggest a criticism of him as subjectivist, is the limitation of the experience of cause to situations of activity, and the experience of one's own activity. While James nowhere denies that there may be other experiences of cause, he gives no other cases, and says of this experience of oneself as active "here is causality at work."[20] Undoubtedly, there are pragmatic reasons for his choice since he has his eye partially, at least, on the problem of how human beings act so as to make the world different. But it might be useful to expand the experience of cause to include the experience one has of oneself as the receiver of the action done to one, as one feels oneself bumped, and the experience of things around one acting upon each other, of changes being observed which one observes as a bystander.

If someone like James addresses himself to reporting experience with all its conjunctions and disjunctions, and if he describes activity as an experienced cause, a critic might say he is reporting activities but not causes. It may be difficult to identify specific connections as causal since cause is an abstract term. But it is not difficult to identify bumpings, burnings, breakings as specific occurrences in experience. To ask for causes in experience is like asking, Do you see visibility? Or, do you experience audibility? The answer must be: "I see red squares and blue streaks; I hear snaps, crackles, and pops, but the other terms are too abstract to be the kinds of things that can be pointed out in experience." Similarly with causes we do experience, as James says, our own actions, our pushings, throwings, drinkings, and so forth; we also experience things done to us, being pushed, being thrown to, being rained upon and so forth; we also experience the goings on around us, things falling and breaking, ice melting, raindrops splashing, waves moving drifting seaweed, and so forth. We may group all these experiences together as experiences of causal connections as given in experience, with the understanding that they are causal in an abstract generalized sense.

Beyond these experienced causes we infer causes from experienced effects, effects from experienced causes, unexperienced causal sequences by analogy and generalization from experienced sequences. From this inferential extension of our experience we develop a concept of causality which may or may not be adequate as a guide to inquiry and action, and may or may not be philosophically consistent with itself and with science and common sense. Such adequacy and consistency are the aims of our philosophical analysis.

In my opinion James held in his hands the tools of an adequate analysis of the experiential basis of causal concepts but uncritically accepted the scientific or pseudo-scientific concept of rigidly determined and uniform causal laws. (Or, at least, if he did not maintain it, he felt that it held the field and had to be argued down by some argument external to itself.) Perhaps this assumption of the rigidity of the compulsive force of causal laws stems from the old definition of cause in terms of necessary and sufficient conditions; at any rate, it seems a concept not only inappropriate to science, as Peirce argued, but even untenable after Hume. I argue that James could have and we can accept the concept of causal laws as correlational and probable statistically without undermining our own experience of causal connections in our own actions, or as done to us, or as experienced as non-participants of the action. We can do so because the two aspects of causality are on different levels; if we experience causal connections, they are what they are experienced to be, and our causal concepts will have to fit the case; but within the range of compatibility we may find a variety of causal concepts which fit the needs of different inquiries, the correlational view is one which does not necessitate any kind of rigidity of determinism and so does not create the problem James thought that it did. The difference of levels also alleviates some of the problems attributed by James to his critics, for example, the requirement of an adequate causal concept that it provide possibility and counterfactuality, seems to be answerable in this way: possibility means only that more than one thing can happen and this merely means an element of indeterminism or chance in the universe, a requirement which in no way conflicts with what James wished to hold – in fact, it is part of his pluralism; the requirement of counterfactuality, as I understand it, refers to the level of inferred causal laws where one wishes to hold that in the absence of the cause, the effect would not have followed, and this, by definition, cannot be found in experience but only in the analysis of causal inferences, since one cannot experience what did not happen.

Whatever the outcome of James' insights, there is much yet to be done, and what is done with the concept of cause will owe much to James' "radical empiricism," his attempt to ground the concept on an experiential base.

NOTES

1. William James, "The Feeling of Effort," in *Collected Essays and Reviews*, edited by Ralph Barton Perry (1880; reprinted, New York: Longmans, Green and Co., 1920; reprinted, New York: Russell and Russell, 1969), pp. 151—219.
2. *Ibid.*, pp. 220—243. "The Sense of Dizziness in Deaf-Mutes."
3. William James, *The Principles of Psychology* (1890; New York: Dover Publications, Inc., 1950), I, pp. 81—83.
4. *Ibid.*, I, Chapter II.
5. *Ibid.*, II, pp. 122—127.
6. William James, "Bain and Renouvier" (1876) in *Collected Essays and Reviews*, pp. 26—35; *ibid.*, pp. 151—219, "The Feeling of Effort" (1880); "The Dilemma of Determinism" (1884) in John J. McDermott, ed., *The Writings of William James* (New York: The Modern Library, 1968), pp. 587—610.
7. James, "Bain and Renouvier," p. 31.
8. James, "The Dilemma of Determinism," p. 592.
9. William James, *A Pluralistic Universe* (New York: Longmans, Green and Co., 1909); see especially "Monistic Idealism."
10. *Ibid.*, pp. 211 ff.
11. William James, *Some Problems of Philosophy* (New York: Longmans, Green and Co., 1911). Chapters XII and XIII.
12. McDermott, ed., *The Writings of William James*, p. 293.
13. *Ibid.*, "The Experience of Activity," p. 282.
14. *Ibid.*, "The Dilemma of Determinism," p. 591.
15. Ronald J. Glossop, "Beneath the Surface of the Free-Will Problem," *The Journal of Value Inquiry*, Vol. V, No. 1 (Spring 1971), 24—34.
16. McDermott, ed., *The Writings of William James*, "The Experience of Activitiy," p. 290.
17. *Ibid.*, p. 290 n.
18. McDermott, ed., *The Writings of William James*, "Some Metaphysical Problems Pragmatically Considered," pp. 390—404.
19. McDermott, ed., *The Writings of William James*, "What Pragmatism Means," pp. 380—381.
20. *Ibid.*, "The Experience of Activity," p. 289.

7

PERCEPT AND CONCEPT IN WILLIAM JAMES

Keith R. David

The object of this analysis is an explanation of the role which percepts and concepts play in the thought of William James, as they apply specifically to his theory of knowledge and truth. An adequate understanding of the nature and role of percept and concept requires some prior knowledge of other aspects of his thought, for example, his view of ultimate reality, the status of relations, the nature of consciousness, and the self. Since the treatment of the subject must be limited, and in as much as some of the subjects will be adequately dealt with by my colleagues sharing the endeavor which this seminar occasions, it must necessarily be assumed that the reader is familiar with those parts of James' position, or can avail himself of the information.

In addition to the main purpose of this study, I hope to point out that James holds a view of truth that is compatible with the realism of the science of his time. There appears to be a need to clarify his scientific theory of truth as it directly relates to the perceptual level of experience, distinguishing it clearly from the psychological and subjective aspects.[1] Since James' theory of knowledge and truth pivots on the relation which concepts have to perception, then, percepts are treated prior to concepts. And even more basic, a brief presentation of James' view of ultimate reality serves as the starting point.

Reality is constituted of one primordial stuff called "pure experience," which is an originally chaotic manifold of non-perceptual experience. It is the world of fact, uncognized by any human mind. The essential nature of pure experience is characterized by its rich, varied, and dynamic field of "given" existence.[2] For James this experience is neutral with respect to being potentially mental or physical, depending on the point of reference from which it is considered.[3] Consciousness arises as a function or relation between the parts of the perceptual flow. Cognition of the experiential flux emerges from this stuff of existence as parts of pure experience transcend themselves in taking account of other parts. All subsequent thought processes and complex conceptualizations depend upon pure experience for the material of their domain and function.

The Nature and Role of Percepts. At the pre-reflective, non-perceptual level of existence pure experience is identified with sensation or feeling. The more intense and outstanding any particular simple quality becomes to the organism, the purer the sensation becomes. However, when the object is cognized in its larger field, that is, taken in relation to the various aspects of its environment, the more likely it will be thought of as perception. In short, sensation varies inversely with perception. Their difference is one of function rather than content. Sensation functions by making us immediately aware of physical objects through their bare natures; on the other hand, perceptions function in making us aware of the "farther facts" associated with the object of sensation. Sensation's function provides an acquaintance with an object; perception provides knowledge about it.[4]

From the vat of the perceptual flow man's experiences emerge and submerge, coming as pulses of feeling which at one moment capture his fullest attention, and at another moment are weak.

The source of percepts lies in the physiology of the human body as the nervous system is aroused by the particular presentations of the surrounding experiential environment. Objects of the external world, when appropriately presented, cause changes in the body, and percepts of those objects are formed as presented. Perception is described as a mental process which

> supplements a sense-impression by an accompaniment or escort of revived sensations, the whole aggregate of actual

and revived sensations being solidified or 'integrated' into the form of a percept, that is, an apparently immediate apprehension or cognition of an object now present in a particular locality or region of space.[5]

This definition allows the body to be its own percept when attention is so directed. In fact, "the objective nucleus of every man's experience, his own body, is, it is true, a continuous percept."[6] That James does allow for *inner* and *outer* perceptions as they relate to specified sensations of the body is aptly discussed by A. J. Ayer.[7]

The perceived relations of similarity and difference provide the notion that there is a variation of quality in the perceptual flow. Thought processes take note of those variations by the power to discriminate between the differences. The later functioning of the mind through memory and reasoning processes will call attention to the particular percepts as real and as leading on to other possible experiences, even to that of language. James says, "Reality consists of existential particulars as well as of essences and universals and class-names, and of existential particulars we become aware only in the perceptual flux. The flux can never be superceded."[8]

Percepts play at least a two-fold role in the cognitive enterprise: first, they make concepts possible, and second, they declare the empirical status of concepts. Regarding the former, just as pure experience permits the possibility of experience on a higher plane, that of the perceptual level, so too do percepts themselves allow for a still higher experience, the conceptual level.

Thus, the order of perception and conception begins in the empirical situation in which perception arises with conceptualization following. By observation and inquiry certain features of the perceptual flow are noted and named by symbols. The names are related to thoughts or ideas of the percepts so encountered. A variety of names is used by James to indicate the objects encountered on each level. In *Some Problems of Philosophy* several synonyms are listed indicating that for "percept" one could equally use "sensation," "feeling," "sensible experience," or the "immediate flow" of conscious life; whereas for "concept," the terms "idea," "thought," and "intellection" would be substituted.[9] The thoughts then, "about" the percepts are "concepts." In the beginning of the intellectual process of abstraction, concepts depend upon percepts, but later, concepts can be treated as independent, for example, as in mathematics. The view that the empirical value of concepts are shown by the percepts to which they lead comprises James' theory of meaning which is discussed later.

The Nature and Function of Concepts. By means of the unique structure of the human central nervous system, especially the brain, conception arises as a result of attention. Consequently, James defines conception: *The function by which we thus identify a numerically distinct and permanent subject of discourse is called CONCEPTION; and the thoughts which are its vehicles are called concepts.*"[10] It is important to notice, with regard to this definition, that conception is neither a mental state nor that to which the mental state refers. Conception is the *function* of signification which obtains between the mental state and the object to which its attention is called. In other words, conception is a relation of the two factors.

The way in which conception functions has an aspect that is sometimes overlooked in reading James in that conception involves the activities, interests, and purposes of the organism as well as a passive aspect. The human organism partly determines what it shall conceive, that is, what its world will be like. Not only do concepts result from attention, but also the nature of mind results from the interests and intentional behavior of the organism.

A comparison of percepts to concepts shows that when the former arise they are already interpreted in some sense by the verbalized inheritance from the social environment. Concepts, too, are influenced to a degree by one's interests and by the social structures, both of which determine what one "should see or feel." Each person perceives, and then conceives his own world. The habits and patterns of conception become an integral part of one's personal biography. As James reminds us, "Concepts flow out of percepts and into them again, they are so interlaced and our life rests on them so interchangeably and undiscriminatingly, that it is often difficult to impart quickly to beginners a clear notion of the difference meant."[11] The greatest distinction, however, is that concepts are separate and discrete, while percepts are constantly changing, having fringes that melt into other percepts, that is, they are continous; concepts are relatively stable and are discontinuous, each one separate from the other. As a part of the stream of feeling, percepts wax and wane in intensity and excitation, being made known by the five senses; concepts maintain a singleness of character, being determined by cognitive processes, as constructions of the mind. Percepts are the particulars of existence, the facts of the empirical world, which vary and even decay; concepts are not facts of the external world, but are units of the inner world, are static, and function as if they are eternal. Being sensible and transient, percepts are of the "here" and "now"; they are real in a temporal way. Percepts are the cases of things presented, whereas concepts concern the remote (past and future).[12] In the world of flux, percepts constitute the singulars which never cease to change and never return exactly as previously experienced. Since they make up the basic elements of the world, as man perceives it, the notion of novelty and chance is a constant impression. Percepts comprise the concrete pieces of man's sensate life, showing the reality of relations perceived, as before mentioned.[13] As to concepts we are told:

> New conceptions come from new sensations, new movements, new emotions, new associations, new acts of attention, and new comparisons of old conceptions, and not in other ways, Endogenous prolification is not a mode of growth to which conceptions can lay claim.[14]

Because each concept is changeless and discrete, it constitutes a discontinuous part of a system made up of ideal cuts or "maps" of the experiential flux. That is, they translate our changing percepts into static and "petrified terms."[15]

Man's ability to form concepts by which to name and refer to the perceptual flux, rather than merely react upon it, has far reaching consequences. James held that for primitive man, in his initial attempts at conceptualizing, "thought proper must have had an exclusively practical use. Men classed their sensations, substituting concepts for them, in order to 'work them for what they were worth,' and to prepare for what might lie ahead."[16] By organizing their perceptual world around concepts which stood for perceived consequences, the earliest thinkers became abler to manipulate their environment according to their interests, one of which was survival. By means of concepts man could adapt himself to an ever-expanding environment, one far beyond that of the lower levels of animal life. It is to this situation that James refers when he claims that concepts originate in utility, that is, their practical usefulness in man's adjustment. In fact, he considers this to be the primary function of concepts.[17] For purposes of clarification, James makes a distinction between the content of a concept and its function. A concept can and usually does consist of three things: a word, a mental image, and some operation.[18] This can be illustrated by the concept "man." There is, first, the word itself which has conceptual value. Then, upon hearing the word "man" a vague picture or image occurs in the mind. Finally, there comes to mind that uniquely human activity of performing abstractions for purposes of symbolizing and representing percepts. In addition, there is that anticipatory activity of being treated humanely upon occasion.

The word and the image associated with it form the substantive content of a concept. The key to understanding James' notion of the functional value of a concept is found in the criterion that concepts must lead beyond themselves in discourse, that is, to percepts which declare their empirical value.[19] A concept is an instrument for leading on to some perceptual experience. In fact, there are concepts which seem to have no value other than the functional. Such terms as

"God" and "soul," besides being words, do not invoke clear images which justify assigning a content to them. But they have a function in the activities of mankind.

A further function of concepts is their usefulness as substitutions for percepts. One great advantage which the rational being has over brute beasts is the ability to pick out pieces of the perceptual flow, to name them, to class them, and to intend them — in other words, to form abstractions.[20] This substitution of concepts for percepts gives man a decided advantage over the lower animals. The latter simply take what comes to them in life and are, consequently, completely at the mercy of nature. Man, the rational being, by using concepts in place of percepts, is not limited to what the chance events of the perceptual flow bring. Concepts allow the mind to take in vast distances of the flow, to separate its parts and perceive new possible relations, to make percepts serve the interests of humanity, and to introduce human creativity as a novelty through an understanding of the *this* by the *what*.

Conceptual substitution is not without its price, however, as James indicates by pointing to both the positive and negative aspects of the process. Concepts, being discrete, static symbols of percepts, provide only a map of the perceptual flow. While it may be true that by conceptual translation we increase our knowledge about percepts, yet, "the map remains superficial through the abstractness, and false through the discreteness of its elements... Conceptual knowledge is forever inadequate to the fulness of the reality to be known."[21] In spite of this limitation to the function of concepts there is a wider role which concepts play in the human enterprise of negotiating with nature for a good life. To employ the term "function" in any given circumstance is the same as to refer to its use. James leaves no doubt as to what he considers to be the overall function of conceptualization. The fundamental use of concepts is adaptation — adaptation to an ever wider range of nature.[22] Probably a more inclusive term than adaptation, and one which is more commensurate with his total philosophy, would be the term "adjustment." Going beyond this, James' general idea is that of man actually changing the natural conditions about him and effecting new forms of circumstance. Whereas the term adaptation implies passive acceptance of things as they are, adjustment carries the idea of an activity on the part of man, making him an agent in the outcome of things.[23] Man, in this sense, has something to say in determining his future. By this function of the mind, in its ability to form and use concepts for adjustment, man becomes a cause rather than a mere effect. This force for human good originates in the function of the conceptual translation of percepts.

Not only are concepts useful for environmental adjustment, but also the process of reasoning is shown to hinge on concepts in the development of language.[24] The trains of images which pass through the brain of brute animals, and men in fancy and reverie, are joined together by empirical connections, that is, by association rather than abstractions.[25] For such two-term acts of thought, James suggests the names "unconscious inference" and "immediate inference" as being suitably descriptive, realizing, of course, that the latter has already found a secure place in formal logic.[26] But that kind of thought is shared by man and beast. Man, however, is able by means of language to assign names to percepts, the consequences of which he remembers. Where animals may remember that fire burns, causing pain, man gives to the perceptual signs of fire a name, substituting that name for real fire. He then acts in terms of the word alone. For example, were a person to enter a public building and convincingly exclaim "Fire," the sane would react as if a real fire threatened them. In view of this kind of human reaction to words – taken-as-percepts, James distinguishes between the lower type of empirical thinking and reason proper. The reasoning of the former is based only on that with which they have had previous experience, while the more rational person in the absence of experience uses concepts to infer successful courses of action. In fact, James goes further by suggesting that we *"make this ability to deal with NOVEL data the technical differentia of reasoning."*[27] By the process of attention, conception, naming and substitution of concept for percept, followed by the substitution of one abstract concept for another, reasoning comes to the fore of human experience. Subsequently, reasoning is defined as "the substitution of parts and their implications or consequences for wholes."[28]

To make explicit that which has been implicit in the consideration of reason, there are two important features to be set forth. First, a part is used to represent the whole. That part is an abstraction of some bit of the perceptual flow, taken as equivalent to the whole of that segment of experience from which it is extracted. The second feature of reasoning is that the abstracted part more evidently gives clues to a consequence than does the whole from which the part was extracted.[29]

The latter feature of abstract concepts, revealing more of reality through consequences than was revealed prior to conceptualization, introduces at least three functions which concepts play in human life.[30] First, concepts have a practical function of guiding us every day by providing a map of the various parts of experience which are encountered. The perceived relations of things get plotted by concepts which are stored in the memory for future reference. And through the sciences concepts have a theoretical function in that by the substitution of concepts for the perceptual flux, we are enabled to understand the latter better. Concepts harness percepts, putting them to work for man's purposes and interests, for good or evil.

A second function which concepts play is that of bringing "new values into our perceptual life." James says that "they reanimate our wills, and make our action turn upon new points of emphasis."[31] This is the function which Andrew Reck calls the "creative function" of concepts.[32] The "revaluation" to which James refers is a deepened appreciation of the richness of the perceptual flow and its service to man, leading to the thrill of discovery in bringing concepts down to percepts and "cashing them in." There is risk, but there is also reward and ends for which to fight.[33] James' open, pluralistic universe offers a continual hope for something better for every man.

Finally, concepts have an interesting and attractive function in their own right. The map which they form of the perceptual flux can itself become an object of study. Concepts possess an existence independent of percepts because of their abstract quality. They have a pristine beauty and order not matched anywhere else. The notion of "eternal truths" constitutes this realm of thought. It is here that meditation and contemplation find a place. Pure concepts, radiant in their glory and connected by relations, lie unstained by percepts. This conceptual structure forms a work of art, constructed and limited only by the logical dexterity of the conceiving mind. James would say, however, that they have their reward only as imagination in the mind's eye unless they are returned to dip into the stream of the perceptual flux to determine their greater reward: practical worth for man.

Percepts and Concepts: The Context of Truth. In the knowing process percepts and concepts are tied to beliefs as guides to action. The knower extends himself into experience by such action and learns whether there has been a successful negotiation with experience by relaying on those beliefs. Knowing is explained by the relations which obtain between our experiences, especially as the mind anticipates and successfully leads out to future experiences.

It was asserted earlier that percepts declare the empirical value of concepts for the inquiring mind. As an empiricist he requires that an idea or concept be tested by locating in time and space the perceptual experience which serves as its referent.[34] To recall his distinction between knowledge by acquaintance (perceptual knowledge) and knowledge by description (conceptual knowledge), it is with reference to the latter that empirical verification renders a service. Given an idea of a physical object in the mind of the knower, the process by which that idea is declared to be true or false is that step by step progress from one percept to another until the final percept is reached which the concept originally intended.[35] Each subsequent experience knows the preceding one establishing a continuity in the cognitive experience from the beginning of the knowing act to the end. The concept is said to be verified by that percept which terminates the inquiry. That percept is what the knower *meant* by his concept prior to the verification process.[36] If the intermediary percepts lead to what the concept intended, then the concept is verified; if not, the concept is false, or at least unknown as to its empirical value. Whatever empirical status a concept may have, its value as such is declared or revealed only by those perceptual termini to which it does or does not lead.

In order to grasp the full import of this idea the word "concept" should be enlarged to include within its definition the notion that it is a plan or guide to action. A concept's significance, then, is determined by the consequences to which it leads. Such consequences include the difference in the way we act or think in terms of the concept. It is here that belief becomes connected to the perceptually real world. By the intentional structure of belief the knower is led by his interests to acquire a particular commerce with the object. The knower can come to know an object by means of an idea when that idea leads through the intermediary experiences which intervene between him and the object. The entire process takes place within the framework of sensible realities with concepts guiding the way. The idea as a plan or an instrument puts the knower into direct sensible possession of the object.

The theory of knowledge, then, which James espouses, can be called appropriately an *a posteriori* theory since the experiential level of existence serves as the first and final judge in all matters of cognition. With his particular type of empiricism the mind experiments with reality and receives either a "yes" or a "no" as to its intentions.[37] Knowledge is, therefore, always open to correction and addition and is relative to the contingencies of experience in time and space.

The distinction, for James, between the completed process of verification and truth is purely a logical one, for verification leads to truth. Truth is not a quality applicable to reality; it is a relation between an idea and its object.[38] An idea may be construed to include opinions, beliefs, statements, concepts, or whatever falls under the same ideational classification. He specified that the property called "truth" belongs to certain ideas, namely, those that agree with reality. An idea had to be acted upon in order to become true or false in the process; it was not true prior to the inquiry. This meant that the mere faithful copying of an object by an idea was insufficient for the title of "truth." Truth and verification become virtually equated in the cognitive process which leads to the agreement of the idea with the intended object. This aspect becomes the crux of James' scientific theory of truth – an aspect which is neglected by many philosophers of his day and many since that time.

Truth, with its close relation to verification, is brought about through the ambulatory process of cognition whereby a concept, as an abstracted percept, leads from one intermediary part of perceptual experience, and on to the next, until the concept is finally dipped back into the perceptual stream and "cashed-in." The intention of the concept, that is, its cash-value, is an object of a particular feeling experience. In his account of truth no aspect of human experience has been omitted, psychological or physical. That is as it should be if a theory of knowledge is to include all experiences possible to man.

As a process theory, allowance is made for representation of dynamic relations actually found in experience, whereas a static idea from the copy-theory cannot be adequately represented. This allows for a modified correspondence theory of truth when the term "agreement" is taken in its broadest sense.[39] James also advocates that the consequences of an idea must fit in with all aspects of reality, including that fund of knowledge constituted by "the whole body of other truths already in our possession."[40] This would in essence include the traditional coherence theory of truth. Furthermore, the pragmatic position lays claim to realism, accepting the view that there is a reality independent of the knower.[41] Truth does not reside in some ideal ethereal realm, with man having only partial and imperfect imitations of it; truth, as James says, "*happens* to an idea," and it occurs in relation to man as the measure.[42]

Another aspect of the pragmatic theory of truth which is of scientific value is in the latitude of the notion of verifiability.[43] The earlier positivists with whom James disagreed sought complete empirical verification of all statements making a truth claim. But for James, an idea may pass for true as long as it is verifiable in principle, either possibly or indirectly. He holds that, *"Indirectly or only potentially verifying processes may thus be true as well as full verification-processes. They work as true processes would work, give us the same advantages, and claim our recognition for the same reasons."*[44] This theory, then, seems consistent with the trends of science in seeking empirical verification of propositions.

NOTES

1. For a discussion of James about his controversial view and his critics see William James, *The Meaning of Truth, A Sequel to Pragmatism* (New York: Longmans, Green and Company, 1911), pp. xix-xx.
2. William James, *Essays in Radical Empiricism* (New York: Longmans, Green and Company, 1912), pp. 4; 16n; 137—138.
3. For an informative quotation from James' notes prepared for a seminar on metaphysics touching on neutral monism see Ralph Barton Perry, *The Thought and Character of William James*, Vol. II (New York: Little, Brown and Company, 1935), p. 385.
4. William James, *The Principles of Psychology*, Vol. II (New York: Henry Holt and Company, 1890), pp. 1—2; 77.
5. *Ibid.*, p. 79. A quotation James borrowed from James Sully.
6. James, *Essays in Radical Empiricism*, p. 65.
7. A. J. Ayer, *The Origins of Pragmatism: Studies in the Philosophy of Charles Sanders Peirce and William James* (San Francisco: Freeman, Cooper and Company, 1973), pp. 218—219.
8. William James, *Some Problems of Philosophy* (New York: Longmans, Green and Company, 1911), pp. 78—79.
9. *Ibid.*, p. 48n.
10. James, *The Principles of Psychology*, I, p. 461.
11. James, *Some Problems of Philosophy*, p. 47.
12. James, *Essays in Radical Empiricism*, p. 15.
13. This comparative description of percepts and concepts is discussed in *Some Problems of Philosophy*, of which the entirety of Chapters IV and VI is devoted.

[14] James, *The Principles of Psychology*, I, p. 467.
[15] *Ibid.*, p. 468.
[16] James, *Some Problems of Philosophy*, p. 63.
[17] *Ibid.*, p. 64.
[18] *Ibid.*, p. 58.
[19] *Ibid.*, p. 59.
[20] James, *The Meaning of Truth*, p. 39.
[21] James, *Some Problems of Philosophy*, p. 78.
[22] *Ibid.*, pp. 66—67.
[23] Lloyd Morris, *William James: The Message of a Modern Mind* (New York: Charles Scribner's Sons, 1950), p. 16.
[24] James' account of language in relation to reasoning is treated in *The Principles of Psychology*, II, pp. 356—358.
[25] *Ibid.*, p. 325.
[26] *Ibid.*, pp. 326—327.
[27] *Ibid.*, p. 330.
[28] *Ibid.*, p. 330.
[29] *Ibid.*, p. 340.
[30] James summarizes these functions in *Some Problems of Philosophy*, pp. 73—74.
[31] *Ibid.*, p. 73.
[32] Andrew J. Reck, *Introduction to William James* (Bloomington: Indiana University Press, 1967), p. 67.
[33] Morris, *William James*, pp. 18—19.
[34] James, *Some Problems of Philosophy*, pp. 57—58.
[35] James, *Essays in Radical Empiricism*, p. 60.
[36] *Ibid.*, p. 61.
[37] Perry, *The Thought and Character of William James*, I, pp. 452—453.
[38] William James, *Pragmatism: A New Name for Some Old Ways of Thinking* (New York: Longmans, Green and Company, 1907), p. 198.
[39] For a brief treatment of various implications of James' thought, see T. E. Hill, *Contemporary Theories of Knowledge* (New York: The Ronald Press Company, 1961), pp. 307—310.
[40] James, *Pragmatism*, p. 212.
[41] James, *The Meaning of Truth*, pp. 217—218.
[42] James, *Pragmatism*, p. 201.
[43] This aspect of James' thought is treated well by George Nakhnikian, *An Introduction to Philosophy* (New York: Alfred A. Knopf, Inc., 1967), pp. 259—266.
[44] James, *Pragmatism*, pp. 208—209.

8

ON WILLIAM JAMES' "RADICAL EMPIRICISM"

Gustav Emil Mueller

> Jede wahrhaft umfassende Philosophie muss Philosophie des uns alle umfassenden Lebens sein.   Heinrich Rickert

In order to understand someone, one must first listen to him; then one must appropriate what one has learned to one's own thinking; then one must respond – enriched by what one has received. In short: Every philosophical understanding is a dialectical process.

My present partner is William James. The brevity of my report is disproportionate with the length of my conversation with him; and my dry account does not reflect the intensity of delight I had in meeting him. There is no more humane and charming philosopher than William James; a master of style, rich, original, infinitely suggestive. But what I present here is mainly a list of perplexities, inconsistencies and contradictions. I am aware of the discrepancy between the whole philosophical personality of James and my logical difficulties with some of his thoughts.

I

Kant's first question of philosophy is: What can I know? And by knowledge he means scientific, intellectual, conceptual knowledge whose possibility is to be founded in its logical principles or categories. Kant's logic is the philosophy of "experience" (Erfahrung). James goes beneath this question by focussing attention on an immediate experience which precedes in time the rational-scientific ERFAHRUNG by an immediate experience (Erlebnis). Before we know we must live. This living, immediate experience is the world-view of babies which they share with animals. Although they are biologically awake, they are spiritually as if they were asleep; as Hegel puts it: "the experience of the waking natural soul is the sleep of the spirit." Hegel also calls this, like James[1]: a magic life, which maintains itself by appropriating other forms of life to sustain its own; physically this appears as eating, drinking and sleeping, in which the natural soul (Hegel's term) is tired of being engaged in the life of others and egotistically refuses contact. Both for Hegel and James trances, hypnosis and telepathy are vestiges of magic life in maturity. In immediate experience there is no world yet, but only an immediate environment. Particular events stand in the center of attention, surrounded by vague fringes. They interact. To be active is to be alive. All things interact among themselves and in reference to the one who is immediately involved and aware of them. They sometimes coalesce, unite, con-fuse; sometimes they separate, divide, get out of sight. Both conjunctive and disjunctive relations are equally experienced; discontinuity is just as real as continuity. My immediate consciousness is not yours, but, on the other hand, one state of consciousness may continuously pass into another; as when I think of a place to be reached and then arrive there.

Things or events as immediately experienced (erlebt) are both relative among themselves as well as subjective with reference to the capacities and organs of the experient; as there are no colours or tones without seeing and hearing them.

As subjective, immediate experience is no less real than are the events that are immediately experienced. The physical room in which I find myself is at the same time my present field of awareness.

This action and reaction, this relative and subjective life of ERLEBNIS is at the same time filled with affectionate values. We live in an affective continuum *and* in affective discontinuum, when we are frustrated, disappointed, and expectations leave us in the lurch. The raw unverbalized life of the natural soul is a flux of unexpected "set of eaches," which are entirely beyond any scientific-rational prediction or control.

Physical, mental, moral accidents break equilibriums. The cruelty of the universe is shocking to morality and upsets religious attitudes. "Of no special system of good attained does the universe recognize the value as sacred. This dogging of everything by its negative, this perpetual undoing and moving on to something future, which shall supercede the present, this is the Hegelian vision of the essential provisionality and unreality of everything empirical and finite. This is accurate."[2]

Reason and its "absolute through and through is too clean for the vast, slowbreathing, unconscious cosmos, with its dread abysses and its unknown tides."[3]

Perhaps the most famous expression of James' feeling of immediate experience is the following:

> If you should liken the universe of absolute idealism to an aquarium, a crystal globe in which goldfish are swimming, you would have to compare the universe to something more like one of those dried human heads with which the Dyaks of Borneo deck their lodges. The skull forms a solid nucleus; but innumerable feathers, leaves, strings, beads, and loose appendices of every description float and dangle from it, and, save that they terminate in it, seem to have nothing to do with one another. Even so my experiences and yours float and dangle, terminating, it is true, in a nucleus of common perception, but for the most part out of sight and irrelevant and unimaginable to one another.[4]

In this middle of the book the title "Radical Emipiricism" shifts to "Humanism." But both titles cover the same meaning. "Humanism" entails a variety of value-pursuits, which are finite, making a difference to their environments with which they interact. Those value-pursuits are risks with no guaranteed outcome; and they are pluralistic, such that the success of one may also be the loss of another, as for example the success of industrialization may at the same time be the loss of a beautiful or festive life. Humanism, to James, means the rejection of transempirical and superhuman standards. This is particularly important with reference to *The Varieties of Religious Experience,* where any "God" is the aspect of the Holy or Sacred in the Universe, one of its parts or "eaches."

Having listened, I now turn to some critical questions: Is "immediate experience" not also mediated? It is that in two ways: First, it is not only immediate, but it is abstracted from the mediated rational, moral and aesthetic "forms of rationality."[5] Secondly, it is mediated in that it has evolved out of the subconscious life of Nature. James shows this most explicitly in his essay on the Earth-Soul in "Concerning Fechner."[6] In James himself, his radical empiricism is mediated through his rejection of a rationalistic block-universe, whose name is F. Bradley. In the next place, James opposes his immediate experience with the rational-scientific experience, where particular experiences are thought as members of their conceptual classes and in accordance of the law of their classes. He admits that scientific experience, which breaks through the narrowness of environments into an objective world, is just as real as is immediate experience. The principle of all scientific knowledge: "Nothing is admitted as a fact, expect what can be experienced at some definite time by some experient in a definite place"[7] is in itself not an immediate experience (Erlebnis) but a universal and formal principle, which defines and limits scientific knowledge.

When he speaks about the "physical world" with its external relations, in contrast to the "spiritual world" with its internal relations, he uses categories of philosophical and dialectical reflection, which are neither immediate experiences nor scientific judgments. He erroneously identifies reason with the reason of scientific object-thinking, and is therefore unaware that his own philosophical reflections are dialectical in distinguishing and relating essential and universal opposites.

When he says: "We are in the end absolutely dependent on the Universe,"[8] then that absolute feeling can hardly refer to the empirical "string of eaches" which is constantly changed by its interacting agents.

And speaking about religion, there is, in James, also a religious mediation, a conversion which has led him to his radical empiricism. It is similar to the conversion of Augustine, who asks in his *Confessions* (Book VIII, chapt. 5) why he should be ashamed to follow the example of the uncultured in accepting piety. Similar also is the conversion of Tolstoy, described by James in *The Varieties of Religious Experience:* Tolstoy threw away his intellectual and artistic life to become a simple farmer. James speaks in a similar vein of the "bankruptcy of the intellect to let life in," and compares this to Luther's "religion of the cross."[9]

Sometimes James seems to be aware of the non-immediacy of immediate experience, as when he says: "Concepts are as real in the realm of space."[10] Or: "Direct acquaintance and conceptual knowledge are complementary."[11] Here he thinks dialectically according to the logic of philosophical reflection. Universal opposites define each other by each not being what its complementary other is. But how does that jibe with the following statement: "For my own part I have finally compelled myself to give up the logic, fairly, squarely, irrevocably."[12] I ask: which "logic"? The logic of scientific intellect (Verstand), or the logic of dialectical self-knowledge of philosophy? I would like to quote another sentence of his against himself: "The empiricists use logic against the absolute, but refuse to use it against finite experiences."[13]

Anyone who disregards logic should quit writing philosophical books which intend to be true and not false – and take to football instead.

II

So far I have followed James' text and have noticed several inconsistencies and self-contradictions; what Hegel calls "immanent criticism." I now turn to the more difficult task of evaluating James as a philosopher. I shall not preface this with the pseudo-modest and redundant remark that such an evaluation must be in terms of what I understand by philosophy. That is self-evident and unavoidable. A physician is not expected to say: According to my subjective opinion this is a case of shingles. It is a case of shingles; and James is a case of empiricism.

An empiricist is perfectly justified in saying: According to my point of view, a philosophy is nothing but an expression of moods and feelings, of healthy or sick, of tenderminded and toughminded souls. The strength of James is his scientific description of states and phases of consciousness; his psychological strength is at the same time his philosophical weakness: psychologism is not philosophy.

I don't recall a single passage which would show an understanding of what is meant by the "concept" in classical philosophy and logic. Concepts are objective contents (Sachverhalte), thought in their universal validity (Geltung) for all their instances. They are known in philosophical reflection on them. It is through concepts and not only percepts that reality becomes articulate. The world of perception is itself a concept of philosophy.

I shall confine my critical remarks to two objections. The first is: his radical empiricism is not radical enough; and the second: his pluralistic universe is not pluralistic enough.

James reiterates time and again that empiricism wants to get hold of the whole of reality from finite and particular experiences, and then never fails to add that this whole is not an experience and its unity nowhere on display. Of course not! Reality is not a jig-saw puzzle! The whole cannot be pieced together of the finite abstractions of immediate experiences. Its spatial span is myopic, its time durations brief and fleeting. And the past is no longer an immediate experience because it is not living anymore, and the future real immediacies are not experienced. In short, the empiricist way of approaching the whole is logically impossible. Radical empiricism *as philosophy* is absurd. The world of perceptions is not reality, but only an appearing section of it.

His empiricism would cease to be absurd, if James would more clearly draw the line between immediate experience as ERLEBNIS, and inferred and logically founded object-thinking. If immediate experience would dialectically reflect on its limitations, it would be more radical and would perform a most valuable service to philosophy in making articulate its own irrationality. This irrationality would then be that ineradicable part of the whole, which contains its own finitude within itself. It would make us forever immune against any rationalism, which is equally one-sided, and against any monism, which would claim to deduce the concept of the whole from one principle. As Hegel puts it: Systematic philosophy is the systematic destruction of falsely absolutized systems. Dialectic is their negation.

A second consideration, which would make radical empiricism more radical, is contained in the proposition of Herakleitos, that "the senses are bad witnesses." This is valid for all perceptions and all percepts. Let me illustrate with the Epicurean example, that in immediate experience the sun has the size of a thumb. This is logically absurd, but in immediate experience it is obtrusively real. We live in this absurd world and get along with it and in it, because we are used to it. It is one of the most profound observations of David Hume that immediate experience is governed by *habit*.

James shuns away from the illusionism of his beloved perceptions; in order to protect them, he rather falls back on a naive realism for which objects are given as they are in themselves, regardless of the many perspectives in which they are thought. This contradicts his pragmatic account of knowledge, according to which objects are fulfillments of practical desires and expectations; and concepts are merely economic shortcuts and substitutions for handling experiences, phases of action. And again he accepts without murmur Bergson's devaluation of this pragmatic view of logic as merely falsifying the stream of life.

I now turn to my other point, that James' pluralistic universe is not pluralistic enough. His term "multiverse" was a stroke of genius. But he does not carry it out. And he cannot carry it out, because he lacks principles by which reality particularizes itself in contrasted spheres or realms of life, each of which is what it is by not being its own complementary other. Actuality and comprehensiveness belong together, as Hegel says. And each of those articulate spheres of reality is represented by individuals who dedicate themselves to them: as the mathematician represents a mathematical order of reality; as an empirical scientist represents an aspect of given experiences which he has isolated; as a statesman represents a legal order; as an artist dedicates himself to beauty which he actualizes in various arts; as religious faith orients itself in the holy – a being which cannot be but good – which in turn is the founding principle of his religious life. "God" is the mythical personification of the absoluteness of Being. We need an ontological anthropology: in man reality becomes systematically articulate and aware of itself.

Conclusion

The Greeks are and remain the founders of PHILOSOPHIA PERENNIS, because they did not think in order to live more comfortably or draw property lines more properly, but they also lived in order to think – to serve truth in all manifestations of cultural life.

Plato's "Idea" of the unconditional whole (anhypotheton) is the absolute standard, in the light of which all levels of knowledge and of insight in all realms of values are justly given their due in their limitations. They are relative approximations and involve contradictions in that lower levels rebel against higher levels of insight. The realms of values are dialectically contrary as well as complementary. His focus of all values is the soul. It is a political one. It incarnates itself in the individual. It builds the organs, enabling communication with others. That is the soul's external politics. Internally it preserves its unity and integrity in the flux of vitality ('Government'). Plato's identity is not "naked," but is the identity of that which is not identical or different. Thus it is "clothed." The same soul also embodies itself in the state, the POLIS, where the same functions of values which are in the individual become visible on a greater scale in the economic, legal and moral institutions of the whole. Every individual is the POLIS in miniature, and the POLIS is the individual soul writ large and therefore more easily discernible. This correlation is the basis for intersubjective communication, which cannot be understood as one starts from the isolated individual, as James is trying to do. The soul is the dialectical unity of I/me, I/we.

Aristotle's One Being in all its kinds and in all individual beings is logically necessary, and ontologically the ground of everything whatsoever. (I disregard here his dualistic and extramundane "God," the darling of scholasticism.)

To think reality as a whole world itself, is the universal and unique task of philosophy, which no other discipline can replace – least of all logistics. It is always logical reflection or dialectical self-knowledge, regardless of whether the content of this self-knowledge be scientific or rational in the sense of formal logic, or non-rational or irrational and negative. "Nonbeing is no less real than being," to mention Plato again. The concrete whole of reality is a whole of opposites; it is not an object, scientific object-thinking is only one of those opposites within it. Reality is dialectical because it posits, cancels and contains all approaches to it within itself.

NOTES

1. William James, *A Pluralistic Universe* (New York: Longmans, Green and Company, New Impression, 1928), p. 31.
2. *Ibid.*, p. 89.
3. William James, *Essays in Radical Empiricism* (New York: Longmans, Green and Company, 2d ed., 1922), p. 277.
4. *Ibid.*, p. 46.
5. *Ibid.*, p. 112.
6. James, *A Pluralistic Universe*, "Concerning Fechner," pp. 131—177.
7. James, *Essays in Radical Empiricism*, p. 160.
8. William James, *Varieties of Religious Experience* (New York: Longmans, Green and Company), p. 51.
9. James, *A Pluralistic Universe*, p. 317.
10. James, *Varieties of Religious Experience*, p. 57.
11. James, *A Pluralistic Universe*, p. 57.
12. *Ibid.*, p. 212.
13. *Ibid.*, p. 243.
14. See Gustav Emil Mueller, *Plato: The Founder of Philosophy as Dialectic* (New York: Philosophical Library, 1968).

9

THE MEANING OF TRUTH IN WILLIAM JAMES

S. Morris Eames

The most controversial part of the philosophy of William James appears to have centered around his conception of truth. In *The Meaning of Truth* (1909), which he regarded as a sequel to his *Pragmatism* (1907), he writes: "The pivotal part of my book named *Pragmatism* is its account of the relation called 'truth' which may obtain between an idea (opinion, belief, statement, or what not) and its object. 'Truth,' I there say, 'is a property of certain of our ideas. It means their agreement, as falsity means their disagreement, with reality. Pragmatists and intellectuals both accept this definition as a matter of course.'"[1]

The definition of truth given above is one version of the correspondence theory of truth. There are interpretations James gave to familiar terms which his critics would not or could not accept; furthermore, he introduced some new notions into the context of the problem of truth. The quotation above suggests questions which James sought to answer. What is meant by "a property of certain of our ideas," by "agreement with reality," and by "the relation which may obtain between an idea ... and its object"? James puts the discussion of truth in the context of a new cosmology, the cosmology of a changing world as envisioned through the evolutionary theories of Charles Darwin. He treats theory of knowledge and theory of truth in the context of a new psychology, a psychology in which consciousness is not an entity, and in which cognition or the knowing process is a function.

How do ideas correspond to reality when, according to the concepts of evolution, reality is changing? Do truths change too? Does correspondence mean something different from the "copy" theory of reality? Does correspondence mean adaptation of mind and organism with environment, and does this correspondence involve a value commitment? Do all beliefs, even true beliefs, arise from human need, and thus have emotional and practical value? How does the mind come to know true beliefs? Why are true beliefs more relevant to human life than false beliefs? How are new beliefs adjusted to old beliefs when they conflict? How do religious beliefs fit into the corpus of true beliefs, if they fit at all? These are some of the problems with which James grappled. Space will not permit a full length study of the development of his ideas on the meaning of truth, but I will indicate what I think are the main developments of his thought, and I will analyze some of the criticisms, early and recent, which neglect his related writings in epistemology.

James's conception of truth developed over the long period of his intellectual activity. As early as 1875 he indicates the general direction of this philosophy when he maintains that truth is to be gained by taking a risk. He writes: "May it not be that in the theoretic life the man whose scruples about flawless accuracy of demonstration keep him forever shivering on the brink of Belief is as great an imbecile as the man at the opposite pole, who simply consults his prophetic soul for the answer to everything? What is this but saying that our opinions about the nature of things belong to our moral life?"[2] This theme has a continuity in his thought until the end of his life.

In 1878 James wrote "Remarks on Spencer's Definition of Mind as Correspondence."[3] Herbert Spencer was the great popularizer of Darwin's theory of evolution by giving it a turn into the subject-matters of psychology, sociology, and ethics. Part III of Spencer's *Principles of Psychology* became the springboard for James's criticism and for putting forth his own views which are germinal to his later thought. Spencer, according to James, defines correspondence as "adjustment of inner to outer relations," mental evolution being a kind of adjustment or correspondence in "space, time, speciality, generality, and integration." What James objects to in Spencer's formulation of "correspondence" is the following:

> In the first place, one asks, what right has one, in a formula embracing professedly the 'entire process of mental evolution,' to mention only phenomena of cognition, and to omit all sentiments, all aesthetic impulses, all religious emotions and personal affections? The ascertainment of outward fact constitutes only one species of mental activity. The genus contains, in addition to purely cognitive judgments, or judgments of the actual – judgments that things do, as a matter of fact, exist so or so – an immense number of emotional judgments: judgments of the ideal, judgments that things *should* exist thus and not so. How much of our mental life is occupied with this matter of a better or a worse? How much of it involves preference or repugnances on our part?[4]

This passage explains part of the context in which James will later place his meaning of truth.

One year later, in 1879, James wrote "The Sentiment of Rationality." The same year he wrote a sequel to this article, "Rationality, Activity, and Faith," which was not published until 1882. These two articles were combined, extracts from the former, with the latter, and published in 1887 under the title of "The Sentiment of Rationality." These writings take up the theoretical and the practical motives. Two other articles should be read in conjunction with the problems of knowledge and truth during this period, "The Function of Cognition," (1885) which later became the first essay he put in the collection, *The Meaning of Truth* (1909), and another essay he wrote in 1889, "The Psychology of Belief," which was reprinted in *The Principles of Pschology*, Vol. II, as "The Perception of Reality" (1890).[5]

James does not separate the knowing process from truth; he is concerned with how statements come to be regarded as true. This procedure involves an extensive treatment of the role that concepts and percepts, along with many other elements in experience, play in the ascertainment of truth. The rationalists center attention on the role of concepts, and they formulate a view of truth which has come to be called the "coherence" theory. The empiricists center attention on the role of percepts, and their view of truth has come to be called the "correspondence" theory. On the side of the rationalists, who emphasize the role of classes, James grants that "classification of things into extensive kinds is the first step, and classification of their relations and conduct into extensive laws the last step of philosophic unification."[6] Obviously, the results are abstract, but some of the living fact is ignored, thus none of our explanations are ever complete.

When he turns to a consideration of the perceptual side of experience, James puts forth a pragmatic principle in this early essay which became important in the whole history of the movement. He says that to explain a thing means that we "pass easily to its antecedents"; to know it is to foresee its consequences. (John Dewey later made this insight the central idea of his philosophy of science.) The first "practical" requirement which a philosophic conception must satisfy is that it must "banish uncertainty from the future." (This requirement will be shown to have tremendous significance in the pursuit of truth, for we want consequences which are fruitful and satisfying.) The psychological basis for this epistemological condition is this: "Our consciousness at any given moment is never free from the ingredient of expectancy." The second practical requirement is that a philosophy "must define the future congruously with our spontaneous powers," and this latter point is related to his view of cognition. James thinks that cognition operates in the lower forms of life as a guide to action and that the only test of intelligence of lower animals is that of acting as if on purpose. (Does James mean by this that animals have "knowledge" or "intelligence"?) At any rate, he believes that cognition is incomplete until discharged in act. In this respect, James's philosophy is an activism, an activism, which follows from the propensities which he assigns to human nature.

The foregoing essay leads us into the ideas put forth in "The Function of Cognition" (1885). In this essay James makes "feeling" the primary experience, and he invents an example to carry his meaning in the simplest terms: he speaks of "the feeling of q," where "q" is representative of the tiniest feeling flowing through the conscious life. The feeling of "q" is given; it is "there." Thus James writes: "Whatever elements an act of cognition may imply besides, it at least implies the existence of a feeling."[7] In this essay, James draws the distinction between *acquaintance with* and *knowledge about*. When this tiny feeling which we call "q" enters into cognition, we find: "It knows q, if q be a reality, with a very minimum of knowledge. It neither dates nor locates it." (So, space and time categories have not been applied to it.) "It neither classes nor names it. And it neither knows itself as a feeling, nor contrasts itself with other feelings, nor estimates its own duration or intensity. It is, in short, if there is no more of it than this, a most dumb and helpless and useless kind of thing."[8] This starting place in theory of knowledge may seem baffling to the reader at this point, so we can only ask for patience. In essays written many years later, James returns to this same point and interprets it more radically than he does here. The point is that he thinks there is a point at which the consciousness simply "feels" something, but no other part of experience "knows" what it is.

This "feeling of q" enters into the cognitive process. But how? "Now, our supposed little feeling gives a *what;* and if other feelings should succeed which remember the first, its *what* may stand as subject or predicate of some place of knowedge – about, of some judgment, perceiving relations between it and other whats which the other feelings may know."[9]

At the time James wrote this essay, he was concerned with the problem of resemblance: Does the feeling of "q" resemble something? How can one tell? Is this bit of experience a dream, a fiction, or does it resemble some reality? James says, "The feeling of q knows whatever reality it resembles, and either directly or indirectly operates on. If it resemble without operating, it is a dream; if it operate without resembling, it is an error." At this stage of his writing, James says that truth is arrived at if the feeling of q operationally leads up to a percept which resembles reality. "We may now express it thus: A percept knows whatever reality it directly or indirectly operates on or resembles; a conceptual feeling, or thought knows a reality, whenever it actually or potentially terminates in a percept that operates on, or resembles that reality, or is otherwise connected with it or with its context."[10]

James reprinted the essay on "The Function of Cognition" in *"The Meaning of Truth"* (1909). In a note he explains how his mind has changed on some things since 1885. He thinks that he had given undue prominence to the notion of resemblance; this notion is related to the "copy" theory of truth which will be discussed later. He thinks he had not treated concepts adequately in this early rendition, and he says in 1909 that he now treats concepts as a coordinate realm with percepts. Another point he had over-emphasized was the operating of the object itself; he had not paid enough attention to the operating of other things related to the object. In this early essay he mentions the "workability" of a feeling or idea, and he thinks that there he had imperfectly developed this notion.

In *The Principles of Psychology* (1890) James puts forth the idea of "the stream of consciousness."[11] Consciousness is a succession of states, or waves, or fields. These states constantly pass and repass; they are "on the move." Consciousness is not a static, but an ongoing affair. James writes in another work: "The existence of this streams is a primal fact, the nature and origin of it form the essential problem of our sciences [psychology]." James shows how within a field of consciousness, we have a focus and a margin. According to our interests, the focus and margins change about. The flow of the stream of consciousness means that the process by which one state "dissolves into another is often very gradual, and all sorts of inner arrangements of contents occur."[12]

The psychological basis for his epistemology was extended and made more explicit in some very important essays: "Does

Consciousness Exist?" (1904), "A World of Pure Experience" (1904), "The Notion of Consciousness" (1905); along with these should be read "The Continuity of Experience" in *A Pluralistic Universe*" (1909).¹³

In these essays James attacks the notion that consciousness is an *entity;* he holds that the primal stuff of experience is a *neutral monism* or *pure experience* in which we no not know at first if each pure experience is physical or psychical until we act upon it. The knowing relation takes place between two parts of experience, one the knower, the other the known. These ideas are put in James's own words: "My thesis is that if we start with the supposition that there is only one primary stuff or material in the world, a stuff of which everything is composed, and if we call that stuff 'pure experience,' then knowing can easily be explained as a particular sort of relations toward one another into which portions of pure experience may enter."¹⁴ Thus, one part of experience knows another part. We can often read an experience in two ways, one part in one context is subject, in another context it is object. These bits of pure experience as they come to us (presentations) are single *thats,* "which act in one context as objects, and in another context figure as mental states." Thus subjectivity and objectivity are functional attributes solely. "If it be the self-same piece of pure experience, taken twice over, that serves now as thought and now as thing."¹⁵ Again he says: "Now I ask you, could we not overthrow quite entirely this manner of viewing the problem? In fact, let us suppose that primary reality is of a neutral nature, and let us call it by some name also ambiguous, such as phenomenon, datum, or *Vorfindung*. As for me, I would willingly use the plural and give it the name of pure experiences. Call this a monism if you will; but it is an altogether rudimentary monism and absolutely opposed to the so called bilaterial monism of scientific positivism and that of the Spinozists."¹⁶ On the relation of the "that" to the "what," he writes: "The presentation, the experience, the *that* in short (for until we have decided *what* it is it must be a mere that) is the last term of a train of sensations, emotions, decisions, movements, classifications, expectations, etc., ending in the present, and the first term of a series of similar 'inner' operations extending into the future, on the readers part."[17]

James says that early in his life he thought of conscious states as too individual and sharply demarcated from each other in their primal states. He later moved toward the view that "The concrete pulses of experience appear pent in by no such definite limits as our conceptual substitutes for them are confined by. They run into one another continuously and seem to interpenetrate. What in them is relation and what is matter is hard to discern."[18] There is a movement of this life of feeling, it comes with a feeling of past and present bound together. "The rush of our thought forward through its fringes is the everlasting peculiarity of its life."

The epistemological implications of the foregoing notions are tremendous. In the first place, it should dawn upon the reader by now that James places all within what he calls "experience." He wrote during this later period in "The Essence of Humanism," (1905): "*one part of our experience may lean upon another part to make it what it is in any one of several aspects in which it may be considered, experience as a whole is self-containing and leans on nothing.*"[19] There is no need to bring in an Absolute which lies beyond experience nor a *ding-an-sich* which lies beneath it. There is no entity called consciousness. Within the stream of what is called "consciousness," all of our knowing relations emerge. Perhaps it would be better to use the term "continuity of experience" or "stream of life." These primal notions set the stage for the development of James's epistemology and theory of truth.

During the five year period, from 1903 to 1908, the controversy over truth was more vigorous than at any other time during the writings of James. In 1903, John Dewey and his Chicago associates published *Studies in Logical Theory*. In a letter of March 1903, Dewey wrote to James that he was sending him some proof from the forthcoming book, and asked James to glance over the pages to see if he "could stand for a dedication to yourself." Dewey wrote to James that he regarded

James's *Psychology* as "the spiritual progenitor of the whole industry; and while we won't attempt to father you with all the weak kidlets which are crying in the volume to be born, it would afford us all (and me in particular, if that doesn't reflect on the pleasure of others) very much satisfaction if you will permit us to dedicate the volume to you."[20] James replied on March 23, 1903: "What you write of the *new school of truth* both pleases and humiliates me. It humiliates me that I had to wait till I read Moore's article before finding how much on my own lines you are working."[21] James's main observation was that the Chicago group had come from Hegel and he had come from empiricism.

F. C. S. Schiller and a group of Oxford professors published *Personal Idealism* in 1903. James reviewed the book in *Mind*, and he had this to say about it: "Here we have Naturalism's concreteness without its lowness, and Absolutism's elevation without its abstractness, for human purposes, of result."[22]

In this same year (1903), Schiller also published *Humanism: Philosophical Essays*, and James reviewed this book for *The Nation* (March 3, 1904). In James's review he presents first an analysis of what has happened in the scientific and philosophical worlds, and how these developments have affected the theory of knowledge and of truth. "Throughout almost the entire past both Science and Philosophy have been accustomed to suppose that 'Truth' must needs consist of a hard-and-fast system of propositions, valid in themselves and eternally, which our minds have only to copy literally."[23] James than points out three developments which have affected the notion of truth. First, the philosophic criticism of Mill, and Sigwart of logic and mathematics, and the laws of physics and chemistry dissolved any absoluteness in these subjects. Second, the doctrine of evolution has shattered our notions of a world of fixities and inflexibilities; this has made us ready "to imagine almost all our functions, even intellectual ones, as 'adaptations,' and possibly transient adaptations, to practical needs." Third, laws are regarded as "not quite true", and men like Pearson, Mach, and Poincaré say "that our sciences are but *Denkmittel* – 'true' in no other sense than that of yielding a conceptual shorthand, economical for our descriptions."[24] (This point about laws being conceptual shorthand "economical" for our descriptions should be kept in mind, for James uses the term "expedient" to designate this view.)

One of the most important points made in James's review of Schiller's book on *Humanism* is the following:

> And the experience consists not in their copying independent archetypes of 'reality,' but solely in the fact of their *succeeding better,* and connecting themselves more satisfactorily with the residuum of life. Truth, in short, lives in the actually felt relations between experiences themselves. It is *in rebus* and not *ante rem*. Error and truth are neither more nor less different than are our happinesses and unhappinesses; and a more 'real' difference than that, it is impossible to conceive.[25]

James was sent a proof by the editor of *Mind* of F. H. Bradley's forthcoming article, "Truth and Practice," which appeared in the journal in July, 1904. Bradley's article written in the summer of 1903, was primarily an attack on Schiller, but he does put in a footnote that since then he had "made acquaintance" with Dewey's *Studies in Logical Theory*. Of the latter he says "that position as a whole has not become clear to me."[26] When James read Bradley's article, he wrote "Humanism and Truth," in the October issue of *Mind* of the same year (1904): "He repeatedly confesses himself unable to comprehend Schiller's views, he evidently has not sought to do so sympathetically, and I deeply regret to say that his laborious article throws, for my mind, absolutely no useful light upon the subject. It seems to me on the whole an *ignoratio elenchi*, and I feel free to disregard it altogether."[27]

The articles on "Humanism and Truth" (1904), "Humanism and Truth Once More" (1905), and "The Essence of Humanism" (1905) are helpful for understanding the ideas James put forth on truth in *Pragmatism* (1907) and *The Meaning of Truth* (1909).[28]

In these articles James continues the line of thought he developed in the review of Schiller's *Personal Idealism*. New developments in logic and mathematics, in the empirical sciences, and in theory of evolution involve much restatement of traditional notions."[29] This is the task James attempts to perform. The notion of truth needs restatement in order to fit into the new notions of science and logic. First, he shows that there has been a breakdown in "the older notions of scientific truth." Logicians no longer believe that "God geometrizes," or that the ideas of Euclid are copies of "archetypes" in the intellect of God. No longer do people hold that there is an eternal and unchanging Reason, and that its voice reverberates in "the syllogistic forms of *Barbara* and *Celarent*." The laws of nature, the natural history of classifications, are not "duplicates of pre-human archetypes buried in the structure of things, to which the spark of divinity hidden in our intellect enables us to penetrate." This older intellectual world is under attack and is collapsing. There have arisen many geometries, many logics, many hypotheses. He says: "We hear scientific laws now treated as so much 'conceptual shorthand,' true so far as they are useful but no farther." (Note the use of the term "useful" here and the context in which it is placed; critics have been prone to select this term, give it a meaning out of context, and make James into some kind of crass materialist, one who is interested in selfish matters.)

James thinks that philosophers must make adjustments to the new developments of science and logic. The older notions of the foundations of science and philosophy are crumbling, yet philosophers still hold to the older views of truth. James's problem is to come to grips with these new developments in science and logic and to formulate a view of truth which is faithful to them. In the first place, this intellectual adjustment requires a new mood and outlook: "Our mind must become tolerant of symbol instead of reproduction (the copy theory of truth) of approximation instead of exactness, of plasticity instead of rigor."[30] James admits that the subject is "unquestionably difficult," and it is the kind of a problem which "never attains a classic form of expression when first promulgated."

James adopts an *experiential* basis for logical relations objects of experience, space, time, and so on. This view is creative, and it is at odds with prevailing views on these topics of his day. Perhaps the best starting place is found in how he thinks the notion of consistency arose in human experience. He says:

> And are not both our need of such consistency and our pleasure in it conceivable as outcomes of the natural fact that we are beings that develop mental *habits* – habit itself proving adaptively beneficial in an environment where the same objects, or the same kinds of objects recur and follow 'law'? If this were so, what would have come first would have been the collateral profits of habit, and the theoretic life would have grown up in aid of these. In point of fact, this seems to have been the probable case. At life's origin, any present experience may have been 'true' – if such a word could then be applicable. Later, when reactions became organised, the reactions became 'true' whenever expectation was fulfilled by them. Otherwise they were 'false' or 'mistaken' reactions. But the same class of objects needs the same kind of reaction, so the impulse to react consistently must gradually have been established, with a disappointment felt whenever the results frustrated expectation. Here is a perfectly plausible germ for all our higher consistencies. Nowadays, if an object claims from us a reaction of the kind habitually accorded only to the opposite class of objects, our mental machinery refuses to run smoothly. The situation is intellectually unsatisfactory.[31]

This naturalistic view of the origin and nature of consistency, of course, is preposterous to those who believe that there is an innate idea of consistency or who hold that, at least, we are born with a pre-existent structure of mind which accounts for the occurence of consistency.

James explains further how intellectual functions and their products arise from an experiential basis. He thinks that there is probably not a single common-sense idea which was not "in the first instance a genuine discovery, an inductive generalization."[32] No one today doubts that the discovery of the atom, of reflex action, or fitness to survive are all notions that can be historically dated in the ongoing of human experience. From human interactions there emerged ideas of *permanent* subjects and *changing* attributes, of classes and sub-classes, and of regular causal connections. James says, "surely all these were once definite conquests made at historic dates by our ancestors in their attempts to get the chaos of their crude individual experience into a more shareable and manageable shape."[33] James says:

> The greatest common-sense achievement, after the discovery of one Time and one Space, is probably the concept of permanently existing things. When a rattle first drops out of the hand of a baby, he does not look to see where it has gone. Non-perception he accepts as annihilation until he finds a better belief. That our perceptions mean *beings*, beings that are there whether we hold them in our hands or not, becomes an interpretation so luminous of what happens to us that, once employed, it never gets forgotten. It applies with equal felicity to things and persons, to the objective and to the ejective realm. However a Berkeley, a Mill, or a Corneilius may criticize it, it *works;* and in practical life we never think of 'going back' upon it, or reading our incoming experiences in any other terms.[34]

Note how the term "works" is used in the above passage. This is the context in which James later says that truth is that which "works."

James exhibits a modern mood when be claims that we can "invent" systems of logic, mathematics, logic, and what not, whose relations are as rigid and just as binding in their functions as those of any other view which claims metaphysical underpinnings or transcendental sanctions. "The whole fabric of the a priori science can thus be treated as a man-made product."[35]

Geometries, logics, mathematical systems, classes and the like can be constructed by human beings; the invariant relations between these theoretic constructs can be as certain and as timeless as we wish them to be. This point of view was put forth in the last chapter of Vol. II of James's *Principles of Psychology* (1890), and he seems disappointed that no one had noticed this point. Truths of this kind are not copies of anything. They are only relations directly found between artificial mental things. They are "useful" if they help us in the determination of "sense particulars" in the ongoing of experience.

Mental functions and their products have arisen from an experiential basis, and they are now so much a part of our intellectual equipment that we cannot ignore them; they make up the very structure of our mental habits. These mental habits have emerged in human experience for four primary purposes; "that we may the better foresee the course of our experiences, communicate with one another, and steer our lives by rule. Also, that we may have a cleaner, clearer, more inclusive mental view."[36]

The experiential basis for the emergence of the notions of consistency, space, time, and so forth, is also the basis for the meanings of terms like *reality, independence, objectivity, correspondence, and agreement.* James says that reality is what we have to take account of in our experience, and this means that " we correspond in some way with anything with which we enter into any relations at all." He continues to list these: "If it be a *thing*, we may produce an exact copy of it, or we may simply feel it as an existent in a certain place. If it be a *demand*, we may obey it without knowing anything more about it than its push. If it be a *proposition*, we may agree by not contradicting it, by letting it pass. If it be a *relation* between things, we may act on the first one so as to bring ourselves out where the second one will be. If it be *something inaccessible*, we may substitute a *hypothetical object* for it, which, having the same consequences, will cipher out for us real results."[37] What is meant by the term "independent" and "objective" on James's experiential view? He says that for a reality to be independent, means that, even if our thought were annihilated, the reality would still be *there*. (It might not be "there" in the shape which our thought makes it, however.) "That reality is independent means that there is something in every experience that escapes our arbitrary control." This is a functional definition of "independent" made within the experiential continuum.

What does the term "correspondence" mean on James view of experience and theory of knowledge? First, we will see how he analyzes the term and what has been connected with it. "The vulgar notion of correspondence," he says, "it that the thought must *copy* the reality." This means either of two views: (1) "propositions are held true if they copy eternal thought"; (2) "terms are held true if they copy extra-mental realities." James raises the question of why our thoughts should "copy" reality. Why should the thought's mission be "to imitate and reduplicate, existence"? Why should not the function of thought be to increase and elevate existence? Mental images may copy realities in some ways that are useful, but, for the most part, much of our "descriptive" truth is put in verbal symbols. "If our symbols *fit* the world, in the sense of determining our expectations rightly, they may be the better for not copying its terms."[38]

Thus, for James, "correspondence" is not a matter of a copy theory of truth. "Correspondence" means adjustments of a present moving experience to other parts of experience. James writes: "The whole system of what the present experience must correspond to 'adequately' may be continuous with the present experience itself. Reality, so taken as experience other than the present, might either be the legacy of past thought or the content of thought to come. Its determinations for us are in any case the adjectives which our acts of judging fit to ist."[39]

Truth and falsehood come to have meanings inside the workings of human experience. James describes how the inquiry can go wrong, how we can indulge in "wayward" thinking, and he indicates that experience itself aids us in our selections of truths over falsehoods. He says: "The only guarantee against licentious thinking is the circumpressure of experience itself, which gets us sick of concrete errors." He goes on to say: "The true is the opposite of whatever is instable, of whatever is practically disappointing, of whatever is useless, of whatever is inconsistent and contradictory, of whatever is artificial and eccentric, of whatever is unreal in the sense of being of no practical account."[40]

In March, 1907, James published "Pragmatism's Conception of Truth,"[41] which was later that year incorporated into his book, *Pragmatism*. There he states his view of truth mentioned in the first paragraph of this essay, and which was restated in *The Meaning of Truth*. This appears to be the view of truth which James wishes to let stand. *"True ideas are those that we can assimilate, validate, corroborate, and verify. False ideas are those that we can not."*[42] It is this article and chapter, however, which stirred up the storm of controversy. James repeats most of the ideas presented previously in our study, but he puts them sometimes rather bluntly and without always preparing the reader for what he has to say. He asks similar questions: "How will the truth be realized? What experiences will be different from those which would obtain if the belief were false? What, in short, is the truth's cash value in experiential terms?"[43] From the foregoing analysis it should be clear that James does not divorce the means of ascertaining truth from the truth itself. Truths are valuable to our lives, and they make a difference. When James uses the term "truth's cash value," he stepped into a hornet's nest of criticism. He meant, of course, as we explained above, that it is important in the continuity of experience that we select the percepts and concepts which will lead us to the result we are expecting. No scientist could operate for one moment in his laboratory without carefully selecting the parts of experience which are of "cash value" in carrying out his experiment. James's choice of the term was a mistake, for it was lifted out of context and by some made to mean that he was really giving expression to American commercialism.

James says: "The truth of an idea is not a stagnant property inherent in it." This point we have covered above in the context of the flow of experience and of the dual functions of percepts and concepts in obtaining knowledge. "Truth *happens* to an idea. It *becomes* true, is *made* true by events. Its verity *is* in fact an event, a process, the process, namely of its verifying itself, its veri-*fication*. Its validity is the process of its valid-*ation*."[44] This process has been explained in the preceding analysis.

I shall consider briefly other aspects of James's theory of truth presently, but now a note can be made about some of the critics of James's theory of truth. In 1909, when he wrote *The Meaning of Truth* as a sequel to his *Pragmatism,* he lists almost a score of critics of his theory.[45] Some of these he answered, some he ignored. An analysis of some of the early critics shows that most of them did not understand the context in which James was writing. (This is why a presentation of his view of experience and theory of knowledge is made in this essay.) For instance, F. H. Bradley after saying he did not understand the pragmatic theory of truth, went on to say that if a humanist understands his own doctrine, "he must hold any idea, however mad, to be the truth, if anyone will have it so." A. E. Taylor shows a classic misunderstanding, for he held that the theory means "believing what one pleases and calling it 'truth'." Bertrand Russell wrote an article and titled it "Trans-atlantik Truth."[46] James answered Russell, but the exchange led nowhere. In a recent book, A. J.Ayer analyzes James' conception of truth and comes to the same conclusion as Russell. He writes: "When we verify a proposition we discover it to be true, but we do not confer truth upon it. Its truth of falsehood belongs to it quite independently of our knowledge, because of its relation to objective facts."[47] We can imagine William James asking Ayer the same kinds of questions he asked H. B. Joseph: What is meant by *independent?* What is meant by *relation?* What is meant by *objective?* What is meant by *facts?*

There is another range of beliefs which are significant for James, and which need some kind of treatment in the total account of truth. These beliefs are those pertaining to religious experiences. Are these beliefs true or false? Some philosophers relegate these beliefs to the "emotive" realm where they have no cognitive significance. For James these beliefs are too important to ignore. First, we must make clear exactly the condition under which James is going to consider this realm of beliefs. In "The Will to Believe" (1896) he wrote: "*Our passional nature not only lawfully may, but must, decide an option between propositions, whenever it is a genuine option that cannot by its nature be decided on intellectual grounds.*"[48] In these cases we risk losing the truth.

James gave the Gifford Lectures, *The Varieties of Religious Experience*, in 1901–02. This was immediately prior to all the intellectual activity over the problem of truth. In this work he seeks to understand the religious experience. The sub-title of the work is "A Study of Human Nature," and it is possible to read the work not as a work on religion, but a work on the various functions of human beings. It uses religious data, but its interest can be taken to be psychological. If we take James's interpretation of belief in the wide behavioral sense, in the sense that beliefs may have good effects or bad effects upon human life, then it can be seen that religious ideas have a profound effect. This analysis by James is not acceptable to those who see the matter this way: "It is its truth, not its utility . . . upon which the verdict ought to depend. If religion is true, its fruits are good fruits, even though in this world they should prove uniformly ill adapted and full of naught but pathos."[49]

In one of the last things James wrote on religion, he said: "On pragmatic principles, if the hypothesis of God works satisfactorily in the widest sense of the word, it is true. Now what ever its residual difficulties may be, experience shows that it certainly does work, and that the problem is to build it out and determine it so that it will combine satisfactorily with all the other working truths."[50] This was a challenge which William James took upon himself. He was not an intellectual coward, and he never backed away from a topic of controversy. Addressing tle Unitarian Ministers' Institute at Princeton,

Mass., in 1881, on the topic "Reflex Action and Theism," he said: "When the invitation of your committee reached me last fall, the simple truth is that I accepted it as most men accept a challenge, – not because they wish to fight, but because they are ashamed to say no."[51] At the time James was professor of physiology, and he sought to make a place for the importance of religious beliefs in their helpfulness to life.

Controversy still rages over James's theory of truth.[52] When one surveys the current literature, however, it is obvious that we are in need of an adequate theory about this important subject. William James may have made some bold statements in his account of truth, but his legacy to us is to find a theory of truth which will encompass all our beliefs in whatever field, and which will be in harmony with the new development of science and logic which our century has developed.

NOTES

[1] William James, *The Meaning of Truth* (1909; reprint ed., Ann Arbor: University of Michigan Press, 1970), p. xxix.

[2] William James, "Lewes's 'Problems of Life and Mind'," in *Collected Essays and Reviews*, ed. Ralph Barton Perry (1920; reprint ed., New York: Russell and Russell), p. 11.

[3] *Ibid.*, pp. 43—68.

[4] *Ibid.*, p. 45.

[5] William James, *The Principles of Psychology* (1890; reprint ed., New York: Dover Publications, Inc., 1950), II, pp. 283—324.

[6] William James, "The Sentiment of Rationality," in *The Will to Believe* (1896; reprint ed., New York: Dover Publications, Inc., 1956), p. 67.

[7] William James, "The Function of Cognition," in *The Writings of William James*, ed. John J. McDermott (New York: Modern Library, 1968), p. 137.

[8] *Ibid.*, p. 140.

[9] *Ibid.*, p. 141.

[10] *Ibid.*, p. 148.

[11] James, *The Principles of Psychology I*, Chapter IX.

[12] William James, *Talks to Teachers on Psychology* (1899; reprint ed., New York: W. W. Norton & Company, Inc., 1958), p. 30.

13 William James, *A Pluralistic Universe* (New York: Longmans, Green & Co., 1909).
14 McDermott, ed., *The Writings of William James*, p. 170.
15 *Ibid.*, p. 179.
16 *Ibid.*, p. 191.
17 *Ibid.*, pp. 173—174.
18 *Ibid.*, p. 294.
19 James, *The Meaning of Truth*, p. 124.
20 Ralph Barton Perry, *The Thought and Character of William James* (Boston: Little, Brown and Co., 1935), p. 521.
21 *Ibid.*, p. 521.
22 James, *Collected Essays and Reviews*, p. 442.
23 William James, Review of F. C. S. Schiller's *Humanism* in *The Nation*, Vol. 78, 175.
24 *Ibid.*, 175.
25 *Ibid.*, 175.
26 F. H. Bradley, "On Truth and Practice," *Mind*, n. s., Vol. XIII (1904), 308n.
27 William James, "Humanism and Truth," *Mind*, n. s., Vol. XIII (1904), 458.
28 The articles should be read in the sequence in which they were written.
29 James, "Humanism and Truth," 458.
30 *Ibid.*, 459.
31 James, "Humanism and Truth Once More," *Mind*, n. s., Vol. 14 (1905), 197.
32 James, "Humanism and Truth," 460.
33 *Ibid.*, 461.
34 *Ibid.*, 461.
35 *Ibid.*, 469.
36 *Ibid.*, 461.
37 *Ibid.*, 463 (Italics mine).
38 *Ibid.*, 468.
39 *Ibid.*, 463.
40 *Ibid.*, 466.
41 William James, "Pragmatism's Conception of Truth," *The Journal of Philosophy*, Vol. IV (1907), 141—155.
42 William James, *Pragmatism* (New York: Longmans, Green and Co., 1907), p. 201.
43 *Ibid.*, p. 200.
44 *Ibid.*, p. 201.
45 James, *The Meaning of Truth*, p. xliii.
46 Bertrand Russell, "Transatlantic Truth," *The Albany Review*, Vol. II (1908), 393—410.

47 A. J. Ayer, *The Origins of Pragmatism* (San Francisco: Cooper & Company, 1968), p. 194.
48 James, *The Will to Believe*, p. 11.
49 William James, *The Varieties of Religious Experience* (1901—1902; reprint ed., New York: Modern Library), p. 369.
50 James, *Pragmatism*, p. 299.
51 James, *The Will to Believe*, p. 111.
52 For instance, see Alan R. White, *Truth* (Garden City, N. Y.: Doubleday & Company, Inc., 1970), pp. 122—127.

10

THE UNITY OF KNOWLEDGE AND PURPOSE IN JAMES' VIEW OF ACTION

Elizabeth F. Flower

It is a commonplace that the past sets the stage for present experience; but somewhat less frequently remarked is that a backward look may not only clarify current issues but also lead to a reassessment of the past, suggesting turning-points that may have gone unnoticed in their day. James' revolutionary approach to consciousness was duly appreciated by such diverse thinkers as Whitehead, Wittgenstein, and Sperry; but James charted a turning-point in the theory of action which launched pragmatism upon a distinctive career.

Critical to contemporary discussion of the theory of action is the question whether an account can be given of action (or conduct) as goal-oriented or rule-directed or purposive behavior. And if so, what kind of psychology is required – a phenomenological psychology, a linguistic analysis of ordinary psychological terms, a behavioristic, an experimental or a cognitive psychology? James clearly recognized the constraints on his problem: the account of action had at least to be consistent with neuro-physiology and experimental psychology and yet not exclude what actually can be done – including such purposes, plannings and experiments as are conditions for psychological inquiry itself. On the one hand, James' work fits into a developing tradition which sought to enrich the view of human nature and its capacities and to rescue it from the passivity of the Lockean subject. But, on the other hand, it represents a dramatic shift in the appreciation of human competencies – the uniquely human ways of learning by rules, of foresight tested in experience, of generative norms, and of shaping and being shaped by cumulative social cultural traditions – and the consequent insistence that there be no insurmountable gulf between the action that psychology studies and the range of human experience and inventiveness. The following has three acts. The first traces the bare manifesto of the activity of the mind in Kant to the rich mapping of his purposiveness in James. The second explores the Jamesian account and finds that it had a sweep which broke through most of the traditional barriers but faltered when it came to the analysis of motor activity. The third suggests the divergent ways in which Dewey and Lewis sought to complete the program.

I

Harvard pragmatism, of course, is one of Kant's children; it owed an enormous debt to his view that the knower is active in constructing the objects of knowledge and that the order we find in nature expresses the order-making or legislation which the mind has first put there itself. However, Kant laid a heavy burden on that philosophy, for he saddled it with an unbridgeable chasm between the two different kinds of legislation – the laws of science and those of value and freedom – a gap which makes almost inexplicable how decisions could issue in the natural world or plans eventuate in action. This division between a natural and a moral world left virtually no purchase for empirical psychology while Kant's prestige additionally helped harden faculty psychology by distinguishing "sense," "reason," "will," etc., just when there was evidence of a thaw in favor of a functional view.

The classic figures of empiricism, Locke and Hume, scarcely leave us better off either as regards purposive thinking or intentional action. Admittedly, Locke's account of the association of ideas (simultaneous rather than sequential) was an effort to import the Newtonian mechanical model into psychology. Generally passive, Locke's individual seems virtually limited to the activities of combining, comparing, and abstracting;

while pleasures and pains, seldom enough even the ideas of pleasures and pains, power behavior. Hume's logical dichotomy between factual and ought premises is backed up by a psychology in which passions are blind and reason impotent. And, on top of it, Hume's sceptical view of induction scarely provides a happy base for confident planning or the pursuit of goals.

Whatever the causes may be, the burdens of all these philosophies did not weigh too heavily on the American Enlightenment. Few doubted the force and primacy of the moral order or the possibilities of reasonable direction and control. They were already reconciled to the uncertainty of knowledge, but they did not draw debilitating consequences for decision-making from this, since they thought that "moral" certainties were sufficient and in any case always corrigible. Thus they early worked on probability theories and the logic of invention. They tended to look first to Bacon (and even Hobbes) and to read their Locke via Berkeley (especially the Berkeley of the *New Theory of Vision*) and via the Common Sense Realists. And in any case they could see that Locke's political achievements and influence were at variance with his limiting view of human nature. And they saw too that Hume would have difficulty in accounting for such a sustained project as his own *Treatise* or for problem-solving generally, on the basis of his own psychology. Indeed, his own analysis of the role of utility in determining moral approvals and the mechanisms governing the flow of trade were expected to lead to practical directives in the moral no less than the economic domain (where they helped displace Mercantilism in favor of laissez-faire in America as well as England). In Bacon, on the other hand, they found the commonplace that knowledge is power and Hobbes supported this by his psychology and further, since the input did not fall on a passive subject but one already in motion, he saw that the response was colored by the person's prior experience, language, and native equipment. Hobbes also distinguished between "reverie," i. e., unguided associations, and those series of controlled thoughts which are essential to plans and strategies. His political thought just as clearly assumes that policy decisions with respect to a foreseeable future are not only possible but imperative for reasonable citizens.

Less concerned than Bacon or Hobbes with the vision of scientific control of the physical and social environment, Berkeley in the *New Theory of Vision* nevertheless added an important dimension of activity. The world of constant objects and relations is essentially a construction derived through sequential associations or suggestions, one sensible experience serving as a sign of, or predicting of, others. Thus we learn to coordinate the visual with muscular feelings (including those of optical convergence) in judgments of distance. This is, loosely, a stimulus-response model where the cue is a stimulus and the expectation and meaning a response. Berkeley even suggested a functional view of responses, for in cases of ambiguous or conflicting sensations we tend to rely on touch over vision because the former has greater utility for self-preservation. Still the *New Theory of Vision* was only a halfway house and Berkeley moved, as we all know, to ideas as archetypes rather than to the testing of our expectations and a fuller theory of learning. If Kant seemed to have had too much faculty, Berkeley, without even a common sensible, appeared to have too little. Does it not seem strange that Berkeley and Hume, no less than Kant in his critical philosophy, should so thoroughly have detoured questions of strategy and planning? It must have seemed even stranger to the Americans for whom planning was a critical part of their experience. For they were absorbed in projects of harnessing laws of physics, psychology, and trade for human ends. They were devising constitutions and designing reform of society. The least they could expect of an empirical philosophy was that it should reflect or match experience.

Surprisingly, the Scottish Common Sense Realists took up the slack. Perhaps this accounts for their popularity and their influence in America. Simple association (argued Thomas Reid) is too impoverished a theory to account for the patent facts of voluntary behavior – for determining means and goals, for regulating the "stream of thought," or for constructing meaningful patterns in art. Even the expansion of sensation to perception involves an activity of the knower for pure sensations are theoretical fictions; we don't have, e. g., visual sensations – our perceiving is functionally a seeing of objects, and the activity of the knower provides the omnipresent cognitive judgment of objective reference. Thomas Brown, who completed medical interests with philosophic ones, so renovated the notion of association (suggestion) that it became powerful enough for larger theoretical needs. He enriched the domain of associables to include all sorts of internal and external affections, emotions, feelings of resistance, of relations, and of resemblance. Furthermore succeeding mental states need not necessarily replace earlier ones, for constant purposes or moods may endure as a fringe along with other trains of thought in the focus. It was especially in conjunction with Brown's works that the newer medical sciences entered philosophic discussion: beside investigations into the sensitivity of muscles, the sheathing of afferent and efferent fibers in a single nerve, important discoveries were made distinguishing reflex behavior from that requiring the higher nerve centers. The general impact of this physiology was to increase radically the domain of the involuntary as opposed to the voluntary in the governance of life processes; but they did not yet appreciate the transfer of once self-consciously learned actions into habitual ones. More dramatically, it shifted interest from the structural aspects of anatomy to dynamic and functional ones. The study of irritability as a property of cells led to the definition of life itself as an aggregate of functions which the several organic systems perform subserviently to the nervous system. It is disease, as well as thinking, willing, etc., that comes to be thought of as *functions* (or malfunctions) – and there is no more need to seek for an entity named "reason" than a "digestion"; one rests with the processes and their functions. Dugald Stewart, friend of Adam Smith and Jefferson, looked rather to mathematics than physiology for philosophic lessons and he added a new perspective to the intentional and decisional. He was impressed by the free way that alternate consistent formal systems and hypotheses could be constructed. Clearly there is needed a shift in the kind of validity involved when such systems or theories are assigned empirical or extentional interpretation, yet even then there may be options between rival hypotheses covering a given set of observations (as in the sixteenth-century Copernican-Ptolemaic controversy). In that case choice depends on considerations of elegance and simplicity.

Now the work of these men flowed into a backwater of British empiricism partly because of John Stuart Mill's rout of Sir William Hamilton's later (and somewhat perverted) accommodation of the Common Sense line to neo-Kantianism and partly because they were blocked in their efforts to account for purposive behavior by the claims of associational psychology and biophysiology. American academics, upon whom Hamilton's impact was marginal, tended to take their Kant straight, and they kept working with a Kantian commitment to purposive activity now placed in the context of psychological problems at the base of knowledge. James was most certainly turned to these problems by his professors (especially Francis Bowen) and by his own "immersion" in Brown and Stewart, but he got a new purchase on them by way of developments in neuro-physiology and, of course, evolution.

II

It has been the fate of James' work, with the differentiation of professional fields, that *The Principles of Psychology* remained largely the possession of psychologists, and that the *Talks to Teachers* was appropriated by educators, neither appreciating that the thin little book is a sophisticated resume of the larger *Psychology*. Philosophers, at least until recently, ignored both these works to get on directly to writings on pragmatism, radical empiricism, and the voluntaristic popular essays. The fact is that James' work is all of a piece.

James' commitments to neuro-physiology led him to see the nervous system as quite literally systematically converting sensory and perceptual stimuli into motor responses. If causal laws governing the flow of awareness are to be found at all, they must be sought in this physiological underpinning, not in the "laws" of association which are not generative. On the other hand, he leans toward the view that mind and body, voluntary and involuntary, are to be taken as functional rather than structural distinctions. It is interesting that James gets other mileage out of his commitments to neuro-physiology: support for that uniqueness of every moment of experience which is a condition for learning and the accumulation of experience; an interpretation of traditional association of ideas as relating objects, events and things "thought of" rather than thoughts and ideas of the things; and a thorough appreciation of how fantastically complex and interrelated knowledge, perception and response in fact are. Finally, the neuro-physiological stress commits him to the view that awareness, mental events, etc., are not nonnatural replicas, but events and functions naturally operating in a natural world. Evolution contributes to this functional view, because consciousness becomes not an entity but a function of an organism grown too complex to regulate itself reflexively. Development on the evolutionary scale in effect means that the stimuli to which a man can respond have become so varied and the alternatives of the response in any given situation so multiple (and possibly conflicting), that consciousness can be viewed as an organ directing the traffic. Built in here, in this naturalistic view of consciousness, are provisions for learning by foresight and self-conscious correction. Above all – men are educatable.

This setting gives consciousness dynamic features, although the richness which James finds in awareness and what it can do is but a further step in the reshaping of the blank tablet passivity of Locke's subject that Hume and the Realists had begun. In addition to being personal, continuous and continually changing, consciousness is also selective and cognitive. It is the relation of these last two that concerns us particularly in the theory of action, especially as they are related to mental capacities and to initiatable behavior. Objective reference, judgments of what is true and real, is assigned even on the most minimal of sensory cues; it is almost never a patch of color but the experience of an object or an event. Selective attending or interest is already at work: the self, the objects of our common world. and even the objects of physics, psychology, and metaphysics are always constructions which might have been seen differently in other contexts and for other purposes, and always may be seen differently as experience accumulates. The persistent sense of relevance, e. g., to a problem, or the sense of alternate and possibly conflicting strategies and even developing criteria for solutions have roots in what is directly experienced. Thus the job that cognitive and selective consciousness effects is the construction of a stable and manageable world out of the uniqueness of each moment of the sensible flux. We come to identify and intend, or mean (and know that we mean), the "same" object, topic, problem as we had intended or meant at some earlier time despite the flow of experience. This talent – to single out and fix for later identification – is the very spine of thinking. We dismiss much of the variety of experience and allow large segments to cue us into a relatively few recurrent items, the names of which become entrenched in language. This ability to generalize and to respond in patterned ways gives order to the world. Were the world chaotic, we should structure it; but without such a talent the world might be orderly and we should never know it.

Sameness, then, is a characteristic of meaning. The grass is the "same" green in the shade and in sunlight although perceptually different. Language, through these labels of reference, functions conservatively; but it not only economizes by making manageable items it also determines in large measure what we expect. We perceive largely what we pre-perceive through these labels; to escape this predisposition and to see what is "simply presented" would be virtually impossible except perhaps for an artist or a philosopher. The posited "simple ideas" of Locke are not simple replicable entities uncolored by learning, set, or interest, but products of sophisticated analysis.

Yet we are not misers, hoarding and economizing only the familiar; we often break through to new discriminations, some of which have their base in felt differences, not in inferences. Some are sought and others occur involuntarily; if a white billiard ball is presented jointly with a red one, we tend to notice color; if it is shown jointly with a tennis ball, then we notice texture, and if we see it with an egg, then shape may "shake out." We do more than make discriminations; we arrange them in linear or transitive orderings. If decreasing pitch always went along with increase in loudness, we might not be able to distinguish pitch from loudness. Unfortunately for the complexity of experience, tones may differ in pitch, loudness, timbre, etc. Everything could be compared, after all, with everything else; the directions of difference are indefinitely great, the linear modalities cross and criss-cross in fantastic ways yet we overlook the number of possible continua because we have labels (concepts) for so very few. We thus go through the world discovering and ordering differences in the like and likenesses in the different. Identity or absolute sameness and absolute difference are not met in experience but are ideal projections of the termini of the continua.

What has been identified, discriminated, and compared is further organized in sequential associations. Sometimes the paths are well-worn as when a lazy man reminds one of a sloth. At other times fresh features are opened up: the oval lid of a cocoa box becomes a mirror in the furnishing of a Victorian doll-house, or induction "a man facing backwards to row a boat forward." James' particular concerns are with associations or sequences that involve insightful reasoning and problem solving. Critical here is the selective way an object can be mutilated and a particular aspect chosen as essential. Sometimes the selection is perceptual, as the choice of squareness from the infinitely many perspective views available, sometimes it is some highly abstract feature, such as number or geometric relation. A truly distinctive capacity of man lies in his deliberate intention to apply signs everywhere, to generalize their use, to construct them into conceptual systems – all the while expanding and correcting in the light of ongoing experience.

In the long run, not only the way, but also the richness of our ways, of proceeding depend on past experience, the ways of processing it and the labels that we have on hand. It becomes apparent that the stock of labels and the choice of "right" ones is crucial. With correctness, a city planner may describe an area as a slum, lacking hardware, etc., while a sociologist may, again correctly, see it as a low-income district worthy of rehabilitating because of its low delinquency and high social cohesiveness. How does one come by new labels? Sometimes they are products of incompatible or rebel experiences or conflicting conceptual systems. Sometimes interest will trigger a perceptual insight as in the case of the doll's house. In any context there is an enormous variety of possible true descriptions; any of a variety of "seeings as" may be appropriate. The whole of our learning takes place through an interaction between the old and the new, between conceptual adjustments and richer perception. New experience is assimilated in categories or classes that we already possess, but often enough the fit is poor, and we have to mould or squeeze the new impression into the old category, forcing it into conformity. When the violence is too great, we invent a new category – and the latter discrimination may, retroactively, illumine the past, leading us to see the new in the old. To describe a Chinese Buddhist sculpture of the Wei dynasty as "gothic" may lead to a fresh perception of it and of the European style as well; while to classify Bach's fugues and the *Monadology* of Leibniz as "baroque" may alter the appreciation of both. Occidentals may think of softness as essential to a pillow until they encounter a Chinese porcelain one. Such an encounter leaves us with the well-known option: that is not a pillow or pillows don't have to be soft. Perceptions may conflict, either with one another or with conceptions, and conflicts needing resolution also occur between conceptual systems. Yet we do manage to get along with conceptual systems which, though not strictly compatible, are still not antagonistic. Thus a physicist's world may deal only with particles in motion, but the common man – who may be the physicist himself off-duty deals with material footballs when he plays with his son.

James' account of the sensory input and its processing via consciousness was in part a strategy for dislodging remnants of Locke's theory of atomic ideas and for stressing the activity of the knower. But when he turns to the production of movement and motor response he is curiously hesitant. James starts out boldly enough:

> The reader will not have forgotten, in the jungle of purely inward processes and products through which the last chapters have borne him, that the final result of them all must be some form of bodily activity due to the escape of the central excitement through outgoing nerves. The whole neural organism ... is but a machine for converting stimuli into reactions; and the intellectual part of our life is knit up with but the middle or 'central' portion of the machine's operations.[1]

Perhaps the writer was exhausted by the time he reached page 1060 of the text. For when he came to efferent processes and the production of motion he missed a serious chance to extend his study into action – to the generalizing of response and what is the "same" response, although these clearly raise issues comparable to the likeness classes of perception. For example, pushing a lever with a right or left hand (paw) is the "same response" if the interest is getting the lever pushed but not if the issue is to discriminate right from left. James loses also the opportunity to exploit robustly the uniqueness of responses and the novelty which arise (even in his own account) from instinctive or from random movements in ever-changing environments. Thus there is a difference between a child's first and admittedly instinctive reach for a brightness, say of a candle, and the intentional reachings on subsequent occasions.

The discrete or atomic character of the ideomotor S-R model, the reflex arc, prevents him from integrating responses into learning. Indeed James' theoretical structure falls so heavily on perception that performance, action, and any learning or learn-how which is dependent upon them is short-shrifted.

Actually, James had the elements needed to go on to a fruitful analysis of intentional or purposive behavior. The purposes and interests which were central to the selectivity and organization of perception work for responses. If guided thinking does not need a directing faculty of consciousness, then directed acting can get by without appeal to a will. Indeed James does go down this track (of excising the will) by locating the question of freedom in attention, that is, in an ability or lack of such to delay an idea by attending to it. Moreover, ideas are already impulsive and thus action does not need to be superadded, while complex ideas may involve incompatible strategies and alternate plans so that there may be conflicting motor tendencies needing reconciliation. One cannot escape this conclusion by shifting to a purely ideational domain since the objects of belief and those of the alleged will differ only in the manner of attending, and both require the same active consent. Indeed, James's later pragmatism depends on a richer theory of action than he provided in the *Psychology*. For in good pragmatic tradition ideas are functional, leadings to, or plans of action, and depend on verification (literally, the making true or testing). The pragmatic view of meaning thus emphasizes the importance of cognition to behavior as well the importance of behavior or action to cognition.

Yet James is fainthearted when he comes to discuss voluntary action, at the close of the *Psychology,* and he concludes that section with a fairly orthodox discussion of the freedom of the will. The will mandates and consents; the early assumption that consciousness can enter causally now becomes a question. Can the will hold an idea before the mind with a right label – the beginning of drunkenness rather than just the last drink? If only attending holds firm, the ideomotor theory can be trusted to do the rest.

The *Psychology* is certainly more than a strategy for unseating Locke's simple ideas as the repeatable items or building-blocks of experience. It is also a confrontation of the traditional dualisms of mind-body, perception-movement, and stimulus-response. It is not, however, a completely successful confrontation, partly because the unit of action remains as atomic as Locke's ideas, and partly because the conceptual and the sensible input are isolated from one another and both from the output (response), and partly because the dualism between thought and action is not thoroughly expelled, although the expulsion order is served under the rubric of "ideo-motor."

III

Interestingly enough, a young Dewey and his associates at Michigan and Chicago read James as having already started a revolutionary trend toward a behavioral account of intelligent conduct, toward integrating thought and action. In the correspondence that led to the dedication of their *Studies in Logical Theory*, Dewey credits James with having given his "thinking new direction and quality," indicating a package of articles which illustrate their mining of the Jamesian vein. Dewey had earlier worked free of anxieties which beset James. He never seriously doubted that intelligent decision makes a difference in the world, that ideas operate as plans of action; this is simply a fact calling for explanation but not denial. Further, he was already prepared to identify the self with concrete and specific activities. And he had been persuaded by the early sections of *The Principles of Psychology* that if the flow of consciousness requires no independent agent, then just as little does purposive action. Dewey went on to seek a fuller account of the role of action in learning.

"The Reflex Arc Concept in Psychology," sometimes titled "The Unit of Behavior," is the critical article in the package. Psychologists, he argues, had been looking for a unifying hypothesis for the understanding of behavior, and they had imported from physiology the notion of the reflex arc. But, in a sense, the distinctions between sensory input, motor output, and intervening mental event, seemed to Dewey to have slipped unnoticed into the seemingly unifying reflex arc. And indeed even the structure of the *Psychology* lends itself to this flat partitioning in which "consciousness" is psychic, movement definitely physical, and sensation a poseur as either or both, although Dewey was polite enough to leave this matter unmentioned. Dewey is looking for a molar view of activity as integrated and coordinated; not only must thoughts, action, and feeling be coordinated but they must find a place in the context of ongoing behavior as a whole and the particular matrix of experience out of which specific stimuli and responses arise. Dewey argues stepwise: Seeing (as even Berkeley had argued) is not merely a sensory matter, it is both optical and ocular. In effect, the sensory or perceptual input already involves motor activities such as the strain of convergence in the eye muscles. Similarly motor reaching (e. g., of the arm) depends throughout on kinaesthetic and visual perception. Dewey's standard example is (again) of a child reaching toward a bright light. Under any circumstances the mere striking of light on the optic nerve doesn't constitute a stimulus; a stimulus fails to be a stimulus without a response, i. e., without the correlation. Lacking this correlation, the "stimulus" is merely one of a sequence of events. The terms "stimulus" and "response" are functional terms; and are meaningless without some reference to one another and to adaptation; furthermore, the reaching-for-a-light is itself a complex process requiring time, and one in which the continuation of the total action depends on a continuous feedback. For example, vision throughout guides the movement of the arm with respect to the light, while the kinaesthetic sense of the location of the hand is, in its turn, a continually changing stimulus which cues further visual activity. One moment's response thus becomes a stimulus to some further response.

Dewey was not out to destroy the stimulus-response distinction but only to inquire into the conditions under which such distinctions arise and are serviceable. As long as habitual coordinations between looking and reaching are successful, the nature of the stimulus may remain unchallenged. It is only when habits fail – when the flow of experience is blocked – that the stimulus becomes important, and then it is as a problem. The child's habits may not be uniformly successful; suppose that after a reasonable number of successful reachings-for-bright-lights, he reaches for a light and is burned. On the next meeting with a light-colored cue, the child hesitates, for he is uncertain whether this new cue is of the burning sort or not. This hesitation provides the opportunity for further discrimination, for a search for discriminating features which will disambiguate the cue. Clearly the "right" description is that which succeeds in reestablishing the smooth flow of experience. Whenever the stimulus occurs again it will be in modified form, carrying piggyback the lessons *and* the traces of the ambiguities of old experience. Does this light cue one to-be-reached-for or to-be-shunned? In effect, it has literally become a yellow-for-caution light. Alternatives serve as primitive working hypotheses which future experience will test. It is indifferent whether we talk about determining (reconstituting) the stimulus, or whether we put the problem in terms of the response. One can ask whether the cue is a flame (a stimulus-description); the experiential test will be the same. These are alternative ways of formulating the same issue. The distinctions between stimulus-response, sensation – overt movement, etc., are made for purposes of analysis, and they function only in this context. They are not entities, ready-made parts of the world. The problems may be located for special purposes in one or another of these places, but they really belong to a larger activity and their resolution involves a reconstruction of the whole pattern.

In substance Dewey has here completed the revolution that he believed James had started. This is evident in the themes that run through Dewey's epistemology (logic) and value theory. Just as an understanding of James' philosophy depends on knowing the commitments of his psychology, so an understanding of Dewey's later philosophy and many points that have puzzled his readers as he tries on now one vocabulary, now another, is immeasurably facilitated by an appeal to this model developed in his early psychological papers. Dewey even uses this pattern (his re-interpretation of the reflex model, which after all originated in physiology) to supplant the vestiges of introspective and mental categories. The intellectual arises from within the flow of experience, mediating stimulus and response, that is, in terms of a problematic situation. Thus the ambiguity of stimuli, and the hesitation in response, are the psychological basis of problem-situations – which situations give context for both the theory of inquiry and that of value. Every inquiry and every appraisal is in some important way unique, being addressed to a particular context which furnishes meaning (or structure in awareness) to the situation, and provides criteria for successful resolution. But we come to no situation empty-handed or empty-minded; we are stocked, as it were, with ways of perceiving and of responding. These habits are not simply separate building blocks, but they always *sum* cumulative experience.

The theory is not so much physiological as biological, because Dewey is thinking, not solely in terms of an organism whose cutaneous boundaries define the total problem, but also in terms of a quasi-ecological view, of an organism responding in and with an environment of which he is a part. Dewey intended more than a simple feedback model, or a set of chemical equations laid out linearly to describe a directional process – he anticipates the kind of inquiry peculiar to modern systems analysis. Dewey continually reminds us that breathing, e. g., is not to be accounted for merely in terms of the structure and function of the lungs; it is equally a matter of the quality of the air. The example, trivial in Dewey's day, is more poignant on present-day reading. Since the environment is also institutional and cultural, his view of evolution also entails cultural anthropology; indeed it is not only that man makes culture, but also that custom and culture make the man.

When Dewey came to seek a unit for social psychology to

James' View of Action

do the job of the reflex arc concept in individual psychology, he called it "habit," meaning by it something similar, in structure or in function, to the events summed under the reflex arc concept. Habits are, naturally, conservative: through them we have access to the store of learned responses. But they are (given his idiosyncratic usage of the term) also dynamic. We do not have to initiate action, or individual response, or social change: these are inevitable and built-in. The problem is rather one of channeling and re-directing, and it is the job of intelligence to modify actions in ways that resolve or avoid conflict. This is done, of course, by novel means, rather than by mere repetition of former expedients. Successful management of ourselves and the world depends now on knowledge of both, together with what changes and controls they both will allow.

Dewey's use of the reflex arc model leads him to reject many dualisms, on the grounds that they misconstrue (almost mispicture) the situation, leading us to hold fast to unduly conservative thought patterns and to neglect that which is novel in our problems. Thus he defines "mind" functionally or instrumentally, as an active search for serviceable meanings. Mental categories are not isolatable from impulses, but translate or convert such impulses into desires or concrete plans which include the manipulating of the environment. But not only mind — also the "self" must be defined functionally; character and conduct are but aspects of one reality, functions of one another.

Even the late (1939) *Theory of Valuation* preserves not merely the general features but even the language of the reflex arc article. The means-end continuum requires that what appears as the end from one perspective may take on the role of means from a different view, it also requires the constant and mutual readjustment of end-in-view and means under the impact of the growing situations. And of course just as means and end can determine each other, so also are principle and situation interlocked. For both epistemology and ethics, principles are not rules to be applied, but working hypotheses to be tested in concrete contexts, while the meaning of the concrete situation depends on the principles used to analyze it. This extended ideo-motor theory sets Dewey irretrievably against all non-cognitivist theories of action, but it leaves him far short of being a "mere cognitivist." There is nothing in appraisals and appraisals of appraisals which pits science against morals.

The world is in the making; ends are never fixed, and the job of morality is to search for new goals and to resolve new problems in a changing environment. Thus the reflex arc concept, with its emphasis on reconstruction and restored coordination of a whole process, is present whenever he looks at an ongoing process blocked by disintegration, conflict, or irresoluteness. He is led always to search for a resolution which will bring about the smooth functioning of the system, and allow for growth. This is even the office of liberalism in social development, as it is the function of intelligence.

IV

The Jamesian vein, of course, was mined in various directions, but especially instructive in these matters are differences between Dewey and C. I. Lewis. Lewis saw in Dewey's reflex arc model, once amplified to include the use of intelligence in planning, Dewey's version of the pragmatic criterion of meaning and verification. Yet Lewis thought that Dewey's suspicion of abstractions and his concern over the mobilization of human resources to meet the particular problem led him to overlook the overwhelming importance of relatively stable conceptual structures in organizing perception and conduct, the ways of correcting by critique and rules, and the role of choice.

Lewis' account of concept formation is of course more detailed than James', but it has its roots in the same concern about epistemology as a learning theory. Concepts of likenesses are ways of transferring a sensible input to an output in rational action. Lewis of course emphasizes the free play of system making, like Dugald Stewart, for example, as in the construction of alternate formal systems or logics. But all our thinking includes such pattern making. Application or empirical interpretation brings other criteria beyond consistency into play, and choice among interpretations will then involve "pragmatic considerations" of utility, interest, etc. which go toward making the world manageable. Even induction already involved in the construction of a stable world of objects, events, and values) does not raise the question of order-making per se but only of how cogent and reliable the order is to be.

Systems of belief involve (strictly imply) consequences and conditions (including contingent testings or action.) They are thus predictive, involving expectations which may or may not come off. This means, also, that the beliefs operate as criteria in mind — rules generating the relevant tests and some sense in advance of whether what does occur satisfies the expectation or not. But such verification is only one part of a larger process of validation, in which the successes and failures must be returned to the base and provide the justifying grounds for later predictions. Thus the base is constantly changing and hence the predictions, relative to it, are always new. This whole process is of course very much like James' quartet of verification, validation, corroboration, and assimilation. Assimilation is carried in Lewis' account by the concept of congruence.

Lewis has thus woven intention and action into his view of knowledge and knowledge-getting. Ideas as plans of action are now wedded to a fairly orthodox epistemology; it remains at base a learning and dynamic feedback model. Since beliefs are dispositions to act and recognize — they are like blueprints or cognitive maps; our ways of patterned response, response by deliberation and rules, form an integral part of the testing of such maps. Since for Lewis there is no sharp distinction between values and facts (valuations are validated in the same manner as empirical judgments generally) they too are woven into the conceptual image or map. Such cognitive structures are relatively stable, and rich in the manner of Boulding's "image." For the most part correction is initiated at the periphery; there are always choices of where to make adjustments. And of course changes may be made in the conceptual part alone, having radical consequences for classification and hence experience.

Lewis, then, is not squeamish at just the point that James was. The search for a stable order lies in the foresight of what would happen without our intervention and of what could happen with it – all these would have no point if the activity of thinking were not effective.

Action thus is not only constitutive for knowledge, but knowledge is for the sake of action and controlled leadings-to. Patterned response and sequential planning are not just by-products since knowledge is the apprehension of the future as qualified by values realizable in action. Lewis does not use such teleology internally, for example, it can not be pressed into service to determine particular questions of validity, cogency, prudence, or justice. Yet it does have a role when questions are raised about why be just, prudent, cogent, and consistent, and whence comes their felt imperative quality. Men live in time, not merely as it is revealed in the dawning of it, but because they can foresee what the future may hold; such foresight makes decision and responsibility unavoidable. Thus the conception that mediates between stimulus and response involves not merely a summing nor even a selective accumulating of past experience, but also a constant reassessment of the ways successes can be utilized and formulated as rules or directions covering like cases. Such rules are themselves criticizable and thus higher-order critiques such as logic and ethics are developed. When critiques are acknowledged as formulating the best of our reflective judgments, they are, by so much, right, i. e., binding or imperative on action. But they are also public and observable.

Of course Lewis' interest in conceptual patterns and their legislative expression in rational imperatives of consistency, cogency, etc., distinguishes his work from Dewey's. But they share a commitment to the cognitive organization of behavior as a central feature of knowledge. The capacity to address problems and competence in self-direction must be assumed if philosophic enterprises are to be sensible. In these matters they are deeply indebted to James. Pragmatism has scarcely said the last word on purposive behavior, strategies and planning; but James has insisted that the first word be heard.

NOTE

1 William James, *The Principles of Psychology* (1890; Dover Publications, Inc., 1950), II, p. 372.

11

THE SELF IN WILLIAM JAMES' PSYCHOLOGY

Felicia Czerwionka

In this paper I will do two things: First, I will give a broad, general view of the self as presented in *The Principles of Psychology*. Second, I will focus particularly on the problem of self-identity. The Jamesian self, located in and one with the stream of consciousness and participating in its smooth lapsing of the past and edging into the future, is best understood when this continuity is kept in mind. Then the categories James uses to render self intelligible – e. g., ME, I, material, social and spiritual me's, successive thinkers – are not construed as presenting discrete parts or segments. Rather, they are understood as telling conceptualizations through which James highlights the multiple aspects and dimensions of the self as it is variously sculpted out of that larger plenum with which is continuous.

The Jamesian Self. In his *Principles* James devotes the whole of Chapter IX to an analysis of "The Stream of Thought." He here unpacks what is for him "the only thing which psychology has a right to postulate at the outset, [i. e.,] the fact of thinking itself."[1] His use of the progressive form of the verb in indicating psychology's "first fact" is significant. Insisting that thought is a stream, a process, he discusses its character under five heads. Under four of these five, he is led to the "fact of self-consciousness."[2]

It is this "'personal consciousness' ... [whose] meaning we know so long as no one asks us to define it"[3] that James takes up in Chapter X, "The Consciousness of Self." Here he approaches the self phenomenologically and linguistically. That is, he attempts to understand self both by describing the experience of self and by examining the common ways of talking about self. He is perceptive that the experience of self is not a rigidly static experience, but one erratically ranging over multiple grades of inclusions and exclusions. He resists the temptation to force what is experienced as fluctuating and vague into rigid and precise formulations. He is content to admit the vacillations both in the experience and in the naming.

Unperturbed that the self is a fluctuating thing, he acknowledges wider as well as narrower senses of self.[4] Despite the variety and range of meanings given to the terms "self," "me," and "I," James notes that they form two major classes. One group of meanings suggests an empirical self, that is, an object known and sorted from all else as 'ME.' The other group indicates a pure ego or 'I' which does the sorting.[5]

The 'ME' is constituted of material, social and spiritual aspects. The "material me" comprises a body as well as the extracorporeal supports and accompaniments of that body. Proceeding from the innermost part of the material me to its widest inclusion, James enumerates the body, clothes, immediate family, home and its scenes, property and wealth, and whatever is the object of one's labor.[6]

The "social me" is the image or set of images one has in the minds of others. A certain set of expectations is built into each of these images. These images are both organismically internalized in the present and collectively stored as one's historic social me.[7]

The "spiritual me," taken concretely, comprises the entire stream of consciousness with all its faculties, dispositions, and activities and all that it reveals over a lifetime experienced as a dynamic unity. James eliminates the present, judging thought from his discussion of the "Spiritual Self, so far as it belongs to the Empirical Me."[8] The spiritual me is at any moment capable of becoming an object for the present judging thought. The abstracted, innermost part of the objective spiritual me is that constantly-active psychic selectivity which welcomes or opposes, appropriates or disowns all that enters consciousness. Upon close introspection, James describes this psychic selectivity in his own case as certain fine and specifiable physical adjustments, cerebral or otherwise.[9]

Such conceptualizations would seem to cut these 'ME's from each other. However, as experienced, the three coalesce, forming one continuous whole which is, furthermore, not dicontinuous with the rest of thought's complex object. These aspects of the self have no absolute demarcations between them. Each involves some features more particularly defining the other. What they all have in common is that they are thought's object.[10]

The 'ME' is continuous with the 'NOT-ME' which, with it, comprises the whole of thought's object. What distinguishes the 'ME' from the 'NOT-ME' is that the 'ME' is an object of interest.[11] As James uses it in this connection, "interest" has a specialized meaning. It is that ongoing and interwoven sequence of preferential attention, instinctual adjustment, emotion and tendency to action which the present thought feels as a matter of fact with respect to certain objects related to survival or development.[12] For man, his body, family, wealth, accomplishments, recognition in the eyes of others, psychic abilities and dispositions are such "interesting" objects. These habitually excite in him instinctive organismic reaction, emotion, and even external activities. On the basis of such preferential interest, he selects from that fullness which comprises his total experience what he identifies as his self.[13] As James puts it with repect to the body: "Now I say that he identifies himself with this body because he loves *it*, and that he identifies himself it because he finds it to be identified with himself."[14]

One cannot absolutely mark the limits of this selective, identifying interest. Rather it seems that this "selective" or "particular" or "intense" or even "extreme" interest[15] is one end of a continuum that shades gradually into disinterest. Identified through interest and fluctuating according to the importance of the object to survival and development as judged by the present thought, one's objective self includes sometimes more and sometimes less.[16] What James has done is to roughly catalog whatever is so included according to its material, social, and spiritual aspects.

It is important to notice that, despite the felt constancy of one's body mass and psychic activity,[17] one's 'ME' is not once and forever constituted of specifically these corporeal features and supports, these persons' recognitions and expectations, this level of psychic capacity and activity. Whereas a conception repeated in logic is successively the same in meaning, the 'ME' – as successive thoughts cut it from the 'NOT-ME' – varies in meaning.[18] The 'ME' as one experiences it or uses the expression, seems to have little static meaning over time.

What is experienced and expressed might be said to parallel rather the dynamic meaning[19] of words met in context: One's 'ME' excludes certain aspects of the objective field; it excludes leaping changes in its material, social, and spiritual constituents. Never finalized, one's 'ME' is experienced as tending toward some yet unrealized possibility of inclusion, not wholly articulable, but continuous with and taking its cues from what one has been and is.[20]

At any point the possibilities that are actualizable are continuous with others ranging all the way to idle wishfulness.[21] One's decision regarding what one backs himself to be and do determines both the direction one's development will take and who will count as his 'set' eliciting this rather than that from him.[22] Given this decision, a certain self regard, i.e., an emotional perception of organismic reaction continuous with one's previous history, becomes the rule.[23]

It is possible to correct mistaken self regard by an intellectual judgment paralleling one's judgment of others.[24] Such judging also orders the rival claims of the material, social, and spiritual constitutents of the 'ME.' With well-being and self-development over the life continuum as the goal, one prefers wider, remote, potential fulfillment over narrower, immediate, actual satisfaction.[25]

All that we have just indicated as selected out, changed through time, and estimated have been objects constituting the empirical self, the 'ME.' But what is it that does the selecting, remembering, estimating? It is the present, passing thought.[26] In his discussion of the "spiritual me," i.e., the collection of states of consciousness, psychic abilities and dispositions taken

The Self in James' Psychology

concretely, James prescinds from the passing, *actual* section of the stream.[27] This present, judging thought is the 'I.' It is the principle of both unity and personal unity in consciousness.[28]

In what way is the present thought "the principle of unity in consciousness"? One puzzle that has troubled philosophers for a long time is that of "the Many known by the One."[29] However, the solutions offered, e. g., theories of soul or transcendental ego, have not been the explanations which they have purported to be. Rather, they have merely thrown the puzzle of how the one can know the many into the transempirical realm.[30] James himself does not pretend to give an explanation. He simply accepts his experience that thought itself combines what is a plurality,[31] and tries to make both the "manyness" of the object and the oneness of the thought more explicit.

What thought thinks of is its "object." Thought's object is all that the thought thinks at any given time, exactly as the thought thinks it.[32] This object is always complex. In that its focus and margin, its inclusions and exclusions, are in constant dynamic flux, this complex object is futher complexified.[33] "*However complex the object may be, the thought of it is one undivided state of consciousness.*"[34]

Thought is a synthesizer. Things, qualities, relations and activities are brought together when we think.[35] Even elements recalled from the distant past or those looked to in the future may be brought together in a single pulse of consciousness.[36] Such synthesizing of what is a plurality is thought's task. "This sort of *bringing things together into the object of a single judgment* is of course essential to all thinking."[37]

Sometimes this synthesizing is a matter of specifically relating things, as, for example, in classifying or identifying; sometimes it is a matter of simply bringing things together in one present section of consciousness. "The things are conjoined *in* the thought."[38] However complex the object whose constituents it brings together or however complex their relations, the present thought is a unity. It is one undivided state of consciousness.

In any moment, thought is functionally distinct from its object. It cannot be thought and object at the same time.[39] Functionally, the just past thought is an object in the present. The present thought itself will pass into the past and become an object for the new present thought.[40] The present thought cannot, however, be its own object. In any specious present, then, 'I' and 'ME' are functionally distinct. For James, "personality implies the incessant presence of two elements, an objective person, known by a passing subjective Thought ... [respectively] *ME and I ... the empirical person and the judging Thought.*"[41]

This functionally complex self is "recognized as continuing in time."[42] That is to say that the functional distinction of thought and object, i. e., of 'I' or 'ME,' in any present does not cancel the continuity to be found in the smooth move from the status of active thought to that of the thought-of object.[43] In the ongoing stream of consciousness, each thought lapses into the past, i. e., lapses into becoming an object for the new present thought. "Each pulse of cognitive consciousness, each Thought, dies away and is replaced by another. ... Each later Thought, knowing and including thus the Thoughts which went before, is the final receptacle ... of all that they contain and own."[44] The expression "dies away," accentuates the gradualness of the lapsing; it indicates that finely graded continuum of movement out of the present into the 'ME' which is complemented on the forward end by a continuous, gradual renewal of the 'I.' That mental procession is itself "the very 'original' of the notion of personality."[45]

This ever-dying-and-renewing thought is all the 'I' there is in Jame's theory of self.[46] It has no substantial unity with the thoughts that it succeeds in that these are irrevocably gone.[47] Yet the 'I' is the principle of personal Unity in consciousness in that each present thought is "aware of the same past in the same way."[48] In every moment it isolates certain aspects of experience as a self.[49] On the resemblance of warmth and intimacy, and the continuity of time and gradual change, it judges the self of differing moments to be the same self enduring through time.[50] We now focus on this "most puzzling puzzle with which psychology has to deal."[51]

Personal Identity. The judgment, "I am the same self I was," has both subjective and objective dimensions.[52] Subjectively, it is an intellectual judgment in which thought isolates a part of its own *sui generis* complex object and relates it to a part of a former object, declaring that the two partial objects of thought are in reality a single numerical thing enduring through time. Objectively, this judgment is based on resemblance in a fundamental respect and continuity. We begin with the subjective, psychological dimension.

The function of singling out "*a numerically distinct and permanent subject of discourse*"[53] from thought's complex object, i. e., from "the mass of matter for thought which the world presents,"[54] is conception. What is abstracted is given a fixed meaning for the purpose of reidentification in later thought.[55] It need only be sufficiently singled out to separate it from other things. Pointing it out or calling it simply 'this' or 'that' will do.[56] "To speak in technical language, a subject may be conceived by its *denotation,* with no *connotation,* attached."[57] This conceiving may be located in the focus or fringe of our thought. "We never can break the thought asunder and tell just which one of its bits is the part that lets us know which subject is referred to [as the same]; but nevertheless we always *do* know which of all possible subjects we have in mind."[58]

The thought articulating such a judgment as "I am the same self" singles out a particular subject whether it be a broader or narrower self.[59] The features on which this singling out is based, and the variety of meanings conveyed in the phrase "broader or narrower self" will become more clear in our analysis of the objective dimension of the identity judgment. For now, we continue in our focus on the subjective dimension: Vis-a-vis a particular singled-out self and some earlier version of it, the present thought judges an identity.[60]

In the case of the 'ME,' i. e., the objective part of the self, the present thought makes a judgment of numerical identity.[61] In a judgment of numerical identity, thought conjoins its partial object at time₁, and its partial object at time₂ and declares the two to be a single thing.[62] That is, a thing thought about at two times is – despite perceptible differences – judged to be one same thing enduring through time.[63] Contrasting it with "subjective synthesis," i. e., thought's bringing two or more things together in a single object,[64] James calls this judgment of numerical identity an "objective synthesis." "It is the sense of a sameness perceived *by* thought and predicated of things *thought-about*."[65]

James is insistent that we guard against the temptation to construe identity too strictly. Unlikeness is an indecomposable relation amongst things, a relation of which there are all degrees.[66] Our conception of absolute sameness is an ideal construction based on the minimum supposable extreme of unlikeness.[67] On a continuum having an entire range of gradations, "Absolute not-sameness would be the maximal degree, absolute sameness the minimal degree of this unlikeness."[68] Whether we compare two things or judge a single, enduring thing James remarks, "No realities ever are absolutely and exactly the same."[69] Since sameness is said of the Self despite changes through time, difference as well as likeness is evident.[70]

Having examined the intellectual or subjective dimension of the identity judgment, we look now with James at its objective dimension, i. e., at whether thought be right or wrong in judging "*I am the same self that I was yesterday.*"[71] In assessing this judgment James admits as data earlier assumed "a past time with past thought or selves contained therein," and as data earlier presented "the present self ... in its various forms."[72] He acknowledges that one must *beg* memory,[73] i. e., knowledge on the part of the present thought of something outside itself, specifically knowledge of past thoughts and their objects.[74]

Despite all the changes in the self over time, thought "calls the present self the same with one of the past selves which it has in mind."[75] What are the features which prompt this identity judgment? James contends that the sameness predicated of self is like sameness said of any other aggregate: "It is a conclusion grounded either on resemblance in the essential respects or on the continuity of the phenomena compared."[76] Appropriation is a further requirement in the case of self-identity.[77] Let me take up each of these three.

What resemblance between the self of yesterday and that of the present does the present judging thought find essential for concluding their numerical identity? James finds an answer in the *warmth and intimacy* felt in both the past and present selves.[78]

Warmth seems to be connected with the body, with its cubic mass and heaviness; intimacy with internal psychic activity, with the spiritual self, both 'I' and 'ME.'[79] However, sometimes James explicitly allows "warmth" to absorb what his ordered pair presentations reserve for "intimacy."[80] Ideas, "warm" to Peter, are those ideas involving both Peter's felt physiological adjustments and his felt psychic activity. Peter's body is one that he feels in all its internal adjustments.

Not only the ideas and body, but the whole of every experience in which these have figured is warm and intimate to Peter.[81] This pervasive character distinguishes experiences of Peter from similar experiences of Paul or of others.[82] It gives all his present or remembered experiences a generic unity, despite their differences in other repects. It constitutes what James later calls the full self, the self in its broadest sense, i. e., the whole field of consciousness.[83] All that I have experienced, all the furniture of heaven and earth insofar as they are my objects, comprise my full self.

But there is a less broad self which is sorted away from the rest of the environment, even that environment which it experiences. James calls this self "the personal and individualized self."[84] In connection with this personal and individualized warmth as 'interest,' i. e., as heightened attention, physiological reaction, emotion and tendency to action.[85] We see this linking of warmth with interest in one's discrimination of the empirical or objective self on the basis of "the passionate warmth of our self-regarding emotions."[86] Or again, when James notes that stories of one's childhood related by another lack warmth and intimacy in that "no sentiment of his little body, of his emotions, or his psychic strivings as they felt to him" comes up with the stories.[87]

What is evident is the fact that when one speaks of one's 'self' extensive "shiftings and expansions and contractions" of the boundaries are possible.[88] When we deal with the self, "we are dealing with a fluctuating material."[89] An analysis of the features which characterize self-identity as it is experienced cannot detach itself from these fluctuations.

One who says, "I am the same self I was yesterday" has bounded the constant that he is singling out in one of multitudinous different ways.[90] In most cases one is not using 'I' in the narrow sense of the present passing thought. Rather, using the 'I' form only insofar as it is the grammatical subject of a sentence, thought may topically include whatever it singles out as self.[91] That topical inclusion could cover the full self, i. e., the totality of all one's experiences to the present.[92] It could focus on the 'ME' in any of the material, social or spiritual aspects we discussed. It could also single out some more delimited aspect, e. g., sameness of profession, or skill, or response, or status, or reputation, etc.[93]

The present passing thought in its self-identifying knows which of these subjects is being referred to, which self – full, or personal, or any of its innumerable aspects – is being held constant by thought's tendency to mean the same. "We never can break the thought asunder and tell just which one of its bits is the part that lets us know which subject is referred to; but nevertheless we always *do* know which of all possible subjects we have in mind."[94] In every case this self is singled out from some larger whole on the basis of warmth and intimacy, and/or interest.[95]

The second characteristic by which the present thought singles out a certain collection of experiences and draws it into a unity called the 'self' is continuity. James discusses three kinds of continuity: continuity of time, of never-abrupt change, and of belongingness. Regarding time continuity James says "distant selves appear to our thought as having for hours of time been *continuous* with each other and the most recent ones of them continuous with the Self of the present moment, melting into it by slow degrees."[96] Even as neural states, never absolutely discontinuous with each other, condition their successors to be somewhat like what preceded them, so also successive psychic states, whether distant or recent, shade gradually into one another, lapsing and incoming by degrees.[97] The self singled out of these continuously renewed thoughts seems continuous.

James also discusses the continuity of never-abrupt change. As one ages, he changes. One's body (its weight, size, organic and emotional tone, material possessions and supports) varies; likewise the persons whose recognition and expectations matter to him, and his mental processes (their quickness, capacity and retention).[98] Yet, however great the changes over the life span, one feels that "the alterations were gradual and never affected the whole of me at once."[99]

Amidst the shifting there is a more constant ingredient: the memories of one's chlidhood. In the comparison of present and distant selves, possession of the same memories is the commonest and most uniform element of all.[100] The elderly man, however different from the youth he was, looks back on the same childhood that his youth remembered and calls it 'mine.' To the degree that these facts disappear in extreme old age, "the person's *me* shrinks."[101]

What makes these earlier memories seem to be one with the very different 'ME' of the present is the third sense of continuity, *belongingness*. The feeling of warmth and intimacy makes the parts "belong," thus giving continuity to even the most separated moments and most altered aspects of the self.[102] Warmth "runs through them all like a thread through a chaplet and makes them into a whole, which we treat as a unit, no matter how much in other ways the parts may differ *inter se*."[103]

The three kinds of continuity complement each other when the question of sameness is being decided: "we think we see an identical bodily thing when, in spite of changes of structure, it exists continuously before our eyes, or when, however interrupted its presence, its quality returns unchanged."[104] These successive phrases contrast gradual change continuity with time continuity, and then time discontinuity with the continuity of belongingness gained through resemblance, each latter kind of continuity complementing the breakdown of the preceding one. The judgment of sameness of self rests then upon continuity of time or gradual change, with resemblance – of memories, but especially of warmth – bridging the gaps.

Judgment of the self's unity and identity in terms of continuity and resemblance in no way disavows difference and plurality in other respects: Continued awareness through time gives a phenomenal unity of connectedness or unbrokenness, but interruptions of awareness are also admitted.[105] The resemblance of the parts in warmth and intimacy in no way reverses the differences in body and thought as we age.[106] No matter what aspect of self the present thought singles out to judge for sameness – whether the entire 'ME' in the fullness of its material, social or spiritual constituents, or any of the more limited aspects we remarked earlier – its identity can be only a relative identity, "a loosely construed thing, an identity 'on the whole.'"[107] The point of view determining the fundamental repect which is unchanging must be maintained. If from this one viewpoint I am the same self, other viewpoints may yield different selves. It is evident that in many ways I am *not* the same.[108]

Common sense insists that the unity of all one's selves involves "belonging to a real Owner, to a pure spiritual entity of some kind."[109] The warm and intimate parts of thought's objects, even in the case of thoughts continuous with one another, do not merely accrete together. "There must be a real proprietor in the case of the selves, or else their actual accretion into a 'personal consciousness' would never have taken place."[110] James contends that the present, passing Thought suffices as this owner.

The present thought, or 'I', is first of all the appropriator of the present Self. In the totality of which it is aware at any time, i. e., its full self, thought identifies and owns the preferentially interesting parts as its self, its individualized or personal self.[111] The present thought is the appropriator of past selves also. It recalls whatever past thoughts are recalled. "Each Thought, ... among the things it knows, knows its own predecessor [s], and finding it 'warm,' in the way we have described, greets it, saying: Thou art *mine*, and part of the same self with me."[112] It recognizes the preferentially interesting parts of all these objects as its self.[113] It concludes the identity of all these more distant selves with its present self on the basis of the continuities of time, never-abrupt change and belongingness.[114] This present thought, or 'I,' is for James, "the hook from which the chain of past selves dangles, planted firmly in the Present, which alone passes for real, and thus keeping the chain from being a purely ideal thing."[115]

Thus far we have spoken of the personal identity that the 'I' finds in its 'ME', i. e., of personal identity only insofar as the present thought singles out some feature – or even the fulness – of the past and the present and judges it to be the same self. But what sense can be made of self identity if we take the 'I' narrowly as the present thought itself, "*as 'that to which'* all the concrete determinations of the 'ME' belong and are known"?[116]

We cannot speak of the 'I's identity in the numerical sense, i. e., an identity "perceived *by* thought and predicated of things *thought-about.*"[117] Since there is no other 'I' but the present thought, and since the 'I' as the present thought is not thought about, the phrase "things *thought-about*" cannot be appropriately said of the 'I.' In what sense then does James speak of the identity of the 'I,' taken "narrowly as the *Thinker, as 'that to which'* all the concrete determinations of the Me belong and are known"?[118]

To clear the ground, he explicitly denies substantial identity; he denies that there is a permanent abiding principle of spiritual activity absolutely one with itself.[119] When the present segment of consciousness remembers and judges, yesterday's states of consciousness as acting 'I's are irrevocably gone. Nevertheless, there *is* an identity between those past states and the present state of consciousness. It is a functional identity, a sameness of function.[120]

Each of these pulses of consciousness was, in its own moment, the "real, present onlooking, remembering, 'judging thought' or identifying 'section' of the stream."[121] The present thought knows the same objects as past thoughts knew. So far as the by-gone 'ME' is among those objects, successive present thoughts react upon it in an identical way, greeting it and calling it *mine,* and opposing it to all the other things they know.[122] The foundation for the 'I's appropriation of the self's remoter constituents is this nascent 'I's immediately taking up the expiring thought and 'adopting' it."[123] It is in owning the just-lapsing 'I' that any present 'I' owns whatever that earlier thought owned. "This functional identity [among successive 'I's] seems really the only sort of identity in the thinker which the facts [i. e., 'all the experience of personal unity and sameness which we actually have,'] require us to suppose."[124]

James admittedly has moved from numerical identity to functional identity. The first is an identity consisting in an objective synthesis of things thought-about at two different times in that the two are, in reality, one thing enduring through time; the second is an identity wherein "successive thinkers, numerically distinct, ... [are] aware of the same past in the same way."[125] In this latter, two things – 'I' at time$_1$ and 'I' at time$_2$ – are said to be not one, but alike.

In what sense are such "successive thinkers, numerically distinct, but all aware of the same past in the same way," adequate to our experience of personal unity? It seems that mere functional identity would be insufficient, except that the function of any 'I' is what it is. It is because successive 'I's include and own all the thoughts which went before, together with all they contained and owned, that personal unity is experienced.[126] Successive 'I's are not only functionally identical, but the function itself of each is such as to unify both the whole of experience as *my* experience and certain parts of that experience as *my* self.

Let me recapitulate briefly. James presents the Self as comprised of a 'ME' which is an object known and sorted from all else, and an 'I' which does the sorting. James catalogs the objective aspects under three headings: the material me, the social me, and the spiritual me. Roughly, these group together the body and its supports, the recognition and expectations of other persons, and the psychic dispositions and activities taken objectively. The last includes all moments but the passing, present section of the stream. As experienced, the three coalesce, forming one continuous whole which is, furthermore, not discontinuous with the rest of thought's complex object. The 'ME' is sorted from the 'NOT-ME' in that, as a matter of fact, it arouses preferential interest, i. e., heightened organismic reaction, emotion, and tendency to act. This interest itself ranges along a continuum of gradations to almost total disinterest.

The present, passing thought is what does the selecting, remembering, and judging of the empirical, i. e., objective, self. It is the 'I.' In any moment this present thought is functionally distinct from its object. Yet it will itself lapse into the past and become an object for the new present thought. What is now 'I' will become 'ME' in the new present.

The present thought's judgment, "I am the same self I was," has both subjective and objective dimensions. Subjectively, it is an intellectual judgment in which thought isolates a part of its own *sui generis,* complex object and relates it to a part of a former object, declaring that the two partial objects of thought are in reality a single numerical thing enduring through time. Objectively, this judgment is based on resemblance in a fundamental respect and continuity.

All the experiences that are one's own resemble each other in the fundamental respect of being or having been warm and intimate. From this totality which comprises its full self, the present thought — the 'I' — discriminates the individualized self or any of its innumerable constitutive aspects on the basis of preferential interest. Despite the multiple possibilities of selection on a continuum ranging from the fullest to the narrowest self, it knows which of these is being referred to and held constant by its tendency to think the same.

Further, the 'I' bases its judgment on experienced continuity. The present thought is continuous in the time sense with its just lapsed predecessor and its incoming successor. Successive past segments of consciousness are remembered as having this time continuity about them. The 'I' is aware of the continuity of never-abrupt change in that alteration of the self in its various aspects is experienced as a slow shifting from youth to old age. Furthermore, even widely time-separated or divergent remembered selves have a continuity of belongingness, i. e., of seeming to belong together in a single whole, because of their warmth, intimacy, and interest.

In determing whether one is or is not the same self as earlier, no transempirical judge is needed. The present thought, which owns all previous thoughts and all that they possessed, suffices. Its own identity through time is a functional identity. It is because its function is what it is, i. e., including and owning previous thoughts and their contents, that such a passing thought is adequate to our actual experience of personal unity.

NOTES

[1] William James, *The Principles of Psychology*, 2 vols. (New York, 1890) I, 224. Hereafter cited as I (or II).
[2] I, 225—227, 241—242, 272—273, 289—290.
[3] I, 225.
[4] I, 291.
[5] I, 291—292, 333, 334, 371; William James, *Psychology. Briefer Course* (New York, 1892), pp. 176—177, 195, 201, 202. Hereafter cited as *BC*.
[6] I, 292—293.
[7] I, 293—296.
[8] I, 296, 297; *BC*, p. 181.
[9] I, 300—301.
[10] I, 289—292, 319, 324—325, 328, 371, 400; *BC*, pp. 176—177, 181.
[11] I, 289—290, 319—327.
[12] I, 318—327.
[13] I, 289—290, 319, 322, 324.
[14] I, 319—320.
[15] I, 320, 324, 323 respectively.
[16] I, 291, 310—316, 324.
[17] I, 333, 319.

[18] I, 291, 324.
[19] See I, 252—266 for static and dynamic meaning.
[20] Cf. I, 259—260, 269, 293—296, 316—327.
[21] I, 309—313.
[22] I, 294—295, 309—310.
[23] I, 306—307, 310—313, 328.
[24] I, 314, 327—328.
[25] I, 314—317.
[26] I, 328, 338—341.
[27] I, 296—297; *BC*, p. 181.
[28] I, 297, 296.
[29] I, 364, cf. 216—218, 272—278, 353—364.
[30] I, 342—347, 360—369; *BC*, p. 200.
[31] I, 499, 360, 364.
[32] I, 360, 364.
[33] I, 240—283.
[34] I, 276; cf. 240.
[35] I, 331—332, 360.
[36] I, 606, 643—644; cf. *BC*, p. 200.
[37] I, 331.
[38] I, 331.
[39] I, 190, 340; cf. *BC*, p. 176.
[40] I, 341; *BC*, 215.
[41] I, 371.
[42] I, 371; cf. 400—401.
[43] I, 339—346, 401.
[44] I, 339.
[45] I, 227.
[46] I, 338—342, 371, 400—401.
[47] I, 345, 338—339; *BC*, p. 202.
[48] *BC*, p. 203.
[49] I, 318—327, 334—342.
[50] I, 333—336.
[51] I, 330.
[52] I, 331.
[53] I, 461.
[54] I, 461.
[55] I, 459—462, 467, 478—482.
[56] I, 462.
[57] I, 463.
[58] I, 480.
[59] I, 459, 334; *BC*, pp. 201—202.
[60] I, 332—336.
[61] Cf. I, 532 and 332.
[62] Cf. I, 331—332, 459.

[63] I, 331—332.
[64] I, 331—332 fn.
[65] I, 332.
[66] I, 493, 533.
[67] Cf. I, 533.
[68] I, 493.
[69] II, 650 ff.
[70] I, 334—335; *BC,* p. 202.
[71] I, 332.
[72] I, 332.
[73] Epistenmologically both resemblance and continuity between the past and the present depend on memory, i. e., the ability of a present thought to revive a past thought, at least partially.
[74] I, 359—360.
[75] I, 332—333.
[76] *BC,* pp. 201—202; I, 334.
[77] I, 338.
[78] I, 333. It seems that thought is not connotatively clear about warmth and intimacy. Being constant and coloring such a multiplicity of associates in so many different contexts, it would seem that we "*recognize* but do not *remember* [warmth and intimacy]" (I, 673; cf. 685). While one may remember what they marked and be able even to verbalize the latter, one seems, ordinarily, to have little more than a denotative recognition of the coloring itself. James's vacillation among separated, co-ordinated, and fused presentations of the two (cf., e. g., I, 333, 334, 335, 341 and 355) elicits a certain tentativeness in my discussion.
[79] I, 333, I use 'seems' rather than 'is' to indicate that James does not consistently cut these two from each other as, respectively, a feeling of body versus a feeling of psychic activity.
[80] I, 355, 333.
[81] I, 335.
[82] I, 334.
[83] William James, *A Pluralistic Universe; Hibbert Lectures on the Present Situation in Philosophy* (1909; Gloucester, 1967), p. 289. Hereafter cited as *PU.* Cl. William James, *Essays in Radical Empiricism* (1912; Cloucester, 1967), p. 170 fn. Hereafter cited as *ERE.*
[84] *ERE,* p. 170 fn.
[85] I, 333; cf. 327, 335.
[86] I, 327.
[87] I, 335. Though James does not adhere to this distinction rigidly, warmth analyzed as a feeling of body mass and psychic activity seems to discriminate whatever experiences are one's own, i. e.,

one's *full* self, whereas warmth analyzed as interest seems to identify the *personal* self.

88 I, 319.
89 I, 291.
90 *BC*, pp. 201—202.
91 *BC*, pp. 201—202.
92 Cf. *ERE*, p. 170 fn.
93 *BC*, pp. 201—202; I, 371—372.
94 I, 480.
95 I, 333—341, 318—327.
96 I, 334.
97 I, 243.
98 Cf. 371.
99 *BC*, p. 201; Cf. I, 371—372, 239—243. As I see it, the continuity of time and of never abrupt change are aspects of a single continuity. "Time continuity" seems primordially experienced as the incoming and lapsing of *all* the content of consciousness, whereas "never-abrupt change continuity" seems more an accent with respect to *certain*, singled-out constituents of consciousness. The first seems most properly said of the "full self," i. e., the "wider sense of self in which the whole 'choir of heaven and furniture of the earth' are ours, because they are our 'objects'" *(ERE,* p. 170 fn.). Correlatively, never abrupt change seems an appropriate description of the individualized self, i. e., the interesting 'ME' constituents.
100 I, 372.
101 I, 373.
102 I, 237, 333—341.
103 I, 334.
104 I, 334; cf. 238—239.
105 *BC*, p. 202; I, 334—335.
106 I, 371—372.
107 I, 372; cf. 335, 352.
108 I, 371—373, 528—529, *BC*, pp. 201—202. It is only conceptually that one can push sameness to its never realized ideal limit, i. e., a sameness which excludes all difference (cf. I, 491—493, 528—529).
109 I, 337.
110 I, 337.
111 I, 333.
112 I, 339; cf. 238—239, 333.
113 I, 319—327; cf. *ERE*, p. 170 fn.
114 I, 333—341.
115 I, 340—341.
116 *BC*, p. 202.

[117] I, 332.
[118] *BC*, p. 202.
[119] *BC*, p. 202, Cf. I, 338—341, 346—350.
[120] *BC*, pp. 202—203.
[121] I, 338; cf. 341.
[122] *BC*, p. 203; cf. I, 339.
[123] I, 339—340.
[124] *BC*, p. 203; cf. I, 337—340.
[125] *BC*, p. 203.
[126] I, 339.

12

JAMES AND THE PROBLEM OF INTERSUBJECTIVITY: AN INTERPRETATIVE CRITIQUE

George Francis Cronk

Introduction

One of the basic problems of modern philosophy is the so-called problem of other minds – the problem of intersubjectivity. This problem may be formulated in two questions: "Is intersubjective experience possible? And if so, *how* is it possible?" These questions arise from many sources in modern thought, but especially from the subjectivist implications of Cartesian Dualism and from the atomistic analysis of experience which is a product of British Empiricism. Descartes drove consciousness inward to a Mind separated from Matter; and then, on the basis of a sensationalist description of perception, the Empiricists atomized consciousness in a thorough subjectification of experience. The philosophy of William James is, in large part, an attack upon these doctrines and an attempt to restore the unity of consciousness and its objects. James' notion of "pure experience," of a neutral "stuff" of which object and subject are merely "functions," is aimed at bridging the gap created by Cartesian Dualism. And his "theory of relations," according to which conjunctions are as characteristic of experience as are disjunctions, is developed in opposition to the atomism of the Empiricist tradition.

But in presenting a non-dualistic account of consciousness and a relational theory of experience, James does not thereby escape the problem of intersubjectivity. On the contrary, the need to discover and explain the nature of intersubjective experience is deep-rooted in James' thought. This is a consequence of the "subjective turn" of his philosophical method. James defines his philosophical perspective as a "radical empirism." "To be radical," he writes, "an empiricism must neither admit into its constructions any element that is not directly experienced, nor exclude from them any element that is directly experienced."[1] The starting-point of James' radical empiricism"is the fact of thinking itself,"[2] or, more broadly, the stream of consciousness. And consciousness, as James describes it, is fundamentally *personal* in nature.[3] From *The Principles of Psychology* to his last writings on radical empiricism and pluralism, James' thought is cast almost exclusively in first-person terms. "Like Augustine, like Erigena, like Descartes, like Husserl, James turns to *the experience of oneself experiencing* as the fundamental fact, the starting point for philosophy..."[4] Given this subjective orientation to experience, the phenomena of human sociality and intersubjective experience are necessarily problematic for James. And his attempt to account for these phenomena, as we shall see, is thoroughly conditioned by his initial commitment to the subjective turn of descriptive (or "phenomenological") psychology.

In the following pages, I shall review (1) James' definition of the problem of intersubjectivity; (2) James' attempt to solve the problem; (3) the description of the "life-world" of perception and praxis, by which James seeks to avoid subjectivism; and (4) James' theory of nonperceptual consciousness. My general contention, throughout this analysis, is that James never quite succeeds in his efforts to solve the problem of intersubjectivity, although he *does* lay the groundwork for a possible solution.

(1) James on the Problem of Intersubjectivity

James' definition of the problem of intersubjectivity is posed in terms of his doctrine of relations, i. e. his view that the relations, conjunctions, and transitions which are felt in experience are just as "real" as are the "substantive *qualities* and *things*"[5] encountered in the stream of consciousness. Now

James is careful to point out that relations may be either conjunctive or disjunctive. In his descriptions of relations between persons, he tends to lay the accent upon disjunction rather than conjunction. It is "a fundamental psychological fact," he writes, that

> No mind can take the same interest in his neighbor's *me* as in his own. The neighbor's *me* falls together with all the rest of things in one foreign mass, against which his own *me* stands out in startling relief.... [The Other] is for me a mere part of the world; for him it is I who am a mere part. Each of us dichotomizes the Kosmos [i. e. draws the line between the "me" and the "not-me"] in a different place.[6]

When it comes to the interaction of different minds, James considers that

> Each of these minds keeps its own thoughts to itself. There is no giving or bartering between them. No thought even comes into direct *sight* of a thought in another personal consciousness that its own. *Absolute insulation, irreducible pluralism, is the law* [italic mine]. It seems as if the elementary psychic fact were not *thought* of *this thought* or *that thought*, but *my thought*, every thought being *owned* [James' italics]. The breaches between such thoughts are *the most absolute breaches in nature* ... [italics mine]. The universal conscious fact is not "feelings and thoughts exist," but "I think" and "I feel."[7]

But James recognizes that human interactions may be, on occasion, conjunctive as well as disjunctive. In his analysis of various types of conjunctive relations, James argues that "merely to be 'with' one another... is the most external relation that terms can have," whereas the "most intimate of all conjunctive relations" is the "passing of one experience into another when they belong to the same self." And when speaking of interpersonal experience as conjunctive, it is "this bare relation of *withness*" that James has in mind.[8] While my intra-subjective experience is "sensibly continuous" in the sense that it is "warm," "intimate," and "immediate," such is not the case with my experience of another person; there, I have only indirect and discontinuous experience.[9] My experiences and your experiences are 'with' each other in various external ways, but mine pass into mine, and yours pass into yours in a way in which yours and mine never pass into one another." Thus, interpersonal relations are infected with an unavoidable "*discontinuity-experience*;" and this (at best) "imperfect intimacy" is at the core of the problem of intersubjectivity.[10]

(2) James' "Solution" of the Problem of Intersubjectivity

"Absolute insulation" or a seriously "imperfect intimacy": are these the alternatives that characterize human interaction? James is disturbed with this possibility and makes several attempts to discover a deeper, authentically *inter*subjective, bond between human beings. These attempts are especially interesting, for they reveal both the suggestive power and the ultimate weaknesses of James' approach to the problem of intersubjectivity.

In his *Essays in Radical Empiricism*, James makes the claim that a radically empirical approach to perception reveals "a world of pure experience," a world that is neither objective nor subjective, a world in which "object and subject *fuse* in the fact of 'presentation' or sense perception."[11] A "pure experience," according to James, is "a bald *that*, a datum, fact, phenomenon, content, or whatever neutral or ambiguous name you may prefer to apply."[12] Experience as such is a neutral "stuff" which can, in retrospect, be defined as either objective or subjective; e. g., a pen can be taken as a physical thing "out there" or as a mental event "in here," but the pen *as such* is a pure (i. e. neutral) presentation, a "that" and not a "what."

In his essay, "How Two Minds Can Know One Thing"

(published in 1905), James turns to a consideration of how a unit of pure experience can be appropriated by two different streams of consciousness. This is a problem because there appears to be a significant difference between the phenomena of consciousness and physical things: i. e., "While physical things ... are supposed to be permanent and to have their 'states,' a fact of consciousness exists but once and is a state." Thus, the question arises as to how "my" phenomenon can be the same as "your" phenomenon. James begins his response to this problem with a description of how a unit of pure experience is appropriated into a single stream of consciousness: The "continuous identity of each personal consciousness," James explains, is "a name for the practical fact that new experiences come which look back on the old ones, find them 'warm,' and greet and appropriate them as 'mine.'" He then breaks this explanation down into four phases: (a) a new experience (e. g. of a pen) "has past time for its 'content,' and in that time a pen that 'was';" (b) the present experience (of a pen) has the "warmth" of pens past, has feelings (especially feelings of "interest") which are associated with pens past, and is *recognized* for what it is on the basis of pens past; (c) these feelings are centered in a self, in a "me;" and (d) associations with pens past (and other past experiences) were and are "mine." The important point here, according to James, is that this appropriation of the pen "is *part of the content of a later experience* wholly additional to the originally 'pure' pen."[13] The "pen-experience in its original immediacy is not aware of itself, it simply *is,* and the second experience is required for what we call awareness to occur."[14] Consciousness requires retrospection.

James notes that pure experiences are unaffected by the appropriative act: the use of a pure experience "is in the hands of the other [conscious] experience, while *it* [the pure experience] stands, throughout the operation, passive and unchanged." On this basis, he continues, it is quite clear how two minds can know the "same thing." "All that we should have to postulate would be a second subsequent [conscious] experience, collateral and contemporary with the first subsequent one, in which a similar act of appropriation should occur. The two acts would interfere neither with one another nor with the originally pure pen." Furthermore, there is no reason why these two streams of consciousness cannot regard their (separate) experiences as being *of* a physical thing which is the same for both consciousnesses. There is, James concludes, "nothing absurd in the notion of its [the pure experience] being felt in two different ways at once, as yours, namely, and as mine." "The paradox," then, "of the same experience figuring in two consciousnesses seems thus no paradox at all," since there is no logical difficulty in the idea that two consciousnesses can appropriate the same object. As experience is presented, i. e. as "pure," an object can be both "mine" and "yours" simultaneously or at different times, can be "owned" by both of us "just as one undivided estate is owned by several heirs."[15]

But while James' analysis of the appropriative act shows how two minds can be conscious of the same objects, it does not make clear how these two minds can *communicate* their thoughts to one another. The radical insulation of consciousness from consciousness is left unremedied in James' description of the mutuality of objective reference. James is apparently aware of this difficulty and, in another (earlier) essay on "A World of Pure Experience" (published in 1904), he makes an explicit attempt to discredit the solipsistic view that there are "no transitions" and no points of contact between different minds, that different minds "are wholly out of connection with each other." One escape from this "'cold, strained, and unnatural'" psychology is the so-called "argument from analogy." James puts this argument as follows: "Why do I postulate your mind? Because I see your body acting in a certain way. Its gestures, facial movements, words and conduct generally, are 'expressive,' so I deem them actuated as my own body is, by an inner life like mine."[16] But the argument from analogy, while it may be a statement of a "reason" for *postulating* other minds, is a theoretical leap beyond the "directly experienced facts" and must therefore be excluded from a radically empirical consideration of the question of intersubjective experience.

Having dispensed with analogical constructions, James turns to the world of lived experience for evidence of true intersubjectivity, and this turn brings him to the notion of what phenomenologists have called the "lived-body." Here, we must digress briefly. In *The Principles of Psychology*, James presents a theory of the self in which he attempts to describe personal experience without reference to a substantial ego or soul which transcends the stream of consciousness. And it is this "non-egological"[17] approach to the self that gives rise to his concept of the lived-body. James makes a distinction "between thought as such, and what it is 'of' or 'about,'" a distinction which he regards as a primal fact of human psychology.[18] It is this distinction that makes possible the "subjective turn" toward a consideration of "the Spiritual Self" (i. e., "a man's inner or subjective being"). We can, James points out, consider the process of thought independently of its objects; we can, that is, *"think ourselves as thinkers."*[19] When we make this turn, we discover that what we call our personality consists of "the incessant presence of two elements, an objective person, known by a passing subjective Thought and recognized as continuing in time." James refers to the objective side of personality as the "me," and to the subjective side as the "I."[20]

On this basis, James contends, we can understand the phenomenon of personal identity without any appeal to a "Pure Ego." James treats the "I" as a "pulse of consciousness" which inherits the self which precedes it; and that preceding self has, in its own right, inherited all that *its* preceding self "owned," and so on. Each "I," then, stands as the *"representative* of the entire past stream," having adopted the "objects already adopted by any [previous] portion of this spiritual stream." This "I" is not an overarching transcendental ego; it "is still a perfectly distinct phenomenon from that Other [which preceded it in the stream of consciousness] ..." "The Thought which, whilst it knows another Thought and the Object of that Other, appropriates the Other and the Object which the appropriated..."[21] "It may feel its own immediate existence ... but nothing can be known *about* it till it be dead and gone. Its appropriations are therefore less to *itself* than to the most intimately *felt part of its present Object, the body, and the central adjustments,* which accompany the act of thinking, in the head. These are the real nucleus of our personal identity..."[22] The self, then, *is* the lived-body. I identify experiences as "mine" on the basis of a felt "warmth and intimacy."[23] Such feelings are *bodily* feelings, e. g. "organic emotion in the shape of quickened heartbeats, oppressed breathing, or some other alteration, even though it be a slight one, in the general bodily tone."[24] Thus, we identify "distant selves" (e. g., past experiences) as "ours" on the condition that these selves are *felt* as warm and intimate, and also on the condition that they are *felt* as "continuous" parts of our total experience of self; and this total experience of self is "embodied."[25] The lived-body is thus the "primitive object... of egoistic interests," and all other objects of interest are derivatives of the body, its social extensions, and its "spiritual [i. e. subjective] dispositions."[26] The concept of the transcendental ego or soul, then, "is at all events needless for expressing the actual subjective phenomena of consciousness as they appear."[27]

Now let us return to James' essay, "A World of Pure Experience," and see how he utilizes the concept of the embodied self in his effort to build a theory of intersubjective experience. He begins by observing that if there *is* a "you" beyond my perception of "your body," then "we belong to different universes...," for my evidence of "you" *is* your bodily expressiveness. But concrete experience militates against the possibility that "you" are disconnected from your body. "... In that perceptual part of *my* universe which I call *your* body, your mind and my mind meet and may be called conterminous."[28] For "your objects," James argues (in an analysis similar to that offered in "How Two Minds Can Know One Thing"), are over and over the same as mine. If I ask you where some object of yours is, our old Memorial Hall, for example, you point to *my* Memorial Hall with *your* hand which *I* see. If you alter an object in your world, put out a candle, for example, when I am present, *my* candle *ipso facto* goes out. It is only as altering my objects that I guess you exist...

Practically, then, our minds meet in a world of objects which they share in common, which would still be there if one or several of the minds were destroyed.[29]

Intersubjectivity, then, is grounded in the lived-body and is focused on objects which embodied minds can hold in common. But what does this account prove? In James' own words, the argument merely demonstrates that "the common-sense notion of minds sharing the same object offers *no special logical or epistemological difficulties*...;" there is nothing absurd or logically contradictory in supposing intersubjectivity to be possible and actual.[30] This leaves dangling in the air the *empirical* question as to whether our minds *do in fact* "terminate" in the same perceptual phenomena. James answers this question negatively. Perceptually, our minds are far apart, even when they are in rough agreement; for we occupy different perspectives and have different interests which condition our perceptions of objects. "Is natural realism, permissible in logic, refuted then by empirical fact? Do our minds have no object in common after all?" At this point, James indicates the *phenomenon of space* as the common perceptual ground (or object) of our minds. "There is no test discoverable," he writes, "by which it can be shown that the place occupied by your percept of Memorial Hall differs from the place occupied by mine." James concludes by grounding his concept of the lived-body in perceptual space and by defining the space of the lived-body as the ultimate matrix of intersubjectivity. Your body-space and my percepts of the location of your body and of points on your body are *in the same place*, "and it is *through* that space that your and my mental intercourse with each other has always to be carried on..."[31]

It is puzzling that James focuses explicitly on the spatial but not on the temporal structure of intersubjectivity since, in the *Principles,* he regards the perception of space and the perception of time as "analogous" and comments that "date in time corresponds to position in space." A radically empirical approach to the phenomena of consciousness would seem to indicate that the "original experience of both space and time is always of *something already given as a unit* . . . ."[32] If James employs the notion of lived-space in his effort to explain how different minds can share the same objects, might not the notion of lived-time be utilized in the same way? Is there any way of determining that the time in which your percept of the present table is located is different from the time occupied by my percept of the present table? Is it not clear that the table is present for both of us "now"? Our present interaction has temporal as well as spatial structure, is taking place both "now" *and* "here," and this spatio-temporal structure is what it is because of the ways in which our bodies are presently oriented. The lived-body, then, carries with it a spatio-temporal aura or halo through which perceptual experiences, which for James are primarily subjective, might become *inter*subjective. In this way, James' description of the "specious present,"[33] i. e., the durational and subjective time of perceptual experience, can be applied to a description of what might be called "dialogical time," i. e., the durational and *inter*subjective time of perceptual experience.

James speaks of the specious present as the "original intuition of time"[34] and regards it as the primary temporal structure of the life-world. Because it is the time of perceptual experience, the specious present is the "original paragon and prototype of all conceived times."[35] James' distinction between perceptual and conceptual time is basic to his account of lived experience and is fruitful for an understanding of intersubjectivity. Conceptual time (e. g., memory, history, clock-time) is, for James, a symbolic extension of lived-time into past and/or future. Beyond the borders of the specious present "extends the immense region of *conceived* time, past and future, into one direction or another of which we mentally project all the events which we think of as real, and form a systematic order of them by giving to each a date."[36]

How can this notion of conceptual time contribute to an understanding of intersubjective experience? In a penetrating passage on James' theory of memory, John Wild attempts to show how the "remote events" of history can enter into and become a part of concrete personal experience. I have a memory of my past, i. e., of past events which I have appropriated to my present experience on the basis of their felt warmth and intimacy. "It is this past that belongs to me," Wild writes, "which gives me a sense of a past direction in time, and makes remote history something more than a mere imaginative construction. No matter how distant these remote events may be, they stretch continuously through historical records and traditions to the past that I remember, and to the present that I am living through and directly know."[37] Thus, a collective time (history) becomes a defining characteristic of the personal time of memory and the specious present.

But Wild does not carry his analysis far enough. I do not only "re-member" (i, e. reconstruct) past events "forward" into my present experience; I also "re-member" my present experience "backward" into my own personal past and thence into the historical past. In this manner, I enter into the experience of others who are no longer living but who, through my appropriative acts, "live on" in the symbolic images of historical thought. This is, of course, a one-sided "communication" since it is I, and not those once living, who define the meaning of the historical past. But there is a sense in which historical consciousness is *actually* intersubjective, i. e. in the sense that different minds may look back to *a common historical past*. When we discuss classical civilization, for example, and even when we disagree about its meaning and significance, do we not in fact occupy a common, although symbolic, world, a world in which we are actually *commun*icating (in the sense of "communing") with one another?

This same sort of analysis can be applied to future time

with reference to which different minds might "live together" in common hopes, fears, expecations, etc. And even clock-time, the most abstract because the least bodily form of time, has intersubjective significance as a method by which different minds coordinate (i. e. make common) their acts. But these and other aspects of James' theory of time which are relevant to a full account of intersubjectivity must be left undeveloped at this point. Reasonable limits on the length of this paper require that I content myself with having suggested a few of the ways by which a Jamesian account of the temporal structure of intersubjectivity might be constructed.

(3) The Problem of Subjectivism in James' Thought

But even when we have supplemented James' spatial analysis of intersubjectivity with an account of the temporal structure of lived experience, a difficulty remains. James defines the self "in its widest possible sense" as "the sum total of all that ... [a man] CAN call his, not only his own body and his psychic powers, but his clothes and his house, his wife and children, his ancestores and friends, his reputation and works, his lands and horses, and yacht and bank-account."[38] It would appear that this definition might lead James to a conception of the self as presupposing aspects of the "not-self," including other persons. But such is not the case. James' description of the self is entirely intra-subjective, a product of his methodological subjectivism: he presupposes the living, experiencing body and attempts to evolve an awareness of others out of that subjective center. Given this orientation, it is inevitable that James must beg the question of authentic sociality and regard awareness of others as "my" awareness. "You" appear as an object, but not necessarily as a subject, in *my* spatio-temporal experience.

The subjectivist tendency of James' theory of the self is mitigated to an extent by his description of the "paramount reality" of lived experience. There is a world in which we live and in which we are conscious. As James points out, consciousness is interested, attentive, and selective. Perceptual consciousness, for example, selects, on the basis of practical interest, certain "sensible qualities" of the world and constructs these qualities into "things" by means of "substantive names" which are given to certain configurations of experience. James compares the operations of the mind to the work of the sculptor who "extricates" his statue from the mass of rock around it.[39] This process of selectivity, of course, has a tendency to "*ignore* most the things before us," and this tendency is perhaps the most important form of selection.[40]

Now, according to James, selective consciousness presupposes a world which offers us "various orders of reality" or "sub-universes" (e. g. the worlds of perception, science, commonsense, madness).[41] It is from these various orders that we must select our "realities." Ordinarily, objects of experience are accepted as real so long as they are consistent other objects that we take to be real. "The sense that anything we think of is unreal can only come," according to James, "... when that thing is contradicted by some other thing of which we think. *Any object which remains uncontradicted is* ipso facto *believed and posited as absolute reality.*"[42] But when two objects *are* in contradiction to one another, on what grounds are we to choose one rather than the other as "real"? Here, James turns to a description of the "world of 'practical realities'" which is the basis of our epistemological choices. "Each thinker...," he writes, "has dominant habits of attention [which are expressions of pratical interests]; and these *practically elect from among the various worlds some one to be for him the world of ultimate realities.*"[43] Objects that appear as "*interesting* and *important*" to us are, generally, considered real; and objects which do not appear as interesting and important are branded as unreal or irrelevant. "*The* fons et origo *of all reality, whether from the absolute or the practical point of view, is thus subjective, is ourselves.*"[44]

But James recoils from the blatant subjectivism of the above remarks and seeks to ground the world of practical interest in the deeper and "paramount" reality of the world of sensation, the world in which objects must compete with one another for recognition as realities. After all, I may be "interested" in discovering a golden mountain without actually finding such an entity in the lived "world of sense;" and I may *not* be "interested" in the Rocky Mountains, and yet they are *there* in perceptual experience. Thus, James concludes, the "world of orderly sensible experience" is the ultimate arbiter of reality,[45] and all other "realities" (objects of imagination, dreams, idealities of science and mathematics, the world of "practical realities" itself) are derivatives of this paramount reality.[46] "Our ideas and concepts and scientific theories pass for true only so far as they harmoniously lead back to the world of sense." [47] If knowledge is conditioned by interest, then interest begins in, arises out of, and points back to the "life-world" of perceptual experience, the world in which we, as embodied selves, live and are capable of "various noetic attitudes"[48] toward the world. And noetic attitudes must be testable against the paramount reality of perception.

But while James' conception of the paramount reality of perceptual experience does ground the lived-body in a lived-world, it does not, by itself, overcome the subjectivist element in James' thought. To accomplish this, James would have to delineate the *social* structure of the life-world. As James ably points out, the "whole function of conceiving, of fixing, and holding fast to meanings, has no significance apart from the fact that the conceiver is a creature with partial purposes and private ends."[49] And he never tires of indicating that the selectivity of consciousness is directed by "habits of attention" which, in turn, are determined by "practical interests." But what determines *interests*? To this question, James provides no answer. To answer this question adequately (which I cannot do in this paper), it would be necessary to uncover the fundamentally *social* nature of the lived-world as the ground of interests. For, as Habermas states, "knowledge-constitutive interests take form in the medium [sic] of work, language, and power;" and these latter are "the definite means of social organization." Habermas defines language in a manner consonant with the findings of Mead and his followers, i. e. as "the communication system of social life-world."[50] Language, as Mead demonstrates, is not merely a logical structure, but also a *social system*.

There is, however, an absence of explicitly social analysis in James' approach to experience. James contends that radical empiricism is "essentially a *social* philosophy, a philosophy of '*co*,' in which conjunctions do the work."[51] But is it a social philosophy in the full sense, i.e. in the sense of an elucidation of human social reality and the forces which form it? Or is James' philosophy of "co" an *onto-psychological* description of first-person experience? On the one hand, radical empirism *does* open the door to a truly social philosophy in that relations between persons are described as *given* in concrete experience and must therefore be taken into account. But, on the other hand, James does not follow up on this opening with a description of the specifically *social* ground of the lived-world – i. e., Those forces ("work, language, power") which determine "interests" and perceptual "perspectives."

Thus, James suffers from a kind of solipsism as a result of his subjective starting-point. Rather than beginning with social experience and moving on to an account of individual consciousness (as do, for example, Marx and Mead), James' method is to attempt to generate an analysis of social experience out of the structures of intra-subjective life. He does not, I have argued, succeed in this attempt, since social experience is a *condition* and not a consequence of personal consciousness. To bring James' analysis of lived experience to a full appreciation of intersubjectivity, it appears that it would be necessary to supplement his intra-subjective descriptions with a *social* theory based upon the work of Mead and Marx. James opens the door to a social critique of the life-world, but he does not pass through.

(4) James' Theory of Conceptions

There is yet another strain that runs through James' writings and which is relevant to the problem of intersubjectivity. In an essay of 1897 on "Human Immortality," James speaks of "an invincible blindness from which we suffer, an insensibility to the inner significance of alien lives . . ." And yet, he goes on, others (including animals and perhaps even plants) "realize themselves with the acutist internality, with the most violent thrills of life." But how can we know this to be the case? As James points out repeatedly, "our private power of sympathetic vibration with other lives gives out so soon . . .,"[52] that we do not recognize the inner lives of others. James, however, states that his comments express the "point of view of *all the other individual beings* . . .,"[53] and that point of view is broad enough to include, not only all human minds, but the "inner lives" of all plants and animals as well! How is this possible, given James' views on intersubjectivity as they have been outlined above? James apparently believes that he has moved beyond the purely private "blindness" of human psychology.[54] By critical reflection on our "blindness," James has rendered it thematic and therefore subject to a higher (and self-transcendent?) consciousness. The reflexivity of consciousness, it appears, can take us beyond our purely privatized existence and can put us in touch with others, indeed with "all . . . other individual beings."

But unfortunately, James does not explain how critical reflection is possible; he simply indulges in it. This leaves the phenomenon of intersubjectivity rather mysterious. This follows from James' failure to develop an explicitly social theory of language and other symbol-systems. For to account for the reflexivity of consciousness, as Mead has demonstrated at length, it is necessary to *begin,* not with personal consciousness, but with the social world out of which individual selves arise; and the means by which selves arise is the incorporation of socially defined symbols into individual consciousness via "symbolic interactions" (i. e. social interactions which take place by means of shared symbols such as gestures, words, definitions, rituals, etc.) in which the individual assumes the roles of others and views himself from the standpoint of these assumed roles. We become capable of self-reflection and self-criticism as a result of taking the attitudes of others toward ourselves.[55] Without this sort of explicit social and symbolic analysis of human existence, James' account of intersubjectivity remains ungrounded.

Now there is present in James' philosophy a framework upon which a theory of language and symbolism might be built, although James himself does not carry the project to fruition. In an attempt to account for the sameness which characterizes different experiences (e. g. my recognition of a table on different occasions, my having the same dream over and over, my thinking the same thought again and again), James formulates what I shall call his "theory of conceptions." According to this theory, I can *conceive* of many objects of thought, and these objects may be either perceptual (e. g. tables) or purely ideal (e. g. mermaids and mathematical functions). James defines conception as "neither the mental state nor what the mental state signifies, but the relation between the two, namely, the *function* of the mental state in signifying just that particular thing."[56] In other words, the conception of an object is the *meaning* of the object, is the way in which a thought *means* ("intends") its object. Moreover, conceptions, unlike thoughts and objects, do not change. "Each conception," James states, "... eternally remains what it is, and never can become another." For example, a piece of white paper which is scorched black does not affect "my conception 'white'," which remains what it is independently of perceptual or intellectual alterations of consciousness. "Thus, amid the flux of opinions and of physical things," James goes on, "the world of conceptions, or things intended to be thought about, stands stiff and immutable, *like Plato's Realm of Ideas*."[57]

The quality of sameness in different thoughts or percepts, then, may be explained by what James calls "the principle of constancy in the mind's meanings." On this principle, "'the mind can always intend, and know when it intends, to think of the Same.'"[58] I can recognize the "same" table, the "same" dream, the "same" mermaid because the *conceptions* of those objects are always present in my mind and ready to be *meant* out toward the appropriate appearances.

In support of his theory of conceptions, which is set out in the *Principles,* James returns to the fray in his later essay, "Does Consciousness Exist?," and now, of course, he is armed with his doctrine of pure experience. And, on the basis of this doctrine, he demonstrates that there is a world of objective consciousness which is "nonperceptual" in nature. In order to do this, he "brackets" the world of percepts, for the association of conceptions with percepts (i. e. as "representative of," as "thoughts of," or as "ideas of" percepts) tends to *subjectify* nonperceptual experience. It is James' contention that "nonperceptual experiences have objectivity as well as subjectivity" and that such experiences, like percepts, may be regarded *either* as objects *or* as mental states depending upon the contexts in which they are taken.[59] Conceptions, like percepts, are "bits of pure experience," *thats* which have yet to become *whats*. A conceived room, for example, may be considered as a "thought-of-an-object" or as an "object-thought-of" – it can *function* as both.[60] The important point to notice is that the world of nonperceptual experience, like the world of perceptual experience, is a world in which objects are "intended" by conscious acts by way of conceptions (or *meanings*).

Now it is clear that these *meanings* are the stuff that language and other forms of symbolism are made of. And there is some evidence that James does indeed notice this implication of his theory of conceptions. But from the standpoint of the problem of intersubjectivity, James' view of language leaves a great deal to be desired. He defines language as a "system of *signs,* different from the things signified, but able to suggest them." He then contrasts human language with the sign-systems of some animals (e. g. dogs): Man, says James, "has a deliberate intention to apply a sign to everything."[61] Language is a result of the ability to conceive of "a *sign as such,* apart from any particular import...,"[62] i. e., to recognize the *general function* of signs as tools of signification. In his description of the development of language in the child, James notes the social context of language acquisition, but puts the emphasis upon the "instincts" of "vocalization," "loquacity," and "imitativeness."[63] Human beings, he implies, have a *natural* ability to acquire and use symbolized *meanings*.

Without denying the role of instinct in symbolic behavior, it appears that James' concentration upon the biology of consciousness prevents him from answering a key question concerning lived experience, i. e. *"Where do the meanings by which consciousness intends its objects come from?"* Are they simply innate ideas? That he does not think so is suggested by James' comment that the mind *"gradually comes into possession of a stock of permanent and fixed meanings, ideal objects, or conceptions, some of which are universal qualities, like... black and white..., and some individual things."*[64] But how does this happen? James never answers this question because he never makes the "intersubjective turn" toward a *social* theory of language nor, for that matter, toward social theory as such. Thus, it was left for Mead to carry out the intersubjective implications of James' theory of conceptions. As we have seen, Mead *begins* his analysis of consciousness with the social process of communication and, on that foundation, makes the other an integral part of self-understanding. Intersubjectivity is to be explained in terms of that "meeting of minds" which occurs in "conversation, learning, reading and thinking...," i. e. in "that part of logic which has to do with the technique of communication either with others or with one's self..." It is on the basis of such socio-symbolic interactions and by means of the conceptual symbols of the communicational process that "successful reference to identical objects... by different selves" is possible.[65]

But this is not a paper on Mead. Suffice it to say that Mead's view that the mind and the self are fundamentally *social* in nature makes possible an approach to human intersubjectivity which is impossible for James. For as Mead's work establishes, other minds and selves are *presuppositions* of, and not phenomena to be discovered by, self-consciousness.

Conclusion

James's failure to explain the possibility and nature of intersubjective experience is based upon his failure to develop a socio-symbolic critique of the life-world. And the absence of social theory in James' work is, in turn, a consequence of his fatal methodological move toward the structures of subjective consciousness. It is for this reason that phenomenological interpretations of James' thought, while they are certainly interesting and valuable, cannot develop the needed critique of his intra-subjective approach to experience; for phenomenology, like radical empiricism, operates from within the "subjective turn." This common starting-point is indeed the basis for the current interest in James' philosophy among phenomenologists. But the phenomenological interpreters do not, by and large, take note of the problem of intersubjectivity in radical empiricism.[66] Wilshire, for example, takes James to task for not formulating a completed theory of intentionality, i. e. a theory of the "necessary and internal relation between act of thought and intentional object."[67] Leaving aside the question as to the accuracy of this appraisal, it is clear that Wilshire's central concern is with the relation of consciousness and its objects; he does not raise the question of the relation of one mind to other minds.

As we have seen, without a systematic elucidation of symbols as *social* in nature and therefore as intersubjective, the phenomenon of intersubjectivity and the necessary and internal character of its relational structure cannot be understood. Consciousness is related to consciousness necessarily and internally through language and other communcative symbolisms. There is evidence that Husserl, in his later work, recognized the limitations of the intra-subjective approach to consciousness and made a preliminary attempt to move to the intersubjective level by viewing language as an intrinsically social phenomenon.[68] But the phenomenological tradition, generally, has not successfully extricated itself from the subjectivist cast of Husserl's hitherto published writings and continues to operate within the context of the subjective turn. Thus, James' phenomenological critics are either disturbed (Wilshire) or elated (Wild) with his treatment of intrasubjective consciousness, but do not point out at any length or depth the limitations of James' analysis of intersubjectivity. Edie, for example, has written an essay on James' "philosophical anthropology" without so much as a hint at the absence of social theory in the Jamesian theory of man.[69] Edie is, however, laudatory when it comes to describing James' subjective (and "phenomenological") point of departure.[70] But, of course, a philosophical anthropology without an explicit account of intersubjectivity, without a *social* critique of the life-world, is a deficient (although perhaps creative) theory of man. The corrective of James' philosophy is to be found, not in Husserl, but in Marx; and its fulfillment is to be found, not in Merleau-Ponty, but in Mead.

NOTES

[1] William James, *Essays in Radical Empiricism* (New York and London: Longmans, Green and Co., 1912); William James, *A Pluralistic Universe* (New York and London: Longmans, Green and Co., 1909). These two works are reprinted with an introduction by Richard J. Bernstein (New York: E. P. Dutton and Co., Inc., 1971), p. 25. The pagination of this reprint edition runs through both volumes.

[2] James, *The Principles of Psychology* (1890; New York: Dover Publications, Inc., 1950), I, p. 224.

[3] *Ibid.*, I, pp. 226—227.

[4] James M. Edie, "Notes on the Philosophical Anthropology of William James," in *An Invitation to Phenomenology*, ed. by James M. Edie (Chicago: Quadrangle Books, 1965), p. 121.

[5] James, *Principles of Psychology*, I, p. 258n.

[6] *Ibid.*, I, pp. 289—290.

[7] *Ibid.*, I, p. 226. Italics added.

8 James, *Essays in Radical Empiricism*, pp. 26—28.
9 James, *Principles of Psychology*, I, pp. 238—239.
10 James, *Essays in Radical Empiricism*, pp. 27—28.
11 *Ibid.*, p. 104.
12 *Ibid.*, p. 65.
13 *Ibid.*, pp. 67—68.
14 *Ibid.*, p. 70.
15 *Ibid.*, pp. 69—70.
16 *Ibid.*, p. 42.
17 James M. Edie, "William James and Phenomenology," *The Review of Metaphysiscs*, XXIII, No. 3 (March, 1970), 509—519.
18 James does not, in this context, attempt to explain this distinction; he simply treats it as "given" in the stream of consciousness. This is one aspect of his nascent theory of intentionality which has aroused so much interest of late in some quarters of the philosophical establishment. See Edie, "William James and Phenomenology," pp. 481—526; John Wild, *The Radical Empiricism of William James* (New York: Doubleday and Co., Inc., 1969); and Bruce Wilshire, *William James and Phenomenology: a Study of "The Principles of Psychology"* (Bloomington: Indiana University Press, 1968).
19 James, *Principles of Psychology*, I, p. 296.
20 *Ibid.*, I, p. 371.
21 *Ibid.*, I, pp. 339—340.
22 *Ibid.*, I, p. 341n.
23 *Ibid.*, I, p. 331.
24 *Ibid.*, I, p. 333.
25 "Whenever my introspective glance succeeds in turning around quickly enough to catch one of these manifestations of spontaneity in the act, all it can ever feel distinctly is some bodily process, for the most part taking place within the head" (*Ibid.*, I, p. 300. James' italics deleted). "In a sense, then, it may be truly said that ... the 'Self of selves,' when carefully examined, is found to consist mainly of the collection of these peculiar motions in the head or between the head and throat. ... [And] it would follow that our entire feeling of spiritual activity, or what commonly passes by that name, is really a feeling of bodily activities whose exact nature is by most men overlooked" (*Ibid.*, I, pp. 301—302; James' italics deleted). See also James' interesting discussion of the relation between consciousness and breathing in *Essays in Radical Empiricism*, pp. 21—22.
26 James, *Principles of Psychology*, I, p. 324.
27 *Ibid.*, I, p. 344.
28 James, *Essays in Radical Empiricism*, p. 42.
29 *Ibid.*, p. 43.

30 *Ibid.*, pp. 43—44; italics added.
31 *Ibid.*, pp. 45—46.
32 James, *Principles of Psychology*, I, p. 610.
33 *Ibid.*, I, pp. 608—610.
34 *Ibid.*, I, p. 642.
35 *Ibid.*, I, p. 631.
36 *Ibid.*, I, p. 643.
37 Wild, *The Radical Empiricism of William James*, p. 172.
38 James, *Principles of Psychology*, I, p. 291.
39 *Ibid.*, I, pp. 288—289.
40 *Ibid.*, I, p. 284.
41 In *The Principles of Psychology*, James outlines seven of the "most important sub-universes": (1) the world of perceptual experience: (2) the world of scientific objects (e. g., atoms, electrons, etc.); (3) the world of "logical, mathematical, metaphysical, ethical, ... aesthetic propositions"; (4) the world of common sense; (5) the world of supernaturalism and mythology; (6) the world of individual opinions; and (7) the world of madness; II, pp. 292—293.
42 *Ibid.*, II, pp. 288—289. Following Brentano, James distinguishes between conception ("imagining a thing") and belief. An object of thought (conception) "may exist as something quite distinct from the belief in its reality" (*Ibid.*, II, p. 286). Belief is an "acquiescence" in the existence of the object thought of (*Ibid.*, II, p. 283).
43 *Ibid.*, II, p. 293.
44 *Ibid.*, II, pp. 296—297.
45 *Ibid.*, II, p. 301.
46 As both McDermott and Wilshire have noticed, James' later writings on "pragmatism" are developments of his early explorations into the lifeworld and the lived-body of concrete experience. See John J. McDermott, "Introduction" to *The Writings of William James*, ed. John J. McDermott (New York: Random House, 1967), p. xxxiv; and Wilshire, *William James and Phenomenology*, p. 19.
47 James, *Essays in Radical Empiricism*, p. 107.
48 Edie's phrase, "William James and Phenomenology," p. 508.
49 James, *Principles of Psychology*, I, p. 482. James' italics deleted.
50 Jürgen Habermas, *Knowledge and Human Interests* (Boston: Beacon Press, 1971), p. 313.
51 James, *Essays in Radical Empiricism*, p. 102.
52 William James, *The Will to Believe and Other Essays in Popular Philosophy* (1897; Dover Publications, Inc., 1956), Appendix, pp. 37—40.
53 *Ibid.*, p. 42. Italics added.

54 He makes the same move in another essay of 1899, "On a Certain Blindness in Human Beeings," in *The Writings of William James*, McDermott, ed., pp. 629 ff.
55 George Herbert Mead, *Mind, Self and Society* (Chicago: University of Chicago Press, 1934), *passim*.
56 James, *Principles of Psychology*, I, p. 461.
57 *Ibid.*, I, p. 462. Italics added.
58 *Ibid.*, I, p. 459. James' italics deleted.
59 James, *Essays in Radical Empiricism*, pp. 10—12.
60 *Ibid.*, p. 14.
60 James, *Principles of Psychology*, II, p. 356. James' italics deleted.
62 *Ibid.*, II, p. 357.
63 *Ibid.*, II, pp. 357—358; 407—411.
64 *Ibid.*, II, p. 644. Italics added.
65 George Herbert Mead, *The Philosophy of the Act* (Chicago: University of Chicago Press, 1938), pp. 52—53.
66 Wild, it is true, goes to torturous lengths to save James from his subjectivism. "My existence," Wild states, "is not enclosed within the limits of an atomic self or substance. I exist in the groups to which I belong, and in the 'relation' of love, my entire 'organic' being exists in the person of the loved." This statement comes at the end of a passage in which Wild discusses James' notion of the "social self." *The Radical Empiricism of William James*, pp. 80—84. This *is* the closest James gets to an authentically social theory of self; he deals with the imagery of oneself in the "minds" of others, and suggests that his imagery is created by our own actions as we act out roles in the various groups to which we belong. *But* there is no analysis of the role of symbols in this context, nor does James deal with role-playing as explicitly interactional. Human relations remain external. *Principles of Psychology*, I, pp. 293—296.
67 Bruce W. Wilshire, *William James: The Essential Writings* (New York: Harper and Row, Publishers, 1971), p. liv and *passim*.
68 Donn Curtis Welton, "The Temporality of Meaning: A Critical Study of the Structure of Meaning and Temporality in Husserl's Phenomenology" (Unpublished Doctoral Dissertation, Southern Illinois University, Carbondale, 1973), pp. 273—281.
69 Edie, "Notes on the Philosophical Anthropology of William James," *passim*.
70 *Ibid.*, p. 121.

NOTES ON THE SEARCH
FOR A MORAL PHILOSOPHY IN WILLIAM JAMES

Abraham Edel

For a philosopher who constantly breathes a moral outlook, there is admittedly little direct discussion of moral theory in Williams James's work. "The Moral Philosopher and the Moral Life" is, of course, the chief exception. Its deceptively diffuse but actually tight-packed pages carry us farther than we may think, but much less than we need or hope. Beyond that we have to look elsewhere. And we have to look with caution, for James himself warns us that "no philosophy of ethics is possible in the old-fashioned absolute sense of the term."[1] Omissions on James's part may therefore turn out to be deliberate and we must look for what it is in his philosophy that rules out such components of a moral theory.

What might a present-day philosopher expect to find in a fully spread-out moral philosophy? Let me suggest at least the following, which constitute in effect a reflective reckoning with the diverse components of a morality and its relation to a general philosophy:

1. A cognitive orientation on man and his world – the metaphysical, scientific and epistomological background of moral thought.
2. A conception of the scope of morality – for example, whether it is universalistic and covers all mankind or local in one or another familiar pattern of national, racial, kin or familial, and so forth.
3. An analysis of basic moral concepts, such as good, obligation, virtue, etc.
4. An analysis of the forms of moral judgment, such as the place of moral "laws", the types of rule that are possible, etc.

5. An analysis of justification, verification or validation for moral judgments.
6. A consideration of the human feelings[2] that operate in moral processes.
7. A consideration of the sanctions that a morality invokes for the development and maintenance of its pattern.
8. An evaluative consideration of modes of decision in morality, and ways of dealing with moral problems.
9. A study of the kind of integration or patterning to be found in morality.

Of course, such a check-list may be constructed in other ways. For example, some would look for the "data" of ethics or the "moral phenomena" as a separate heading; here they would be found under 3 and 6–8. Again, there are questions about the psychology and history of morality itself, including explanatory accounts of how morality functions in the individual and society, whether moral formulations are in individual or social terms, whether historically there has been "moral progress" and so forth. Such questions about morality itself would constitute part of the cognitive orientation – the view of man and the world and its operations in which morality is enmeshed.

It may be said that I am simply presenting my own view of what moral philosophy is[3] and asking how much James contributes along its lines. But such a procedure would be sanctioned by James himself. For he says of the moral philosopher that his purpose is an ideal of his own, to get the ideals he finds existing in the world into a certain unified form.[4] My present paper is guided by the hypothesis that there is much more to be elicited from James for the understanding of pragmatic moral philosophy that we have been prone to think, that much more of the basis that was articulated in Dewey's fuller work – in spite of differences – should be assigned to James. Studies of James's ethics, such as Brennan's and Roth's[5] have stressed largely the cognitive orientation, metaphysical and epistomological, as well as bringing out the values and virtues that emanate from the cognitive orientation. I want to look, if possible, for James's technical answers to technical questions of moral philosophy, extorted if necessary from his studied disparagement of the technical. How often, for example, does he pour out a whole is of examples which, if we stop to examine them carefully, encapsulate a history of the development of the subject or a rich diversity of phenomena in which a common lesson suddenly emerges. Take, for instance, his short paragraph on the various essences of good.[6] Or compare the way he throws together scattered phenomena to make a point: love of drunkenness, bashfulness, terror of high places, ... the passion for poetry, for mathematics, for metaphysics.[7] Nietzsche would have written at least an exuberant essay for each paragraph. Aristotle would have given a systematic characterization (as indeed he does in his *Rhetoric*).

I propose in what follows, therefore, to look first at "The Moral Philosopher and the Moral Life" to see what it yields, and then suggest further directions to go.

I

"The Moral Philosopher and the Moral Life" distinguishes the *psychological, metaphysical,* and *casuistic* questions of ethics.

The psychological question asks about the origin of moral sentiments. James approves the exhibition that many of our secondary moral reactions arise from association with pleasure and pain and from evolutionary development. But he insists that a large assortment comes from purely inward forces, that higher ideals are revolutionary and oriented toward the future rather than lessons of the past. This is part and parcel of his familiar cognitive orientation of the individual as constantly creative.

The metaphysical question concerns the analysis of "good," "ill," "obligation." Here he offers a simplified model for the entry of value in the universe. It would be absent in a purely inorganic world and appears only with the occurrence of consciousness in a sentient being. First he posits a "moral solitude" of one individual, in which "so far as he feels anything to be good, he makes it good."[8] Problems arise when a second individual is introduced and there is conflict. Consciousness develops feelings of right and wrong; obligation is the reaction to a claim actually made by a concrete person, every *de facto* claim creating in so far forth an obligation.[9] In analyzing both goodness and obligation James is concerned with naturalizing them as against theories of *outside* validity, over and beyond the feelings of satisfaction and imperativeness among men. There is no doubt about the primacy of goodness or value in his moral theory. James somewhere speaks of the sober hand of obligation that German philosophers have imposed on us, and in contrast he stresses the character of joyousness at the root of the moral.

But more is involved in his giving the feelings a *prima facie* validity. It expresses the familiar 19th and 20th century individualistic liberalism in which the individual's subjective reaction is the ultimate source of all ethics, and the bulk of moral problems concern the harmonizing of conflicting demands. James's position here is basic also to his later Harvard contemporaries – Santayana and R. B. Perry – who make the point in much greater detail. For Santayana every human impulse and for Perry every interest have already a moral status, and Perry goes so far as to consider love to be an interested support of another's preexisting and independently existing interest, whatever its object.[10]

The casuistic question is that of comparative value, finding a measure for application to decide what should give way to what in solving a moral problem. Denying that there is any essence for good to guide in this, other than simply to satisfy demand, James offers the standard of satisfying as many demands as we can, getting the best whole "in the sense of awakening the least sum of dissatisfactions"[11] and calls on us to invent modes of realizing ideals that satisfy this. He does not, like Santayana in *The Life of Reason,* survey the institutional and cultural ideals for the harmonizing and maximizing of human impulse. Nor like Perry in his *General Theory of Value* does he go into precise analysis of criteria of harmony and integration. Professor Roth has suggested[12] that we should not disparage the sketchy character of James's presentation, because if we look at the date of the essay (it was first published in the April 1891 issue of the *International Journal of Ethics*) we can see its ground-breaking character as compared to these later elaborations. This is indeed true. But of course James was not the first to state the individualistic liberalism. Bentham had accompanied it a century earlier with the hedonic calculus, and the theory of maximization of pleasures already had strong economic foundations.

I suspect that we would be missing James's point in such comparison. He is really intent here on only one thing – on showing us that institutions and social forms have *experimental* moral character. He goes on to a quite kaleidoscopic view of social forms,[13] with a glance at the risks in experimental departure from established ways – a man must not fear "to stake his life and character upon the throw."[14] And he concludes[15] that "All this amounts to saying that, so far as the casuistic question goes, ethical science is just like physical science, and instead of being deducible all at once from abstract principles, must simply bide its time, and be ready to revise its conclusions from day to day." Here he reckons with abstract rules as aids, but not more, for "every real dilemma is in literal strictness a unique situation; and the exact combination of ideals realized and ideals disappointed which each decision creates is always a universe without a precedent, and for which no adequate previous rule exists."[16] Having thus disposed of rules, he ends with virtue, distinguishing the easy-going and the strenuous mood.

I suspect that Peirce, with the same respect for the particular situation would be more appreciative of the cumulative character of knowledge in the long run. And Dewey not merely shares the uniqueness of good in each situation and the experimental character of institutions, but studies the specific areas of human experience from which we can get light and aid for our moral decisions. Even more importantly, Dewey applies his psychology to see the problematic character of desire, impulse, and interest, so that each individual demand cannot so blithely assert itself as moral without having its credentials investigated. James recognizes[17] that even in a moral solitude the lone consciousness can compare the ideals expressing its demands and desires for greater pungency and consistency, for regrets they may generate. But Dewey goes further: he sees the desire as a proposed means to resolving an underlying problem or concern. Hence, in effect, demands and claims become starting-points for analysis and evaluation rather than moral atoms for casuistry. Reconstruction and experiment can thus go beyond even the scope that James envisaged.

This is, however, an extension that is not our present concern. Let us then revert to our check-list. James's central essay on moral philosophy has dealt with a fair range. It touched on the implications of cognitive orientation (1), it offered a schema for analysis of two major moral concepts (3), it at least rejected laws as the form of moral judgment in favor of individual moral judgments expressing unique situations (4), it proclaimed the experimental character of moral validation (5), it projected the basic place of feelings (6) though it did not examine which did the heavy work of morality. It remains a sketch, mostly a bare sketch, but significant because it was plunging into fresh directions. Where then shall we look for more?

II

One direction furnishes a temptation to be avoided. It might be said that James's treatment of moral philosophy seems limited precisely because it is pervasive: we do not note it because it is everywhere! For does he not define truth as what proves to be good in the way of belief? Hence all discussion of epistemology is grist to our moral mill.

Yes and no. James is, of course, a pioneer in calling attention to the value-base of science and of rationality, not merely in its focus and selection of problems, but in its criteria of judgment of adequacy in results. In some respects this has become commonplace by this time – that there is a pragmatic base of human purposes of order and control underlying decision among different theoretical approaches. James perhaps put it over-subjectively, leading some philosophers to talk as if rationality were simply an arbitrary emotional commitment. But in any case, these values underlying rationality are much wider than morality. They constitute a purposive set, as wide as Münsterberg's "eternal values" in his book of that name, which are presupposed in the very idea of a world as the object of knowledge. Morality, whatever it is, is something less than that.

Our search in James's work has therefore to be more focused than to his epistemology generally. This means looking specifically for his contributions to moral philosophy in his psychological work and in his writings on religion. Both of these would seem to be contributing to the cognitive orientation for morality, and indeed they do. But they also provide materials and suggestions for the other specific questions of moral philosophy. Let us take as illustrations in what follows, three of the components not touched on or barely touched above: the scope of morality (2); the theory of virtue (3) which was not analyzed by him in the essay we explored, but which we should have expected to accompany goodness and obligation; and the theory of decision-making (8).

III

We sense at many points in James that his view of the moral community is, like Kant's, universalistic. There are two sides to such a conception. One is the positive recognition that every person counts. James's argument that utilitarianism cannot be correct is expressed in the intuition that if millions were to be kept permanently happy at the expense of a certain lost soul leading a life of lonely torture on the far-off edge of things (Is this an echo of Prometheus bound?) it would be a hideous thing.[18] There is also the negative side, that in order to enter a world community the individual has in some sense to loosen the bonds of family, kin, nation, etc. – anything less than the whole of mankind. These may impose special obligations, but they no longer define the human being. The universalistic moral community involves thus the shedding of narrower qualifications as the essence of a person. James, in his opposition to an imperialistic turn of nationalism, clearly showed his universalistic attitude.

Now where in James do we find a conception of man which shows us how to focus on the all-human and set aside the differences? Surprisingly, (or not surprisingly?) the topic arises in the last chapter of the *Psychology*. He is examining the rise of categories and general precepts, denying they come in the front-door of associated experiences, grappling with oversimplified view of brain structure, finding the principles to be surreptitiously born in the house of man's thought, analyzing the activity of discerning differences and similarities in comparison and the generation of classes in the activity of the mind. In this context of constructive activity not wholly dictated by outside impression he turns at last to aesthetic and moral principles. He takes judgments of justice or equity[19] and traces the dawn of such a principle as that "nothing can be right for me which would not be right for another similarly placed." It is not instinct, for that makes us judge differently for ourselves, nor empirical conclusion, for we see others behaving in an equally self-centered fashion. The dawn of the universal judgment overturns the habitual. It is a question of how we classify ourselves with other men. We come to pass over the differences, and recognize that if what we have in common is our essence, we should be mutually substitutable in moral judgment. "The more fundamental and common the essence chosen, and the more simple the reasoning, the more wildly radical and unconditional will the justice be which is aspired to."[20] Note that he has not asserted our common essence, but argued from "if these things be our essence."[21] For he is equally sensitive to the demands of the particular situation. He goes on: "Life is one long struggle between conclusions based on abstract ways of conceiving cases, and opposite conclusions prompted by our instinctive perception of them as individual facts." Sometimes the abstract treatment is the better way, sometimes it is morally useful to treat the concrete case as *sui generis*.

This concern for the particular is not of course rejecting the concern for justice. To respect a person as a person also involves respecting what is different about him, and what he finds important. And James is not merely sensitive to differences but also to the fact that it is precisely when we classify things together that we begin to look for differences, just as when we classify them as different that we begin to look for similarities.

That James adhered to the universalism of the moral community is, of course, perfectly clear from his usual setting of the lone individual on the frontier of decision as the moral situation. What is significant about James's discussion here, however, is the recognition that the principle of universality is a *human construction* built up by people with the same processes that take place in all their thinking.[22] A philosopher more attentive to the social and historical setting of our ideas would see it on a social scale as expressive of a generally growing one world. But he would share with James the constructed character of the principle in human life and thought, and so the methodological pragmatic lesson that moral principles are to be understood in the whole fullness of relation to how men operate in the formation of thought and feeling.

IV

Our second brief illustration raises the question of the theory of virtue. The concept was not analyzed alongside of goodness and obligation in the essay we examined, but the essay ended in a contrast of the easy-going and the strenuous mood – a basic point of character of the self as a whole. Now since a virtue is, in the old definition, a state of character, we should expect to find some treatment of it in the *Psychology*. We do – a bit. The chapter on "Habit" (Vol. I, Ch. IV) has scattered references to good and bad habits. But although he does not underemphasize the importance of habits, as (he says) a chapter in physics,[23] James's heart is less in habit than on fashioning and modifying habit and making it an ally instead of an enemy.

The treatment of attention (Vol. I, Ch. XI) and that of will (Vol. II, Ch. XXVI) seem more promising, especially when James gives rich sketches of types of will, and focuses finally on effort of attention as the core phenomenon of will, the attention being directed to an idea. Will is thus seen as a relation between the self and its states of mind. By regarding the effort as an independent variable,[24] he is able to formulate a theory of free will, supported in Kantian fashion as a presupposition of obligation being meaningful. This leads to his well-known statement that "Freedom's first deed should be to affirm itself."[25] Such a sense of freedom brings James to what he regards as basic in one's attitude to the world. It is a courageous, even heroic, coming to terms with the world. In so facing it a man becomes "one of the masters and the lords of life. He must be counted with henceforth; he forms a part of human destiny."[26] And by our responses our effort measures our worth as men.

This is not an elaborated theory of virtue, but it is clearly a psychological foundation for it. James, given this basis, cannot be expected to list fixed traits in the style of Aristotle's virtues. He is more like Augustine, or Kant for that matter, in whose ethics virtue is a constant effort of the total self. Dewey's conception of virtue has the same dynamic whole-self character in that (in his *Theory of the Moral Life*) he looks to the features of the pursuit of interest rather than character items. His basis is, however, broadened, including not only the psychologically unified nature of the self but the historical change of content in specific virtues, and the institutional reference in human character-formation, as well as the broad recognition of constant change in human life.

For James's fuller picture of virtue, writ large in action, we have to go to his writings on religion. They are too familiar to be recapitulated here. A constant theme running through all the essays included in *The Will to Believe and Other Essays in Popular Philosophy*, as well as in *The Varieties of Religious Experience* is the difference between an energetic optimism and a pessimistic indifference. There is thus a clear continuity between the picture of man in the *Psychology* as selecting, discriminating, constructing, guided by purposes in cognitive and practical activity alike, building and maintaining and testing and refining a world, and the active willing of a world in which effort counts.

It is, of course, not surprising that so much of the writing on religion should be ethical in character. For James is one of the notable heirs of the great Kantian reversal in the relation of religion and ethics. Once Kant had set going explicitly the view that our religious ideas are reached through our moral consciousness, not as independent cognitions to which morality is then made to conform, it was a short step for a pragmatic treatment to assume that religious beliefs are to be actively fashioned in the light of moral demands – in the sense of required attitudes to the world and life. (Hence, for example, comes James's experimentation with the idea of a finite God.) James does not, however, carry it as far as Dewey or Santayana, who see religion, respectively, as a quality of feeling and as a cultural language or system of symbols for the moral ordering of life.

V

Our last example is in the theory of moral decision. This is different from justification or verification of moral judgments which might provide lessons of experience to be used for decision. It refers rather to the ways of resolving a moral problem in the actual context of making up one's mind what to do and how to act. James's fullest treatment of this question is to be found in the essay "The Will to Believe." Its general ethical import is sometimes overlooked because it is classified in the religious context to which he was applying it. But, as we have seen, religion in his pragmatic view is ethically oriented, and the discussion in that essay can – when divorced from the specific context – be seen to constitute a general model for situations involving risk and insufficient knowledge, one of the central areas of contemporary decision theory now being highly metricized.

The model needs little recapitulation here. It does not refer to choices where evidence can settle the problem or is available on further inquiry, although it may conceivably be applied to individual cases of present unavoidable decision where there is no time for further inquiry. James describes the features of a situation of choice which call for the model. The options or alternatives must be living, not dead; they must, he says, make some appeal to your belief. They must be forced, not avoidable: that is, not to choose at all is equivalent in its effect to choosing one of the options. (To ask whether I will enjoy going to a theatre as a basis for going or not going, and not to make up one's mind, is equivalent to not going.) The option must, in terms of the differential consequences, be momentous, not trivial: in an extreme case, the result is life or death, war or peace. James calls an option genuine when it is forced, living, and momentous. It should be added that though he speaks of the options as beliefs, belief and action are close on his view. In any case, an action is in such a question dictated by the beliefs (including value judgments) on which it rests.

Now James's decision procedure in such cases is to let our "passional nature" decide between the options, and he gives a vivid picture of the rising ladder of self-conviction from the perhaps to the must. This suggests to many the arbitrary holding of belief on emotional grounds. This is not, of course, what James meant, for he argued in "The Sentiment of Rationality" that our passional nature likewise underlies the quest for rationality and scientific knowledge. What is needed in order to avoid misunderstanding is a more precise reckoning with which passional elements or basic human purposes the use of the method is compatible. There is also need for a classification of types of contexts of possible use. James often argues for the plastic character of the situation in which the model is applied – areas in which the beliefs help create the fact. This clearly suits some fields (for example, self-fulfilling judgments where confidence helps determine the result) and not others, where over-optimism or over-pessimism may face a stubborn fact.

The character of the model is perhaps best seen in medical or political problems. Medical emergencies obviously may dictate trying out uncertain remedies in dire cases, where the alternative of inaction might spell death – even apart from cases where the fact of continued effort may build the patient's will to live. In international politics, a "cold war" situation clearly fits the model: each side bristles with mistrust of the other and sets as criteria of proof of good faith steps equivalent to surrender. A will to believe that the other side is ready for more peaceful relations (even though coupled with caution) may itself be the decisive factor in breaking the impasse and releasing forces for peace. James himself gives enough human illustrations. My point is not to evaluate his model of decision here, but to recognize that he is moving in a domain of inquiry that has since been subject to stern logical analysis, once it is regarded as a hypothesis for a mode of moral decision. And he is tackling it at its hardest point – not the easier job where probabilities are applied to groups in a frequency interpretation, but the singular situation in which differences of values and particular contexts coupled with probabilities will lead to different choices. For this is of greatest importance to an ethics which insists on the uniqueness of particular cases.

VI

Even with all the different directions in which we have looked, James's moral philosophy remains sketchy. I have no doubt that further scanning could produce material on the subtle human emotions and feelings that enter into morality (for example, his highlighting of regret in "The Dilemma of Determinism" or his occasional debunking of a frothy sympathy that issues in no action), and of the sanctions that operate in human conduct. However, none of the items in our initial check-list is without some material. Let me conclude with some remarks on the first (1) and the last (9) – the cognitive orientation and the kind of integration or patterning to be found in morality.

There has been no need to discuss the question of cognitive orientation because so much of James's work fits into it. His whole psychology is both background and foreground for his ethics. It is as close as Bentham's hedonistic psychology is to his moral theory, or Plato's picture of human nature is to his moral and social conceptions. The central difference between the ethics of James and Dewey is to be located in this area. Dewey went on to find room in his psychology for the growth of the social sciences, and the outcome was a formulation of moral theory in social terms: morality itself is regarded as basically a social phenomenon, and individuality itself as a moral aim. These differences, great as they are, do not alter their community in a pragmatic outlook. They do, however, mean their going in different directions with respect to the unity or patterning to be found in morality.

The unity that James finds in morality is not thus one of social development but of individual frontier decision. It is a unity – strangely strong for a metaphysical pluralist – that sees the individual somewhat alone, and capable of creative action, on the perilous edge. All James's ethics seems intended to equip this individual to face this ultimate battle. Whether this is a fair account of human life, or a myth to sharpen our perception of the more customary social reality, is not a question we can here pursue.

Finally, whether the kind of search I have suggested will yield a comprehensive moral philosophy in James – one that gives technical answers to technical questions – cannot be answered merely on the basis of pointing a direction. I am confident, however, that it would show a straighter line between James and the mainstream of pragmatic ethics. James did more than clear the grounds and leave to Mead, Dewey, C.I. Lewis and others to do the planting. In any case, we can reap the harvest.

NOTES

1 William James, "The Moral Philosopher and the Moral Life" in *The Will to Believe and Other Essays in Popular Philosophy* (New York: Longmans, Green and Company, 1897; Dover paperback edition, 1956), p. 209.
2 James, of course, opposes the old faculty psychology that would distinguish sharply cognitions, intuitions, and feelings. For him these are instrumental distinctions for which there might be alternatives.
3 See May and Abraham Edel, *Anthropology and Ethics*, rev. ed. (Cleveland: The Press of Case Western Reserve University, 1968), and Abraham Edel, *Method in Ethical Theory* (Indianapolis: The Bobbs-Merrill Company, 1963), Chapter IX.
4 James, "The Moral Philosopher and the Moral Life," p. 181.
5 Bernard P. Brennan, *The Ethics of William James* (New York: Bookman Associates, 1961); John K. Roth, *Freedom and the Moral Life: The Ethics of William James* (Philadelphia: The Westminster Press, 1969).
6 James, "The Moral Philosopher and the Moral Life," p. 200.
7 *Ibid.*, pp. 186—187.
8 *Ibid.*, p. 190.
9 *Ibid.*, p. 195.
10 George Santayana, *The Life of Reason* (New York: Charles Scribner's Sons, 1905); Ralph Barton Perry, *General Theory of Value* (New York: Longmans, Green and Company, 1926), p. 677 f.
11 James, "The Moral Philosopher and the Moral Life," p. 205.
12 In conversation, discussing the present paper.
13 James, "The Moral Philosopher and the Moral Life," pp. 205—208.
14 *Ibid.*, p. 206.
15 *Ibid.*, p. 208.
16 *Ibid.*, p. 209.
17 *Ibid.*, p. 191.
18 *Ibid.*, p. 188.

[19] William James, *The Principles of Psychology* (Henry Holt and Company, 1890), II, p. 673.
[20] *Ibid.*, II, p. 674.
[21] In any case, he does not believe in fixed essences. Cf. *ibid.*, II, p. 325. What is essential is relative to purposes.
[22] See the treatment of characteristics distinguishing man from animals in the chapter on "Reasoning," *ibid.*, II, pp. 348—369.
[23] *Ibid.*, I, p. 105.
[24] *Ibid.*, II, p. 571.
[25] *Ibid.*, II, p. 573.
[26] *Ibid.*, II, p. 579.

14

WILLIAM JAMES' THEORY OF EDUCATION

John Albin Broyer

It is generally agreed that William James has made a lasting contribution to human knowledge by way of the fertility and originality of his insights. To argue that James produced no system, and that inconsistencies may be discovered does little to damage the value of his contribution. Rather, it testifies to the originality and perpetual open mindedness of James' investigation. And James himself advanced the doctrines of "radical empiricism" which holds that we live in and know a pluralistic universe,[1] and "pragmatism" which holds that truth is situational and evolutionary.[2]

One way to understand William James is to see him as he saw himself, namely as a mediating figure, bridging the gaps between (1) what he identifies as the two great classical traditions of speculative philosophy ("Idealism" and "Materialism," or "Intellectualists" and "Sensationalists"), and (2) the unique new perspective created by the application of experimental science to the understanding of human behavior. His personal biography as well as his writings display examples of unsystematic wanderings which inevitably accompany an ambitious attempt to come to grips with a radically new situation on its own terms. This inconsistency is not indicative of shoddy scholarship or insufficient intellect to cope with the problem, but rather is the result of his perception of the plurality that constitutes experience, his lack of categories adequate to express the new, and his unwillingness to apply old category systems which failed, as he saw it, to correspond to the new state of affairs. James left a large fund of insights which served and still serve as rich resources for subsequent investigation.

His theory of education, like the other features of his philosophy, ventures to pioneer new ground, contending that a rough sketch of new lands at hand is at least as important as the most ornate diagrams of frequently traveled regions. For convenience, our considerations of James' theory of education will be divided into four parts. First, we shall consider the extent to which James is concerned with the problems of education, and with the interrelationships he sees among philosophy, psychology, and practical experience in forming an adequate theory of education. Second, we will outline educational implications of James' resolution of various classical problems of philosophy. Third, we will develop a statement of James' psychology of education, following his own method of moving from a general psychological principle to the derivation of its educational implications. Fourth, we will close with some critical comments which might help one to evaluate James' theory of education in the perspective of some subsequent historical developments.

James and the Problems of Education

For 35 years, from his appointment in 1872 until his retirement in 1907, James was an able and popular teacher of physiology, psychology, and philosophy at Harvard University. He was deeply and directly concerned with the problems of education. George Santayana recalled that James "believed in improvisation, even in thought; his lectures were not minutely prepared. Know your subject thoroughly, he used to say, and trust to luck for the rest."[3] However, James was very concerned with the problem of effective teaching, and with developing philosophical and psychological principles of a theory of education which would make that possible. His most explicit publications on the problems of education are found in three works: the two volume *Principles of Psychology*, published in 1890; *Psychology*, published in 1892; and *Talks to Teachers*, written in 1892 and published in 1899. These form a relatively consistent and organized block of writings. Our analysis here of his theory of education will draw heavily on these works. In addition, educational implications may be found throughout his general philosophical writings.

As early as 1876, James was dealing with the problem of defining the aims of education, when he suggested that education seeks "wider openness of mind and a more flexible way of thinking...."[4] James saw both education and philosophy as serving to promote the development of a person's distinct individuality, and aiding in the search for meaning in life. It is around these values of individuality and meaning that James built his theory of education. And it may be argued that these values remained essentially constant throughout James' intellectual career, thus giving a consistency to the content of his long span of educational theorizing. Since these values of individuality and meaning also seem to be central to the development of James' general philosophy, they appear to suggest strongly the connection and integrity of his theory of education to his general philosophy.

James' individualism was rooted both in his own personality and in his philosophical convictions. Horace Kallen has observed that the most "particular devotion" and "most precious value" James held was "individuality: it is novelty and variation and difference of whatever kind."[5] For it is from the novelty, variation, and difference of individuals that life draws its interest and society draws its progress. Above all, philosophy, psychology, and education must serve to preserve and promote individualism. In his philosophy, this principle of individuality became his doctrine of "pluralism," that the world contains real variety, which makes an adequate closed metaphysical system impossible. James believed that "There is no point of view absolutely public and universal," and that as a consequence one must respect "the sacredness of individuality."[6] We must respect pluralism in individual persons as well as throughout the universe. We must be cautious of the influence of institutions, including education. Institutions tend to be based on points of likeness among people. James wants to stress the constructive value of differences between people. Psychologists and educators must learn to study, accept, and help to enrich the variety of individual experience in many diverse areas such as religion, employment, and life style. James says "Hands off: neither the whole truth nor the whole good is revealed to any single observer."[7]

James also valued highly the achievement of meaning in life. As with his value of individuality, this quest for meaning was rooted both in his own personality and in his philosophical convictions. Horace Kallen has remarked that James finally attained "a new sense of his place in the world..." after a long and painful search for meaning in his life, and that "What healed him was the attainment of his philosophy."[8] Philosophy is the search for meaning in life, and as such, there is nothing more important in life than having an adequate philosophy. Education is an instrument for learning and relating meanings. Therefore, the test of a philosophy and of a theory of education are similar: do they work in practice to increase the range and depth of meanings in our life? James wrote of a "Certain Blindness in Human Beings," which is our tendency to pronounce as meaningless "forms of existence other than our own."[9] We need to *see* that other people have value meanings which may differ from our own. We need to accept and respect these differences of value meaning as legitimate in our pluralistic universe. We need to establish a creative interchange between our present value meanings and the diverse value meanings of other people, for it is from the unfamiliar perspective that we can learn something new. Psychologists and educators can help us to achieve a more meaningful life through aiding us to overcome our blindness to the value meanings of other people.

James was a scientist by training, and he invited his students to adopt the "biological conception" of man,[10] rather than the traditional speculative perspective. He helped to introduce the scientific approach to the study of psychology and of education. It is clear, however, that his main interest was in the *principles* of psychology and of education, and that this is eventually a philosophical concern. For James, philosophy and science need not be in conflict, and philosophy need not produce a closed system in our pluralistic universe. When James decided to accept an appointment in Biology at Harvard University, he wrote in his diary, on February 10, 1873, that "Philosophy I will nevertheless regard as my vocation and never let slip a chance to do a stroke at it."[11] It seems that James continued to regard philosophy as his permanent vocation throughout his career, and it appears reasonable to include James' psychology and his theory of education as parts of James' overall philosophy.

Philosophical Principles of Education

Having considered the general context of James' concern for educational theory, we will now look at his views of the philosophical principles of education. Because he did not advocate constructing closed philosophical systems, it seems most appropriate to outline his overall philosophical position, as it is relevant to educational theory, in terms of six organizing insights, drawn from his response to several traditional problems of philosophy.

The first question at issue is James' concept of experience. He recognized two dominant historical definitions of experience, the "spiritualist" and the "associationist." The former interpreted Real experience as that of universals; changing empirical data appeared as an inferior shadow of the universal. The latter interpreted experience as the reception of discrete atomic sensations, giving as such no clew of relation, and therefore branded proposed relations as artificial. The "spiritualists" would see my dog Fido as an imperfect appearance of the universal essence Dog from which Fido gains his relative identity. The "associationists" would speak of sensations such as warm, brown, or barking, from which I infer the presence of a constructed Fido. James "rejects both..." of these theories of experience.[12] James claims that there is a primitive reality or "givenness" of Fido himself. The Fido that I experience is neither appearance nor inference: Fido is actually Fido. Primary experience is necessarily empirical, inevitably involves perception of qualities and organic relations, and brings the fund of past experience and future purpose to bear in interpreting the present event. Experience is neither of discrete atomic particulars nor of universals, but is the empirical perception of an organic whole out of which attention selects certain characteristics, from which reason may subsequently abstract either universal qualities or particular sense qualities. The "radical empiricism" of primary experience compels one to take change seriously, and suggests the value of the experimental method of investigation. The organic nature of primary experience testifies to continuity, relation, and identity which persists throughout change. An answer is given to the problem of "causality" which puzzled classical empiricists. Here also is a solution to the appearance-reality problem. Echoing the Aristotelian doctrine that there can be no change unless something abides, James observes that the abiding cannot be interesting unless something changes. So it is that "every year must bring its slight modification of last year's suit...."[13] Chaotic caprice and mechanistic determinism are both rejected as metaphysical doctrines. James adopts a process view of reality which, he thinks, combines the attributes of regularity and novelty in relative coexistence. As process *is* primary experience, experience is dynamic, relational, and never finished. Since education claims experience as its subject matter, the radical empiricist view of experience will necessarily require a reconstructed view of education. The fact of change and the fruitfulness of the experimental method in dealing with change become the epistemological groundwork of James' theory of education.

A second philosophical principle of James' theory of education is his view of consciousness and the nature of the self. While his concept of "society" lacks the depth of its contemporary meaning, he conceived of the human organism and its environment as functionally interrelated. This active interrelation is the existential substance of consciousness. James observes that "minds inhabit environments which act on them and on which they in turn react..."[14] The important implication here for education is that learning is not seen as separate from life, but rather as a function related to the life process. James says that the mind "cannot... be regarded as primitive."[15] The self is not an original entity whose essence can merely be drawn out, but rather the self is functionally evolved and created by education, and hence in large measure by teachers. Thus teachers have great moral responsibility, since an effective teacher is a creator of human consciousness and fulfillment in his or her students.

Thirdly, his refusal to make entities of behavioral processes offers an answer to some instances of the problem of universals in education. We do not simply think, but think about some object, i. e. some objective; we do not simply remember, but we remember something. As James says, we need a "cue."[16] In refusing to acknowledge an abstract Reason, Memory, or Consciousness, and so forth as entities apart from behavior, he renders the question meaningless as to what or where is Reason when it is not reasoning about something. Educationally this suggests that pedagogy deals not with abstract faculties, but rather is relating a present stream of behavior toward an end in view. The implicit conclusion is that education equips the student to solve problems, and James says that "the solution of problems is the most characteristic and peculiar sort of voluntary thinking."[17] Educational universals are to be defined in terms of generic types of recurrent problems and generic types of recurrently effective methods of problem solving. Educational universals are not to be defined as the training of the abstract entities of Reason, Memory, or Consciousness, and so forth.

Fourthly, the classic philosophical and educational debate about conceptual categories and about truth is answered when these are seen as teleological rather than ontological issues. A rigid set of *apriori* conceptual categories is rejected in favor of a flexible category system functionally related to one's present purpose. The thing in my hand may really be a walking stick, firewood, or a weapon depending on my purpose. James claims that "All ways of conceiving a concrete fact, if they are true ways at all, are equally true ways. There is no property *absolutely* essential to any one thing."[18] From this observation that conceptual categories are not ontologically *apriori*, it does not follow that categories cannot be useful in interpreting experience. Similarly, James gives "truth" a functional rather than an ontological definition. This is presented in his doctrine of "pragmatism," the view that truth is a function of successfully fulfilled purpose. If truth is made and changes objectively, i. e. relative to objectives in a situation, then educators must teach students to create truth in their own experience. When we act on a fruitful belief as if it were really true, then he says "it will infallibly end by growing into such a connection with our life that it will become real."[19] If, as James suggests, categories are teleological, it follows that one's conceptual system will arise out of one's interests. Our lives will have meaning for us if they have purposes, and purposes are the result of seeking to actualize interests. It is a function of education to give us numerous, broad, and fruitful interests. James says that "neither the old nor the new, by itself, is interesting; the absolutely old is insipid; the absolutely new makes no appeal at all."[20] It is the job of education to relate novelty and continuity so as to produce the interests which give rise to purposes, and thus expands the experience of meaning in our lives.

Fifthly, by his proposing the Law of Diffusion,[21] James rejects the traditional formulation of the body-mind problem, in philosophy and in education. This means that when we act, we act as total organisms, any possible feeling producing a movement, which is a movement more or less of every part of the whole. Mental activity is teleological and demonstrates a "choice of means,"[22] and thus distinguishes it from the "activity" of a rolling stone or the "activity" of elm trees defoliating in fall. James says that unlike other animals, man inherits "no settled instinctive tendencies . . . ." and is able therefore "to settle every novel case by the fresh discovery by his reason of novel principles. He is, *par excellence,* the *educable* animal."[23] But mental activity is inseparable from neurology.

James says that "The causes of our mental structures are doubtless natural, and connected, like all our other peculiarities, with those of our nervous structure."[24] His psychology is therefore behavioral rather than transcendental. Under this view, education is not the training of Mind, but of behavior, and must take into account the total activity of the organism. A behavioral program of education must progressively develop specialized mental activity through relating its ideas or conceptions to resolving what James calls "the largest possible variety of the emergencies of life. A lack of education means only the failure to have acquired them, and the consequent liability to be 'floored' and 'rattled' in the vicissitudes of experience."[25] If this is true, then a fixed subject curriculum is too inflexible. The actual curriculum must adjust itself to the requirements of the particular existential situation. Routine activities may become habitual then, an automatic trained neurological response. James believes that "The great thing, then, in all education, is to make our nervous system our ally instead of our enemy."[26] Here we have a careful and educationally pertinent distinction between the positive and negative functions of habit. When we have made routine behavior habitual, we are free to notice and attend to new and peculiar problems. Only by abolishing the traditional body-mind dualism can education effectively "make automatic and habitual, as early as possible, as many useful actions as (it) can,"[27] since habituation is as much a matter of neurology as of mind. The teacher does not train minds, but instructs habits of behavior. Habits of behavior are useful to the extent that they resolve satisfactorily the wide variety of problematic situations we experience. Therefore an educationally adequate curriculum should deliberately reflect this wide variety of our existential experience.

A sixth philosophical principle relevant to education is his solution of the free will – determinism problem, suggested by his analysis of habit. Traditional philosophy seems to present the alternatives of acknowledging ex-nihilo willed activity in man, or of accepting fatalistic determinism. For James, will can only operate when its *"ex-abrupto"* character is denied.[28] We are "free" to the extent that meaningful alternative possibilities of behavior are present. "Will" is the force of attending to these options, and selecting from our repertoire of knowledge, habits, and associations, that mode of behavior which best fits the case at hand. James says that this freedom depends directly "First, on what the stock of ideas is which we have; and, second, on the habitual coupling of the several ideas with action ...," i. e. the manner in which they are related.[29] It is the business of education to supply these required conditions, and these are the principles which should guide the development of the permanent aspects of an educational curriculum. In so doing, education becomes the prerequisite of an individual's freedom. This is a sufficiently persuasive reason for concern with finding the most effective modes of pedagogy. Further, there is an important moral implication here. If education can make us free to direct the practical course of our lives, then the moral responsibility is ours for increasing good and combating evil within our own spheres of influence. This depends upon the range of our value appreciations, which in turn are supplied by the educative process. In order to will the good we must know the good, or more accurately how to discover the "goods," since there may be several value perspectives present in any moral problem. For James, the teacher's "task is to build up a *character* in (his or her) pupils; – an organized set of habits of reaction."[30] The teacher is an active agent in the pupil's moral development, and thus the teacher plays a critical role in determining the moral character of individuals and the society which they constitute. Good education and good teachers are required conditions of achieving good citizenship. James once approved of the view that when a landlady considers a lodger, it is "important to know his income, but still more important to know his philosophy."[31] Teachers affect directly the character formation of students. When considering a teacher, it is most important to know his philosophy. James thinks that for a person's character and for a country's welfare, "teachers ... have its future in their hands."[32]

Psychological Principles of Education

Having considered some general principles of James' philosophy relevant to educational theory, we will turn to considering James' theory of behavior, and its central position in his philosophy of education. Taking contextual behavior itself as the given experience, metaphysical universals or atomic sense qualities are both seen as constructs not found in immediate existential experience. The "spiritualist" (idealist) and "associationist" (materialist) epistemologies are thus equally faulty; both are incapable of speaking of a process of behavior, the former because it calls change an illusion, the latter because it denies continuity of atomic sense qualities.

Behavior is the epistemological foundation of James' psychology. There *is* activity: the organism thrusts itself upon its environment by impulse, the environment is perceived by the organism. We act, or more properly, "it" acts.[33] The interaction of organism and environment produces experience. Sensation is bare consciousness of particular physical things. Perception is the interrelated association of sensations that we actually experience. Our conscious articulate experience always begins with perception since James thinks that "A pure sensation... (is) an abstraction never realized in adult life."[34] Then we explore the meanings of our experience, based on past experience and developed habits. The novel perception meets this waiting conceptual framework, and consciousness becomes thought. Education is the means through which we seek to deliberately enlarge and make more effective our repetoire of behavior and consequently our thoughts. Thus it is important that teachers understand the psychology of human learning.

Consciousness is a stream of activity which seeks a "perching" spot, a regular channel. It carries with it a learned conceptual scheme. A novel event is perceived, and consciousness takes "flight" in search of a new "perch." We seek consciously to know the meaning of an experience and to discover a solution to its problematic aspects. The new perch can never be identical to the former one, since conceptual experience is cumulative.

Once things are learned, James says that "we are different for having once learned them."[35] Thus learning has an evolutionary effect. These alternative states of flight and perching represent the two facets of the stream of consciousness, which characterizes human behavior. Flight represents movement, process, change, the problem solving part of thought. Perching represents rest, continuity, the substantive part of thought. Flight gives a feeling of relation, perching a feeling of objects. James sees the main use of this flight as the means of "leading us from one substantive conclusion to another."[36] It is this element of flight which most previous epistemological schemes ignored. Flight yields what James terms "knowledge about" (wissen, savoir), when this means a conceptual relationship called meaning. This "knowledge about" is not the images of distinct things, but the identification of implication and relation, the filling of the gaps in perception. Perching yields what James terms "acquaintance with" (kennen, connaître), when this denotes the direct acceptance of given experience.[37] Flight is consciousness focused on what James terms "doubt and inquiry,"[38] perching is "belief" and "affirmation." Each facet requires the other for its completion. Together they exhaustively describe the stream of consciousness; both are subject to empirical study.

The stream of consciousness is present in each of us, its scope and depth depending in part upon the quality of our native perceptual and intellectual potential, and in part upon our education. James sees the former as relatively immune to alteration, particularly in the case of memory which capacity James says "he can never hope to change."[39] Our education, however, is extremely subject to change. Education enters the psychological process at the point where the stream of consciousness becomes selective, attending to some specific phenomena. Once attention has been fixed, the stream of consciousness moves to make the experience meaningful through defining the object of attention with the frame of referential past experience held in memory. Association is the work of joining the new and the old in synthesis, which we earlier called consciousness in flight. An experience is meaningful to us to the extent that it has clarity and associations in our consciousness. It is a task of education to supply us with a wide range of experience to serve as a basis for our meaning associations.

Meanings may be analytic or synthetic. Analytic thinking is the process of drawing distinctions, discovering the relatively unique features of an experience. Analysis proceeds by discrimination and comparison.[40] Discrimination is analysis of unique factors of difference of the experience from other experiences; comparison is analysis of unique factors of likeness or resemblance within an experience.

Synthetic thinking is the associative process of establishing relative relationship between different experiences. Synthesis may be by either contiguity or similarity.[41] I observe that a rash appears on my face when and only when I eat eggs. This regular contiguity between egg eating and my rash strongly suggests a relationship between them. This is an example of association by contiguity. Association by similarity occurs when I reason that different phenomena are synonymous for a particular purpose or state of affairs. If I am unable to find the hammer with which I habitually drive nails, I look about me and select a rock or walking stick for the purpose. James believes that "Compared with men, it is probable that brutes neither attend to abstract characters, nor have associations by similarity."[42] The "brutes" are tied to concrete signs to communicate, and solve problems. Humans can break out of this stagnant cycle because we can use abstract symbols which can make it possible for us to "see" associations or meanings based upon functional similarity.

Education provides the conditions necessary for association to progress, and especially those aspects of association by similarity that underlie the uniquely creative aspects of the human level of existence. These educational contributions to the associative process are two. First, education must provide the widest possible range of experience, both concrete and symbolic, since the number of associations possible in any given case is directly determined by the available range of potential associates which have been experienced. Learning the subject matters of history, mathematics, language, and so forth furnishes a broad reservoir for association to draw upon. Second, education must provide the tools of inquiry, and form habits by which association may occur as thoroughly, frequently, and quickly as possible.

When association occurs, both the perceived object and the perceiving subject contribute to the process. The perceived object must contribute the quality of interest, or more properly have the capacity to be interesting. Whatever possesses interest to a student is a legitimate subject matter for his or her study. Not only science, but also religion, art, values, and the practical problems of our lives may become objects of thought, and legitimate subjects of education. In much the same way that Hume and Kant showed respectively how the senses and the intellect help to determine our experienced reality, so James suggests that *interest* performs a similar function. The learner may contribute to increasing his or her knowledge by willful attention. According to James, "will" is to "attend to a difficult object and hold it fast before the mind."[43] Thus the interesting character of the perceived object, plus the willed act of attention by the perceiving subject unite to focus attention upon an event, and this attention introduces association.

The teacher must capture a native interest, or pair a new event with a native interest to stimulate the associative process. Education should lead to sustaining curiosity and to making a wide range of things habitually interesting. James believes that regarding curiosity and interest, "there is a native tendency to assimilate certain kinds of conception at one age, and other kinds of conception at a later age."[44] During the first seven or eight years of childhood, sensible properties of material things will generate the most interest. A child should come to feel at home in his or her physical world. By early adolescence the student should be master of the basic subject matters, of which James thinks a "large mass ... must be dull and unexciting, and to which it is impossible in any continuous way to contribute an interest associatively derived."⁴⁵ Mastery of this material will not only equip one with alternatives for association, but will also train us to will the habit of attention. Finally, furnished by education with a habituated capacity for interest, a trained will, the subject matter reserve necessary for association, and the techniques of association themselves, the student is prepared by advanced adolescence to plunge into systematic inquiry in general abstract fields such as morals, sociology, and metaphysics. James has thus provided a psychologically grounded outline of the "stages of education," which suggests interesting similarities to Whitehead's later analysis.⁴⁶

James believes that human life has the distinctive possibility of "progress."⁴⁷ "Progress" requires the combination of "ideals," which are our symbolized ideas of what could possibly be realized, and "virtues," which are plans of practical means to realize our ideals. Education aids progress through multiplying our ideals and through developing our ability to truly realize them. For James, education and progress are each measured primarily as means to developing a person's individuality and sense of meaning in life. They are primarily individual rather than institutional or social traits. For what gives individuality and meaning will differ from person to person. It is a mistake to suppose that all people see an event the same way. It is, therefore, a mistake to suppose that one form of education can serve all people.

Paul Woodring notes that James' psychology is frequently termed functionalism," since it "defines mental phenomena as processes or activities rather than mental content, and emphasizes the usefulness of these activities or *functions.*"⁴⁸ James describes education in functional terms as seeking to promote the "organization of acquired habits of conduct and tendencies to behavior."⁴⁹ In this, James believes that "psychology ought certainly to give the teacher radical help."⁵⁰ He says that the science of psychology can tell the teacher in advance "that certain methods of instruction will be wrong . . . ,"⁵¹ and may suggest a range of promising alternatives consistent with psychological laws. But knowledge of scientific psychology is not sufficient to guarantee success in the art of teaching. The inventive ingenuity of the teacher is required, to apply the general rules of psychology to particular situations and individual students, which for James always possess novelty. Thus the effective teacher will likely be one who has mastered the scientific principles of behavior, and who also possesses the ability to capture the interest of students. There may be varied teaching techniques that prove equally effective. James thinks that "the fact remains that some teachers have a naturally inspiring presence, and can make their exercises interesting, while others simply cannot."[52] Instruction in teaching methods can produce no easy formulas to guarantee student interest.

The key teaching method which *can* be learned is to graft a new event by association onto an already existing interest. James says that "The great maxim of pedagogy is to knit every new piece of knowledge on to a pre-existing curiosity...."[53] If the proper thinking habits have been formed, the interest will then join with will to focus attention on the event, and the process of creative association will be triggered. This supposes that the teacher must select the event to which he or she hopes to attract attention. Thus the teacher must be competent enough in the subject matter he or she is instructing to distinguish the essential from the trivial. This demand for competence in the subject matter is not only a practical, but also a moral requirement, since the teacher must take the initiative of evaluating what shall be made interesting. In this way the teacher assumes the responsibility of a form of influential control over the welfare of the pupil.

James says that "our mind is essentially an associative machine."[54] The education of our mind occurs by forming diverse and multiple associations within our experience. This is a neurological process, subject to empirical study. In any analysis of the learning process, James feels "the physiological formulation is everywhere the simplest and the best."[55] As we age, the associative process becomes increasingly habitual, each new performance strengthening the habit. In fact, James believes that "The ideas gained by men before they are twenty-five are practically the only ideas they shall have in their lives. They *cannot* get anything new. Disinterested curiosity is past, the mental grooves and channels set, the power of assimilation gone."[56] The primary function of formal education is thus to develop habits that will serve the student for a lifespan. Good habits are those which enable us to meet the widest variety of situations in the most effective manner possible. This complex of habits is called "character." A person's formal education has been satisfactory if he or she develops an individuality of character, and develops an expanding sense of meaning in experience throughout life.

To do his or her part, the student can make habitual four pedagogic maxims to offer the teacher his or her maximum cooperation. James observes, "The great thing ... in all education, is to make our nervous system our ally instead of our enemy."[57] The four pedagogic maxims for students are:

(1) In seeking to acquire or shed a habit, launch yourself with as strong and decided an initiative as possible.
(2) Never suffer an exception to occur till the new new habit is securely rooted in your life.
(3) Seize the very first possible opportunity to act on every resolution you make, and on every emotional prompting you may experience in the direction of the habits you aspire to gain.
(4) Keep the faculty of effort (or will) alive in you by a little gratuitous exercise every day.[58]

Succinctly put, James says you "Sow an action and you reap a habit; sow a habit and you reap a character; sow a character and you reap a destiny."[59]

Critical Comment

Some broad critical comments on James' theory of education will close this exposition. There are several areas of theory in which important advances in knowledge have been achieved recently. From the perspective of these subsequent historical developments, some expansion of James' theory of education might be fruitful. We will note three of these developments in the study of symbols, the unconscious, and society.

First, it can be argued that James did not investigate sufficiently the role of symbols in shaping our experience, and in the educational process. James knew that human language is a symbol system, and that symbols contributed to freeing humans from the bondage of an immediate situation. He did not elaborate the pervasive extent to which symbols (e. g. status, class) control our motivation and behavior. He did not discuss how symbols for the nonexistent can instigate horrors, e. g. the "witches of Salem" or Hitler's "super race." He did not appreciate the great potential power of symbols as rewards in education (e. g. recognition among peers, etc.), as associative devices to make interesting otherwise dull subject matter.

Secondly, James did not consider thoroughly the role of the unconscious in behavior, which has become an increasingly important issue. James makes passing references to the unconscious,[61] and hints at its importance in his treatment of memory and habit. Nevertheless a full exposition of this question had to wait for later investigation. The contemporary study termed "motivational" or "depth" research shows the importance of the unconscious elements in the learning process.[62] Certainly a full knowledge of the operation of these hidden forces will enlarge the teacher's qualification both to protect and to lead the student. James' theory of education must be supplemented in this area.

Finally, James did not sufficiently emphasize the role of society in shaping the individual. James was an individualist who believed strongly that the main changes in communities from generation to generation are "due to the accumulated influences of individuals....," and concludes that the "causes of production of great men lie in a sphere wholly inaccessible to the social philosopher."[63] He saw education in personal rather than institutional or social terms. He suggests an interaction between individual and environment, saying that "minds inhabit environments which act on them and on which they in turn react...."⁶⁴ Yet his use of traditional introspective language along with meager reliable sociological studies upon which to draw, prevented him from giving close attention to the social acts in which each individual participates. For example, the work of John Dewey and George Herbert Mead have immeasurably enriched the concept of society, and the individual's place in the social act.⁶⁵ Later ventures in social psychology such as these have opened whole new vistas in educational theory to which James devoted relatively little attention.

In general, James' theory of education remains compatible with contemporary knowledge in the sciences of psychology and education. Having stood well the test of several generations of scientific advance, his theory of education has become a classic. James' theory of education continues to be an important and useful subject for study by both teachers and philosophers.

NOTES

1 William James, *A Pluralistic Universe*, (New York: Longmans, Green and Company, 1909). See esp. Chapters I, II.
2 William James, *Pragmatism (Lowell Lectures)*, (1907; New York: Meridian Books, 1963). See esp. Lectures II, VI.
3 George Santayana, *Character and Opinion in the United States*, (New York: Charles Scribner's Sons, 1920), p. 66. For a detailed description of James' performance as a teacher see Henry James, *The Letters of William James*, (Boston: The Atlantic Monthly Press, 1920), Vol. II, pp. 1—17.
4 "The Teaching of Philosophy in our Colleges," *The Nation*, XXIII (September 21, 1876), 178. This unsigned essay is attributed to William James by Ralph Barton Perry in *The Thought and Character of William James: Briefer Version*, (New York: George Braziller Publisher, 1954), p. 144.
5 Horace M. Kallen, "Introduction," *The Philosophy of William James*, ed. Horace M. Kallen (New York: Modern Library, 1953), p. 44.
6 William James, *Talks to Teachers*, (1899; New York: W. W. Norton & Company, 1958), p. 19.
7 *Ibid.*, p. 169.
8 Kallen, *The Philosophy of William James*, p. 30.

9 James, *Talks to Teachers*, p. 169.
10 *Ibid.*, p. 34.
11 Quoted in Ralph Barton Perry, *The Thought and Character of William James: Briefer Version*, (New York: George Braziller Publisher, 1954), p. 134.
12 William James, *The Principles of Psychology*, (New York: Dover Publications, 1950), Vol. I, p. vi.
13 James, *Talks to Teachers*, p. 82.
14 James, *The Principles of Psychology*, Vol. I, p. 6.
15 *Ibid.*, Vol. I, p. 273.
16 James, *Talks to Teachers*, p. 87.
17 James, *The Principles of Psychology*, Vol. I, p. 584.
18 *Ibid.*, Vol. II, p. 333. (Italics his.)
19 *Ibid.*, Vol. II, p. 321.
20 James, *Talks to Teachers*, p. 82.
21 James, *The Principles of Psychology*, Vol. II, Ch. XXIII.
22 *Ibid.*, Vol. I, p. 11.
23 *Ibid.*, Vol. II, p. 368. (Italics his.)
24 *Ibid.*, Vol. II, p. 688.
25 James, *Talks to Teachers*, p. 103.
26 James, *The Principles of Psychology*, Vol. I, p. 122.
27 James, *Talks to Teachers*, p. 58.
28 James, *The Principles of Psychology*, Vol. I, p. 594.
29 James, *Talks to Teachers*, p. 125.
30 *Ibid.*, p. 125. (Italics his.)
31 James, *Pragmatism*, p. 17.
32 James, *Talks to Teachers*, p. 21.
33 James, *The Principles of Psychology*, Vol. I, p. 224.
34 *Ibid.*, Vol. II, p. 76.
35 James, *Talks to Teachers*, p. 100.
36 James, *The Principles of Psychology*, Vol. I, p. 243.
37 *Ibid.*, Vol. I, see pp. 221, 259, 588.
38 *Ibid.*, Vol. II, p. 284.
39 *Ibid.*, Vol. I, p. 664.
40 *Ibid.*, Vol. I, Ch. XIII.
41 *Ibid.*, Vol. I, Ch. XIV.
42 *Ibid.*, Vol. II, p. 348.
43 *Ibid.*, Vol. II, p. 561.
44 James, *Talks to Teachers*, p. 103.
45 *Ibid.*, p. 80.
46 Alfred North Whitehead, *The Aims of Education*, (New York: Macmillan Company, 1929), Ch. II.
47 James, *Talks to Teachers*, p. 187.
48 Paul Woodring, "Introduction," in James, *Talks to Teachers*, p. 10. (Italics mine.)

49 James, *Talks to Teachers*, p. 37.
50 *Ibid.*, p. 22.
51 *Ibid.*, p. 25.
52 *Ibid.*, p. 81.
53 James, *The Principles of Psychology*, Vol. II, p. 110.
54 James, *Talks to Teachers*, p. 86.
55 James, *The Principles of Psychology*, Vol. II, p. 30.
56 *Ibid.*, Vol. II, p. 402. (Italics his.)
57 *Ibid.*, Vol. I, p. 122.
58 *Ibid.*, Vol. I, pp. 123—126.
59 William James, *Psychology*, (New York: Fawcett Publications, 1963), p. i.
60 James, *The Principles of Psychology*, Vol. II, p. 305, and James, *Talks to Teachers*, pp. 73—76.
61 See James, *The Principles of Psychology*, Vol. I, pp. 164—176, 199—213, 229, and James, *Talks to Teachers*, p. 134.
62 See Vance Packard, *The Hidden Persuaders*, (New York: Mentor Books, 1961).
63 William James, *The Will to Believe*, (New York: Longmans Green and Company, 1897), pp. 218, and 225—226.
64 James, *The Principles of Psychology*, Vol. I, p. 6.
65 See John Dewey, *Human Nature and Conduct*, (New York: H. Holt and Company, 1922), and George Herbert Mead, *Mind, Self and Society*, ed. Charles W. Morris (Chicago: University of Chicago Press, 1934).

15

WILLIAM JAMES AND CONTEMPORARY RELIGIOUS THOUGHT: THE PROBLEM OF EVIL

John K. Roth

You deserve a warning before reading this paper. My original intention was to write an objective report about James's influence on recent work in religion. Special attention was to be given to his treatment of the problem of evil and the suggestions that this offers for current religious thought. Although these early plans have neither been scrapped completely nor left entirely unfulfilled, the mood and content of this essay have taken unexpected turns.

This round with William James became an occasion to express some personal feelings about a number of religious issues. The thoughts set down here remain imprecise. No clinching arguments or iron-clad conclusions are to be found. My effort has produced a subjective – sometimes polemical, aways vulnerable – piece of writing which provided some "mind-clearing" for me. I offer it here only because the essay does point out some crucial problems that are worthy of serious discussion. William James would quarrel with much that I have to say. You may too. But he would, I think, follow the ideas thoughtfully and present helpful reactions as well. Having bared my soul, I hope that it will be handled with a similar sensitivity.

I. James's Influence on Recent Developments in Religious Thought

Speaking of religion, William James once said that "the life of it as a whole is mankind's most important function."[1] James's philosophical concerns did not always focus on religious themes, but a persistent interest in the emergence, hope, frustration, and destiny of the human spirit always kept him in touch with religious life. Belief in particular creeds played no significant part in his experience. He often found himself in the role of critic and rebel against the dominant religious practices and theologies of his day. For religious *experience,* however, – which he defined as "any moment of life that brings the reality of spiritual things more 'home' to one"[2] – he always retained the highest respect.

James understood that religious experience – sometimes well, sometimes badly – tries to discern and communicate the basic nature of existence and attempts to honor all that is good. For him, then, the life of religion could be man's most important function, because to live authentically and to live religiously were very close, if not identical. As a result of this outlook, James's philosophical work often aims at describing and evaluating the religious aspect of human experience, at criticizing conceptual and behavioral patterns that hinder its best development, and at suggesting new ways to think about our existence and destiny.

George Santayana believed that James's "excursions into philosophy were... in the nature of raids."[3] He meant that James was neither a system-builder nor a thinker limited to a single theme. James experimented. His universe was pluralistic; so was his thought. Both were characterized by variety and novelty. There were structure and unity in both, but no rigidity to preclude something new. Both are left open-ended and unfinished.

This analysis applies to James's work as a philosopher of religion. He developed no finished system that interprets religion exhaustively. Even his detailed study, *The Varieties of Religious Experience,* is rather thin in the area of fully developed conclusions. Its strength, as far as contemporary thought is concerned, lies more in the host of provocative suggestions that it contains regarding human experience and reality itself. In all of his work, James asked questions in new ways, provided flashes of insight, and blazed fresh trails. This fact is illustrated by recent religious thought, where his influence – direct or indirect – continues to be important.

First, James pioneered a phenomenological approach to religious experience. He always tried to understand experiences as persons actually lived them through. For him, this task was a necessary prerequisite to any causal analysis or moral evaluation of the experiences themselves. This ideal serves as a principle in some contemporary studies of religious life, and it stands as a criticism of others. In either case, James's influence is present. Today *The Varieties of Religious Experience* makes timely reading. In the midst of scientific sophistication and the secular city, religious experience has reappeared with unexpected intensity and in surprising places. It involves a variety which suggests that the universe - at least in terms of religious life – is increasingly pluralistic. Traditional church life may remain tepid, but mysticism, "speaking in tongues," and conversion experiences give the 1970's an interesting religious flavor. Another William James is needed to make an assessment.

The renewed religious interest in many circles comes fast on the heels of two other recent developments. These are the "death of God" movement and the influence of linguistic analysis on religious thought. The former was more public in its effect, but it was also linked closely to more esoteric philosophical questions concerning the meaningfulness, verifiability, and falsifiability of religious language. James's thought figures in the emergence of both trends.

Pragmatism is a form of linguistic analysis – or perhaps *vice versa*. In any case, it is not very far from certain aspects of James's philosophy to some of the linguistic concerns that have characterized much contemporary philosophy of religion. Is "God-talk" verifiable or falsifiable? Is it meaningful? These questions are at least first cousins, if not direct offspring, of James's basic pragmatic principles: (1) that a concept or theory is meaningful only to the degree that there are specifiable practical consequences in future experience that the object of the concept or theory leads us to anticipate, and (2) that a claim is true or false just to the degree that the consequences it leads us to anticipate are fulfilled or unfulfilled. In addition, the suggestion – derived from Wittgenstein – that religious discourse constitutes a special form of "language game," where the meaning of religious concepts is determined by their special use, may be understood as a dimension of the phenomenological study of religious experience which James helped to encourage.

If James thought that religious claims were not conclusively verified in this life, he certainly believed that they were sufficiently grounded in experience so as to be meaningful. He was reluctant to dismiss any religious report or theory as an impossibility on technical philosophical grounds. He did, however, find that some religious attitudes and beliefs failed to fit his understanding of reality and human needs. As a result, James anticipated the "death of God" movement which dominated much religious discussion in the late 1960's.

That movement was not so much an argument for atheism as it was a criticism of certain theological traditions and a tortured plea for new concepts. James did not discard God completely, but he did precede many recent spokesmen in regarding "the 'omniscient' and 'omnipotent' God of theology ... as a disease of the philosophy-shop."[4] This particular God was dead because of an inability to fit with human experiences of freedom, evil, and hope. James would not have felt like a stranger in the theological debates of the late 1960's. He helped to create them.

This takes us to a fourth way – for me the most significant – in which James still influences contemporary religious thought. James had an exiting and bold vision of reality. Always more a sketch than a complete picture, it emphasized the qualities of freedom, open-endedness, and change in existence. This universe included a God. Indeed it involved many spiritual forms of existence above and beyond our usual states of awareness, so that James sometimes thought of himself as a polytheist. In any case, James spoke of God as "a combination of Ideality and (final) efficacity,"[5] and to the end he used the concept to refer to a being who is individual as well as complex and multi-faceted.

James was reluctant to be a theologian, and he never developed his view of God in much detail. What he does say, however, is both interesting and, as we shall see later, full of problems. If James's God was the highest of beings in a basic sense, he was not supreme in the traditional theological manner. Not only subject to influence and change, this God was "finite, either in power or in knowledge, or in both at once."[6] At the same time, James thought that God was an active force ("He must *do*.") and personal in the sense of being "cognizant and responsive in some way."[7] In addition, James understood God "as a more powerful ally of my own ideals."[8] God was identified only with the good, the ideal, and not with the whole of existence.

Although still partly blurred at James's death, his idea of a pluralistic universe-in-process has helped to shape present attitudes, and it has provided the grist for many philosophical papers and books. James's suggestions about God, in particular, have been a stimulus for "process theology." This elaboration of Whitehead – who regarded James as a very great thinker indeed – stands as one of the most significant theological positions developed on American soil in this century.

II. James's Influence on Me

Perhaps more important than all of his connections with recent schools of thought, William James was simply a person who thought long, hard, and creatively about man's hopes and fears and about the ways in which reality might fit them. He is a magnificent "man for all seasons," and I am glad that a considerable portion of my life has been spent wrestling with him. From graduate school in 1963 to my most recent teaching and writing, hardly a day passes without some inner dialogue with this man I never knew. At the beginning of my acquaintance with his thought, I experienced the joy of discovering someone who said forcefully so many of the things I had been feeling. My reading of his works also introduced me to new and captivating ideas about freedom, consciousness, belief, truth, emotion, and religion. I became James's vigorous defender on almost every count.

In a world of flux, heroes retain no fixed position. My familiarity with James has bred no contempt; my enthusiasm for his thought remains high. However, my thinking has changed over the years, so that my agreement with him is now less than complete. The points in question are not technical. They involve instead a fundamental orientation toward the structure and destiny of existence. I find myself following James up to a point, but then I go another way. My difficulty with James stems from a religious issue: the problem of evil.

Before discussing that problem, I should explain one thing about myself. If I have a philosophical style of my own, it is to try to understand existence by thinking about God. Such an approach may not be the most in vogue these days, but it puts one in distinguished company as far as philosophical tradition goes. To think about God – his existence or nonexistence, his possible nature and relation to the world, his sense of purpose or lack of it, etc. – is one way in which a person can try to fathom who he is, what his place within nature and history amounts to, and what his ultimate end may be. I believe that James sensed this too, although I would never argue that the concept of God haunted him as it does me. I may not be God-intoxicated, but I cannot get God out of my mind any more than I can William James.

Quoting again from his essay on James in *Character and Opinion in the United States,* Santayana makes two more perceptive comments. First, he says of James that "the unlovely secrets of nature and the troubles of man preoccupied him."[9] A little later he writes: "Like most Americans, however, only more lyrically, James felt the call of the future and the assurance that it could be made far better, totally other, than the past."[10] The fact that James acknowledged the frequent brutality of nature and the deep suffering of men without being consumed by despair is a major reason for his greatness. His courage to hope is inspiring. Indeed, he convinces me that to be fully human a person must hope that his best ideals ultimately receive a sympathetic hearing in existence instead of simply returning to dust. On the other hand, James's defense of hope also leads to my disagreement with basic elements of his treatment of the problem of evil.

In a basic sense, James's optimism about men far exceeds my own, although as my analysis will show, perhaps I am the one who is ultimately more optimistic about existence. His open-ended universe places much responsibility on men. How people use their freedom makes a vital difference to the qualitiy that reality will have. I share that view with James, but at this point in the 1970's, I find it difficult to share even James's level of optimism about what men will do with their freedom.

Make no mistake. James was no Pollyanna who found man's free choices making the world ever better. He could say that "life *is* evil. Two souls are in my breast; I see the better, and in the very act of seeing it I do the worse."[11] He even asserted that "the scourge of life is *responsibility*."[12] An example of the "sick souls" he had described in *The Varieties of Religious Experience*, James gazed into life's pit and felt the depths of despair. Yet he lived hopefully, with zest and courage.

No matter how devastating his attack on the Absolute Idealism of his friend and colleague Josiah Royce, James always acknowledged that a world embraced by Royce's God of sovereign power, complete knowledge, and total goodness could offer a sense of assurance that his open-ended, pluralistic universe did not allow. Still, James opted for the freedom and risk of the latter. If he had doubts about the final outcome of human responsibility, he urged it on us as a factor basic to the significance of our lives.

James is right: Responsibility is both a scourge and something that makes life significant. It is a scourge because existence forces us to choose and we often do so blindly and selfishly. Our decisions often destroy others and torture ourselves. Too often we try to dodge responsibility for destructive acts, but we feel it nonetheless. Responsibility gnaws at us. James knew all of this, but he was spared the traumatic events of 20th century life that have driven these facts home with a vengeance.

On the other hand, responsibility does allow for a unique sense of significance in life. Only when men can experience responsibility can they feel the joy of creative accomplishment. Only if men can feel responsibility is there the possibility of love and community that nurture life and make it blossom. James knew these things too, and in the end he retained the hope that the positive qualities of human responsibility would dominate. He held fast to the vision of a world that grows, largely through good human intentions and actions, toward an increasingly improved condition. Failure always lurked nearby, but James placed his bet on men. God stood by as an ally. The decisive cards, however, remained in our hands, and how we played them really determined the outcome.

Because James taught me to hope, I find it difficult to follow him at this point. The idea that men are going to transform themselves, that they will rid the world of injustice and brutality by changed intentions and that the world will move toward anything like utopia, strikes me today as sheer fantasy. James never encouraged anyone to hope for something that seemed incompatible with the facts of existence. The facts I read today are perhaps different from those that James discerned. At any rate, I become increasingly convinced that life in this world never has been – and never will be – more than an ambiguous, but essentially unchanged, mixture of good and evil, ecstatic joy and needless suffering, nobility and injustice. Men may know more than they did at earlier times. They may even "know better," and from time to time individual lives may change dramatically for a good. But the record of selfish consumption, power-grabbing, corruption, and slaughter stands unscathed in all but a few of us.

These days it is a little hard to trust in man's potential for goodness. Any revival of religious interest in American life today may be a symptom that the humanism which James and other pragmatists helped to encourage has been found wanting in crucial spots. Our freedom is a burden as much as it is a source of joyful creativity. Real progress remains elusive. Some of us are perhaps closer to a Puritan than to a pragmatic view of man. In any case, neither manifestoes nor orations on "the faith of a humanist" stir people as they might have once.

This is not to suggest that humanism is dead or that I have written man off completely. A humanistic outlook remains indispensable if men are not to "do each other in" altogether. Narrow self-interest is a dominant human characteristic. Thus, only if men and women work very hard indeed toward humanistic goals will a worthwhile continuation of life on this earth be possible. Furthermore, since I find that life can be very good – to the extent even that I have chosen to father two children in these recent years of turmoil – I do follow James's faith in trying to use my energy to make life worth living for others as well as for myself. But my mood, and I believe that many of my contemporaries share it, is profoundly anti-utopian. That this world will move substantially toward ideal conditions seems a remote possibility. Camus puts it well: "For twenty centuries the sum total of evil has not diminished in the world. No paradise, whether divine or revolutionary, has been realized."[13] The future of this world, no matter how open-ended, is not likely to be much different.

III. God and Hope

Where does this leave things? My differences with James lead me to reconsider the role that God plays in his thought and the part the God might play in another metaphysical vision related to, but not identical with, James's own. We can start this analysis by elaborating some implications of two important ideas that James holds about God: (1) God is identified with the ideal, the good, so that he bears no responsibility for evil. (2) God acts and responds. He is aware and knows. But in spite of the fact that James asserts God's existence to involve "final efficacity" (a concept which is never clarified very well), he stresses the view that God's power and/or his knowledge are finite, limited.

James opts for a God who has personal qualities of knowledge and action, and whose work always supports the good. In addition, the good is understood in a way that makes it very close to human ideals of justice and integrity in this life and of triumph over death as well. I share much of this orientation with James. At this point, my hope is similar to his.

A legitimate function of philosophy, according to James, is to help make life meaningful. God, therefore, fulfills a dual function in his thought. First, the affirmation of God's existence is an expression of James's hope that man's existence is not an ultimately futile sputter in a cruelly destructive void. Second, James found that belief in the right kind of God could be a source of courage that would help to release man's moral energy into the world. A sound theology could help to prevent moral indifference – James called it the "don't care mood" – which always lurks within a purely naturalistic outlook.

For James, human energies alone were insufficient to redeem existence. He could feel the power of moral ideals as keenly as his more naturalistic colleagues, Santayana and Dewey, but he always remained convinced that no relation – however active – between the human spirit and its ideals would be strong enough to transform reality. To be sure, James thought that these factors might accomplish more than I do, but he felt the need of a God supernatural and transcendent in basic ways as a necessary condition for the overcoming of negative features in existence.

There will never be a consensus among men on matters of this kind. Our experiences are too varied and ambiguous for that, and each person must find his own way to cope as best he can. But I share James's feelings very strongly at this point. Unless reality is ultimately in the control of a force – I use the word "God" to designate it – that cares deeply enough for human life so as to rescue it from destruction and death and to reconstitute us individually on a nobler level, then I confess that life seems to me to come off in the end as an absurd waste.

Life does have its beauty, grandeur, and nobility. For specific persons, it may be very rich indeed. But when I survey the whole span of human history, the negative categories – hunger, disease, death, injustice, slaughter, slavery, greed – seem to dominate. Man's moments of nobility are the exceptions that prove the rule. Everything returns to dust and ashes. There is high tragedy in that fact, but little solace and satisfaction, even if the evolutionary process goes on to infinity.

Camus's rebellion, Santayana's piety toward nature, and Dewey's "religious" humanism all have grandeur, and they help to convince me to avoid a debilitating pessimism. Still, the kind of optimism that they preach – the nobility of human life in spite of absurdity and natural finitude – leaves me depressed. In the end it all adds up to silence in a void. James's optimism depresses me too. He counts on men unrealistically, but I am with him against the romantic tendencies that characterize more naturalistic humanism.

Problems haunt my feelings, I know. If the facts of existence are so bleak, how can one's mind turn to God? Moreover, how is the negativity of the facts compatible with the hope about God that I have professed? How does the dominance of evil in this world jibe with the hope that God's nature is ultimately characterized by a saving love for individuals? A few words about hope itself figure into the answers.

James's study of religious experience teaches that the most profound religious life is based on the experience of need. This life has roots in the emotions and feelings of persons. Moreover, these emotions and feelings are usually deeply grounded in the experiences of suffering, pain, and loss which are the correlates of joy and happiness at every turn of human life. The reason that it is difficult to demonstrate – or to destroy completely – the validity of any specific religious claim, then, is the fact that the claims tend very often to emerge out of experiences which seem to stand directly in conflict with them. Immortality or resurrection is affirmed in the face of death. Salvation comes only with destruction and guilt as preconditions. Visions of a wholesome existence are shaped in contrast to horror.

To some degree, religious faith is always hope-in-spite-of-facts. This leads to the criticism that the evidence not only fails to support religious convictions but runs squarely against them. It leaves religion open to the charge of escapism or failure of nerve to accept things as they are. James's analysis, however, puts the issue a little differently. He outlines it in a more helpful way, one that is closely in touch with human sensitivity, which may be quite a different thing from philosophical precision.

Less concerned about uniformity of opinion than about individual authenticity, James recognized different emotional needs in persons and defended the right of individuals to develop varied "overbeliefs" to meet them. His guideline was this: Hope for as much as is honestly possible and admit that the resulting overbelief is a hope which may have substantial evidence against it. On the other hand, James also held that there could be evidence for the truth of our overbeliefs in the experiences and feelings of persons. The results, however, would remain ambiguous. One's hope might provide a kind of assurance, but never total certainty.

A religious person might be an escapist if his hopes were not honestly evaluated. At the same time, religious hope could be the most realistic and profound stance toward life if it emerged from a critical appraisal of one's own needs, the possibilities that the facts would allow, and the highest ideals that men are capable of imagining. At its best, and this is why James gave the highest marks to religion when it was profound, religious faith pointed toward the most worthwhile qualities in life and encouraged people to live for them in the present.

In a world of horror and terror, James invites one to cultivate religious hope. This is one reason why I find my mind turning toward God when I survey the bleakness of life as it is lived here and now. Deep inside, I very much want something more. Without some divine power that transcends nature, my need is likely to be unmet. It may remain unmet forever, but I hope because things are bleak. I also try to live in terms of the ideals that my hope supports. The result is a mixture of success and failure, which corroborates my sensitivity about human weakness. In this sense, my hope is not verified by experience, but it is intensified.

Is my hope mere wishful thinking? Is it a dodge, an insulation against realities that I am too weak to face? Perhaps I deceive myself, but I like to think that I am as tough-minded and realistic as anyone about the facts of life. I admit that I do not want the negative features to have the last word, but I think that is less a sign of weakness than a sensitivity that is worth cultivating. Still, in terms of sheer evidence that would support my hope, am I not living in bad faith?

I do not know myself well enough to answer conclusively. I suspect that none of us do where our basic hopes and fears are concerned. From time to time, however, I do have feelings of assurance that things are "all right" with reality in a way that I can interpret in terms of my idea of God. These feelings come unexpectedly and not at my own calling. I do not understand them completely, but I take them seriously. Most often they come in quiet times of reading, writing, and reflection, in the presence of people I love and respect, and in worship and prayer. I am also encouraged by friends who share similar needs and experiences, and by people who express interest, if not agreement, about my religious conceptions.

Personal feelings and reports from other persons – those have long been held in ill-repute as sound reasons for religious faith. The subjectivism involved is notorious. Philosophers have for years drummed out of court claims based on anything so flimsy. But William James did a good job on me. He urges one to take such experiences seriously – not blindly and uncritically, to be sure, but with the recognition that all evidence ultimately comes in these forms and that truth does not always reside in the obvious or with the majority. For reasons such as these, I find myself thinking about God in the darkness of human life, believing that my hope is not escapist but a worthwhile risk directed toward high ideals.

IV. God and Evil

Feelings lead to theories; so we must return now to James's concept of God and the ways in which I appropriate and reject it. I have applauded James's reasons for incorporating God as an individual being in his philosophy. My reaction to the characteristics he ascribes to God is more mixed. James suggests that God is not responsible for all that exists. He is limited in power and/or knowledge. The motives behind these ideas are clear. The problem of evil figures into all of them.

Reacting against the view that God is both omnipotent and omniscient, James believes that God's knowledge must be limited if man's freedom and God's goodness are to be assured. A world known completely in every possible detail by an all-powerful God was understood by James as a world finished and complete. It could contain no genuine news. Men might feel free, but in fact they would not be. Their lives would be complete before they were lived, formed through divine omniscience. Evil and suffering, too, would be constituted in accord with God's knowledge. Such a God would be consciously demonic. To guard against such undesirable conclusions, God must be conceived as one who has novel experiences. Thus, temporality enters God. His future, as well as ours, contains elements of indeterminateness. A perspective of eternity can still apply to his vision of possibility, but not to everything that will become actual. God's knowledge of reality develops as the members of a pluralistic universe move, choose, and act on their own.

Only partially did these limitations on God's knowledge satisfy James's moral sensitivities. He hoped that the universe was moving toward ideal ends, not as the result of conformity to some divine plan enforced from without, but through the free cooperation of its members with God. On the other hand, James saw that the degree of evil in the world was substantial. The obstacles toward overcoming evil with good were sufficiently great that failure might be the final word. Thus, James provided two additional qualifications for God.

We have touched on the first already: James aligned God with the ideal. This was done partly to modify the limitations placed on God's knowledge. James wanted a God for whom novelty and even play would be real categories. But he did not want God to become a bumbling fool, acting out of ignorance, any more than he wanted God to be consciously demonic. God's awareness of past and present could be complete. His understanding of possibilities for the future could be without gaps. In addition, James suggested that God's actions and hopes for reality would always be motivated by ideals to which sensitive minds would respond warmly.

At the same time, the implication of James's reflections is that God's power must be limited. This move follows from the identification of God with the good. If God were omnipotent in the traditional sense and totally aligned with the ideal, he would be at fault if he did not create a situation in which the ideal and the actual are one. For James, the reality he experienced was anything but such a merger. Thus, the result for God was that he became finite in power as well as in knowledge. Struggling with forces that provided real obstacles, God became an all-important but finite figure in a moral battle.

James's God seems incapable of making choices that would unleash sheer cruelty and destruction in the world. His nature is more limited than that. Only in a very restricted sense, therefore, can such a God be understood as the creator of this violent world. The boundaries within which he determines his own actions remain fixed by melioristic ideals. In a complex and wild world, James's God is an instance of purity and relative simplicity. If he could do more now to make the world ideal, it would be out of character not to do so. To tolerate needless suffering, injustice, senseless pain, and wasteful conflict – if they could be avoided – would be inconsistent for him, if not impossible.

Human freedom is sometimes offered as the reason for God's reluctance to eliminate negative factors in existence. God's respect for freedom, his high evaluation of it, precludes him from tinkering too much with actions, even if their outcome is destructive. To be sure, James's God does not tinker too much with human actions either. But this is not so much out of self-restraint as it is because of the fundamental limits on God. James's God is always doing the best he can. This means that if he could control man's freedom, channel it in less destructive ways, he would do so. This God may respect and value human freedom highly, but he seems incapable of altering it radically except through the persuasion of mopping-up operations after the damage has been done.

If God tolerates evil in the world more from necessity than from choice, this raises interesting problems for James's unclarified claim that God is in some sense finally efficacious. Coupled with all that James says about the open-endedness of the universe and human responsibility, his limitations on God lead toward these issues: If God is now doing all that he can to eradicate evil, are there good reasons to think that he will be finally efficacious in a way that would fit James's own hopes? If God really cannot prevent the triumph of negative forces when it occurs in the present world, which is what James implies, then is he likely to have power sufficient to recreate things according to James's dream? To both questions my answer is negative.

What are we to make of this situation? Everything depends on the assessment that one makes of nature and human life. In spite of his acquaintance with their darker side, James remains ultimately very optimistic about their future. If that is one's attitude, it is easy to live with a finite God of the type sketched by James – or to live with no God at all. If one's analysis of nature and human life is more pessimistic, the decision may also be to live without God, since no factors of final salvation are decisively clear. At the same time, one's negative assessment may produce a yearning for God, as instances in our own culture indicate. This time, however, the God who is sought is not very likely to be finite in power, at least to the degree that James's theory suggests.

How James could get from his analysis of "sick souls" to

the humanistic optimism of his particular finite God and melioristic universe is something that I cannot quite understand. The negative experiences of the human spirit, which he describes so well, and the limitations he places on God seem not to fit very well with his hope that this world may achieve lasting ideal ends. James suffered from a defect – it became more pronounced in John Dewey – common in American thinkers. After describing in depth very serious problems in the human situation, he tended to assume that all of these could really be swept away by greater human diligence, integrity, education, and effort. It is a noble vision, but naive as well. Such optimism is depressing in the end, because the facts always fall so far short of the dream.

The only healthy optimism about this life is one based on a good dose of pessimism about what is probable. It is likely that only a God of substantial power can really redeem this world. If James sensed this, it is true nonetheless that his attachment to optimism about human potentiality and freedom dominated his thought. God became a finite partner in man's struggle for the good. In the late 20th century, that is a precarious role indeed. It is one which may make everyone a loser.

As I have said, my inability to share even James's degree of optimism about man leads me to seek a stronger God than he offers. But there are dangers in such a search. One may find nothing at all. Nature – violent, cruel, and wasteful in the end, especially in its human forms – may be all that there is. In addition, if one does find something, he has to be aware that his theories about it are hypotheses which may be false and which are always liable to oversimplify the negative experiences that helped to prompt the search in the first place. In a word, Gods of love can be seductive, substituting false appearances for painful realities.

A song popular some years ago asserted that "the best things in life are free." That is wrong, of course. Everything in this life exacts a price. If existence kills humanistic optimism, leading one to reflect on a God of power who might have something better in store for us than this world alone suggests, a high toll may be taken in terms of shattered illusions concerning what that God might be like. No simple God of goodness and love can emerge from a critical estimate of the facts and one's most personal hopes. What will be discovered is this: If there is a God of love with sufficient power to redeem the waste of a world that has produced Auschwitz, Hiroshima, Vietnam, and Watergate in my short lifetime alone, this is also a guilty God.

V. *God and Guilt*

In what ways might God be guilty? By human standards, at least two dimensions appear. First, God could be guilty of *criminal negligence*. This would be true if there are any ways in which he could prevent or correct injustice and needless suffering but fails to do so, or if he fails to take any other action at his disposal that would make the world better now. Second, he could also be guilty of *criminal intent* – and sometimes of murder. This would be true whenever he knowingly and freely creates or allows a situation which, in his own estimate, is likely to produce an outcome more negative than would probably follow from other available possibilities.

In God's case, criminal negligence would imply criminal intent and *vice versa*. If God fails to prevent or correct a negative situation when it is possible for him to do so, he will know that this is the case and thus intend something more negative than is necessary. By the same token, if he intends something more negative than is necessary, he fails to actualize better options. On the other hand, the dimensions of guilt in question here are not identical. God may be negligent in his intentions, and he may intend to be negligent. But criminal negligence points toward only one quality – failure to do all that is possible to support the good – which would be linked to criminal intent in God.

James's God cannot be guilty in either of these senses. He simply lacks the power that makes guilt – or the full overcoming of evil – possible. On the other hand, if we consider the

James and Contemporary Religious Thought

world's structure and a God sufficiently powerful so as ultimately to overcome its negativity, it is likely that we will conclude that God is guilty in both of these ways. Men, it is true, are responsible for much of the world's horror. We blight the good gifts that God provides. But God, too, must share his rightful portion of the blame.

Among the options that life presents, you can think of God as strong and guilty or as weak and innocent. You can also turn to some form of naturalistic humanism. Any of them, however, tends to leave the negative forces in existence as the ultimate victors. One of my students recently expressed the opinion that all human choices are made among undesirable possibilities. Perhaps that is too strong, but there may be some truth to it in this case. A powerful but guilty God, an innocent but weak God, or a humanism that crashes headlong into the deadned of death itself – these three leave us in a twilight zone. The options may be wider than that, of course, but it is unlikely that any allows us an exit into clear, warm daylight. The problem of evil and individual destiny puts every religious and moral hope on the rack.

The dilemma of humanism is this: Either it becomes utopian, in which case it does not square with human nature, or it confesses its potential as largely restricted to mopping-up operations, in which case the world will probably continue to creak along in the same tired way. An innocent God would provide a breath of fresh air in the world, but innocence at the price of weakness may be too much to pay. It, too, leaves the world muddling along or dying, either with a bang or a whimper.

A powerful but guilty God leaves one with all manner of questions and doubts. This option may be the most demonic of all, because it suggests that we could be dealing with a God whose basic characteristic is cruelty. He creates and sustains a world subtly adjusted so as to permit moments of real joy and beauty – only to have them swallowed up in pain and grief. Moreover, the performance is carried on from generation to generation. New hope is raised in each, but frustration dominates. This God refuses to let hope die. He seems to have created us as beings who hope. But this only figures into the overall strategy of cruelty. Small boys sometimes torture and kill animals for fun. A powerful but guilty God may do the same, using human lives for his play.

That picture is not very pretty. A naturalistic humanism or a Jamesian outlook might offer more consolation by removing the maliciousness that could characterize a God of evil. There is, however, another side of the coin in the case of a powerful and guilty God. In the end, I suppose my own attitude is like grabbing that coin and flipping it, hoping that the right side will come up.

What would the right side of that coin look like? For one thing, there might be an inscription on it saying, "In God We Trust." The meaning, however, would not be a "God-bless-America" kind of trust. It would be much more akin to the kind of trust found in the Old Testament figure of Job. This man deals with a God of power who is unquestionably guilty of allowing conditions in his life that are unjust and unnecessary. Job protests, but does not get a fully satisfactory accounting from God. Ultimately he must accept God's sheer power as final, however it is used.

At the same time, Job's laments sometimes emphasize a note of trust. In part at least, they express a hope that reality is not finally capricious and malevolent.

"This I know: that my Avenger lives,
 and he, the Last, will take his stand on earth.
After my awaking, he will set me close to him,
 and from my flesh I shall look on God.
He whom I shall see will take my part:
 these eyes will gaze on him and find him not aloof."[14]

Perhaps God was unworthy of Job's trust, or perhaps God's actions killed it. But I like to think that Job's hope never ceased, even though his pain might have diminished if it had.

The story suggests that God permitted pain, suffering, and

James and Contemporary Religious Thought

injustice to fall on Job's head in order to test him. The idea that life is a test is very old and not especially popular any longer. My own disposition, however, is to see life more and more in those terms. Life is always demanding. It constantly spews up problems, questions, and dilemmas. Some are challenging and creative. A few are just good fun. Others produce frustrations, destruction, and bitterness. At any rate, life usually involves some sense of testing for me. If I could rid myself of that feeling, perhaps life would be simpler, more carefree. But I do not think that I can eliminate the feeling because of the way that life itself is structured.

If you think of life as a test, it is natural to be hopeful that the test means something worthwhile and that the outcome will be positive. Furthermore, you have to hope that the examiner is ultimately benevolent, no matter how tricky, frustrating, and disheartening the examination may be. God sets needlessly difficult tests. He allows them sometimes to torture and destroy many persons. Some victims hardly have a chance. The whole course of human life shows this wasteful side. In addition, even among those who endure the tests and meet them well, there is often no equity in terms of earthly rewards. God restored Job's earthly fortune – at least that is the report with which the story ends. Probably it is an appendage produced by some "healthy-minded" editor. At any rate, the rewards of this life are not consistently handed out according to merit. This life, then, provides no final and satisfactory resolutions for the experiences that we have lived through.

Still, the testing – with all of its suffering and waste – could be positively significant and judged good overall. This could be true if there is life beyond death in which persons are changed by a God whose harshness is finally tempered by care and love so that our pasts become the prelude to a life of creativity and joy which could be an end in itself. I do not hope for such a transformation on any broad scale in this life. There are too many facts against it. In addition, I see a more powerful God than James's as the factor needed to make such change possible beyond death. Neither men nor James's God seem capable of substantially reducing the negative factors in existence. It is all they can do to hold the line against them. Only a God who could decisively alter things in this life – and now – seems to me capable of recreating it beyond the grave. So I live with a guilty God of power, hoping that he is also, in ways now hidden, a God of love.

Two concluding comments are needed. First, I want to emphasize that I am not totally weary of this world – only a little. As I have worked on this essay, interrupted from time to time by the laughing faces of my wife and children, I keep having feelings which tell me that this life is genuinely good and joyous. Even as I lament, I know that is true in a fundamental way. So I try to live with cheerful concern in this life right now, however difficult this may sometimes be. Finally, it is precisely feelings of this kind, which are often fostered in me by other persons (some religious, some not), that help me to understand my existence in terms of a God who is loving as well as harshly powerful. William James is one of those persons. For good or ill, he has shaped my spirit. I hope it is for good.

NOTES

1 From a letter to Miss Frances R. Morse, dated April 12—13, 1900. See Henry James, ed., *The Letters of William James* (Boston: Little, Brown and Company, 1926), II, p. 127. Original copyright 1920. Hereafter this collection is referred to as *Letters*.
2 Part of James's response in 1904 to a questionnaire on religious belief sent to him by Professor James B. Pratt of Williams College. See *ibid.*, II, p. 215.
3 George Santayana, *Character and Opinion in the United States* (New York: Charles Scribner's Sons, 1921), p. 67.
4 From a letter to Charles A. Strong, dated April 9, 1907. See *Letters*, II, p. 269.
5 Another part of James's response to the Pratt questionnaire. See *ibid.*, II, p. 213.
6 William James, *A Pluralistic Universe* (New York: Longmans, Green and Company, 1909), p. 311.
7 From James's reply to the Pratt questionnaire. See *Letters*, II, p. 213.

8 Also from James's reply to the Pratt questionnaire. See *ibid.*, II, p. 214.
9 Santayana, *Character and Opinion in the United States*, p. 65.
10 *Ibid.*, p. 88.
11 From a letter to Shadworth H. Hodgson, dated December 30, 1885. See *Letters*, I, p. 245.
12 From a letter to Miss Grace Norton, dated August 29, 1902. See *ibid.*, II, p. 174.
13 Albert Camus, *The Rebel*, trans. Anthony Bower (New York: Vintage Books, 1956), pp. 303—304.
14 Job 19:25—27. From *The Jerusalem Bible* (Garden City, New York: Doubleday & Company, Inc., 1971).

16

EIGHT SPOTLIGHTS ON «THE WILL TO BELIEVE» BY WILLIAM JAMES

Hans F. Geyer

I intend to quote some passages from the essay mentioned and from other essays which made up the collection James published under the title, *The Will to Believe and Other Essays in Popular Philosophy*. Each quotation will correspond to a spotlight, a small circle of intensive light which shows perhaps better than a general survey some particularity of the thought of William James. It is my intention, too, not to neglect the element of surprise. William James shall spring into existence, spring on you, shall spring into your eyes, as we say in German; his manifestation or materialization shall have the spontaneity of life. He will be present among us. I shall speak, too, about the context of the text, the context of the citation, and then, after the philosophical business, I shall try to philosophize about the philosophy of William James. And now, after this short introduction, to work.

Spotlight Number One:
M plus x

This sounds a little bit mysterious, but we shall see clearly about it presently. James writes: "Suppose that in looking at the world and seeing how full it is of misery, of old age, of wickedness and pain, and how unsafe is his own future, a human being yields to the pessimistic conclusion, cultivates disgust and dread, ceases striving and finally commits suicide. He thus adds to the mass of mundane phenomena, independent of his subjectivity, the subjective complement x, which makes of the whole an utterly black picture illumined by no gleam of good."[1]

We find this passage in James' essay, "The Sentiment of Rationality." Sentiment, yes, and emotion, too, power and dynamics of the *sursum corda,* the *sursum corda* of any religion, of any philosophy and science, because science, too, has its sentiments and very different they are in the different sciences! All this is represented by the little x in front of the great, of the overwhelming M which stands for the mass of mundane phenomena. William James shows the subjective disposition in sharp contrast with the world. We ask ourselves: Does the world begin with the will to believe, or the will to believe with the world? This question seems preposterous. Isn't the world the first datum, the datum of data? Isn't man, the latest newcomer, bold and impudent enough to pretend that a God of his own creation created the world, a God, too, who must have believed in what he created, who started the whole creation with his belief? An aerial structure which can't explain in the least the existence of the earth, of the sun, of the whole universe and all things being! But the whole universe in our equation is M, the totality of phenomena in the world. Unexplained or explained, it explains neither the presence of man in the world nor the tricky little x, the other element of our equation, which adds itself in a rather peculiar fashion to the totality of mundane phenomena. X will never be explained simply because it is itself the principle of explanation. And James believes – and believes with a will – that this principle of explanation is in its heart of hearts an emotion.

Spotlight Number Two:
The Leap in the Dark

I confess that I read James with real emotion because I'm too, like James, a man who leaps and likes to leap in the dark, which is amply proved, I think, by the book I'm publishing this year. But now, dutifully, about the leap of William James.

James writes:

> Suppose, for example, that I am climbing in the Alps, and have had the ill-luck to work myself into a position from which the only escape is a terrible leap. Being without similar experience, I have no evidence of my ability to perform it successfully; but hope and confidence in myself make me sure I shall not miss my aim, and nerve my feet to execute what without those subjective emotions would perhaps have been impossible. But suppose that, on the contrary, the emotions of fear and mistrust preponderate; or suppose that, having just read the Ethics of Belief, I feel it would be sinful to act upon assumption unverified by previous experience, – why, then I shall hesitate so long that at last, exhausted and trembling, and launching myself in a moment of despair, I miss my foot-hold and roll into the abyss.[2]

Faith is the magical character of this enterprise of one moment and one life, of this "terrible leap." James sees faith as creating its own verification, which means that it is one entity, the man and his deed. And he is firmly convinced that just this evidence has never been clearly pointed out. I think that he is quite right about it. And I think, too, that his truth hasn't since been found again. James was in advance of his century, and he is in advance of ours. We just begin to see again what he saw; his truth dawns upon us. What about science? James is of the opinion that belief outstrips scientific evidence. And why? My answer is: Because it creates the man and creates his deed. Man is the subject, his deed is the object. But subject and object are, in this case, indistinguishable. Subject and object form a whole of which Aristotle has said that it is more than the addition of its parts. Faith is certainly inner experience. Couldn't we admit the possibility of a science of inner experience which wouldn't have any business outstripping scientific evidence? Science now begins to guess at the inner experience of animals, which is the great theme of ethology. And what about inner experience, what about the ethology of man? Faith, certainly, would be an important trait of it.

Spotlight Number Three:
Oxford Street or Divinity Avenue?

James writes: "What is meant by saying that my choice of which way to walk home after the lecture is ambiguous and matter of chance as far as the present moment is concerned? It means that both Divinity Avenue and Oxford Street are called; but that only one, and that one *either* one, shall be chosen."[3]

We find this passage in the essay, "The Dilemma of Determinism." James is interested in the following problem: The professor, after his lecture, might go home through Divinity Avenue or Oxford Street. Which of the two will it be? Will the course of events in the universe be changed if he decides for the one or for the other? After the fact of his return, we know the answer; but viewed before the fact, there is the possibility of a universe characterized and influenced by the first or by the second choice. And James asks himself and his hearers: "But looking outwardly at these universes, can you say which is the impossible and accidental one, and which the rational and necessary one?"[4] The philosophy of William James is a philosophy of chance, and a philosophy which takes a chance. The expression "philosophy of chance" means a *genitivus subjectivus* and a *genitivus objectivus*. On the one hand, James isn't a systematic philosopher in the manner of Hegel. His philosophy has an aphoristic quality. On the other hand, "chance" is an important concept in his loose system. He couldn't do without it, because there is always, as we have seen, the little x of subjective disposition in front of the great mass M of mundane phenomena. The subjective and the objective chances that the microcosmos of man and the macrocosmos of the universe would be other than seen and foreseen by the determinist are overwhelming.

Spotlight Number Four:
The Natural History of the Mind

James says: "We shall merely have investigated a chapter in the natural history of the mind, and found that, as a matter of such natural history, God may be called the normal object of the mind's belief. Whether over and above this he be really the living truth is another question."[5] We see that William James isn't quite sure about God, but for practical reasons he is inclined to tolerate and even to welcome the hypothesis. And one of the practical reasons, but certainly not the foremost, might well be that he is addressing an assembly of Unitarian ministers. He has, as he says, the "physiological view of mentality"[6] and finds that the cognitive faculty "appears but as one element in an organic mental whole."[7] The attempt of James at what might be called the "conjugation in the singular" of the universe is interesting. For him, the infratheistic way of looking at the world leaves God in the third person, a mere "it"; theism turns "it" into a "thou," and "other theories try to cover it with the mantle of the first person, and to make it a part of *me*."[8] This first person could have been, for James, who studied medicine and especially physiology, the human body, the human body being in the virtue of conscience a "thou," in virtue of its organic immensity an "it," part of the world, a world in itself, a microcomos. The human body, as the sole body of the universe we know of, has inner and outer discerning experience, the inner experience of religion, the outer experience of science. And now, quite independently of William James, must we not admit that the feeling of some sort of perfection in our body, it may be of the physiological, of the psychological or of the mental kind, has nothing to do whatever with every conceivable variety of historic religion and its patent errors about man and the world? And couldn't we say then that these feelings, these emotions and these thoughts are part of the natural history of the human body, of the human soul and the human mind?

Spotlight Number Five:
The Idiosyncrasy of Genius and Molecular Chance

James says, "The environment *preserves* the conception which it was unable to *produce* in any brain less idiosyncratic than my own."[9] I see the essay "Great Men and their Environment" as a remarkable application of Darwinian theory on the cultural history of man. James identifies the idiosyncracy of genius, that is, his molecular chance with the Darwinian tendency to spontaneous variations which we call today "mutations." James says: "The causes of production of great men lie in a sphere wholly inaccessible to the social philosopher. He must simply accept geniuses as data, just as Darwin accepts his spontaneous variations."[10] In short, the absolute history of man is a combination of the element of chance in the natural history of man with the element of chance in the cultural history of man, because, originally, all essential institutions of human society were "flashes of genius in an individual head."[11] Now there seems to me to be a contradiction of a Hegelian kind in the philosophy of William James, between his conception of human history (which is to say, cultural history) and of human natural history, a contradiction which does not annihilate truth, but quite to the contrary, permits us to find the truth. A great aphorism in the "Great Logic" of Hegel runs like this: Der Widerspruch treibt in die Tiefe: it is a contradiction which opens up the depth of truth. On the one hand, James sees the molecular chance of individual man which in the form of the great man might happen to influence considerably the social environment. This corresponds to an influence of the natural history of man on his cultural history. On the other hand, it's the conviction that natural science is very important that tends to hinder or even to prevent the historic influence of individual molecular chance because natural scientists, as a rule, aren't inclined very much to believe in genius. They see the nature of nature which in its macrophysical results is determination; they don't see enough the nature of man which is not determination in this sense. The depth of the contradiction seems to prove that the height of the natural history of man coincides with the height of his cultural history. Natural science and natural scientists haven't yet paid enough tribute to this elementary truth.

Spotlight Number Six:
The Maggots

James says: "It gives us a pluralistic, restless universe, in which no single point of view can ever take in the whole scene; and to a mind possessed of the love of unity at any cost, it will, no doubt, remain forever inacceptable. A friend with such a mind once told me that the thought of my universe made him sick, like the sight of the horrible motion of a mass of maggots in their carrion bed."[12]

James is a pluralistic type of philosopher. He is a man of religion and a man of natural science; he is a man of inner and of outer experience; he is a man of natural and of cultural history. He begins with medicine and ends with philosophy; he begins with the anatomy of the body and ends with the anatomy of the mind. Maggots, maggots, maggots! He is the kind of loose philosopher who begins with an aphorism and ends with a system; then, mistrusting the system, returns to the aphorism which now, enriched by its past, wields systematic power. He is a man of the earth and a man of the stars; he believes what he sees, but what he sees hides the unknown. He is a rationalist and at the same time a potential mystic. And last and not least, he is a philosopher and a brilliant author too. The brilliancy of his style has the Shakespearean character of the unexpected. His essays are of the best I know in the English literature. His style is impending. I mean by this that it brings the unexpected but we expect it. His style is sudden because it combines aphoristic incisiveness with the width of a systematic horizon.

Spotlight Number Seven:
Admit Plurality and Time May be Its Form

James writes: "Is not, however, the timeless mind rather a gratuitous fiction? And is not the notion of eternity being given at a stroke to omniscience only just another way of whacking upon us the block-universe, and of denying that possibilities exist? – just the point to be proved. To say that time is an illusory appearance is only a roundabout manner of saying there is no real plurality, and that the frame of things is an absolute unit. Admit plurality, and time may be its form."[13]

There is a relation and an affinity of materialistic determinism and of the theistic theory of Providence which James underlines in this passage. In both cases the conception of time and, we may add, the conception of future assume the character of absolute unity. Deus sive natura! In Spinoza we find this conception in its purest form. Isn't it rather curious that we are quite prepared to see the historic past of humanity not as a unity but as a very complex whole, whereas we are inclined to what James calls "closet solutions"[14] regarding the future? And James adds most characteristically: "Better chaos forever than an order based on any closet-philosopher's rule, even though he were the most enlightened possible member of his tribe."[15] So as every century in the past has its definite character, so will every century in the future have its character too. So as every century in the past had its liberty before God, being "unmittelbar zu Gott" in the words of the German historian, Ranke – so every century in the future will have its liberty before God too. Plurality in the past, plurality in the future, time has brought and time will bring it.

Spotlight Number Eight:
The Nulliverse

You won't find this word "nulliverse" in any dictionary; James has invented it *ad hoc*, for a good purpose, one might say. James writes: "Nevertheless, many persons talk as if the minutest dose of disconnectedness of one part with another, the smallest modicum of independence, the faintest tremor of ambiguity about the future, for example, would ruin everything, and turn this goodly universe into a sort of insane heap or nulliverse, no universe at all."[16] To the deterministic philosopher the universe in which chance takes a role is a nulliverse because an indeterministic future means the abolition of causal determination in the past, in the present, and in the future. It is not a universe in order any more; it is a universe thoroughly out of order; it is an unpredictable universe, a universe with a whim, a universe in psychologic disorder, a universe which might have to fear at any moment an annulation and annihilation by a decision out of the depth of free will. It is a casual universe and its "casualty" in a double sense is the result of the inner experience of man, of his free will. The universe, for James, runs the risk to be free which means that it is not free of chance. James says: "We have seen that chance, the very name of which we are urged to shrink from as from a metaphysical pestilence, means only the negative fact that no part of the world, however big, can claim to control absolutely the destiny of the whole."[17] James finds himself in the vicinity of Schopenhauer who revealed the depth of will but which, unlike James, doesn't see as a free will. According to James, we could explain this metaphysical difference psychologically, that is, by the difference of the emotional base of philosophic thought. But might not there be a logical explanation too? We know that in the microphysical theory there is a chance that something may happen or not. On the other hand, macrophysical theory is, in spite of the fortuitiousness of microphysical theory, strictly deterministic. Now, couldn't we admit an analogy between nature as a whole and mankind in this sense that the motivation of the somatic microcosmos of human body comes out of the microphysical region, ruled by statisical laws, to enter the openness of the macrophysical region, governed by deterministic physical laws? The process of the brain which builds up the human decisions has certainly a microphysical side to it from which we get psychologically the specific feeling when we are in suspense between two possible decisions. Should this hypothesis be true, then the inner experience of man would have for ages and ages corroborated the result of quite recent discoveries of the outer, that is, the microphysical experience of man. And the consequence of it? There is no necessary contradiction between the universe and a supposed nulliverse as well as there is no contradiction between mass and energy, between mass particles and wave motion. And wasn't the universe once a nulliverse which exploded into a universe? The most modern theories of the origin of the world seem to permit this conclusion. The origin of the universe in the nulliverse? In a double-edged, ironical manner of speaking, this is a vindication for William James.

NOTES

1 William James, *The Will to Believe and Other Essays in Popular Philosophy* (1897; London and Bombay: Longmans, Green and Co., 1907), "The Sentiment of Rationality," pp. 100—101.
2 *Ibid.*, pp. 96—97.
3 *Ibid.*, "The Dilemma of Determinism," p. 155.
4 *Ibid.*, p. 156.
5 *Ibid.*, "Reflex Action and Theism," p. 116.
6 *Ibid.*, p. 142.
7 *Ibid.*, p. 140.
8 *Ibid.*, p. 134.
9 *Ibid.*, "Great Men and their Environment", p. 250.
10 *Ibid.*, pp. 225—226.
11 *Ibid.*, p. 253.
12 *Ibid.*, "The Dilemma of Determinism," p. 177.
13 *Ibid.*, p. 181.
14 *Ibid.*, "The Moral Philosopher and the Moral Life," p. 207.
15 *Ibid.*, p. 204.
16 *Ibid.*, "The Dilemma of Determinism," pp. 154—155.
17 *Ibid.*, p. 159.

17

WILLIAM JAMES AND HIS FATHER: A STUDY IN CHARACTEROLOGY[1]

Gérard Deledalle

That William James suffered from insomnia and that this was related to his neurotic temperament is a fact. The suggestions which have been made that James's search for an identity of the self can be explained by the duality of his own character, or that James's *Open Universe* has its origin in the author's claustrophobia, sets the following problem: Is there a relation between an author's character and his work?

In point of fact, no psychological explanation can account for a system of thought, nor any other kind of explanation either, were it only for the fact that, to take the case of claustrophobia, all other persons suffering from it have not worked out a theory of the *open universe*. It is none the less interesting, even if it is only a game, in the manner of Wittgenstein, to relate a system of thought to a character, while taking care not to put the cart before the horse; in other words not to try to deduce thought from character, for, as we shall see, in the case of the two Jameses, their philosophies, although dissimilar, are rooted in the same type of character.

It was while reading, some time ago, Frederic Young's book on Henry James, Sr.[2] that I had the impression that there existed a kind of harmony between father and son, that their respective philosophies seemed, however, to belie, and that I began to wonder of what nature this unity, over and above concepts, might be.

I have applied the method of analysis of character invented by the Dutch psychologists Eymans and Wiersma, which has been systematized in France by the philosophers R. Le Senne, G. Berger and P. Mesnard. Contrary to the psychological methods used in America which are mostly based on factorial analysis, the Dutch method is typological. However, if one examines closely the questions of the Dutch questionnaire, one will see that they correspond fairly well to the factors or traits of the American psychologists of "personality." It will be noted that what is called in France "character" is what is more usually called "personality" in America.

The characterology of the Franco-Dutch school can be exposed in a few words. Let it suffice to remember that its terminology must be divested of all psychological connotations in their traditional sense, philosophical as well as literary: E or emotionality means, to quote G. Berger *(Traité pratique d'analyse du caractère)* "a disposition to experience strong and repeated emotions," A or activity, which it would be more appropriate to term effective activity (for it means creative or innovating activity), "the relative facility with which one carries out what one wants to do," S or secondary, "the retention of impressions." As for the combinations of these three factors or of their contraries[3] (nE lesser emotionality, nA lesser activity, P lesser secondarity, therefore primarity, non-retention of impressions), they are not stable, on the one hand, because characters evolve, and on the other hand, because a so-called Passionate character, for instance, corresponding to the formula EAS, is at variance with itself, EA denoting an explosiveness which is smothered by the secondarity.

With this in mind, we can say that the Jameses belong to the characterological category of the Nervous: emotional, non-active, primary (EnAP). They are emotional: they are easily moved to enthusiasm. H. James was literally carried away on reading Swedenborg's treatise on *Love and Divine Wisdom;* W. James embraced pragmatism with transports of delight.

The flow of words and the epic tone of the father' writings are equalled only by the communicative warmth of the son's lectures; in 1906 people flocked to hear W. James's lectures on pragmatism, and the ladies were already raving about him.

W. James was susceptible, and could not bear criticism, even when it was justified. What he wanted from the other philosophers was just a sympathetic attitude. He was convinced that pragmatism needed only that to be accepted. He felt sorry for those who did not understand it. Of Bourdeau, who had written an article on pragmatism inspired by the papers of Lalande published in the *Revue philosophique,* he said: "Poor man! He seems not to be able to get rid of the subject; but the pragmatism that lives inside of me is so different from that which I succeed in wakening the idea inside of other people, that theirs makes me feel like cursing God and dying."[4] The incomprehension of the public towards H. James was just as great. The critics were little concerned with his work except to ridicule it when they had a chance. "Henry James wrote *The Secret of Swedenborg,*" said one of them, "and he has kept it well." But H. James seems to have suffered far less than his son from this incomprehension. His escape into a dream-world, which is characteristic of the Nervous type, softened the harshness of the contact with the public and left the universe of his visions unexplored by others.

However they both suffered from a fundamental sadness, a sadness which was dispelled or rather shaken off by spurts of enthusiasm. The biographer of W. James has made this quite clear. Ralph Barton Perry distinguishes three Jameses: the neurasthenic, unstable James with his "sometimes morbidly, vivid and lawless imagination ... and his aversion to rigorous intellectual procedure ... ; the radiant James, vivid, gay, loving, companionable and sensitive"; and a third James "in whom the second of these is deepened and enriched through being united with the first."[5] The impression of graciousness and kindness made on people by W. James, like his father whose affability was as well-known as his eccentricity, does not contradict what we have already said about the congenital emotionality of our two philosophers.

In characterology this is in fact usually the case when emotionality is combined with secondarity or to broadness of the field of consciousness. In the case of the Jameses who were primary, it is to the broadness of their fields of consciousness that we must attribute their graciousness and kindness. It is to this also that we must impute the lack of intellectual rigor in William James and in his father "who argued freely from analogy, took figures of speech literally, and produced a blend of poetry and science which was neither the one nor the other."[6]

The essential test of emotionality is as follows: "Do you take to heart little things which you know to be of minor importance? Are you sometimes upset by trifles?" To which our philosophers reply in unison "Yes!" each of them relating a characteristic and astonishingly identical experience. That of H. James occurred in 1884. It is described in *Society the Redeemed Form of Man* (pp. 44–46) quoted by F. Young:

> One day ... having eaten a comfortable dinner, I remained sitting at the table after the family had dispersed, idly gazing at the embers in the grate, thinking of nothing, and feeling only the exhilaration incident to a good digestion, when *suddenly – in a lightning-flash* as it were – "fear came upon me, and trembling, which made all my bones to shake." To all appearance it was a *perfectly insane* and abject terror, *without ostensible cause, and only to be accounted for, to my perplexed imagination, by some damned shape squatting invisible to me within the precincts of the room, and raying out from his fetid personality influences fatal to life. The thing had not lasted ten seconds before I felt myself a wreck, that is, reduced from a state of firm, vigorous, joyful manhood to one of almost helpless infancy.* The only self-control I was capable of exerting was to keep my seat. I felt the greatest desire to run incontinently to the foot of the stairs and shout for help to my wife, – to run to the roadside even, and appeal to the public to protect me; but by an immense effort I controlled these frenzied impulses, and determined not to budge from my chair till I had recovered my lost self-possession. This purpose I held to for a good long hour, as I reckoned time, beat upon meanwhile by *an ever-growing tempest of doubt, anxiety, and despair,* with absolutely no relief from any truth I had ever en-

countered save a most pale and distant glimmer of the Divine existence, – when I resolved to abandon the vain struggle, and communicate without any more ado what seemed my sudden burst of inmost, implacable unrest to my wife.
Now, to make a long story short, this ghastly condition of mind continued with gradually lengthening intervals of relief, for two years, and even longer...[7]

The experience undergone by William James is described by himself in almost the same terms in *The Varieties of Religious Experience* in the chapter on "The Sick Soul."[8] It was the same terrifying inhuman vision of "an epileptic... with greenish skin, entirely idiotic" who "sat there like a sort of sculptured Egyptian cat or Peruvian mummy." The vision gripped W. James "suddenly without any warning, just as if it came out of darkness," with a horrible fear of his own existence, and he identified himself with it: "That shape am I, I felt, potentially." It all lasted only a few seconds, says James, but "it was as if something hitherto solid within my breast gave way entirely, and I became a mass of quivering fear."

These experiences prove perhaps too much in that they seem to belong rather to the field of pathological psychology than to that of characterology. If the Nervous man is often taken for a sick man, not all experiences of emotionality have this morbid aspect. The Jameses, although not exceptions, were excessively emotional and tormented by the beyond in its evil form, by what we might call "transdescendance" to use Jean Wahl's term. H. James was haunted by the problem of evil and W. James by that of metaphysical phenomena. The author of *the Varieties of Religious Experience* wrote a good deal on psychical research and he played a great part in the founding of the Society for Psychical Research.

The emotionality of the two Jameses is a morbid hyperemotionality because it is combined with strong primarity and definite non-activity. These factors, of course, can be distinguished from each other only by a mental analysis and even then we cannot describe the explosive and evanescent emotionality of the Nervous type while pretending to ignore the primarity which gives emotionality its violent but sporadic aspect, its alternation of calm and storms, the calm itself being the effect of the non-activity; neither can we describe the deep and lasting emotionality of the Sentimental type (EnAS) without taking into account the secondarity, which in this case allies with the non-activity and gives it calmness and seriousness. In the Nervous type the non-activity is dominated by the primary emotionality: $EP>nA$, while in the case of the Sentimental type, secondarity combined with non-activity overcomes the inclination to revolt produced by emotionality: $AS>E$. This is why the mobile Nervous type sometimes gives a false impression of activity, which is not the case with the Sentimental type.

The two Jameses were primary, and therefore mobile and improvident. The pleasure-trip which, according to them, was always undertaken for reasons of health, was a family institution. It was not just a trip, in fact. At the least sign of failing health, they were off to the capitals and spas of Europe. But they would soon weary of it all and return home, only to be off again after a short while. Henry James led the way and the family imitated him, especially William who, at every journey he made, regretted his lost tranquility. In 1865 W. James joined an expedition of naturalists to Brazil, but regretted it immediately: "I thrill with joy," he wrote to his family, "when I think that one short month and we are homeward bound. Welcome ye dark blue waves! Welcome my native slosh and ice and cast-iron stoves, magazines, theatre, friends and everything! even churches."[9] But the following year he went to Europe to have treatment for his back. Two years later he was home again: "I have a better chance of getting well in the quiet of home than in tossing about Europe like a drowned pup about a pond in a storm," he commented.[10] This did not prevent him from going to Switzerland in 1892 with his wife and four children of whom the eldest was thirteen and the youngest two. No sooner had he arrived in Europe than he wrote to a friend, "How could (your nephew and his wife) see us off and not raise a more solemn word of warning?"[11]

Another characteristic of primarity is the changing of one's profession. Were it only by this characteristic James would be a hundred, percent primary. In turn he felt a calling for painting, chemistry, nature study, medicine, physiology, psychology and philosophy (never for logic). While studying chemistry, he went to the lectures of the naturalist Agassiz; on becoming a doctor he taught physiology and afterward psychology; on becoming a professor of psychology, he taught philosophy and launched pragmatism. As for Henry James, he practised no profession. His health made it impossible, his fortune made it unnecessary, and his non-activity could amply dispense with it.

Their primarity made the Jameses unmethodical. To prove the eccentricity of Henry James, people often relate how at table he had the knack of bringing up all kinds of problems about which the emotional and primary members of the family would quarrel, without unpleasantness but violently, to the dismay of the guests, whom Mrs. James, who had been endowed by Nature with the secondarity of the perfect hostess, would endeavor to reassure. There was always a happy ending, the antagonists possessing the tenderness of the broad Nervous type.

It was a blessing for our two philosophers to have both married secondary women who set their affairs in order and ran their houses well. Would William James ever have written his *Principles of Psychology* or the *Briefer Course* if his wife had not protected him from unwelcome visitors and organized his time and work?

The Nervous type is non-active. It is surprising to be able to say that the Jameses were inactive; they wrote a lot, not so much as if they had been of the Choleric type, who produce one pamphlet after another, or of the Sentimental type, scrupulous diary-keepers, but their works are there to speak for them. Our surprise turns into suspicion when we learn that they were prolific letter-writers. Is not the letter characteristic of the active type? And how shall we account for the continual voyages across the Atlantic?

That is all true. And yet letters and books are as much a sign of inactivity as the restlessness of the primary emotional type is. But before explaining their apparent activity let us point out several biographical traits of non-activity. William James and his father were capable of remaining for a long while without doing anything, simply day-dreaming; Henry James would stare at the glowing coals in the fire-place and his son, while in Germany, often spent his time with his face pressed against the window-pane dreaming about the girls he could see in the houses opposite. They both preferred contemplation to action. William James did not like working in laboratories; although in 1876 he founded the first laboratory of psychology in America, he hardly ever worked there and in 1892 gave over the direction of it to Munsterberg. His main conclusion after the expedition with Agassiz was that he was "cut out for a speculative rather than an active life."[12] To which his father replied that he himself was inclined by nature to love and to think rather than to act, and that time spent on real actions like sewing on a button lay heavy on him.

H. James, like his children, had excuses; he had been amputated of one leg and suffered from backache like the rest of the family. He could not remain standing for any length of time; neither could W. James, which explains why, for the latter, laboratory work must have been most painful.

Finally, and this is the last characteristic we shall deal with, the Jameses were clumsy and impractical. It was owing to his clumsiness that Henry James lost his leg. He injured himself while attempting to put out a fire in stable. A similar accident occurred to Henry James, the novelist, but he was luckier and came out of it with no more than a strained back. As for William James, his lack of practical common-sense was responsible for the illness which proved fatal to him; while out walking he got lost; he tried to retrace his steps but could not find the way nor orientate himself; he walked for thirteen hours and arrived home with a strained heart.

We shall now reply to the question: Why did these inactive people write? The reply is simple: they were compelled to. But the compulsion may take on two different aspects according to its internal or external character. When it is internal, it is an expression of the intellectual passion of primary emotionality: Henry James was carried away by Sandemanism and defended it; he became enthusiatic over the doctrine of Swedenborg and wrote a defense of it. William James rushed head-first into psychology and then into philosophy; the stream of consciousness was his property, pragmatism belonged to him. No one might touch them without the pen-wielding Cerberus, their owner, protecting them. That is one form of external constraint: to defend one's property; it is negative. There is another form, more positive and more compelling: the publisher and his contract. In the fire of his ardor for psychology, W. James signed a contract with Henry Holt for a book to appear within two years at the latest. *The Principles of Psychology* (the book in question) was actually published after great difficulties eleven years later in 1890. Then the author had to prune it and produce the *Briefer Course*. But psychological faith had already been sacrificed a long time before to philosophical faith. It was thus not surprising that W. James needed a lot of coaxing to complete his work on psychology.

Characterology shows that the inactive type neglects work imposed by his profession in favor of work which is not imposed. Have we not already seen the professor of physiology preparing his work on psychology and the professor of psychology preparing his work on philosophy?

The simple formula of the Nervous type EnAP is thus personalized: the Jameses are primary emotional and non-active, with a broad field of consciousness and strong intellectual passions. What can their readers expect from philosophers belonging to this category? Certainly not systematic treatises nor analytical works. The broadness of the field of consciousness is incompatible with the dry and objective thesis. What is best suited to them is the essay, which does not demand pompous objectivity but allows the author to make digressions and personal syntheses, felt rather than proved, in a lively, direct, exclamatory style which is what the Jameses have left us in fact. Most of their writings are based on, when they are not merely the reproduction of, lectures and letters. One can feel in them the warmth of contact with a real individual of flesh and blood, be he listener or correspondent. *The Principles* have the importance and the value of a treatise on psychology but they are, in the words of a critic who cannot be suspected of partiality, Stanley Hall, the work of "an impressionist in psychology: his portfolio contains sketches, old and new, moral, literary, scientific and metaphysical; some are exquisite and charming in detail and even in colour, others are rough charcoal outlines, but all together stimulating and suggestive."[13] And Stanley Hall adds: "This is through and through a 'tendence' book."[14]

As for the *Briefer Course,* James had a poor opinion of it: "I have cut out of *The Principles* the most interesting part," he said to his publisher, "the Humor and the pathos."

These essays do not aim to establish an objective truth which is indifferent to the incomprehension of human beings; they try to persuade, to convince affectively. Objective truth is sometimes given rough treatment: the Jameses are not logicians; they care little about the objective value of the argument as long as it attracts as many people as possible to the "faith" that the missionary is called to preach. But the Jameses being Nervous missionaries sacrificed the faith to the faithful and the Swedenborgism and the pragmatism they preach are heresies.

Before we examine these "heresies" and in order to be able to do so, we shall try to decide what the themes of Nervous thought are. Let there be no mistake, however: we are not saying that the Jameses' philosophies were inevitably determined by their characters. Temporal and logical histories have their word to say here. Let the reader not suspect us, either, of trying to attribute to the Nervous type what the Jameses said. It is the themes that we are going to bring out and nothing more; they follow a historical line which may disguise them but does not deform them. The Nervous philosopher, because he is emotional, gives preference to the qualitative over the quantitative and the rational. His qualitative is *felt*. One would say today that it is "existential." It is not a category as with Aristotle, one might say it is rather in the nature of the "tertiary qualities" of Santayana. Because he is primary, the Nervous philosopher has a natural tendency to valorize what is spontaneous, alive, and moving. Because he is non-active, he is often an idealist, but his idealism is mystical and experienced; values do not exist up in the Platonic world of ideas, they live in us. To be noted also in the Nervous type is the facility with which he gets hold of new ideas which he appropriates shamelessly to himself without any care for objectivity.

It is this lack of objectivity which makes the Nervous type into heretics. William James's pragmatism has nothing of the logical theory of Peirce continued by Dewey. James saw in pragmatism the negation of the value of reason and the affirmation of the primacy of life. This is quite consistent with his character. He appropriated pragmatism and defended it with his interpretation of it against all comers, including Peirce and Dewey who had to give it up to him lock, stock and barrel. Peirce re-baptized his doctrine by the name of "pragmaticism" and Dewey called his "instrumentalism."

This taste for novelty had other and happier consequences: it made W. James the initiator of experimental (non-quantitative) psychology and the creator of religious psychology. If pragmatism suffered from it, it was because James was not the first in the field, but we must admit that his name has remained attached to this affective pragmatism which philosophy has never whole-heartedly accepted.

That one of the Nervous type, non-active by definition, can defend a pragmatic theory might seem paradoxical, and it would be tempting to call this "sublimation," as has already been done in the case of Maine de Biran's theory of effort, if James's pragmatism were a real theory of action; but this is not so: the only action of ideas that James ever conceived of by himself was the subjective satisfaction of the thinker.

James is thus the philosopher of affectivity, of feeling, and of life, because he is a Nervous philosopher. This is further confirmed by his conception of God and the after-life. As for his theory of the stream of consciousness, it is that of a Nervous type, but a broad Nervous type who is more sensible to the continuity of life than to the discontinuity of his primarity, and to the affective unity of his ego than to the plurality of its states. Strictly speaking, the theory of the stream of consciousness owes more to the broadness of its author's field of consciousness than to the typically Nervous character; since a Phlegmatic type like Bergson (formula nEAS, the contradiction of the formula of the Nervous type EnAP) can profess it. That is also why James's philosophy is a pluralistic monism. Describing the broad Nervous type, Le Senne, without having William James in mind, wrote the following lines in which we see a proof of our argument:

> Through the narrowing of the field of consciousness, the passing from one instant to another is, in the narrow Nervous type, discontinuous... On the other hand, through the broadening of the field of consciousness the stream of the latter becomes continuous and fluid. Experiences and ideas follow one another smoothly. *There is not the systematized construction of thought implied by secondarity, but an uninterrupted metamorphosis of the mind along certain themes which always appear, even when intellectualized, to be moments of a dream in which association and a certain affective tonality are dominant.* The will seems to have disappeared: *consciousness is a stream impelled by its own force.* Everything is blurred. The mental atmosphere is not a brillant light which shows up clear-cut shapes, but the soft haze of a diffused light. There are no well-defined outlines, no sharp edges, few interruptions.[15]

The doctrine of the stream of consciousness, like pluralistic monism, is thus the faithful image of its theorist's consciousness.

Henry James's philosophy is an original and therefore heretical synthesis of Swedenborgism. The theory of the scientific Swedenborg was too analytical, too abstract for a Nervous individual like Henry James, Sr. Swedenborg is often thought to have been illuminated and people speak often of his "mysticism." This shows an ignorance of his doctrine which is expressed in a dull report in thirty volumes on the structure and the administration of the celestial universe, written in a style which is almost as bald as that of an official document. This baldness could not suit Henry James, who gave the doctrine that life it proclaimed while not possessing it. Whereas Swedenborg deals mainly with the Esse, Essence and Existere of the Divine being, James is interested almost exclusively in the Divine in its Existere and its *procedere* as they are manifested in its creative activities. The name of theo-pragmatism is therefore quite apropriate.[16] Thus one is justified in seeing in the father's philosophy the origin of the son's pragmatism. All the more so, we would say, in that the pragmatism of of Henry James, active as it may be, is no more practical than that of his son. It is the philosophy of a broad Nervous individual, sensible to the continuity of action. Henry James sees and thinks everything which exists *sub specie creationis*.

The incarnation of values, the primacy of life, the sense of continuity, such are the characteristics of Henry James's philosophy. They are also those af William James's. They qualify the thought of the broad Nervous type. If we add the obsession with evil laid down as the principle of "spiritual evil," "spiritual evil which I am," as Henry James says,[17] and the taste for scatological terms which he shares with Swedenborg, such as "fetid," "excretory," "excrementitious," "putrid," "stinking," and so on,[18] the philosophy of the thinker will bear a good deal of resemblance to the characterological portrait of the man.

At the beginning of this paper I explained how I came to undertake a characterological study of the Jameses as philosophers. It is now possible to say, and I shall draw no other conclusion from this analysis, that their respective philosophies are closely connected with their broad Nervous type of character. William James's romantic pragmatism is thus rather characterologically than historically related to the "Americanized Swedenborgism" of his father.

NOTES

[1] This is a revised and shortened translation of a paper published in French in *Les Etudes philosophiques* (October—December 1955), 634—646.

[2] Frederic H. Young, *The Philosophy of Henry James, Sr.* (New York: Bookman Associates, 1951).

[3] These combinations give eight types of character:

EAP	the Choleric	nEAP	the Sanguine
EAS	the Passionate	nEAS	the Phlegmatic
EnAP	the Nervous	nEnAP	the Amorphic
EnAs	the Sentimental	nEnAS	the Apathetic

[4] Ralph Barton Perry, *The Thought and Character of William James* (Boston: Little, Brown and Company, 1935), II, p. 468.

[5] *Ibid.*, II, p. 699.

[6] *Ibid.*, II, pp. 150—151.

[7] Young, *The Philosophy of Henry James, Sr.*, pp. 6—7.

[8] William James, *The Varieties of Religious Experience* (1901—1902; New York: The Modern Library), pp. 157—158. For his work on psychical Research, see *William James on Psychical Research*, Compiled and Edited by Gardner Murphy and Robert O. Ballou (New York: The Viking Press, 1960).

[9] Perry, *The Thought and Character of William James*, I, pp. 225—226.

[10] *Ibid.*, I, p. 288.

[11] *The Letters of William James*, edited by his son, Henry James (Boston: Atlantic Monthly Press, 1920), I, pp. 320—321.

[12] *Ibid.*, I, p. 62.

[13] Perry, *The Thought and Character of William James*, II, p. 108.

[14] *Ibid.*, II, pp. 108—109.

[15] René Le Senne, *Traité de caractérologie* (Paris: Presses universitaires de France, 1949), p. 207. The italics are mine.

[16] Young, *The Philosophy of Henry James, Sr.*, p. 284.

[17] *Ibid.*, p. 249.

[18] *Ibid.*, p. 59.

18

THE RELATION BETWEEN JAMES AND WHITEHEAD

Victor Lowe

We can say with fair assurance that William James and Alfred North Whitehead shared certain philosophical convictions – if we phrase them carefully and in broad terms; and we can then considerably improve our understanding of both thinkers by comparing what they did with these convictions in their published writings. Many years ago I wrote something along these lines.[1] The fact that Whitehead produced his philosophy after James died, however, makes the question of *influence* a natural one. I have examined this too, and presented the conclusion that the effect on Whitehead of reading William James is better called sympathetic appreciation than influence, for there is no evidence in Whitehead's published writings that he *derived* any of his philosophic ideas from James.[2] In the eight years preceding the meeting of this Seminar I have been hunting private materials for a biographical study of Whitehead, and I should now like to report and discuss the result as it bears on his relation to James, first so far as the question of influence is concerned, and then more generally.

I

Was there any direct communication between the two men, (a) by correspondence or (b) in conversation? It would please me to be able to report one or two finds. Alas, neither correspondence nor references to conversations seem to exist. Let me show why we should accept this negative conclusion, fallible though it is, and what significance we should attach to it.

(a) In the voluminous papers of William James at Harvard's Houghton Library there are no letters from Whitehead. This is good evidence that Whitehead never wrote to him. Also, it decreases the possibility that James wrote to Whitehead; unlike Whitehead, he was a man who answered letters. We can never be assured that Whitehead received none, for the letters that he kept until his death at the end of 1947 were, with very few exceptions, destroyed along with his unpublished manuscripts by his widow in obedience to his wishes. The exceptions do not include any letter from any member of the James family. And there are not drafts of letters to Whitehead in William James's papers.

The careers of these two men make it quite improbable that the destroyed letters included any from James. Whitehead, we must always remember, was professionally a mathematician until long after James died. James probably *heard* of him from Bertrand Russell. In 1896, when Russell stayed with him at Harvard, we may suppose that Russell mentioned at least the kindness and great helpfulness of his mathematical teacher, who was also the mathematical reader of his 1895 Trinity College fellowship dissertation on the foundations of geometry. (The philosophical reader was his tutor, James Ward.) And in the spring of 1908, at Oxford or nearby Bagley Wood, Russell might well have said something to James about his collaborator on "the mathematical treatment of the principles of mathematics," to quote from the first sentence of *Principia Mathematica* – a work which, as James knew from his reading of *The Principles of Mathematics,* was being "addressed exclusively to mathematicians."[3] Add the fact that Whitehead was not involved in any psychical research, and we must doubt that James would have had any occasion to write to him. Whitehead's intimates knew that he was always a man of many interests, but no correspondent; he loved to *talk* about politics, history, and literature with his Cambridge friends. But Cambridge was not one of the places which James frequented on his trips to England.

(b) In all probability Whitehead never met James. As he

was born in England in 1861 and did not visit America until 1922 (two years before his migration to Harvard), no meeting could have occured in America, and none in Europe before the time, 1882–83, when James made many professional contacts there, especially in England. I mention this date only because it sets an outer limit to the remote possibilities. I say remote, because Whitehead was then still an undergraduate, reading mathematics for honors at Cambridge, and not yet a member of the "Apostles." The list of places in Britain where James stayed on later visits is long; the important and sufficient point is that the people with whom he is known to have had serious talks in Oxford or Edinburgh or London or Rye do not, so far as I know, include any of the people in Whitehead's circle. There *was* one in Cambridge, where Whitehead was teaching all these years: the psychologist and philosopher James Ward. (Henry Sidgwick and Frederic Myers were acquaintances rather than friends of Whitehead.) Ward was a good friend of long standing, though not an intimate, of Whitehead's. He was also an old friend of James, and for three days somewhere between the 20th and the 26th of September, 1908, James visited him in Cambridge. September was part of the Long Vacation at the University; the entire Whitehead family was in Switzerland and did not return until the 29th,[4] by which time James was in Oxford. Had a meeting been possible and occurred, James might have got from Whitehead a perspicacious explanation of Russell's persistent criticism, and a fresh view of the supposedly unresolvable conflict between logic and pragmatism; for Whitehead was a logician but not a member of the Moore-Russell school. It is a pity that men who are, or become, distinguished philosophers show so little consideration for the chroniclers who would like to relate them to each other.

The possibility that at some time James and Whitehead at least shook hands can never be eliminated, because too little is knowable about Whitehead's movements; if he kept any diary in these decades, none is extant. If a meeting occurred which meant something to James, a mention of it should be discoverable in James's diaries and papers. I have not been through all those things in Houghton; but James's recent biographer, Gay Wilson Allen, tells me that he found no reference to Whitehead in them. Ralph Barton Perry, who had been Whitehead's colleague for ten years when he finished *The Thought and Character of William James*, and who appreciated the similarities between their philosophies, never mentions Whitehead in that book. In the hundred odd letters from Whitehead, and not quite half as many from his wife and children, which are in the Russell Archives, there is no mention of James, and in the small correspondence between James and Russell there is no mention of Whitehead.

Indirectly, our two men knew *something* of each other, but not in any depth. Doubtless there was some talk about William James when the Russells were staying with the Whiteheads or *vice versa*, and occasionally at other times in the dozen years preceding James's death. Russell and Whitehead talked about almost everything under the sun, but I believe that the talk that was not concerned with their joint work was less about current philosophical issues than about the House of Commons. It is a mistake to suppose that the intellectual interests of Russell and Whitehead in those days were identical. Whitehead was never Russell's philosophical side-kick; Moore was. Russell and Moore were immersed in the battles over pragmatism, realism, and idealism; Whitehead was not. He did not attend the meetings of the Cambridge Moral Science Club, and he did not join the Aristotelian Society until 1915, nineteen years after Moore and Russell had done so.

We ought, then, to drop any hopeful supposition of a personal relation between Whitehead and James, and to conclude that their mutual friendship with Bertrand Russell did not provide much of a substitute.

Did they know each other through their writings? James could not have read Whitehead's, which were entirely in mathematics and mathematical logic. Probably Whitehead read some of James's, but did not study them until he turned toward philosophical writing. I shall say a bit more about this later.

II

To see the relations and non-relations between James and Whitehead, a view of what they were separately doing in the last two decades of James's life is indispensable. 1890 was an important year for both. His *Principles of Psychology* completed, James's continuing concerns were fideism, psychical research, and abnormal psychological phenomena; his chief new work was on the varieties of religious experience, human immortality, radical empiricism and its allied "pure-experience" theory, Bergson's alternative to intellectualism, an attempt in notebooks (unsuccessful, I think) to figure out a pluralistic metaphysics of experience that would finally satisfy him, the unfinished introductory textbook in metaphysics, and above all the advocacy of pragmatism as a liberator of philosophy and religion from the claims of rationalistic, absolute idealism. Whitehead's works in this period were entirely mathematical. I shan't list them, but I would call attention to three little-known facts about him.

(1) In 1890 Whitehead, whose background was solid Church of England, was seriously considering going over to Rome – something William James could never have dreamt of doing. After much reading and mulling over Christian theology, Whitehead sold his theological library in 1897 or '98, and for the next two decades was an outspoken agnostic.[5] When *The Varieties of Religious Experience* came out in 1902, Russell read it with some of his friends, not including Whitehead, whose marked-up copy of the book is a 1929 reprint. If Whitehead did read an early printing of the book, he must have agreed with Russell that James's conclusions were quite unjustified.[6]

(2) By the end of our period, mathematician Whitehead had already done some thinking about how the teaching of mathematics should be reformed[7]; he would publish his ideas later, with emphasis on the power of general, abstract ideas, precisely understood, in application to the world.

(3) Whitehead entertained an over-all view of his research as a mathematician. His statement of this view – the only

statement I have discovered – occurs in a letter he wrote to the Provost of University College, London on March 16, 1912.[8] Whitehead said:

> During the last twenty-two years I have been engaged in a large scheme of work, involving the logical scrutiny of mathematical symbolism and mathematical ideas. This work had its origin in the study of the mathematical theory of Electromagnetism, and has always had as its ultimate aim the general scrutiny of the relations of matter and space, and the criticism of the various applications of mathematical thought. The scheme perhaps has been overambitious, ...

These facts, Whitehead says, are known only to his intimate friends and immediate associates. He adds that his large scheme of work is only partly published; "much remains yet in project." He was then wrestling with the fourth volume of *Principia*, on geometry, which he never finished; instead, his later work in England on the foundations of physical science concluded his published writings that fall under this scheme, except for a late revisionary comment on *Principia Mathematica*.

We should not be content with thinking that the difference between Whitehead's work in England and William James's work is simply that one man was a mathematician, the other a philosopher. That *is* a big difference. But what is interesting is the kind of mathematician Whitehead was, and the kind of philosopher James was.

A glance at Whitehead's mathematical bibliography is enough to show that, though it is an exaggeration, it is not a great one to say that he left the workaday pursuit of mathematical research to others. The passage I have quoted from his letter of 1912 suggests what he was after. Such work seemed required by the great proliferation of symbols, formulae and methods, all more or less clear and in some competition with each other, in mathematics and mathematical physics after 1843,[9] and by the formulation of logic itself as an algebra. On the first page of the first product of Whitehead's large scheme of work, the *Treatise on Universal Algebra* (1898), he says that comparative study of the newer algebras should throw light "on the general theory of symbolic reasoning."

The phrase, "the various applications of mathematical thought" in the letter was not used just because Whitehead was writing as a candidate for a chair of applied mathematics.[10] He had used just that phrase at the beginning of his article, "Mathematics," in the eleventh edition of the *Encyclopaedia Britannica* (1911): "MATHEMATICS, the general term for the various applications of mathematical thought, the traditional field of which is number and quantity."[11] Whitehead's emphasis on applications recurs in parts of his letter which I have not quoted, and it indicates to me a difference between his attitude and one of Russell's. The author of "A Free Man's Worship" tended to place mathematics above the sordid world of actuality, whereas for Whitehead there was never more than one world. Most of the courses he taught were in applied mathematics, which he never deemed inferior to the pure variety. In his view of the nature of mathematics, however, I can find no touch of any pragmatism or of Bergsonism.

The possible mathematical "relations of matter and space" form the subject of Whitehead's Royal Society memoir, "On Mathematical Concepts of the Material World," which he published in 1906. It is easy to imagine what James's reaction would have been on reading the passage which raises the question of the perceivability of the material world (in one mathematical Concept), only to dismiss it as "a philosophic question with which we have no concern"[12] – no concern in that memoir; Whitehead would give the perception of nature much attention from 1914 on.

What is it about James as a philosopher that would have made him an opponent of Whitehead's "large scheme of work," had he been aware of it? There is the obvious, general fact that to James the symbolization of mathematical ideas produced at best useful distortions of the real world, i.e., the perceptual world. His addiction to the British empiricist view that a thing is what it is perceived or perceivable as, reinforced by his enthusiasm for Bergson, made him blind to the possibility of devoting oneself to mathematical symbolism without cutting oneself off from the real world. He enjoined his friend Bertrand Russell: "My dying words to you are 'Say good-by to mathematical logic if you wish to preserve your relations with concrete realities'."[13] This reveals less about Russell than about what Ralph Barton Perry called James's "temperamental repugnance to the processes of exact thought."[14]

Another characteristic of James led him to a particular repugnance. He was always a psychological philosopher. Like the psychologist Bain before him, he took belief as primary: doubt and the entertainment of an idea as a proposition were secondary features of our mental life.[15] The great problems of philosophy were problems of what to believe, and the problem of truth to which he addressed himself was that of spelling out the relation between reality and beliefs – beliefs, *not* propositions. In a letter of 1908 to a former pupil who was studying Russell's work, James wrote that "propositions ... are mongrel curs that have no real place between realities on the one hand and beliefs on the other."[16] In *The Meaning of Truth*[17] James disputed the view, held by Russell, Moore, and others (among whom I would include Whitehead), that truth and falsity are properties of propositions. When he added, "I do not say that for certain logical purposes it may not be useful to treat propositions as absolute entities, with truth or falsehood inside of them respectively, ... " he made a concession to a travesty of the role of propositions.[18] The trouble is that James was a militant, almost obsessed with commitment; and so he also wrote, in the letter from which I have just quoted: "'Propositions' are expressly devised for quibbling between realities and beliefs."[19] He *would not* see that in mathematics, and for that matter in all theoretical disciplines, it is not beliefs but *propositions* whose components, interrelations, and then truth, are investigated.

Difference between James and Whitehead concerning propositions does not disappear when we come to *Process and*

Reality. Though propositions are there given their real-life place as "lures for feeling," and belief is discussed, truth is presented as a relation between actual entities and propositions.

III

When did Whitehead first come to appreciate William James? I do not find a mention of James, or an appeal to any of his views without naming him, in any book or article before *Science and the Modern World* (1925).[20] From talk with Russell and other Cambridge friends in the *Principia* period, Whitehead surely knew of James's pragmatic theory of truth, and knew that he was a lively critic of the metaphysics of monistic idealism and of the kinds of arguments by which Bradley and Royce claimed to demonstrate its truth. But how much of James's work did Whitehead know at first hand before he received (and promptly accepted) Harvard's offer of a philosophical appointment in February, 1924? The almost complete dispersion of his library and the absence of notes and diaries makes it impossible for me to give an answer, except this: he may have known a good bit, but it is somewhat more likely that he knew only a bit. From 1911 to 1924 Whitehead was pretty much preoccupied with space, time and relativity, the anguish of the war, full-time teaching, administrative duties in the University of London and other institutions (in 1970 Goldsmiths' College named its new science building after him in recognition of what he had done for it in the early 'twenties), and the aims of education in English schools (not only mathematical education; Whitehead was the only scientist on a committee appointed by the Prime Minister in 1919 – it held eighty-five meetings, and he was almost always present – to inquire into the position of classics in the educational system). In short, he was too busy to be able to attend much to the work of James or of any other American philosopher. Whitehead was an active member of the Aristotelian Society from 1915 to 1924, but its programs for those years show that he could not have heard there more than passing references to James's philosophic positions; in fact, interest in James declined sharply in England after his death. It *probably* took the Harvard appointment to stimulate Whitehead to study James.

However, there was one philosopher outside Britain who the busiest man (with an interest in philosophy) could not ignore: Bergson. Whitehead probably came to him late; I know only that he was reading *Creative Evolution* in 1912 or soon thereafter, and that in the ten or twelve subsequent years he often discussed Bergson's philosophy with his friend Wildon Carr. Carr defended Bergson in print against Russell, and published a book on him in 1914. When James set forth the continuity of experience in *A Pluralistic Universe*, he ranged himself alongside Bergson; yet he was not a mind-matter dualist, as Bergson was but Whitehead did not want to be. Thus Bergson's description of experience as process may have served as one of the roads that took Whitehead eventually to James.

Another road, of which I am quite sure, is a desire that was natural for Whitehead to act upon when he decided to come to Harvard's department of philosophy: the desire to acquaint himself with the thought of its former great men. This meant James, first of all. In the back pages of his 1924 appointment book Whitehead wrote down a miscellaneous list of sixteen books, all but one in philosophy. He also wrote down the names of Royce, Descartes, and Hume – the last two underscored. The book list does not look as if it sprang from a single purpose; but I think that the listing of James's *A Pluralistic Universe* and *Some Problems of Philosophy* indicates an intention to read them.

A third and strong stimulus toward gaining that pointed knowledge of James which Whitehead shows in *Science and the Modern World* came from new colleagues. Five of them had been James's students and, in different ways, admirers: Ralph Barton Perry, W. E. Hocking, James H. Woods, C. I. Lewis, and H. M. Sheffer. Woods had known James longest, and was the colleague of whom Whitehead saw the most in his first half-year at Harvard. Whitehead was adept at learning by conversation; before he wrote those Lowell Lectures in his first winter there, he would have learned much about his reading of James from Woods and Perry, and something from the others.

Appreciating James was something that continued through Whitehead's subsequent years at Harvard. As a sort of addendum to this paper, let me note in what respects he appreciated him. Whitehead gave one broad answer in a 1936 conversation with me: James was the man who had the idea that philosophy required a new departure − with his radical empiricism. Whitehead added that the hurry Americans are always in caused James (and Dewey too) to hurry up and set down the finished idea. "The finished idea" seems rather an odd phrase to use concerning the man who whole-heartedly endorsed the words, "There is no conclusion. What has concluded, that we might conclude in regard to it?"[21] But when we think of "Does Consciousness Exist?" (an article that Whitehead knew well[22]), some of James's other *Essays in Radical Empiricism*, and the writings of Dewey that take a similar line, Whitehead's remark makes good sense. James *was always* in a hurry, and Whitehead knew that philosophy must not hurry.

Still, however inadequate James's sensational article and his pure-experience theory were, they began a new departure. Whitehead gave James a critical place in his history of philosophy as the psychological philosopher who challenged the Cartesian Ego at just the right time.[23] And Whitehead appreciated the non-Humian untraditional character of James's radical empiricism.[24] James's descriptions of the moment of experience as an integration of feelings (in his *Psychology* and later) were at hand, if Whitehead's readers needed an outside empirical support for the analysis of experience into "prehensions." And James was the vivid describer of the central place of purpose and emotion in human experience. When we read about "subjective forms" in Whitehead, i. e., about the affective tone with which a datum given to experience is felt, James is the supporting psychologist. In 1971 a book was published entitled *The Unifying Moment: The Psychological Philosophy of William James and Alfred North Whitehead*.[25] It is tempting, but not justified, to call these two philosophies one.

Let us notice some parts of James's work which were not, for Whitehead, matters to appreciate – in addition to the hurriedness which I have mentioned.

The motives behind James's theism were so different from those behind Whitehead's that I cannot believe that the former's "piecemeal supernaturalism" struck any responsive chord. (Apart from the denial of omnipotence, their concepts of God are also quite different. But I cannot undertake to discuss this subject.)

Whitehead never refers to the "pure-experience" theory which James set down to resolve the dualism of thought and things. Was it a hasty theory, to be set aside by anyone with Whitehead's conceptual equipment for dealing with that problem? I think so. Again, in the last chapters of *Some Problems of Philosophy* James presented what he called "the conceptual view," and then, rejecting that, his own view, "the perceptual view," of the problems of infinity and causation. Whitehead had a more balanced outlook. And James found the original of causation, efficient as well as final, in the experience of striving against obstacles. Whitehead knew well that we feel our experience as *both* creative of novelty *and* as derived from that of the historic process of the universe; and he was able to produce a theory in which this effecient causation, and our final causation, are coordinated. James was too one-sided; as I suggested before, too partisan.

I know of no evidence that Whitehead ever came to share James's attitude toward mathematical logic, or what would have been James's attitude toward Whitehead's "large scheme of work" (work from 1890 to 1923). True, he uses James's discussions of the problem of novelty, in which James had naturally brought in Zeno's paradoxes and rejected "the new [Cantorian] infinite."[26] This occurs in Whitehead's argument (in which Zeno also appears) that an act of experience is not infinitely divisible: "The authority of William James can be quoted in support of this conclusion."[27] But before the end of the paragraph Whitehead makes this characterictically mild remark: "I do not think that he allows sufficiently for those elements in Zeno's paradoxes which are the product of inadequate mathematical knowledge."

In Whitehead's written and oral comments on James, appreciation was customary, criticism rare. He saw James's intellectual life as a "protest against the dismissal of experience in the interest of system."[28] Perhaps he valued him as much for this as for any other reason. It was a valuing of James that came best from a systematic philosopher, and it could come from Whitehead because he was gifted with a fine sensitivity to experience and with real intellectual humility.

NOTES

[1] Victor Lowe, "William James and Whitehead's Doctrine of Prehensions," *Journal of Philosophy* 38 (1941): 113—126. A later version appeared as Ch. 13 of my *Understanding Whitehead* (Baltimore: The Johns Hopkins Press, 1962).
[2] See p. 289 f. in Lowe, "The Influence of Bergson, James and Alexander on Whitehead," *Journal of the History of Ideas* 10 (1949).
[3] Bertrand Russell, *The Principles of Mathematics* (Cambridge: Cambridge University Press, 1903), Preface.
[4] Letters from Whitehead to Bertrand Russell (now in the Bertrand Russell Archives at McMaster University), Sept. 10 and Sept. 30, 1908.
[5] See Lowe, *Understanding Whitehead*, p. 231 f. Ignorance of Whitehead's agnostic period can result in jumps to unjustified conclusions when a scholar finds the word "God" in something Whitehead wrote in that period. Thus, some anticipation by Whitehead of his *Process and Reality* doctrine of God's twofold nature has already been "found" in a 1904 letter to Russell on the question of whether they should handle a certain type of proposition as a series of ideas or as one entity. I mention this danger because philosophical theology is the part of Whitehead's work on which American scholars are now most busy.
[6] See Bertrand Russell, *Autobiography*, Vol. I (London: George Allen & Unwin, 1967), p. 167.

7 Whitehead says this in the letter cited in n. 8.
8 University College London, Professorial Board file 1884—1916, folio 151; quoted with the permission of Whitehead's heirs and the Secretary of University College. This file was thought to have been destroyed by bombs in the First World War, and was rediscovered only recently. Whitehead's letter was prompted by his wish to be considered for the chair of applied mathematics which Karl Pearson had vacated.
9 Hamilton's creation of his system of quaternions dates from December 1843. For Whitehead the other key figures in this history were the mathematicians Grassmann, Riemann and Boole, and Clerk Maxwell. In 1884 Whitehead wrote his Trinity College fellowship dissertation on Maxwell's *Treatise on Electricity and Magnetism* (and was thereafter regarded at Cambridge as an *applied* mathematician). Maxwell's distrust of mathematical symbols in separation from physical meaning is well known; yet Helmholtz was puzzled to explain what an electric charge was on Maxwell's theory beyond being the recipient of a symbol. And Maxwell liked quaternions but was troubled by quaternion "methods." — These are some of the things that suggested the desirability of an extensive study such as Whitehead undertook.
10 See n. 8, above.
11 The point of the last clause is that Whitehead is about to question the limitation of mathematics to this field.
12 *Philos. Transactions, Royal Society of London*, series A, 205, 480.
13 Letter from James to Russell, Oct. 4, 1908, as published in Russell's *Autobiography*, Vol. I, p. 198.
14 Perry, *The Thought and Character of William James* (Boston: Little, Brown & Co., 1935), Vol. II, p. 680.
15 See, e. g., James's *Principles of Psychology* (New York: Henry Holt & Co., 1902; first published 1890), Vol. II, p. 318 f.
16 *The Letters of William James*, ed. Henry James (Boston: Atlantic Monthly Press, 1920), Vol. II, p. 353. The letter is dated Jan. 26, 1908; its recipient is not named.
17 (New York: Longmans, Green & Co., 1909), p. 282 f.
18 If James read Russell fairly, Russell invited the travesty when he wrote that "the correct view" was "that there is no problem at all in truth and falsehood, that some propositions are true and some false, just as some roses are red and some white." (Quoted by James, *ibid.*, p. 285.)
19 James does not show this scorn for *hypotheses*, but he keeps them within the context of belief and its refusal. Thus, on the second page of the essay, "The Will to Believe," we read that 'hypothesis' names "anything that is proposed to our belief." His Hibbert Lectures, he courteously told his audience, were meant only to

present pluralism as a hypothesis to place alongside monism, i. e., as a worthy alternative for belief. The pity of it is James's inability to see that a hypothesis should be put in the form of a set of analyzed propositions before its believeability is put up for decision; such formulation was not his *forte*.

[20] New York: Macmillan Co. The two chapters in which Whitehead uses James are among the eight (the core of the book) which he delivered as Lowell Lectures in February, 1925. This makes it likely, but in the absence of a transcript of the lectures or a manuscript of the book does not prove, that Whitehead was "up on James" within a year of his acceptance of Harvard's offer and within five months of landing in Boston.

[21] James, *Memories and Studies* (New York: Longmans, Green & Co., 1911), p. 411. The words were those of his friend, the "pluralistic mystic" Benjamin Paul Blood.

[22] See Whitehead, *Science and the Modern World*, Ch. IX, beginning with the eighth paragraph.

[23] *Ibid.*, as in the preceding note.

[24] See James, *Essays in Radical Empiricism* (New York: Longmans, Green & Co., 1912), pp. x, 42 f. The essay was first published in *Journal of Philosophy*, 1 (1904). The connection with Whitehead is discussed in Ch. 13 of my *Understanding Whitehead*.

[25] Craig R. Eisendrath (Cambridge: Harvard University Press, 1971).

[26] James, *Some Problems of Philosophy* (New York: Longmans, Green & Co., 1911), Ch. XI.

[27] Whitehead, *Process and Reality* (New York: Macmillan Co., 1929), p. 105 (Part II, Ch. II, Sect. II, tenth paragraph).

[28] Whitehead, *Modes of Thought* (New York: Macmillan Co., 1938), Lect. I, Sect. 1.

19

AN APPRECIATION OF WILLIAM JAMES: PHILOSOPHER, PSYCHOLOGIST, AND EDUCATOR

Mohammed Fadhel Jamali

I

William James was a philosopher in the literal sense of the term. He was a man of wisdom who worked to radiate his wisdom. Besides, his philosophy aims at contributing to human welfare. It is not a maze of abstract thought nor does it swim in the clouds. He was a down-to-earth man, a clear thinker and a charming writer. He spoke and wrote common sense. It is a pleasure for those interested to open any of his books and enjoy reading them.

Philosophers, in every time and place, present their wisdom in relation to the time and circumstances in which they exist. Every philosopher may have a contribution which he makes to his own society. Some philosophers may be forerunners in human thought. Some may contribute to humanity at large. Others may have a local and temporary influence. It may be interesting to see what elements of lasting value to human welfare exist in the philosophy of William James.

To begin with, we wish to express appreciation for James's openmindedness and courage in facing the facts of the universe as a whole. He does not shrink from dealing with the world of the visible and the invisible. He does not deny the existence of the mysterious and the invisible. He recognizes the fact that some people are more adept in the field of the invisible than others. He is not a "materialist." To him philosophy should not *stop* at the confines of the exact sciences for it has a greater function to achieve which includes the relating of the exact sciences to the life of humans and their concern for their own destiny.

James's philosophy is primarily concerned with life and not with abstractions and polemics that have no influence on human action. It is a fact that much of what goes in the name of philosophy in the thousands of volumes that bear the name of philosophy has only distant relation, if any, to human life and human destiny. Intellectualism divorced from the reality of life characterizes some of the classical systems of philosophy.

America, in its age of vitality and construction of a new civilization, needed James's *pragmatic* method of philosophy. *Pragmatism* is not a new discovery in philosophy. It has been with man from his early emergence on this earth. Man has always to test his beliefs, traditions and assumptions in action and by results. Various philosophers, from Socrates onward, have used the pragmatic method. But all of that was piece-meal and occasional. James's great contribution to philosophy is that he generalizes the application of the pragmatic method and makes it a standing guide for human thought and human action. If an idea is true, it must yield fruitful results. "By their fruits ye shall know them"[1] is a sound principle. "*The attitude of looking away from first things, principles, 'categories,' supposed necessities; and of looking towards last things, fruits, consequences, facts*"[2] forms the essence of pragmatism. It is a useful and practical approach to problems of life. But one may ask: By what measures does one choose the last things, fruits, consequences and facts? Pragmatism was the philosophy fitted to the United States of America while she was trying to build a new civilization based on action, invention, adventure and competition. The developing nations, or the so-called third world, need pragmatism in their present stage of development.

Pragmatism as a philosophical method will always remain useful in the life of man, but it has to answer at least two questions. One concerns universality and the other concerns authenticity.

Universality. A certain act may be good for me if it works for me. Is it good for my community and my nation also? Supposing it is good for me, my community and my nation, is it good for the rest of mankind? In the days of William James the world was not so interrelated and interdependent as it is today. Pragmatism could well afford to be individualistic in those days. But since then, the world has changed and changed very rapidly. Restricted and localized pragmatism has already contributed to some of the serious problems of the world including some of those in the United States of America. James's pragmatism needs a world consciousness and brotherhood. This in no way detracts from the significance of pragmatism as a method, but it does call for its broader application in terms of man's relation to man, man's relation to Nature and the environment, and man's relation to the universe and the universal order. Much of this was provided by John Dewey's democratic and international thinking.

Authenticity. The other question which pragmatism has to face is more serious, in our view, and it is the one on authenticity. I do an act thinking it is good for me. I enjoy it at the time. I do not see its danger to my health, my family or other people. Its danger is not seen at the time. I keep doing it, thinking it is good, but sooner or later the tragedy falls and I suffer, my people suffer and the whole peace of the world is endangered. For example, I may think my patriotism or my philanthropy is true and good as judged by pragmatic standards. All of a sudden I find I have been moving on the wrong track, on a very risky and dangerous track. Pragmatism wants me to see the *end*. But suppose my farsight has been shortsight. It has been blurred by ignorance and selfishness. How can pragmatism save me without my being armed with moral standards? Moral standards themselves can be attained by human consciousness of the unity and brotherhood of man and faith that man on this earth is not a mere bubble nor is he meant to be a brutal beast or a wasteful and destructive agent. He has a noble and constructive role on this earth, a role emanating from a sense of love and unity with the universe and its creator. Fortunately the pragmatism of James leaves the door to heaven wide open for those faithful and mystic who choose to enter it. We submit that pragmatism needs idealism; it needs a system of moral, social and economic values.

An important philosophical issue which James treats is the one he calls, "The Dilemma of Determinism." James masterfully rejects determinism in favor of indeterminism. He stands for free will and human choice with all the pluralism which that entails. We agree with James that mechanistic determinism reduces man to submission and irresponsibility. James's indeterminism is quite suitable for a humanity that cherishes freedom, individual initiative and creativity. James's philosophy expresses the new spirit which America presented to the world, the spirit of optimism and frontier adventurous life.

Indeterminism is certainly more consonant with the dignity of man. We wish to submit, however, that indeterminism requires a great effort on the part of the individual to realize his freedom. He needs much knowledge and great self-control to achieve freedom. Indeterminism with ignorance and moral irresponsibility could lead to man's doom.

James assumes that one may choose either determinism or indeterminism and he opts for the latter. We submit that man has to combine both. He has to exert the greatest effort within his realm to be indeterminate, free and creative. But man's capacity is limited and controlled by basic elements including water, air, light, climate, food, etc. His destiny is bound up with the resources of this earth and the conditions required for life on it. No matter how much effort and freedom man exerts, life is determined by some ultimate bounds. Thus, while indeterminism is to be maintained to the farthest limits possible, it is never absolute. While determinism may be rejected within the practical bounds of human experience, it cannot be ruled out of ultimate human destiny, individual or collective.

As for James's pluralism, while it encourages human freedom, variety and individuality with all the tolerance and open-mindedness which has to go with it, the word today needs to move a step farther and encourage inter-communication and integration in the moral, cultural and economic fields. The world has advanced to such an extent in the realm of communication and transportation as to require new planning on an international scale.

James's thoughts were quite adequate and progressive for his days. Now we have to complement his thoughts with those found in John Dewey's philosophy which goes a long leap beyond James in the social, educational, and international fields.

II

One hears voices raised here and there saying that psychology should be considered at least two sciences, one being a biological science and the other, a human science, both being legitimate fields of study. The reason for this trend seems to be that some modern psychologists restrict themselves to the study of observable behavior which they study as they do animal behavior. The human science should take into account the study of man as a free creative agent with a will endowed with purpose and ideals. It should include the study of the subconscious. Furthermore, it should investigate the spiritual religious aspect of human behavior.

William James was one of the great psychologists who applied the scientific method to the study of the whole man, his animal as well as his human aspects. His view of the unity and integration of human behavior, the stream of consciousness, his study of human sentiment, will, and religious life, certainly answers the call of some modern writers who find that the study of psychology as a biological science does not do justice to the study of man. It is true that man has the attributes of a living animal, but he is much more than that. To neglect introspection as a method, to neglect the recognition of the role of the invisible and the unmeasurable phenomena like the subconscious, insight, creativity and spiritual experience is certainly an injustice rendered to psychology. William James deserves to be considered as a great psychologist who treated the subject both as a natural science and as a human science.

The Will to Believe and *The Varieties of Religious Experience* contain a wealth of case studies and reports which describe objectively and accurately the religious phenomenon in man. William James rightly establishes the fact that man is capable of believing in the invisible and that this belief may awaken and activate his great potential and relate him to a superpower which helps him achieve his hopes or cure him of his ills.

I myself have had a religious experience which corroborates William James's findings. I am a Muslim believer in God and I practice my daily prayers. I was condemned to death by the High Military Tribunal after the coup d'etat in Baghdad of July 1958. I remained under sentence of death for over a year expecting to be hanged any night. My faith in God and my prayers provided me with *hope* and *support*. I preserved my mental health and faced the imminent danger with patience and equilibrium. The death sentence was commuted through the intervention of several highly placed personalities and the prayers of hundreds of my friends. Faith and religious life played a positive role in my case. William James's findings on the role of religious experience in human affairs is very well substantiated in my experience.

It is my considered judgment that the modern world, with its multiple problems and ills, needs a revival of faith, – faith in God, in human brotherhood, honesty, justice and freedom, – faith which is a fountain of peace and a dynamo for action. This is an aspect of human psychology which might easily be ignored now-a-days by psychologists of the mechanistic school. Modern psychology should study the whole man, especially the highest faculties of man of which faith and religious experience form a significant part.

While respecting and admiring James's defense of the religious nature of man, I wish to remark that religious life does not rest on human feelings and sentiments alone. A sound religion is one which integrates human feelings with reason. Faith in the existence of God can be both sentimental and rational. I, as a Muslim, am required by Islam to use reasoning and the study of Nature in order to sustain my faith. Personally I reached my faith in God by reasoning over the mystery and wonders of the creation on the one hand, and by observing the interrelationship and interaction between the various aspects of the creation, on the other. I believe that it is the power of God that continues the creative activity as revealed in the process of evolution. It is the will of God that makes the natural phenomena interact and be integrated with each other.

I do not agree with William James that Darwin's theory of evolution weakened the rational foundation of faith in God. On the contrary I believe that the process of evolution itself is a great argument for faith in the Invisible Creator.

I wish to go one step farther and state that, although experience has proved that religious belief works and is a help, my faith in God does not depend exclusively on the benefit I draw from this faith. In other words, my faith is well established by my reason, irrespective of the consequences of this faith.

As a matter of fact, *faith* divorced from *reason* may lead to great human sacrifice and suffering as we see happening in the Holy Land today. The whole world has gone to the brink of catastrophe because of national and religious fanaticism. There is a danger that man may not survive with faith divorced from reason nor can he do much with reason without faith. Reason and faith integrated should lead to positive action. We wish to emphasize again the need for an integral and integrated view of man, a view which integrated reason, sentiment and the will to act into one behavior pattern.

We welcome James's call to "deanthropomorphization of imagination." This is very much in line with the teaching of Islam. We also welcome James's attempt in *Varieties of Religious Experience* to find a common solid ground for faith. It is an attempt in the direction of finding a "common faith." We thus think that James's contribution to the study of man has been immense.

III

William James was a great *educator*. His lectures entitled, *Talks to Teachers on Psychology and to Students on Some of Life's Ideals*, contain a mine of wisdom and guidance for the educators of today. He is realistic when he states: "The renovation of Nations begins always at the top among the reflective members of the state and spreads slowly outward and downward. The teachers of this country, one may say, have its future in their hands."[3]

James was well acquainted with the educational systems of western Europe, especially with those of Germany and Great Britain to which he sometimes refers. But he was very proud and optimistic concerning American education which, in his day was entering its glorious epoch. This is some of what he says about it:

> The outward organization of Education which we have in our United States is perhaps, on the whole, the best organization that exists in any country. The State school systems give a diversity and flexibility, an opportunity for experiment and keenness of competition, nowhere else to be found on such an important scale. The independence of so many of the colleges and universities; the give and take of students and instructors between them all; their emulation and their happy organic relations to the lower schools; the traditions of instruction in them, evolved from the older American recitation-method... (to say nothing of that coeducation of the sexes in whose benefits so many of us heartily believe), all these things, I say, are most happy features of our scholastic life... in a generation or two America may well lead the education of the world. I must say that I look forward with no little confidence to the day when that shall be an accomplished fact.[4]

I think that James's prophesy did come true to a great extent. American education did make a direct impression on the systems of education in many parts of the world in the first half of this century, and it is still doing so today.

James rightly thinks that teaching is an art of which he says, "The art of teaching grew up in the schoolroom, out of inventiveness and sympathetic concrete observation."[5] This statement certainly implies the qualities of a progressive teacher. Knowledge of the science of psychology may prevent a teacher from committing some errors, but it does not by itself make good teachers, just as study of logic does not necessarily guarantee logical thinking.

One of the best pieces of advice James gives to teachers, (advice which was developed at length by John Dewey), is the following:

> you must simply work your pupil into such a state of interest in what you are going to teach him that every other object of attention is banished from his mind; then reveal it to him so impressively that he will remember the occasion to his dying day; and finally fill him with devouring curiosity to know what the next steps in connection with the subject are.[6]

This advice puts James with the forerunners of progressive education.

In short, William James was a great leader in American life and thought. He was wise as a philosopher, truly scientific as a psychologist, and great as a teacher.

NOTES

1 *The Gospel According to St. Matthew*, 7:16.
2 William James, *The Moral Philosophy of William James*, edited and with an introduction by John K. Roth (New York: Thomas Y. Crowell Co., 1969), p. 280.
3 William James, *Talks to Teachers on Psychology and to Students on Some of Life's Ideals* (New York: Dover Publications, Inc., 1962; originally published by Henry Holt and Company, New York, in 1899), p. 1.
4 *Ibid.*, pp. 1—2.
5 *Ibid.*, p. 3.
6 *Ibid.*, p. 4.

20

HEALTHY MINDS WITH SICK SOULS

Herbert W. Schneider

In the diction of William James "mind" is cerebral and "soul" is emotional; neither is a substance or entity, but together they constitute human nature. Mind is consciousness, the pursuit of ends, by perception and conception and by will (will is attention plus effort). Soul is appetites, passions, motives, interests, morals. A healthy mind is the life of reason; a sick soul is a life of fear, frustration, and folly. A sick soul is apt to turn to "saintliness" both for the expression of its sickness and for cure. A healthy mind turns to a reasonable self-confidence and "will to believe," and its will turns to the heroic virtues. The mind is biologically at the service of the soul, but when it is feeble and under the power of suggestion, it may develop a kind of blind optimism which calls itself "mind-cure" or religious healthy-mindedness, the soul being freed of its sickness by a mental anaesthetic. A feeble mind plus a sick soul are a pathetic, helpless combination. But a healthy mind may be able to live with a sick soul, provided the self is not divided in two, which is a real danger, but not a helpless condition. This is a brief outline of James' clinical psychology.

Instead of illustrating and developing this theme by references to his writings, I shall attempt to psycho-analyze James himself in these terms. It would be natural to make such analysis into a kind of biography, but this would be a more ambitious task than I can undertake. Suffice it to select four important stages in his career in order to tell my story: his youthful experience of the dualism; its formulation in *The Principles of Psychology* (c. 1890); its detailed exposition in *The Varieties of Religious Experience* (The Gifford Lectures at Edinburgh in 1901–2); and his final formulation in *Radical Empiricism* and in *A*

Pluralistic Universe (1909). Though his pragmatism is an important aspect of his healthymindedness, I shall ignore it, since it is very familiar.

I. *The Healthy Mind and Sick Soul of the Youthful James*

After William James had given up his ambition to become a painter, and had heard his father expound at length the moral weaknesses of artists, he asked his father to help him prepare for medical science. To see his son descend to a still lower level below the "spiritual life" and devote his life to the care of the body, was a severe trial for the elder Henry James. But with his usual generosity he gave William the best of opportunities in Europe to study physiology and pathology. The strenuous devotion which the youth showed not only to medical science but to materialist philosophy was typical of the way in which the accentuated differences of mind between father and son strengthened their emotional ties to each other. But William's excessive devotion to science created in himself a divided loyalty. He confessed early and repeatedly that he could not devote himself to science alone, and that the "deepest moral" philosophic speculations were basic for him. His mind and his clinical studies in physiology conflicted with his emotional concern for moral philosophy. The tension, partly nervous and partly conscientious, threw him into both an ardent mental pursuit of medicine and a moral hypochondria or sickness of soul. It occurred to him that a combination of the two in physiological and introspective psychology might solve the dilemma, and he began to say to himself: "psychology or die." But in 1868 there was no academic demand in the United States for such a combination, especially not in the Harvard Medical School.

In despair he finally decided to give up (1870) his materialistic conception of physiological psychology and to pretend to believe in morals and free will. Fortunately, a sug-

Healthy Minds with Sick Souls

gestion from Renouvier enabled him to interpret free will in terms of natural spontaneity (as used by Darwin) and he tried to demonstrate scientifically that the energy generated in the mind by a given stimulus was not invariant. Such ideas helped him to justify the introduction of moral and philosophical issues into his clinical courses at the Harvard School of Medicine. But despite this healthy-minded psychology, he continued to worry about his professional obligations and his moral distractions. His inner tension continued. It was not until 1880 that Harvard finally let him teach in the Philosophy Department without sacrificing his "principles of psychology."

This story is told with emotional intensity in the letters of William James during these years. To Wendell Holmes, May 15, 1868, he wrote:

> I had hoped until the end of my visit to Teplitz last winter that I might be able to get working at physiology. ... But I now see that I can probably never do laboratory work, and so am obliged to fall back on something else. ... I nevertheless feel the want of some particular outward responsibility to prevent my wasting time. I shall continue to study, or rather *begin* to, in a general psychological direction, hoping that soon I may get into a particular channel. Perhaps a practical application may present itself some time – the only thing I can now think of is a professorship of 'moral philosophy" in some western academy, but I have no idea how such things are attainable, nor if they are attainable at all to men of a nonspiritualistic mould.[1]

> I am tending strongly to an empiristic view of life. I don't know how far it will carry me, or what rocks will block my future path. Already I see an ontological cloud of absolute idealism waiting for me far off on the horizon, but I have no passion for the fray. I shall continue to apply empirical principles to my experiences as I go on and see how much they fit.[2]

To Thomas Ward, May 24, 1868:

> I am naturally almost as sceptical as you, and from not having come into contact for the past year with any living human reason, had sunk ever deeper into the drifting slough of indifference and disrespect for individual manifestations of life, which seems to me to be the Devil's own drug with which he benumbs our souls before catching them. ... Life is *such!* And what have I been making it? About! my heart, my brain! This *Auseinandersetzen* of the everyday occurrence of a man's having his soul aroused and inspired at the sight of the good, true, or beautiful, may amuse you. But it is nevertheless a goodly experience. The only trouble is that the reverberation dies away so soon in the soul and the bog closes around one again. Nothing is so efficacious as the actual, sensible intuition of these portions of the unveiled absolute ...[3]

To Thomas Ward, Oct. 9, 1868:

> I am poisoned with Utilitarian venom. ... There will remain and live ... some shreds of manhood (thoughts, smiles), and, shreds though they be, they are worth more to the world than the fermentations and chemical reactions that might replace them. They are not worth more for the consciousness of your individual self, perhaps, – more of pain than of pleasure will follow in their train – but taken as existence theirs is a nobler category than the other. ... All in all, even the sweepings of morality are better than chemical reactions. – Thus do I lash my tail and start myself up again.[4]

To Henry James, June 1, 1869:

> I wrote you that my bottom rather fell out two and a half months ago. I've not picked up since much of any. ... This summer with *no* study and hardly any reading may start me up again. If not, I genuinely don't much care, for I have

loosed the lock-jaw-grasp with which I clung to the hope of accomplishing external work, and transferred my interest in the game of life to the subjective attitude, i. e., become moralized, in some sort.[5]

In his Diary, Feb. 1, 1870, he wrote:

Shall I *frankly* throw the moral business overboard, as one unsuited to my innate aptitudes, or shall I follow it, and it alone, making everything else merely stuff for it? I will give the latter alternative a fair trial. Who knows but the moral interest may become developed.[6]

Diary, April 10, 1873:

Yesterday I told Eliot I would accept the anatomical instruction for next year, if well enough to perform it, and would probably stick to that department. I came to this decision mainly from the feeling that philosophical activity as a *business* is not normal for most men, and not for me. To be responsible for a complete conception of things is beyond my strength. To make the *form* of all possible thought the prevailing *matter* of one's thought breeds hypochondria. Of course my deepest interest will as ever lie with the most general problems. But as my strongest moral and intellectual craving is for some stable reality to lean upon, and as a professed philosopher pledges himself publicly never to have done with doubt on these subjects, but every day to be ready to criticize afresh and call in question the grounds of his faith of the day before, I fear the constant sense of instability generated by this attitude would be more than the voluntary faith I can keep going is sufficient to neutralize. ... That gets reality for us in which we place our responsibility, and the concrete facts in which a biologist's responsibilities lie form a fixed basis from which to aspire as much as he pleases to the mastery of the universal questions when the gallant mood is on him; and a basis, too, upon which he can passively float, and tide over times of weakness and depression, trusting all the while *blindly* in the beneficence of nature's forces and the return of higher opportunities. ... Of course one may say, you could make of psychology proper just such a basis; but not so, you can't divorce psychology from introspection, and immense as is the work demanded by its purely objective physiologic part, yet it is the other part rather for which a professor thereof is expected to make himself publicly responsible.[7]

To Henry James, May 11, 1873:

I believe I told you in my last that I had determined to stick to psychology or die. I have changed my mind, and for the present give myself to biology. ... The fact is, I'm not a strong enough man to choose the other and nobler lot in life, but I can in a less penetrating way work out a philosophy in the midst of other duties.[8]

II. *Mind and Soul in the Natural Science of Psychology*

By the time James was ready to publish his *Principles of Psychology* (1890) the problem of mind and soul had taken a new form. He insisted that physiological psychology is a thoroughly natural science and implies the idea that there is no mind-stuff. Mind is a type of action which pursues ends, and such action is a "brain-process." When he came to the analysis of "will" and its consciousness, he analyzes it in terms of acts of attention and feelings of effort. They compose the deliberate pursuit of ends by conscious choice of means. There is no need of a "soul-substance" to account for the union of mind and brain process in life; it would explain nothing. Nevertheless the popular use of "soul" for behavior that centers in "the heart" rather than in the mind and brain is needed in naturalistic psychology to distinguish feelings and processes that are not "cerebral" but emotional; they are non-cognitive, neither perceptions nor conceptions. They are motivational, but not the causes of mental processes; rather they are the effects of external stimulation and are not useful in the pursuit of ends. Apart from the theory of their relation to cerebral processes, the emotions receive scant attention in the *Principles of Psychology*. The "heart and soul" of emotions is a type of feeling distinct from mental consciousness, but it is physiological. James even suggests that the physical heart rather than the cerebral nervous system may be its center.

The more James explains that voluntary, spontaneous acts of attention and effort are essential aspects of a healthy mind, the more he realizes that he is approaching the field of "moral philosophy." And in his desire to confine psychology to the mind, he was obviously neglecting the soul and portraying only a half of human nature. In other words, the "whole man" is still divided, as in the classical tradition, into intellect and passion, mind and soul.

A few selections from the *Principles of Psychology* will serve to show James's awareness of the old contrast in him between the science of mind and the philosophy of morals:

> The ultimate of ultimate problems, of course, in the study of the relations of thought and brain, is to understand why and how such disparate things are connected at all. But before that problem is solved (if it ever is solved) there is a less ultimate problem which must first be settled....
>
> What shall we do? Many would find relief at this point in celebrating the mystery of the Unknowable.... It may be a constitutional infirmity, but I take no comfort in such devices for making a luxury of intellectual defeat. They are but spiritual chloroform. Better live on the ragged edge, better gnaw the file forever!...
>
> But is this my last word? By no means. Many readers have certainly been saying to themselves for the last few pages: "Why on earth doesn't the poor man say *the Soul* and have done with it?" But the plain fact is that all the arguments for a "pontifical cell" or an "arch-monad" are also arguments

for that well-known spiritual agent in which scholastic psychology and common sense have always believed....

I confess, therefore, that to posit a soul influenced in some mysterious way by the brain-states and responding to them by conscious affections of its own, seems to me the line of least logical resistance, so far as we yet have attained.
If it does not *explain* anything, it is at any rate less positively objectionable than either mind-stuff or a material-monad creed. *The bare PHENOMENON, the IMMEDIATELY KNOWN thing which on the mental side is in opposition with the entire brain-process is the state of consciousness and not the soul itself.*... We shall abide there in this book, and just as we have rejected mind-dust, we shall take no account of the soul.[9]

Concerning the stream of thought, James writes:

The stream of thought is like a river. On the whole easy simple flowing predominates in it, the drift of things is with the pull of gravity, and effortless attention is the rule. But at intervals an obstruction, a set-back, a log-jam occurs, stops the current, creates an eddy, and makes things temporarily move the other way. If a real river could feel, it would feel these eddies and set-backs as places of effort.... Just so with our voluntary acts of attention. They are momentary arrests, coupled with a peculiar feeling, of portions of the stream. But the arresting force, instead of being this peculiar feeling itself, may be nothing but the processes by which the collision is produced.... When we come to the chapter on Will, we shall see that the whole drama of the voluntary life hinges on the amount of attention, slightly more or slightly less, which rival motor ideas may receive. But the whole feeling of reality, the whole sting and excitement of our voluntary life, depends on our sense that in it things are *really being decided* from one moment to another, and that it is not the dull rattling off of a chain that was forged innumerable ages ago. This appearance, which makes life and history tingle with such a tragic zest, *may* not be an illusion.... Under these circumstances, one can leave the question open whilst waiting for light, or one can do what most speculative minds do, that is, look to one's general philosophy to incline the beam. The believers in mechanism do so without hesitation, and they ought not to refuse a similar privilege to the believers in a spiritual force. I count myself among the latter, but as my reasons are ethical they are hardly suited for introduction into a psychological work.[10]

We can leave the free-will question altogether out of our account.... And although such quickening of one idea might be *morally and historically* momentous, yet, if considered *dynamically,* it would be an operation amongst those physiological infinitesimals which calculation must forever neglect....

Our strength and our intelligence, our wealth and even our good luck, are things which warm our heart and make us feel a match for life. But deeper than all such things, and able to suffice unto itself without them, is the sense of the amount of effort which we can put forth. Those are, after all, but effects, products, and reflections of the outer world within. But the effort seems to belong to an altogether different realm, as if it were the substantive thing which we *are*, and those were but externals which we *carry*. If the "searching of our hearts and reins" be the purpose of this human drama, then what is sought seems to be what effort we can make. He who can make none is but a shadow; he who can make much is a hero.... The deepest question that is ever asked admits of no reply but the dumb turning of the will and tightening of our heart-strings as we say, *"Yes, I will even have it so!"*

The world thus finds in the heroic man its worthy match and mate; and the effort which he is able to put forth to hold himself erect and keep his heart unshaken is the direct measure of his worth and function in the game of human life. He can *stand* this Universe.... He must be counted with henceforth; he forms a part of human destiny. Neither in the theoretic nor in the practical sphere do we care for, or go for help to, those who have no head for risks, or sense for living on the perilous edge. Our religious life lies more, our practical life lies less, than it used to, on the perilous edge. ... We draw new life from the heroic example. The prophet has drunk more deeply than anyone of the cup of bitterness, but his countenance is so unshaken and he speaks such mighty words of cheer that his will becomes our will, and our life is kindled at his own.[11]

III. *Healthy and Sick Religious Appetites*

When William James was invited to give the Gifford Lectures on Natural Religion at Edinburgh (1901 and 1902), he announced that he would divide the twenty lectures into two parts: the first, On Man's Religious Appetites; and the second, On Their Satisfaction through Philosophy. The first series would be descriptive, the second "metaphysical." As it turned out Part II is confined to the last twenty pages of a 527 pages volume, and of these twenty-seven, seven are entitled "Postscript."

It is evident, and clearly stated in the final pages, that James regards what is "natural" in religions a matter of "soul" rather than of "mind," of "feeling and conduct" rather than of experiences that can be satisfied through philosophy. He writes:

Both thought and feeling are determinants of conduct, and the same conduct may be determined either by feeling or by thought.... But the feelings on the one hand and the conduct on the other are almost the same, for Stoic, Christian, and Buddhist saints are practically indistinguishable in their lives. The theories which Religion generates, being thus variable, are secondary; and if you wish to grasp her essence, you must look to the feelings and the conduct as being the more constant elements.[12]

Again, he says:

> We have been literally bathed in sentiment. In re-reading my manuscript, I am almost appalled at the amount of emotionality which I find in it. . . .
> I took these extremer examples as yielding the profounder information. . . . We have next to answer, each for us for himself, the practical question: what are the dangers in this element of life? and in what proportion may it need to be restrained by other elements, to give the proper balance?[13]

This bath in sentimentality seems to be an attempt by James to be empirical about the emotional side of human nature, which he had neglected in *The Principles of Psychology* as not mental.

Central lectures in the descriptive presentation of religious experiences are: "The Religion of Healthy-Mindedness," "The Sick Soul," and "The Divided Self and the Process of its Unification." The reader will understand that the minds of those who embrace the cult of healthy-mindedness or "Mind-Cure" are portrayed as unhealthy, but these persons, though afflicted with feeble minds and carefree wills, may heal their sick souls. Whereas the sick souls, in their morbid fears and desperate awareness of evil, are apt to be more healthy-minded. In general James is satirical about "optimism" and is sympathetic toward "pessimism" in both morals and religion.

In his long "empirical" evaluation of "saintliness" he discusses the health or sickness of saints, not in terms of a critical moral philosophy, but in terms of "common sense" standards of mind and soul, and of their healthy balance.

Noteworthy is his aim throughout the Lectures to keep clear of "the science of religion" and of religious institutions, in order to focus on particular, personal "appetites" in great variety and in such extreme cases of emotional expression as invite clinical analysis. This applies even to the "insights" which mystics claim; they seem to James to be a kind of supernatural "excitement" rather than a revelation of truth.

The following selections from *The Varieties of Religious Experience* are intended not only to give more detail concerning the above comments, but also to illustrate their relation to James's own experience as a healthy mind and sick soul:

> We must address ourselves to the unpleasant task of hearing what the sick souls, as we may call them, in contrast to the healthy-minded, have to say of the secrets of their prison-house, their own peculiar form of consciousness. Let us then resolutely turn our backs on the once-born and their sky-blue optimistic gospel; let us not simply cry out, in spite of all appearances, ... "God's in his Heaven, all's right with the world." Let us see rather whether pity, pain, and fear, and the sentiment of human helplessness may not open a profounder view and put into our hands a more complicated key to the meaning of the situation.[14]

> When a superior intellect and a psychopathic temperament coalesce ... in the same individual, we have the best possible condition for the kind of effective genius that gets into the biographical dictionaries. Such men do not remain mere critics and understanders with their intellect. Their ideas possess them, they inflict them, for better or worse, upon their companions or their age.... What, then, is more natural than that this temperament should introduce one to regions of religious truth, to corners of the universe, which your robust Philistine type of nervous system, forever offering its biceps to be felt, thumping its breast, and thanking Heaven that it hasn't a single morbid fibre in its composition, would be sure to hide forever from its self-satisfied possessors?[15]

> The systematic cultivation of healthy-mindedness as a religious attitude is therefore consonant with important currents in human nature, and is anything but absurd. In fact, we all do cultivate it more or less, even when our

professed theology should in consistency forbid it. We divert our attention from disease and death as much as we can; and the slaughter-houses and indecencies without end on which our life is founded are huddled out of sight and never mentioned, so that the world we recognize officially in literature and in society is a poetic fiction far handsomer and cleaner and better than the world that really is.

The advance of liberalism, so-called, in Christianity, during the past fifty years, may fairly be called a victory of healthy-mindedness within the church over the morbidness with which the old hell-fire theology was more harmoniously related....

In that "theory of evolution" which, gathering momentum for a century, was within the past twenty-five years swept so rapidly over Europe and America, we see the ground laid for a new sort of religion of Nature, which has entirely displaced Christianity from the thought of a large part of our generation. The idea of a universal evolution lends itself to a doctrine of general meliorism and progress which fits the religious needs of the healthy-minded so well that it seems almost as if it might have been created for their use....[16]

To my mind a current far more important and interesting religiously than that which sets in from natural science towards healthy-mindedness is that which has recently poured over America and seems to be gathering force every day.... I will give it the title of the "Mind-cure Movement."...We can overlook the verbiage of a good deal of the mind-cure literature, some of which is so moonstruck with optimism and so vaguely expressed that an academically trained intellect finds it almost impossible to read it at all.

The plain fact remains that the spread of the movement has been due to practical fruits, and the extremely practical turn of character of the American people has never been better shown than by the fact that this, their only decidedly original contribution to the systematic philosophy of life, should be so intimately knit up with concrete therapeutics.[17]

Yet I believe a more careful consideration of the whole matter... ought to rehabilitate it in our esteem. For in its spiritual meaning asceticism stands for nothing less than for the essence of the twice-born philosophy. It symbolizes... the belief that there is an element of real wrongness in this world, which is neither to be ignored nor evaded, but which must be squarely met and overcome by an appeal to the soul's heroic resources, and neutralized and cleansed away by suffering.... We saw in our lectures on melancholy how precarious [the attempt to sail through life happily on a healthy-minded basis] necessarily is. Moreover it is but for the individual; and leaves the evil outside of him, unredeemed and unprovided for in his philosophy.... The real deliverance, the twice-born folk insist, must be of universal application. Pain and wrong and death must be fairly met and overcome in higher excitement, or else their sting remains essentially unbroken. If one has ever taken the fact of the prevalence of tragic death in the world's history fairly into his mind, – freezing, drowning, entombment alive, wild beasts, worse men, and hideous diseases, – he can with difficulty, it seems to me, continue his own career of worldly prosperity without suspecting that he may all the while not be really inside the game, that he may lack the great initiation....

The wild and the heroic are indeed such rooted parts of life that healthy-mindedness pure and simple, with its sentimental optimism, can hardly be regarded by any thinking man as a serious solution. Phrases of neatness, cosiness, and comfort can never be an answer to the sphinx's riddle.

Asceticism must, I believe, be acknowledged to go with the profounder way of handling the gift of existence.... One hears of the mechanical equivalent of heat. What we now need to discover in the social realm is the moral equivalent of war: something heroic that will speak to men as universally as war does, and yet will be as compatible with their spiritual selves as war has proved itself to be incompatible.... May not voluntarily accepted poverty be "the strenuous life," without the need of crushing weaker peoples?... We have grown literally afraid to be poor.... The desire to gain wealth and the fear to lose it are our chief breeders of cowardice and propagators of corruption. ... Think of the strength which personal indifference to poverty would give us if we were devoted to unpopular causes. We need no longer hold our tongues or fear to vote the revolutionary or reformatory ticket....

I recommend this matter to your serious pondering, for its is certain that the prevalent fear of poverty among the educated classes is the worst moral disease from which our civilization suffers.[18]

The debate is serious. In some sense and to some degree both worlds must be acknowledged and taken account of; and in the seen world both aggressiveness and non-resistance are needful.[19]

Our abandonment of theological criteria, and our testing of religion by practical common sense and the empirical method, leave it in possession of its towering place in history. Economically, the saintly group of qualities is indispensable to the world's welfare. The great saints are immediate successes; the smaller ones are at least heralds and harbingers, and they may be leavens also, of a better mundane order.[20]

To the medical mind [mystic] ecstasies signify nothing but suggested and imitated hypnoid states, on an intellectual basis of superstition, and a corporeal one of degeneration and hysteria.... To pass a spiritual judgment upon these states, we must not content ourselves with superficial medical talk, but inquire into their fruits for life.... Since denial of the finite self and its wants, since asceticism of some sort, is found in religious experience to be the only doorway to the larger and more blessed life, this moral mystery intertwines and combines with the intellectual mystery in all mystical writings.... There is a verge of the mind which these things haunt; and whispers therefrom mingle with the operations of our understanding even as the waters of the infinite ocean send their waves to break among the pebbles that lie upon our shores.... The mystic is, in short, *invulnerable,* and must be left, whether we relish it or not, in undisturbed enjoyment of his creed.... We have no right, therefore, to invoke his prestige as distinctively in favor of any special belief, such as that in absolute idealism, or in the absolute monistic identity, or in the absolute goodness of the world. It is only relatively in favor of all these things – it passes out of common human consciousness in the direction in which they lie.... Mystical states merely add a supersensuous meaning to the ordinary outward data of consciousness. They are excitements like the emotions of love or ambition, gifts to our spirit by means of which facts already objectively before us fall into a new expressiveness and make a new connection with our active life. They do not contradict these facts as such, or deny anything that our senses have immediately seized.... It must always remain an open question whether mystical states may not possibly be such superior points of view, windows through which the mind looks out upon a more extensive and inclusive world.... The wider world would in that case prove to have a mixed constitution like that of this world, that is all. It would have its celestial and its infernal regions, its tempting and its saving moments, its valid experiences and its counterfeit ones, just as our world has them; but it would be a wider world all the same.[21]

IV. *Radical Empiricism and Moral Pluralism*

The "bath in sentimentality" of the *Varieties of Religious Experience* made William James aware of his previous neglect, as a psychologist, of the emotional life of man and of his natural "appetites." He shifted his attention from the scientific study of the physiology of mind, and by a more "radical" empiricism tried to describe the "whole man" existing among other beings. He now took seriously what he had preached in the early 1880's, when he pointed out that even rationality is a sentiment: "The whole man within us is at work when we form our philosophical opinions. Intellect, will, taste, and passion co-operate just as they do in practical affairs.... The absurd abstraction of an intellect verbally formulating all its evidence ... is ideally as inept as it is actually impossible."[22] And he goes on to say: "The ultimate philosophy, we must therefore conclude, must not be too strait-laced in form.... There must be left over and above the propositions to be subscribed ... another realm into which the stifled soul may escape from pedantic scruples and indulge its own faith at its own risks."[23]

He now enlarged his theory of the stream of consciousness into the larger, more elemental, "stream of life"; and he enlarged his empirical study of "mind" to a study of the self or person, mind and soul, in their biological unity. However, this study developed in two directions, which reflected his double interest in health of mind and in the intricacies of "affectional facts." The former led to pragmatism and the latter to pluralism; the former, to scientific methods of verification of beliefs, and the latter, to a "moral" individualism opposed to absolutistic, rationalist, abstract monism. Underlying both was his "radical empiricism" and the theory of "pure experience," which expressed his revolt against the dualism of subject and object, inner and outer, mind and body.

In the revision of his analysis of "the stream of consciousness" with its emphasis on sense-perception and volition, he unfortunately, in his analysis of "the stream of life" called it "pure experience." He attempted to do justice to the emotional life and to non-cognitive feelings by putting the whole person into his natural environment and by describing the conscious pursuit of ends as an emergence in the complex of desires, needs, and interests. This entire stream of life he conceived as "pure" or "neutral" experience, as something alternately physical and mental, subjective and objective. This led him into a number of controversies and misinterpretations; it was commonly assumed that "pure" experience was still "phenomenal." But when he denied the existence of consciousness, his analyses of the life processes were more explicitly expressed as forms of action or behavior, and "experience" was evidently wider than consciousness.

His emphasis on the living self led him to a deep hostility to all abstractions, to absolutism, and to all forms of a metaphysical monism. His Hibbert Lectures of 1908 delivered at Manchester College in Oxford, published in 1909 under the title, *A Pluralistic Universe,* were devoted chiefly to a development of pluralistic philosophy, both in morals and ontology. These lectures gave a popular expression to his individualism and character, without the technicalities of his "radical empiricism." But he admitted that his final, healthy form of empiricism was only one aspect of his conflict with monism as an enemy of morality. His militant pluralism was his attempt to be "a faithful soul," defending moralism as his father had" faithfully" defended spiritualism and monism. James says:

There is a pluralism hardened by reflection and deliberate; ... it seems to me that the deepest of all philosophic differences is that between this pluralism and all forms of monism whatever.... Any absolute moralism must needs be such a healthy-minded pluralism.... But healthy-mindedness is not the whole of life, and the *morbid* view ... asks for a philosophy very different from that of absolute moralism. To suggest personal will and effort to one "all sicklied o'er' with the sense of weakness, of helpless failure, and of fear, is to suggest the most horrible of things to him. What he craves is to be consoled in his very impotence.... We are all *potentially* such sick men. The sanest and best of us are of one clay with lunatics and prison-inmates. And whenever we feel this, such a sense of the vanity of our voluntary career comes over us, that all our morality appears but as a plaster biding a sore it can never cure, and all our well-doing as the hollowest substitute for that well-being that our lives ought to be grounded in, but, alas! are not. This well-being is the object of the *religious* demand. . . . So that of religion and moralism, the morbid and the healthy view, it may be said that what is meat to the one is the other's poison. Any absolute moralism is a pluralism; any absolute religion is a monism. It shows the depth of the religious insight of Henry James, Sr. that he first and last and always made moralism the target of his hottest attack, and pitted religion and it against each other as enemies. . . . The accord of moralism and religion is superficial, their discord radical. Only the deepest thinkers on both sides see that one must go. . . . Meanwhile, the battle is about us, and we are its combatants. . . . It will be a hot fight indeed if the friends of philosophic moralism should bring to the service of their ideal, . . . a spirit even remotely resembling the life-long devotion of my father's faithful heart.[24]

In *Essays in Radical Empiricism,* James writes:

It is by the interest and importance that experiences have for us by the emotions they excite, and the purposes they subverse, by their affective values, that their consecution in our several conscious streams, as "thoughts" of ours, is mainly ruled. Desire introduces them; interest holds them; fitness fixes their order and connection. . . . It thus appears that the ambiguous or amphibious *status* which we find our epithets of value occupying is the most natural thing in the world. . . .[25]

In *A Pluralistic Universe,* James says:

Pluralism lets things really exist in the each-form or distributively. Monism thinks that the all-form or collective unit form is the only form that is rational . . . . In the each-form, on the contrary, a thing may be connected by intermediary things, with a thing with which it has no immediate or essential connection –. . . . the type of continuity, contiguity, or concatenation. . . . It forms a definitely conceivable alternative to the through-and-through unity of all things at once, which is the type opposed to it by monism. This fact of coalescence of next with next in concrete experience... is what distinguishes the empiricism which I call "radical."[26]

The Oxford brand of transcendentalism seems to me to have confined itself too exclusively to thin logical considerations, that would hold good in all conceivable worlds, worlds of an empirical constitution entirely different from ours. It is as if the actual peculiarities of the world that is were entirely irrelevant to the content of truth. But they cannot be irrelevant; and the philosophy of the future must imitate the sciences in taking them more and more elaborately into account.[27]

NOTES

[1] Ralph Barton Perry, *The Thought and Character of William James* (Boston: Little, Brown and Company, 1935), I, pp. 275—276.
[2] *Ibid.*, p. 516.
[3] *Ibid.*, pp. 276—277.
[4] *Ibid.*, pp. 287—288.
[5] *Ibid.*, p. 298.
[6] *Ibid.*, p. 322.
[7] *Ibid.*, p. 343.
[8] *Ibid.*, p. 344.
[9] William James, *The Principles of Psychology* (1890; New York: Dover Publications, Inc., 1950), I, pp. 177—182.
[10] *Ibid.*, I, pp. 451—454.
[11] *Ibid.*, II, pp. 576—579.
[12] William James, *The Varieties of Religious Experience* (1901—1902; New York: The Modern Library), p. 494.
[13] *Ibid.*, p. 476.
[14] *Ibid.*, p. 133.
[15] *Ibid.*, pp. 24—26.
[16] *Ibid.*, pp. 89—90.
[17] *Ibid.*, pp. 92—94.
[18] *Ibid.*, pp. 354—361.
[19] *Ibid.*, p. 365.
[20] *Ibid.*, p. 368.
[21] *Ibid.*, pp. 404—419.

22 William James, *The Will to Believe and Other Essays on Popular Philosophy* (1897; New York: Dover Publications, 1956), pp. 92—93.
23 *Ibid.*, p. 110.
24 William James, ed., *The Literary Remains of the Late Henry James.* Introduction by William James (Boston: Houghton Mifflin Co., 1885), pp. 116—119.
25 William James, *Essays in Radical Empiricism* (New York: Longmans, Green and Co., 1912), p. 153.
26 William James, *A Pluralistic Universe* (New York: Longmans, Green and Co., 1909), pp. 324—326.
27 *Ibid.*, p. 331.

NACHWORT DES HERAUSGEBERS

> *"It is a fair presumption, that the cards of humanity have not all been played out."*
> William James

Nirgends wuchert der Ismen-Wald bunter Fahnen, Flaggen und Paniere so reich wie in der Domäne der Philosophie. Es sind die Anschriften, Embleme, Schibbolethe, Lock-, Warn- und Schlachtrufe der alten und altneuen Denkerparteien, die das Rätsel des gemeinsam Vorhandenen durch kühne und kühnste Konstruktionen des Erdachten zu lösen suchen. Der vielberufene «Weltgeist» bezeugte ein merkwürdig geringes Interesse, dem Menschen auch nur etwa die Einsicht in das eigene Herkommen zu erleichtern. Er geizte mit der Latimeria, dem Archaeopteryx, ließ das Formenheer der Anthropoiden im Tier–Mensch-Übergangsfeld wahllos aussterben. So fehlten dem antiken Menschen die hilfreichen Zwischenformen, etwa eine fortlebende große Kultur der Neandertaler, als einleuchtende Beweise des phylogenetischen Zusammenhanges. Er stillte sich seinen Erklärungshunger mit selbsterdachten Märchen, Mythen, Hypothesen und Theorien. Im Fortgang der Forschung erwies sich das meiste davon als bloße Fabel. Auch der Weltgeist selbst, der ihn mit absichtlichen Erschwerungen narrt und verwirrt. Dennoch wirken die alten Mythopoesen als mächtige Fermente des Denkens fort. Sie entsprechen inneren, durchaus natürlichen Bedürfnissen. Die sinnsuchende Unruhe des Menschen, sein metaphysisches Verlangen hascht nach Erklärungen, welchen Ranges auch immer. «Die Natur wollte wissen, wie sie aussieht, und sie erschuf Goethe» – so Heine in einer flinken Formel.

Der «series of muses», von der John Dewey einmal spricht, kann der erkennende Mensch offenbar nicht entrinnen. Gleich Thales bei der nächtlichen Betrachtung der Sterne in den Brunnen, fällt er immer wieder in die Gruben der Widersprüche, in die Verlockungen verheißungsvoller Aspekte. Eine

Theorie leuchtet ihm auf, ein erklärendes Modell, ein fruchtbarer Gedanke - und schon vergewaltigt er damit Natur, Mensch und Gott. Der gnoseologische Lustgewinn ist so groß wie das Machtbewußtsein, die Wahrheit gefunden zu haben.

Der Pragmatismus - «a new name for some old ways of thinking», wie William James immer wieder einschärft - stellt das Leben, die Praxis, das Handeln in die Mitte - nicht das Denken, diesen Spätling der «Entwicklung». Das Leben zwingt zur Aktion, durch Hunger und Durst, durch das Treiben der Triebe, in der Feindvermeidung und Feindbekämpfung, im Drang zur Lust, zur Geborgenheit. Es übte sich im Lösen alltäglicher Probleme durch Versuche, Modelle, Experimente - was dabei zum Erfolg führte, war gut, was sich bewährte, wahr, das Nützliche oft genug existenzrettend. Heute erwächst dem genetischen Pragmatismus in der vergleichenden Verhaltenslehre, der Ethologie, der längst erwartete große Helfer. Die Darwinschen Impulse gelangen in ihre letzte Reife. Was sich im menschlichen Bewußtsein ausfaltet, hat sich im tierischen Werden vorbereitet. Es ist kaum mehr einzusehen, warum die sog. «höheren» Funktionen des seelischen und geistigen Seins nicht mit den nämlichen Methoden untersucht werden sollen, die sich für die «niederen» ergiebig erweisen. Zu seinen Ahnen zählt der Pragmatismus Heraklit und Protagoras, die Sophisten überhaupt. Er siedelt am Ufer des Sensualismus, Empirismus, Relativismus und Nominalismus. Er steht dem Biologismus, Psychologismus, Voluntarismus nahe, dem Utilitarismus, Meliorismus, Optimismus und Aktivismus. Er überschneidet sich vielfach mit dem frühen Marx, der Kritik am Tun des Philosophen überhaupt, wie mit seiner Deutung der Ideologie. Der Empiriokritizismus von Avenarius ist ebenso zu erinnern wie der Fiktionalismus Vaihingers; Nietzsche, Bergson und Simmel sind unvergessen. Ebenso, daß Kant der praktischen Vernunft den eindeutigen Primat vor jeder spekulativen festlegte. Die Arbeiten F. C. S. Schillers (1864-1937), der den Pragmatismus als «Humanism» auslegte, harren noch der verdienten Auswertung.

Trotz verheißungsvoller Vorarbeiten fehlt uns immer noch eine zureichende Geschichte und Kritik der Ismen. James versuchte sie aus den «Temperamenten» zu erklären, Jung spricht von psychologischen Typen, Leisegang von Denkformen, Kretschmer sah das Fundament tiefer in Konstitutionstypen schon des Körpers. Anlagen entfalten sich aber nicht nur im Sonderzufall der physischen Umwelt, wirksamer sind die prägenden Ismen des sozialen Feldes, in dem wir aufwachsen. Wir alle werden in eine Welt wirkender und kämpfender Weltanschauungen hineingeboren, müssen uns mit religiösen, philosophischen, politischen, sozialen Ideologien auseinandersetzen, die allesamt um uns werben, da sie von aktiven Gruppen getragen werden, die ihren Machtraum im Kampfe um ihre «Wahrheit» zu vergrößern suchen. Zu den heterom determinierenden Mächten gehören die Sprache, sämtliche Traditionen, Wertungen, bis zu den kämpfenden und bekämpften Sitten und Gebräuchen. Alle entscheidenden geschichtlichen Vorgänge lassen sich reduktionistisch auf reinen Machtwillen zurückführen, der Stärkste siegt nach dem Prinzip des survival of the fittest. Im Bereich des Menschen fällt auf, daß er seine Kriege gern der bedrohten oder heilbringenden Ideologien wegen führt, oder diese damit verbrämt. Das als wahr Erkannte ist auch wert, verteidigt zu werden, es vermag ein Sendungsbewußtsein zu schaffen, andere damit zu beglücken, die im Gefängnis einer «unwahren» Ideologie vegetieren. So erhalten Wertungen welcher Art immer ihre Brisanz. Gewiß werden Ideologien wie materielle Waffen als Instrumente verwendet und tragen dann ein starr dogmatisches Gesicht. Hier läßt sich der Pragmatismus ins Verhängnisvolle stilisieren. Die Wahrheit ist nie eine bloße Funktion der Macht. Nicht alles Nützliche muß eo ipso wahr sein, aber die Wahrheit kann sich sehr wohl mit dem wahren Guten und dem wahren Nützlichen vertragen. Diese sind uns nicht gegeben, sondern unserem forschenden Erkennen aufgegeben. Der Pragmatismus ist weniger eine Doktrin als eine Methode, mehr ein Suchen als ein Haben; wo er dogmatisch wird, hebt er sich auf. Die Wirklichkeit, in der wir als Wirkliche leben, ist eine solche des Werdens. Auch die Wahrheit wird, das Erfassen der werdenden Wahrheit in der Freiheit zeigt sich als Sinn unseres Daseins.

«The task of future philosophy, schreibt John Dewey, is to clarify men's ideas as to the social and moral strifes of their own day. Its aim is to become so far as is humanly possible an organ for dealing with these conflicts. That which may be pretentiously unreal when it is formulated in metaphysical distinctions becomes intensely significant when connected with the drama of the struggle of social beliefs and ideals. Philosophy which surrenders its somewhat barren monopoly of dealings with Ultimate and Absolute Reality will find a compensation in enlightening the moral forces which move mankind and in contributing to the aspiration of men to attain to a more ordered and intelligent happiness». («Reconstruction in Philosophy», 1920, pag. 26.)

* * *

Dank der großzügigen Bestimmung der Volkart-Stiftung kann das «Archiv für genetische Philosophie» weiterhin in seinem Winterthurer Heim an der Römerstraße 29 domiziliert bleiben. Unter den über 30 000 Titeln seiner Bibliothek befinden sich auch bedeutende Bestände amerikanischer Philosophie, die uns Herbert W. Schneider vermittelt und mit einzigartigen Supplementen aus eigenem Besitze erweitert hat. Am 24. Juni 1976 wurde das Archiv der ihr entwachsenen «Akademie für ethische Forschung» geschenkt. Damit ist nun auch der Weg für seine intensivere Nutzung freigeworden.

Es führte vier Seminare mit amerikanischen und europäischen Freunden Herbert Schneiders durch. Die erste dieser Studienwochen galt «Peirce, James and C. I. Lewis» (1966), die zweite stand unter dem Thema «Ethics and scientific methods» (1968). Dank der selbstlosen Mühe und Geduld von S. Morris Eames konnten die Arbeiten des «George Herbert Mead»-Seminares von 1970 als Buch erscheinen (1973). Ihm reiht sich nun 1976 der Band «William James» der Tagung von 1973 an, beide Werke wurden vom Felix Meiner-Verlag in Hamburg übernommen. Damit beginnen sich vieljährige private Mühen zu stabilisieren und Früchte zu tragen.

Alle diese Arbeitswochen standen im Sternzeichen einer schöpferischen, freimütigen Freundschaft, einer wohlerfahrenen Vertrautheit mit den tender-minded Bostonians, ebenso wie mit den Rocky Mountaintoughs, von denen James mit Behagen spricht. Wer im Kristallpalast des Apriorismus seinem platonisierenden Glasperlenspiel frönt, als positivistischer Kahlschläger das gesamte metaphysische Bedürfnis auszurotten sucht oder den Pragmatismus nur als nackte Erfolgslehre privater Praxis verfocht – solche Extremformeln gerieten im witzigen und weisen Humor der Diskussionen ganz von selbst in die Enge. Durchgehend aber war die besorgte, aufgeschlossene Bereitschaft zu spüren, alles Philosophieren am leidenden, verirrten und bedrohten Menschen zu messen.

Winterthur, 4. Juli 1976 Walter Robert Corti

BIBLIOGRAPHY OF WRITINGS BY AND ABOUT WILLIAM JAMES

Compiled by Charlene Haddock Seigfried

I. Principal Works of William James

Collected Essays and Reviews. Edited by R. B. Perry. New York: Longman's Green and Co., 1920.
Essays in Radical Empiricism. Edited by R. B. Perry. New York: Longman's Green and Co., 1912.
Essays on Faith and Morals. Edited by R. B. Perry. New York: Longman's Green and Co., 1943.
The Meaning of Truth. New York: Longman's Green and Co., 1909.
Memories and Studies. Edited by Henry James, Jr. New York: Longman's Green and Co., 1911.
A Pluralistic Universe. New York: Longman's Green and Co., 1909.
Pragmatism: A New Name for Some Old Ways of Thinking. New York: Longman's Green and Co., 1907.
The Principles of Psychology. 2 Vols. New York: Henry Holt and Co., 1890.
Psychology. Briefer Course. New York: Henry Holt and Co., 1892.
Some Problems of Philosophy. Edited by Henry James, Jr. New York: Longman's Green and Co., 1911.
Talks to Teachers on Psychology and to Students on Some of Life's Ideals. New York: Henry Holt and Co., 1899.
The Varieties of Religious Experience. New York: Longman's Green and Co., 1902.
The Will to Believe and Other Essays in Popular Philosophy. New York: Henry Holt and Co., 1897.

II. Recent Editions of William James

Collected Essays and Reviews. Edited by Ralph B. Perry. New York: Russell and Russell, 1969.
Essays in Pragmatism. Edited by Alburey Castell. Riverside, New Jersey: Hafner Press, 1974.
Essays in Radical Empiricism and A Pluralistic Universe. Edited by Ralph B. Perry. Intro. by Richard J. Bernstein. New York: E. P. Dutton and Co., Inc., 1971.

Essays on Faith and Morals. New York: New American Library, 1974.
In Commemoration of William James, 1842—1942. New York: A. M. S. Press, Inc., 1942, 1974.
The Meaning of Truth. A Sequel to Pragmatism. Intro. by Ralph Ross. Ann Arbor: University of Michigan Press, 1970. Also New York: Greenwood Press, 1968. Cambridge: Harvard University Press, 1976.
Memories and Studies. Grosse Pointe, Michigan: Scholarly Press, 1970. Also New York: Greenwood Press, 1968. Folcroft, Pennsylvania: Folcroft Library Editions, 1973.
The Moral Equivalent of War and Other Essays; and selections from *Some Problems of Philosophy.* Edited and intro. by John K. Roth. New York: Harper and Row, 1971.
The Moral Philosophy of William James. Edited and intro. by John K. Roth. New York: Apollo Editions, 1969. Also New York: Thomas Y. Crowell, 1969.
On Some of Life's Ideals. On a Certain Blindness in Human Beings. What Makes a Life Significant. Folcroft, Pennsylvania: Folcroft Library Editions, 1973.
A Pluralistic Universe. Folcroft, Pennsylvania: Folcroft Library Editions, 1973.
Pragmatism. Edited by Ralph B. Perry. New York: New American Library, 1965. Also Cambridge: Harvard University Press, 1976.
Progmatism and Four Essays from The Meaning of Truth. New York: Meridan Books, 1955.
The Principles of Psychology. New York: Dover Publications, Inc., 1950. Also Chicago: Encyclopedia Britannica, 1952, 1955.
Psychology: Briefer Course. Riverside, New Jersey: Macmillan Publishing Co., Inc., 1962. Also edited by Gorden Allport. Scranton, Pennsylvania, 1974.
Some Problems of Philosophy. Edited by H. M. Kallan. New York: Greenwood Press, 1968.
The Varieties of Religious Experience. Riverside, New Jersey: Macmillan Publishing Co., 1961. Also New York: New American Library, 1974.
The Will to Believe. New York: Dover Publications, Inc., 1974. Also Folcroft, Pennsylvania: Folcroft Library Editions, 1974.
William James on Psychical Research. Edited by Gardner Murphy and Robert O. Ballou. New York: Viking Press, 1960, 1969.
A William James Reader. Edited and intro. by Gay Wilson Allen. Boston: Houghton Mifflin Co., 1972.
The Writings of William James. Edited by John J. McDermott. New York: The Modern Library, 1968.

III. Letters of William James

Hardwick, Elizabeth, ed. *The Selected Letters of William James.* New York: Farrar, Straus and Cudahy, 1961.

James, Henry, ed. *Letters of William James.* Boston: Atlantic Monthly Press, 1920. New York: Kraus Reprint, 1969.

Kaufmann, Marjorie K. "William James's Letters to a Young Pragmatist [H. V. Knox]." *Journal of the History of Ideas,* 24 (1963), 413—421.

Kenna, J. C. "Ten Unpublished Letters from William James, 1842—1910, to Francis Herbert Bradley, 1846—1924." *Mind,* 35 (July, 1966), 309—331.

Le Clair, Robert C., ed. *The Letters of William James and Theodore Flournoy.* Madison: University of Wisconsin Press, 1966.

Nethery, Wallace, ed. "Pragmatist to Publisher, Letters of William James to W. T. Harris." *Personalist,* 49 (Fall, 1968), 489—508.

Perry, Ralph Barton. *The Thought and Character of William James.* 2 vols. Boston: Little, Brown and Co., 1935.
Contains some five hundred letters by William James not found in the earlier edition of the *Letters of William James.*

Thiele, J. "William James und Ernst Mach. Briefe aus den Jahren 1884—1905." *Philosophia Naturalis,* 9 (1965), 298—310.

IV. Selected Bibliography, with emphasis on the years 1965-1975

For a complete, annotated bibliography of the writings of William James through 1966, see:

McDermott, John J., ed. *The Writings of William James.* New York: The Modern Library, 1968, 811—858.

Allen, Gay Wilson. *William James: A Biography.* New York: The Viking Press, 1967, 1969.

—, ed. and intro. *A William James Reader.* Boston: Houghton Mifflin Co., 1972.

Anderson, Paul Russell and Fisch, M. H. *Philosophy in America from the Puritans to James, with Representative Selections.* New York: Octagon Books, 1969.

Ayer, A. J. *The Origins of Pragmatism.* Studies in the Philosophy of Charles Sanders Peirce and William James. San Francisco: Freeman, Cooper and Co., 1968.

Baumgarten, Edward. *Der Pragmatismus: R. W. Emerson, W. James, J. Dewey.* Frankfurt am Main: V. Klostermann, 1938.

Beard, Robert W. "James and the Rationality of Determinism."

Journal of the History of Philosophy, 5 (April, 1967), 149—156.
—, "James' Notion of Rationality." *Darshana International*, 6 (1967), 6—12.
—, *"The Will to Believe* Revisited." *Ratio*, 8 (1966), 169—179.
Beck, Lewis White. *Six Secular Philosophers:* Religious Themes in the Thought of Spinoza, Hume, Kant, Nietzsche, William James, Santayana. New York: The Free Press, 1966.
Bentley, Arthur F. "The Jamesian Datum." *Inquiry Into Inquiries*. Edited by Sydney Ratner. Boston: The Beacon Press, 1954, 230—267.
Bixler, J. S. "'Relevance' in the Philosophy of William James." *Religious Humanism*, 9 (Winter, 1975), 38—44.
Bixler, Julius Seelye. *Religion in the Philosophy of William James*. Boston: Marshall Jones Co., 1926.
Blomberg, Jaakko. "James on Belief and Truth." *Ajatus*, 31 (1969), 171—187.
Boutroux, Emile. *William James*. London: Longmans, Green, 1912.
Brennan, Bernard P. *The Ethics of William James*. New York: Bookman Assoc., 1961.
—, *William James*. New York: Twayne Pub., 1968. New Haven: College and University Press Services, 1971.
Bridges, Leonard Hal. *American Mysticism:* from William James to Zen. New York: Harper and Row, 1970.
Browning, Douglas, ed. *Philosophers of Process*. New York: Random House, 1965.
Carnap, Rudolf. "Empiricism, Semantics and Ontology." *Pragmatic Philosophy*, Edited by Amelie Rorty, 396—411.
Chamberlain, Gary L. "The Drive for Meaning in William James' Analysis of Religious Experience." *The Journal of Value Inquiry*, 5 (Summer, 1971), 194—206.
Compton, Charles Herrick. *William James, Philosopher and Man*. New York: Scarecrow Press, 1957.
De Aloysio, Francesco. *Da Dewey a James*. Roma: Bulzoni, 1972.
Delaney, Cornelius F. "Recent Work on American Philosophy." *New Scholasticism*, 45 (Summer, 1971), 457—477.
Dilworth, D. "The Initial Formations of 'Pure Experience' in Nishida Kitaro and William James." *Monumenta Nipponica*, 24 (1969), 93—111.
Dooley, Patrick K. "The Nature of Belief: The Proper Context for James' *The Will to Believe.*" *Transactions of the Peirce Society*, 8 (Summer, 1972), 141—151.
—, *Pragmatism as Humanism:* The Philosophy of William James. Chicago: Nelson-Hall, 1974.
Edie, James M. "The Genesis of a Phenomenological Theory of the Experience of Personal Identity: William James on Consciousness and the Self." *Man and World*, 6 (September, 1973), 322—338.

—, ed. and intro. *An Invitation to Phenomenology:* Studies in the Philosophy of Experience. Chicago: Quadrangle Books, 1965.

—, ed. and intro. *New Essays in Phenomenology.* Studies in the Philosophy of Experience. Chicago: Quadrangle Books, 1969.

—, "William James and Phenomenology." *The Review of Metaphysics,* 23 (March, 1970) 481—526.

Eisendrath, Craig R. *The Unifying Moment:* The Psychological Philosophy of William James and Alfred North Whitehead. Cambridge: Harvard University Press, 1971.

Essays Philosophical and Psychological: in Honor of William James, by his colleagues at Columbia University. London: Longman's Green and Co., 1908.

Fairbanks, Matthew. "Wittgenstein and James." *New Scholasticism,* 40 (1966), 331—340.

Fernandez, Pelayo Hipolito. *Miguel de Unamuno y William James; un Paralelo Pragmatico.* Salamanca: Cervantes, 1961.

Fisher, John J. "Santayana on James: A Conflict of Views on Philosophy." *American Philosophical Quarterly,* 2 (1965), 67—73.

Flournoy, Theodore. *The Philosophy of William James.* Freeport, New York: Books for Libraries Press, 1969. Reprint of 1917 edition.

Gini, A. R. "Radical Subjectivism in the Thought of William James." *The New Scholasticism,* 48 (Autumn, 1974), 509—518.

Giuffrida, Robert. "James on Meaning and Significance." *Transactions of the Peirce Society,* 11 (Winter, 1975), 18—36.

Gobar, Ash. "History of the Phenomenological Trend in the Philosophy and Psychology of William James (1842—1910)." *American Philosophical Society Yearbook,* (1968), 582—583.

—, "The Phenomenology of William James." *Proceedings of the American Philosophical Society,* 114 (1970), 294—309.

Gould, James A. "R. B. Perry on the Origin of American and European Pragmatism." *Journal of the History of Philosophy,* 8 (October, 1970), 431—450.

Grattan, Clinton Hartley. *The Three Jameses, A Family of Minds: Henry James, Sr., William James, Henry James.* New York: University Press, 1962.

Hare, Peter H. and Madden, Edward H. "William James, Dickinson Miller and C. Ducasse on the Ethics of Belief." *Transactions of the Peirce Society,* 4 (Fall, 1968), 115—129.

Hertz, Richard A. "James and Moore: Two Perspectives on Truth." *Journal of the History of Philosophy,* 9 (April, 1971), 213—221.

Hocks, Richard A. *Henry James and Pragmatic Thought;* a Study in the Relationship Between the Philosophy of William James and the Literary Art of Henry James. Chapel Hill: The University of North Carolina Press, 1974.

Høffding, Harald. *Moderne Philosophen.* Vorlesungen, gehalten an der Universität in Kopenhagen im Herbst 1902. Leipzig: O. R. Reisland, 1905.

Johnson, Ellwood. "William James and the Art of Fiction." *The Journal of Aesthetics and Art Criticism,* 30 (Spring, 1972), 285—296.

Kallen, Horace M., ed. *In Commemoration of William James. 1842—1942.* New York: Columbia University Press, 1942.

—, *William James and Henri Bergson:* A Study in Contrasting Theories of Life. Chicago: University of Chicago Press, 1914.

Kauber, Peter. "The Development of the New Pragmatic Theory of the *A Priori." Kinesis,* 3 (Fall, 1970), 9—33.

—, "Does James's Ethics of Belief Rest on a Mistake?" *Southern Journal of Philosophy,* 12 (Summer, 1974), 201—214.

—, "The Foundations of James's Ethics of Belief." *Ethics,* 84 (January, 1974), 151—166.

Kauber, Peter and Hare, P. H. "The Right and Duty to Will to Believe." *Canadian Journal of Philosophy,* 4 (December, 1974), 327—343.

Kersten, Fred. "Franz Brentano and William James." *Journal of the History of Philosophy,* 7 (April, 1969), 177—191.

Linschoten, Johannes. *On the Way Toward a Phenomenological Psychology;* the Psychology of William James. Edited by Amadeo Giorgi. Pittsburg: Dusquesne University Press, 1968.

MacLeod, William J. "James' Will to Believe, Revisited." *Personalist,* 48 (April, 1967), 149—166.

Madden, Edward H. and Chakrabarti, Chandana. "James' 'Pure Experience' versus Ayer's 'Weak Phenomenalism.'" *Transactions of the Peirce Society,* 12 (Winter, 1976), 3—17.

Marshall, G. D. "Attention and Will." *Philosophical Quarterly,* 20 (January, 1970), 14—25.

Martland, Thomas R., Jr. *The Metaphysics of William James and John Dewey:* Process and Structure in Philosophy and Religion. New York: Philosophical Library, 1964.

Mathur, Dinesh Chandra. *Naturalistic Philosophies of Experience.* Studies in James, Dewey and Farber against the Background of Husserl's Phenomenology. St. Louis: Warren H. Green, 1971.

McDermott, John J., ed. *The Writings of William James.* New York: The Modern Library, 1968.

Meyers, Robert G. "Ayer on Pragmatism." *Metaphilosophy,* 6 (January, 1975), 44—53.

—, "Meaning and Metaphysics in James." *Philosophy and Phenomenological Research,* 31 (March, 1971), 369—380.

—, "Natural Realism and Illusion in James's Radical Empiricism." *Transactions of the Peirce Society,* 5 (Fall, 1969), 211—223.

Moore, Edward C. *American Pragmatism:* Peirce, James and Dewey. New York: Columbia University Press, 1961.
—, *William James.* New York: Washington Square Press, 1965.
Mullin, Richard P., Jr. "Does Speculative Philosophy Make a Difference: Jamesian Approach to the Justification of Metaphysics." *Journal of the West Virginia Philosophical Society,* (Spring, 1975), 19—21.
Murphey, Murray G. "Kant's Children, the Cambridge Pragmatists." *Transactions of the Peirce Society,* 4 (Winter, 1968), 3—33.
Myers, Gerald E. "William James on Time Perception." *Philosophy of Science,* 38 (September, 1971), 353—360.
Newman, Jay. "The Faith of Pragmatists." *Sophia.* 13 (April, 1974), 1—15.
Novak, Michael, ed. *American Philosophy and the Future.* Essays for a New Generation. New York: Charles Scribner's Sons, 1968.
Pancheri, Lillian U. "James, Lewis and the Pragmatic *A Priori.*" *Transactions of the Peirce Society,* 7 (Summer, 1971), 135—149.
Perry, Ralph Barton. *In the Spirit of William James.* Bloomington: Indiana University Press, 1958.
—, *Present Philosophical Tendencies.* New York: Greenwood Press, 1968.
—, *The Thought and Character of William James.* 2 vols. Boston: Little, Brown, and Co., 1935.
Phillips, D. C. "James, Dewey, and the Reflex Arc." *Journal of the History of Ideas,* 32 (1971), 555—568.
Reck, Andrew J. "Dualism in William James's *Principles of Psychology.*" *Tulane Studies in Philosophy,* 21 (1972), 23—38.
—, "Epistemology in William James's *Principles of Psychology.*" *Tulane Studies in Philosophy,* 22 (1973), 79—115.
—, *Introduction to William James.* An Essay and Selected Texts. Bloomington: Indiana University Press, 1967.
—, "The Philosophical Psychology of William James." *Southern Journal of Philosophy,* 9 (Fall, 1971), 293—312.
—, *William James et l'attitude Pragmatiste.* Paris: Seghers, 1967.
Reeve, E. Gavin. "William James on Pure Being and Pure Nothing." *Philosophy* 45 (January, 1970), 59—60.
Riconda, Giuseppe. "L'empirismo radicale di William James." *Filosofia,* 16 (1965), 291—332.
—, "La filosofia della religione di James." *Filosofia,* 15 (1964), 241-277.
Riepe, Dale. "A Note on William James and Indian Philosophy." *Philosophy and Phenomenological Research."* 28 (June, 1968), 587—590.
Roberts, James Deotis. *Faith and Reason;* A Comparative Study of Pascal, Bergson, and James. Boston: Christopher Publishing House, 1962.

Roggerone, Giuseppe Agostino. *James e la crisi della conscienza contemporanea.* Milano: Marzorati, 1967.
Rosenthal, Sandra B. "Recent Perspectives on American Pragmatism: Part I." *Transactions of the Peirce Society,* 10 (Spring, 1974), 76—93. Part II. 10 (Summer, 1974), 166—184.
Roth, John K. *Freedom and the Moral Life;* the Ethics of William James. Philadelphia: Westminster Press, 1969.
Roth, Robert J. "Is Peirce's Pragmatism Anti-Jamesian?" *International Philosophical Quarterly,* 5 (1965), 541—563.
—, "The Religious Philosophy of William James." *Thought,* 41 (1966), 249—281.
Royce, Josiah. *William James and Other Essays on the Philosophy of Life.* Reprint of 1911 edition. Freeport, New York: Books for Libraries, 1969.
Scheffler, Israel. *Four Pragmatists:* A Critical Introduction to Peirce, James, Mead, and Dewey. New York: Humanities Press, 1974.
Schirmer, D. B. "William James and the New Age." *Science and Society,* 33 (1969), 434—445.
Schmidt, Hermann. *Der Begriff der Erfahrungskontinuität bei William James und seine Bedeutung für den amerikanischen Pragmatismus.* Heidelberg: C. Winter Verlag, 1959.
Schrag, Calvin O. "Struktur der Erfahrung in der Philosophie von James und Whitehead." *Zeitschrift für philosophische Forschung,* 23 (1969), 479—494.
Shields, Allan. "On a Certain Blindness in William James and Others." *Journal of Aesthetics and Art Criticism,* 27 (Fall, 1968), 27—34.
Shouse, J. B. "David Hume and William James: A Comparison." *Journal of the History of Ideas.* 13 (1952), 514—527.
Singer, Marcus G. "The Pragmatic Use of Language and the *Will to Believe.*" *American Philosophical Quarterly,* 8 (Januray, 1971), 24—34.
Smith, John E. "The Reflexive Turn, the Linguistic Turn, and the Pragmatic Outcome." *Monist,* 53 (October, 1969), 588—605.
—, *The Spirit of American Philosophy.* Oxford University Press, 1963.
—, *Themes in American Philosophy.* Purpose, Experience and Community. New York: Harper Torchbooks, 1960.
Spicker, Stuart F. "William James and Phenomenology." *The Journal of the British Society for Phenomenology,* 2 (1971), 69—74. Bruce Wilshire, "A Reply," 75—80. S. F. Spicker, "Brief Rejoinder to Mr. Wilshire," 80.
Stettheimer, Ettie. "*The Will to Believe* as a Basis for the Defense of Religious Faith." *Archives of Philosophy,* 2 (December, 1907), 1—97.

Stevens, Richard. *James and Husserl:* The Foundations of Meaning. The Hague: Martinus Nijhoff, 1974.

Strout, C. "William James and the Twice-born Sick Soul." *Daedalus,* 97 (1968), 1062—1082.

Ten, Sing-Nam. "Has James Answered Hume?" *Journal of Philosophy,* 49 (1952), 160.

Thayer, H. S. *Meaning and Action:* A Critical History of Pragmatism. Indianapolis: Bobbs-Merrill, 1968.

Tibbits, Paul. "The Philosophy of Science of William James: An Unexplored Dimension of James' Thought." *Personalist,* 52 (Summer, 1971) 535—556.

Weinstein, Michael A. "Life and Politics as Plural: James and Bentley on the Twentieth Century Problem." *Journal of Value Inquiry,* 5 (1970—1971), 282—291.

Wertz, Spencer K. "On Wittgenstein and James." *The New Scholasticism,* 46 (Autumn, 1972), 446—448.

Wickham, Harvey. *The Unrealists.* James, Bergson, Santayana, Einstein, Bertrand Russel, John Dewey, Alexander and Whitehead. Reprint of the 1930 edition. Freeport, New York: Books for Libraries, 1970. Also Port Washington, New York: Kennikat Press, 1971.

Wild, John. *The Radical Empiricism of William James.* Garden City, New York: Doubleday and Co., Inc., 1969.

—, "William James and Existential Authenticity." *Journal of Existentialism,* 5 (1964—1965), 243—256.

Wilshire, Bruce. "Protophenomenology in the Psychology of William James." *Transactions of the Peirce Society,* 5 (Winter, 1969), 25—43.

—, "A Reply to Stuart Spicker's 'William James and Phenomenology.'" *The Journal of the British Society for Phenomenology,* 2 (October, 1971), 75—80.

—, *William James and Phenomenology;* A Study of the *Principles of Psychology.* Bloomington: Indiana University Press, 1968.

INDEX

Agassiz, L. 323 sq.
Alexander, S. 23
Allen, G. W. 87, 334
Aristotle 71 sq., 155, 247, 254, 309, 327
Augustine 151, 222, 254
Ayer, A. J. 112, 135, 173

Bach, J. S. 188
Bacon, F. 181 sq.
Bain, A. 338
Bentham, J. 249, 258
Bentley, A. 85, 94
Berger, G. 317 sq.
Bergson, H. 54, 62, 66, 94, 116, 154, 328, 335, 338, 340
Berkeley, G. 38—42, 55, 57, 113, 123, 169, 181 sq., 192
Bernstein, R. J. 78, 241
Blood, B. P. 21, 30, 345
Boole, G. 344
Bourdeau 319
Bowen, F. 184
Bradley, F. H. 41, 150, 166, 173, 339
Brennan, B. P. 246, 259
Brentano, F. 71 sqq., 243
Brown, N. O. 86
Brown, Th. 183 sq.
Broyer, J. A. 7
Buber, M. 94
Buddha 20 sqq., 24
Butor, M. 24

Cage, J. 24, 29
Caillois, R. 23
Camus, A. 86, 291, 293, 305
Cantor, G. 58
Carr, W. 340

Carus, P. 11
Chisholm, R. M. 115
Cioran, E. M. 86
Clarke, D. S. 7
Clay, E. R. 51 sq., 76 sq.
Cooley, Ch. H. 19 sq.
Corneilius 169
Corti, W. R. 7

Darwin, C. 157 sq., 312, 353, 359
Dedekind, R. 58, 60
Descartes, R 38 sq., 71 sq., 74, 221 sq., 340
Dewey, J. 26, 28 sq., 34, 43, 54, 78, 81, 83, 90, 94 sqq., 98, 160, 164, 166, 180, 191—196, 198, 246, 249 sq., 254 sq., 258 sq., 279, 281, 292 sq., 299, 327, 341, 349, 351, 355
Dretske, F. I., 116
Ducasse, C. J. 115
Duchamp, M. 29
Duras, M. 24

Edel, A. 259
Edel, M. 259
Edie, J. M. 241—244
Edman, I. 29
Ellul 86
Emerson, R. W. 17, 30
Erigena, J. 222
Euclid 167
Eymans 317

Fichte, J. G. 14
Flournoy, Th. 81
Flower, B. 20
Freud, S. 90 sqq.

Grassmann, H. G. 344

Habermas, J. 234 sq., 243
Hall, S. 326
Hamilton, W. 184, 344
Hegel, G. W. F. 14, 38, 148, 152 sqq., 165, 310, 312
Heidegger, M. 86
Helmholtz 344
Herakleitos 153
Hitler, A. 278
Hobbes, Th. 181 sq.
Hocking, P. 15
Hocking, W. E. 340
Hodgson, S. H. 102, 305
Holmes, W. 359
Holt, H. 325
Huizinga, J. 23
Hume, D. 18, 39, 40, 47, 55, 57, 73, 86, 101, 103, 109 sqq., 123, 125, 131, 153, 180 sqq., 185, 274, 340
Husserl, E. 71—74, 222, 240 sq.

Iklé, H. 7

James, H. 18, 29, 279, 304, 360, 362
James, H. Sen. 20, 317—325, 329, 358, 375
Jaspers, K. 86
Jefferson, Th. 183
Joseph, H. B. 173
Joske, W. D. 116
Joyce, J. 86

Kallen, H. M. 263 sq., 279
Kant, I. 22, 26, 54, 86, 96, 147, 180, 182, 184, 251, 254 sq., 274

Lalande, A. 319
Lamprecht, S. 108 sq.
Lange, K. 22
Lee, H. N. 54, 77 sq.
Leibniz, G. W. 188
Le Senne, R. 317, 328, 330
Lewis, C. I. 15, 60, 180, 196 sqq., 259, 340
Locke, J. 38—41, 123, 180 sq., 185 sq., 189, 191

Long, W. H. 115
Lowe, V. 343
Luther, M. 86, 151

McDermott, J. J. 7, 243 sq.
Mach, E. 165
Madden, E. H. 11
Maine de Biran, F. P. Gonthier de 327
Marcel, G. 86
Marx, K. 86, 90, 235, 241
Maxwell, C. 344
Mead, G. H. 9 sqq., 13, 17, 20, 23, 26, 28, 54, 67, 70, 73 sq., 77 sq., 81, 83, 235 sq., 239, 241, 244, 259, 279, 281
Meinong, A. 72
Merleau-Ponty, M.-J. J. 29, 241
Mesnard, P. 317
Michotte, A. 108 sqq.
Mill, J. S. 113, 165, 169, 184
Miller, D. 20
Montessori, M. 90, 98
Moore, G. E. 114, 165, 334, 338
Morris, C. W. 281
Morris, W. 26 sq.
Morse, F. R. 304
Münsterberg, H. 251
Mumford, L. 26 sq.
Murphey, M. 12
Myers, F. 333

Nietzsche, F. 86, 247
Northrop, F. S. C. 54, 77
Norton, G. 305

Packard, V. 281
Pearson, K. 165, 344
Peirce, C. S. 14 sq., 29, 34 sq., 56, 60, 67, 78, 81, 131, 249, 327
Perry, R. B. 27 sq., 48, 248, 259, 279 sq., 319, 330, 334, 338, 340 sq., 376
Pillon, F. 84
Plato 154 sq., 237, 258
Poincaré, H. 165
Pratt, J. B. 304 sq.

Ranke, L. v. 314
Reck, A. J. 141
Reid, Th. 182

Renouvier, C. 35, 48, 102, 115, 121, 125, 127, 359
Rickert, H. 147
Riemann, B. 344
Robbe-Grillet, A. 23
Romanes, G. J. 79
Roth, J. K. 246, 249, 259
Rousseau, J. J. 90
Royce, J. 38, 81, 289, 339 sq.
Russell, B. 57, 173, 332—335, 337—340, 343 sq.

Santayana, G. 30, 81, 248, 255, 259, 262, 279, 284, 288, 292 sq., 304 sq., 327
Sartre, J. P. 86, 90
Schelling, F. W. J. 14
Schiller, F. 22, 26
Schiller, F. C. S. 165 sqq.
Schopenhauer, A. 25, 315
Sheffer, H. M. 15, 340
Sidgwick, H. 333
Sigwart, C. 165
Smith, A. 183
Socrates 348
Spencer, H. 158 sq.
Sperry 179
Spinoza, B. 314
Stewart, D. 183 sq., 196

Stonemark, E. 7
Strong, C. A. 304
Sully, J. 77, 145
Swedenborg, E. 318, 325, 329

Taylor, A. E. 173
Thoreau, H. D. 18
Toffler, A. 24
Tolstoy, L. N. 21, 151

Wahl, J. 321
Ward, J. 332 sq.
Ward, Th. 360
Weightman, J. 24
Welton, D. C. 244
Whitehead, A. N. 15, 27, 53 sq., 60, 62, 94, 116, 179, 275, 280, 287, 331—345
Wiersma, E. D. 317
Wild, J. 231, 241 sq., 244
Wilshire, B. W. 241—244
Wittgenstein, L. 57, 179, 286, 317
Woodring, P. 275, 280
Woods, J. H. 340 sq.
Wright, F. L. 26

Young, F. 317, 320, 330

Zen 20 sqq., 29 sq., 51, 57, 342 sq.

LIBRARY OF DAVIDSON COLLE